The Short Version

THE SHORT VERSION

An ABC Book

Stan Persky

Stan Persky!

New Star Books
Vancouver

NEW STAR BOOKS LTD.

107 – 3477 Commercial Street | Vancouver, BC v5n 4e8 | CANADA
1574 Gulf Rd., #1517 | Point Roberts, WA 98281 | USA
www.newStarBooks.com | info@NewStarBooks.com

Publication of this work is made possible by grants from the Canada Council, the British Columbia Arts Council, and the Department of Canadian Heritage Book Publishing Industry Development Program.

Conseil des Arts   Canada Council   Canadä   BRITISH
du Canada   for the Arts   COLUMBIA
                                                   ARTS COUNCIL

Printed and bound in Canada by Houghton Boston Printers
First printing, August 2005

LIBRARY AND ARCHIVES CANADA CATALOGUING IN PUBLICATION

Persky, Stan, 1941–
The short version : an ABC book / Stan Persky.

ISBN 1-55420-016-4

I.Title.

PS8581.E75S56 2005   C814'.54   C2004-907018-5

for Lanny Beckman

in memory of Czeslaw Milosz

Contents

Perhaps my ABC's are instead of: instead of a novel, instead of an essay on the 20th century, instead of a memoir. Each of the individuals remembered here sets into motion a network of mutual allusions and interdependencies linked to the facts of my century. In the final analysis, I do not regret that I have dropped names so cavalierly (or so it must seem), or that I have made a virtue of my casual way.

CZESLAW MILOSZ
Milosz's ABC's

A

ABC books

I got the idea of writing an ABC book from reading the Polish poet Czeslaw Milosz's version of this genre, *Milosz's ABC's*.* An ABC book is a literary form composed in alphabetically arranged entries of indeterminate length that can run from an aphorism to a complete essay or story.

Milosz's ABC's was originally published in two volumes in Polish in 1997-98, when its author was, remarkably, in his mid-eighties. It is a miscellany that consists of character sketches and literary profiles, mostly of figures little-known to us and long dead; descriptions of places that have had meaning in Milosz's personal geography; and reflections on broader themes, often of a quasi-theological character. His motive in writing his *ABC's* was simply to recoup something of a world he'd once known that had by the end of the 20th century almost completely vanished. His memory is haunted by "disappearance, of people and objects . . . My time, the 20th century, weighs on me as a host of voices and the faces of people whom I once knew, or heard about, and now they no longer exist. Many were famous for something, they are in the encyclopedias, but more of them have been forgotten, and all they can do is make use of me, the rhythm of my blood, my hand holding the pen, in order to return among the living for a brief moment."

---

* Czeslaw Milosz is one of my pantheon — the set of writers that everyone who writes gradually acquires over a lifetime — and I feel as close to his work as I do to the circle of my intimate friends. Since Milosz is indisputably one of the great poets of the 20th century, most poetry readers know who he is. Unfortunately, there aren't a lot of poetry readers these days. So, just to be on the safe side:

Milosz was born in 1911, and raised in Wilno (now Vilnius), Lithuania. After World War II, he served as a cultural attache in the Polish diplomatic corps in France, but around 1950, Milosz made a dramatic break with Poland's Communist government. His book-length essay, *The Captive Mind* (1953), is one of the early and most important post-war anti-totalitarian books, joining a list that includes Arthur Koestler's *Darkness at Noon*, George Orwell's *1984*, and Hannah Arendt's *The Origins of Totalitarianism*. After several years of asylum in France, Milosz accepted a professorship at

Thus, *Milosz's ABC's*. As soon as I was partway into reading it, I conceived the notion that any writer might do something similar, since all of our worlds inevitably disappear. It is not only the dead who are on our minds, but also our condition as human beings. As Milosz says in "Adam and Eve," a passage on our enduring fascination with the story of the expulsion from the Garden of Eden, "In our deepest convictions, reaching into the very depths of our being, we deserve to live forever. We experience our transitoriness and mortality as an act of violence perpetrated against us. Only Paradise is authentic; the world is inauthentic, and only temporary. That is why the story of the Fall speaks to us so emotionally, as if summoning an old truth from our slumbering memory." Conversely, we could say, only the world is authentic and it, instead of the illusion of paradise, should be eternal.

Born in imitation of, and as homage to, Milosz's book, this ABC book too, then, is the record of what I think about certain people, places and ideas, part of what I want to leave to posterity, for its use and to prevent forgetting. As well, it is my vain protest against the "act of violence perpetrated against us."

Like many writers nowadays — and by "nowadays" I mean ever since Denis Diderot wrote *Jacques the Fatalist* in the mid-18th century — I think of the relationship between author and content as an ever-present part of the subject matter. Diderot was among the first modern writers I know of to step into the frame of the picture he was making and say, more or less, "Here I am." Even this preface is an instance of that interest in making visible the author's role. (Conveniently enough, the preface is also the first entry in my ABC book.) As for the corollary issue of the content's relation to the form of the writing, the Charles Olson-Robert Creeley dictum about the shape of poetry — "form is never more than an extension of content" — is

---

the University of California at Berkeley in 1960 and lived in the West Coast American college town until the appearance of the Solidarity movement in Poland and the subsequent fall of Communism in 1989. In the 1980s, he was again able to visit his native Wilno and began to divide his time between Berkeley and Krakow, Poland, eventually settling in the city of the Jagiellonian kings.

Milosz is one of those writers — like Jean-Paul Sartre, Jean Cocteau, or Günter Grass — who is enviably competent in many genres. He's written novels, volumes of essays, screenplays, memoirs such as *Native Realm*, literary history, and he's edited anthologies, mostly of Polish compatriots. His major works, though, are poetry, and range from particular volumes, such as *A Treatise on Poetry*, *Bells in Winter*, and *Road-side Dog*, to the various editions of his *Collected Poems*. In 1980 he was awarded the Nobel Prize for Literature. He died in Krakow, August 14, 2004.

basically true, but at a certain point in the composition of a book the structure of the work itself informs or feeds back into the content. The relationship becomes dynamic rather than one-sided. There's a bias toward the who, what, where, why, and when, i.e., content, but even the initial content of what we write is dependent on culturally existing forms: lexicons, sentences, concepts, syntax, etc.

The English-language edition of *Milosz's ABC's* is a selection from the original two-volume Polish publication. That leads me to reflect that one feature, and difficulty, of an alphabetically organized book is that it will inevitably be "the short version," so to speak, of everything it treats. Every entry in it could be infinitely long. And there could be dozens of additional entries. In fact, an ABC book gives rise to the notion of "the ABC game." It's a game of inclusions and exclusions: What's missing, what other entries might have been made, or, more important, what would be in *your* ABC book? But given the ever more limited horizon afforded to me by the approach of old age and death, the short version may be the best I can do, a protest, symbolic and physical, against dying with a host of imaginary, unwritten books extinguished along with me.

No sooner is the notion of "the short version" invoked — it's a phrase I often use in conversation, my version of "to make a long story short" — than a hazy outline of the contents of such a book begins to form, like a small but persistent cloud. The compositional problem is that a book of this kind is an abridgement, something short of "the whole story" or all the possible people, cities, and themes I could write about. At the same time, an ABC book suggests an infinite, ideal text: I could write about anything at all; about everything.

In addition to its textual opportunities and constraints, an ABC book is perforce the short version of another, conceptually amorphous entity, just as life itself is the short version of the dream of immortality. That entity is one that includes both a database — the sum of all my vocabularies — and the events of my life; together, they provide the locus in which I experience the world. I sometimes see my life as an obscurely connected continuum in which I can never consistently locate the narrative. Remembering the etymology of "narrative" in the Greek word for "knowing," I mean that it is now our epistemological condition to be on uncertain ground, to not be able to know for sure what and where we are.

That condition is pretty much what we mean by the contemporary term "postmodernism." Nor is it the first time in history that human beings have found themselves in such circumstances, although each particular historical conjuncture of "the cloud of unknowing" is unique.

The uncertain grounding of what I know is itself a primary subject matter, rather than something to be overcome by a declaration of will. It almost goes without saying — but I'll say it anyway because this point is frequently misunderstood — that the recognition of epistemological uncertainty is not an assertion of relativism or skepticism, moral or otherwise, nor is it an invitation to mysticism. That is, I'm prepared to make judgments, and justificatory arguments for those judgments, even though the justifications themselves are ungrounded in any absolute sense. There is groundwork, but no ultimate ground. Finally, the arbitrary order imposed by an alphabet book conveniently stands in for the obscurity of the connections in the continuum.

Probably no one is able to tell the whole story, but even in the short version one inflexible rule obtains: I'm not permitted to hold anything back. Some things may drop out of the text, more or less naturally in the course of composition, but I can't save anything for later. Ideas, aphorisms, stories, entire imaginary books, whatever I have, must be surrendered to the work at hand. I won't say, Oh, I'll hang on to this neat little idea, or grand thesis, for my next book, for my comfortable old age.

Once I began writing my ABC book, I soon encountered the obstacle of interminability. Since any entry could run from an aphoristic paragraph to a full-length essay, if I were to treat the project with bloody-minded literalness, I realized it would run to an unmanageable, and unpublishable, length. One day, a solution presented itself. Why not be literal about an ABC book, and thus merely suggest, or gesture at, the whole of the alphabet? So, for now, just A, B, C. That's enough, I think, for a coherent memoir, a tour of fabled cities (i.e., the places I've been that have meant something to me), a core sample of reflections about persons and ideas. Perhaps one day I'll write D.

Once, at dinner, when I mentioned my effort to imitate *Milosz's ABC's*, one of my table companions astutely and reasonably asked, "But wouldn't you have to be as famous as Milosz?" I got his point. If you weren't Milosz, wouldn't your choice of persons, places and topics to write about merely be idiosyncratic? I saw that to make up for the author's obscurity, the writing would have to be "interesting."

S.P.

VANCOUVER – BERLIN

2001 – 2005

Aboutism

Sometime around the beginning of what we call "the third millennium" (the year 2000 in the Western system of dating years), my long-time friend, the San Francisco-born, Vancouver poet George Stanley half-jokingly invented "aboutism." Among other things, aboutism proposes that a poem — or any other literary work for that matter — should be, after all, about something. Aboutism stands in contrast to the contemporary poetries of linguistic abstractionism or verse containing no more than local anecdotal significance, and whose context is restricted to the expressive self rather than connected to the world. And underlying that dictum about poetry is the suggestion that one's life, too, should be about something.

In his book *At Andy's*, George Stanley's poems are described (in a back cover blurb) as being "about movies, ballparks, hockey, dogs, sex, aging" and various trips Stanley had made "to Calgary and Veracruz, Ireland and Scotland, his return to Terrace, B.C., where he lived for fifteen years . . ."

And so they are. But I immediately noticed something peculiar about the whole idea of aboutism. When you read one of Stanley's poems, one, say, ostensibly about a few half-stoned men watching hockey on TV, or the comings-and-goings of Terrace, a small town in northwestern British Columbia, Canada, it turns out that the poem is also about capitalism, about television, about the phenomenological events in the poet's mind, about advertising ("the car drives into your head & is wedged there, & the beer pours through your veins —"), about the nature of language, about one's decentered location in the cosmos, about the problems of writing, about ruthless mortality and about "the huge surrounding fucked reality." (I especially like that last, big, fuzzy concept, "the huge surrounding fucked reality.") The poems are not only about something, they're also almost always about everything.

Aboutism is George Stanley's reminder — to himself and others — that art is, finally, about the world. A related but slightly different idea appears in contemporary philosophy in one of Richard Rorty's essays, when he says, "Certainly we should not think of our [philosophical] claims answering to how anyone or everyone takes things to be, but neither should we take them to answer to how things really are. The alternative is to take them as about things, but not as answering to anything, either objects or opinions . . . Aboutness, like truth, is indefinable, and none the worse for that."

In relation to art, aboutism is a game, but within it is a fairly serious parody of contemporary literary movements. In fact, were it not saved by its playful aspects, aboutism would be a slightly reactionary doctrine — though not actively retrograde, like the so-called New Formalism in poetry (or, the "New Formaldahyde," as Stanley calls it). But aboutism is reactive in the sense that it rejects a lot of the outcomes, if not the intent, of the late 20th century literary movement known as Language Poetry. That movement proposed a kind of writing that would be self-consciously critical of the banal characteristics of much of contemporary poetry, including its tendency to regard itself as making priestly pronouncements, all of which had only served to remove poetry even further from public consciousness and reduce it to a minor art understood solely by a select readership. In the "pomo-speak" style that Language Poetry critical writing favoured, the movement argued for "a self-critical poetry, minus the short-circuiting rhetoric of vatic privilege" that "might dissolve the antinomies of marginality."

Aboutism doesn't object to that idea. But what was wrong with a lot of the poems by the Language Poets is that you couldn't make head or tail of what they were saying; the results were often *irreferential*, in the sense that they didn't seem to be about anything, or anything most people could understand, despite the effort to break "the automatism of the poetic 'I'." Language Poetry wanted to get rid of the authorial voice, to produce a kind of "view from nowhere," on the grounds that the "I" inevitably distorted the world. Whether the storyteller can be eliminated from the story and its telling is arguable (I think it's a dubious proposition) but, in any case, Language Poetry seemed just as marginal as any other marginal writing. Does any of this matter? Yes, of course, it does. How we tell the story, what we write about, our understanding of the function of writing are all issues for every writer, to which the idea of aboutism offers one possible response.

Like other ideas, aboutism is not just an abstraction existing in a vacuum, but is part of a discourse whose context is both autobiographical and about the world. In the mornings, at the college just outside of Vancouver where I work, before we go off to teach our 8:30 classes to sleepy-headed students, Ryan Knighton, Reg Johanson, and I imagine aboutism. Ryan and Reg are the next generation of writers and teachers at the college, while George Stanley and I, in our sixties, are just about to be put out to pasture. Reg, though not an

Aboutist, is willing to humour Ryan and me. He or Ryan, conjuring up the yet-to-be-written "Aboutist Manifesto," cites the movement's first axiom: "Theory guards us from error. We are for error." I.e., art wants to risk making mistakes.

Ryan insists that the name of the doctrine be pronounced in the French manner — "*a*-boo-*tisme*." Its practitioners can then be known as "*Aboutistas*," he says. The quirky shift from French to Spanish is a comical way of celebrating the current Mexican Zapatista political movement, or a comment on Starbucks coffee shops referring to its workers as *barristas*. Ten years from now, I think, this semantic fooling around, which enlivened a few of our mornings (and thus gave us courage to talk to the students), will no doubt be inscrutible to readers. I imagine a project to recover — from the secret crannies and undervalued protocols of literary production — a history of lost literary jokes, and the pleasures they invoke.

Just before we leave for class, I suddenly cry out from my flimsy-walled office cubicle, imitating the strangled voices of dinosaurs I heard in "prehistoric" movie melodramas when I was a teenager. The movies had names like *100 Million B.C.*, and though they were far less "realistic" than contemporary digitalized dinosaur movies, they were much more scary. My high-pitched wail — a sort of "Wrrraghurrooaa" — echoes down the fibreboard corridor of the Humanities Division to Ryan's office at the far end. Though my unpremeditated outburst is just a goofy, anti-professorial mockery of us academics studiously preparing our lesson plans before class, there's something curiously authentic from my childhood under its surface. Maybe those movies gave me my first sense that, as George Stanley puts it in another poem, "Things cry out against each other — / the world, the image / I have of it, whirled back / in time, into nothing —."

"The sounds of professors in their cages," I say, but think: *We cry out.* I can hear Reg, in a similar cubbyhole across the hall, chuckling at my send-up of classroom "preparation" (an activity solemnly invoked in union contracts between the college and the teachers). Perhaps I'm hinting that these days professors have been reduced to the evolutionary obsolescence of dinosaurs, but the immediate point of making fun of preparation is that there's no way to be prepared for anything. Then we head off to our classes, perfectly unprepared *Aboutistas*, energetically ready to talk about the world.

PS: Predictably, as soon as a few people started taking aboutism half-seriously, Stanley announced that aboutism was over. He proposed an academic conference: "Aboutism: What Was It All About?"

Acknowledgements

I'm one of those readers devoted to the paraphernalia of books. I like prefaces, forewords, introductions, contents pages, epilogues, afterwords, appendices, bibliographies, indexes, even the "running heads" of authors' names and chapter titles, and the fine print data on the verso of the title page. Of all the extra-textual materials, I'm particularly fond of acknowledgements and often find myself reading long lists of the names of those people who helped the author, as if I'll run into someone I know (or even myself). Acknowledgements usually appear at the beginning or end of the book, but in an ABC book, of course, they enter the text itself.

Most of the writings in this book were first read, criticized and edited by Brian Fawcett, and early versions of many of the pieces here were initially posted on the Dooney's Café website, dooneyscafe.com, the digital space over which Fawcett has presided. Other pieces also appeared elsewhere, and I'm particularly grateful to Stephen Osborne and *Geist* magazine in Vancouver, and Frank Berberich and *Lettre International* in Berlin for their attention and encouragement. Several people read and were kind enough to comment on parts of this book, or assisted me in other ways. Among them: Lanny Beckman, Robin Blaser, Carellin Brooks, John Dixon, Daniel Gawthrop, Mark Johnson, Ryan Knighton, Don Larventz, Thomas Marquard, Rolf Maurer, Audrey McClellan, Ilonka Opitz, Bob Perrey, Renee Rodin, Tom Sandborn, Nikolai Schmarbeck, Bruce Serafin, and George Stanley.

Finally, I like the traditional last line of acknowledgements, in which those who aided the author are absolved of blame for his mistakes, and the writer declares, "Whatever errors of fact or interpretation that remain are the responsibility of the author."

Adam

In Jan van Eyck's *Ghent Altarpiece* (*c.* 1432) — which I saw in St. Bavo's Church in Ghent, Belgium in spring 2002 — in the upper left-hand panel of the triptych, there's a portrait of a naked Adam, driven from Paradise, taking the first irreversible step out of the Garden of Eden. What I notice are the sole and carefully rendered toes of Adam's right foot, lifted in a step that, through an optical trick of van Eyck's art, steps out of the narrow frame of the picture. I think of the old saw: The hardest step on any journey is the first. To which George Stanley tartly responded: "The hardest step on every journey / is the last, and every step is the last". The aphorism can bear one more addendum: And every step, first or last, is the expulsion.

Adolescence

While I was an adolescent, everything that is crucial to my identity happened. Because those adolescent experiences were so vivid, I could never accept the notions of the determining impact of either the unconscious or the affective power of early childhood traumas with any enthusiasm. So, I'm not a Freudian even though it was the reigning psychological ideology during the 1950s when I was growing up. The general ideas of Freud are plausible in the abstract if not in the specifics, but I remain deeply resistant to the concept that we are primarily shaped by our infantile experiences.

Adolescence as the determining period of the creation of the self seems more common-sensically true. As an adolescent, my relationships with the boys with whom I played sandlot baseball and went to Marshall, and then Austin High School in Chicago — the Murphy brothers, Eddie Lacy, Bob Greenspan, Abe Dorevich, Nick Kinnis, Elliot Goldman, Mel Weisberg — set the parameters of my notions of friendship, loyalty, physical beauty and desire. Adolescence is when I first contemplated the nature of the starry universe; became engrossed in politics (the McCarthy-Army U.S. Senate hearings on communism were on TV and I watched them after school); and acquired a taste for "bohemian" company — in drama class with Sandra S., "Bunny," Chuck Harris. Adolescence is also when I began to write.

One day, age 13 or so, around the onset of adolescence, I was working — inkily and ineptly — in the school mimeograph room (Sumner Elementary School) with Bob Perna, a local "tough" of Mediterranean lineage. He told me about an uncle of his who was an artist. I looked up blankly from the clicking drum of the mimeo and registered his disappointment that I failed to recognize the name of his relative, Salvador Dalí, or the remarkableness of being so related. After all, I was supposed to be a "brain." I was awed by Perna's sophistication, his assumption that one should surely know who Dalí was, by the intimation that a larger world existed and could be the concern of people like me. Much later, coincidentally, I became particularly fond of Dalí's paintings — just the other day I was again looking at his Narcissus — notwithstanding the contempt in which he's held by the official art world, which regards him as something of a fraud.

Adonis

Here's the sort of thing that not infrequently happens to me: I'm sitting in Berlin one rainy summer afternoon reading, in a desultory way, the electronic edition of the *New York Times*. I happen upon an article about an Arabic-language poet who, the headline says, "dares to differ." I click onto it thinking no more than, OK, some guy who dissents from the madness of Islamic politics. Good.

But in the article, apart from its topical account of an Arab literary dissenter, I learn that 72-year-old Adonis, a Syrian-born writer named Ali Ahmad Said until he took the name of a Greek god as his nom-de-plume at 19, is "widely considered the Arab world's greatest living poet." Among other things, he lives in exile in Paris but is spending the year in Berlin (so we're in the same city, as I'm reading the article); he's a modernist, as important to 20th century Arab-language poetry as T.S. Eliot is to poetry in English; he rejects Islamic ideology, and is also critical of equivalent Western nonsense; etc.

A few lines of a prose poem, "Remembering The First Century," are quoted: "We blunder through prophecy as if through sand. 'Brother, show us a sign that shall prevail.' History crumbles downhill like a babble of ants that choke on their own dust, on the filth of snails, on shell after shell . . ."

All of the article's claims about the greatness of Adonis strike me as completely believable. And I'm thunderstruck. Maybe I shouldn't be, but I am. It's as if the newspaper article is announcing the discovery of a whole new continent. I perhaps had heard Adonis's unusual pen-name, but paid no attention. I think I confused him with some African or Caribbean "dub" poet. How is it possible that I've lived a relatively long life that includes knowing quite a bit about poetry and yet I knew, until that moment, nothing about Adonis? There is no end to ignorance, or at least no end to my ignorance. I'll have to reconfigure my picture of the world, my *mappa mundi*, not only now, this very minute, but probably right up to my very last breath.

Irene Aebi

Memory, quick as a gift: In the copy of Marguerite Duras's *Practicalities* that Irene Aebi gave me (because she knew of my fondness for Duras), I find her inscription in French, "For my friend Stan (who always remains the young man that I knew), affectionately, Irene."

We were both young. It was in Naples, Italy, around 1960. I was in the U.S. Navy, stationed near Naples, and she was a Swiss girl, working as an assistant to a biologist doing research in immunology, studying chicken eggs under a microscope. The three of us met because he was looking for help in writing up his findings. Irene and I became friends. She was tomboyish, with short-cropped blond hair and strong cheekbones — a look that was made fashionable by the actress Jean Seberg when she appeared in Jean-Luc Godard's *Breathless*. As a Swiss, Irene was quadrophonic, speaking a melange of English, French, Italian and German. She was the first European I knew.

A couple of years later, Irene visited me in San Francisco. Then there was a gap of many years. When she reappeared — it was in Vancouver in the 1980s — her life was transformed. In her new incarnation, she was a singer and occasional violinist who performed with her partner, the famous jazz soprano saxophonist, Steve Lacy. They lived together in Paris, but Irene often found periodic refuge at the Sylvia Hotel in Vancouver. That's where she gave me the Duras book. We were no longer young, but our conversations, about books, art, ideas, retain the adolescent excitement of a lifetime.

Of African descent

My father owned or worked in a series of more or less failing grocery stores in black neighbourhoods on the South Side of Chicago for some twenty-five years, roughly between 1940 and the mid-1960s. His stores foundered because of the appearance of large, new, chain supermarkets, a feature of post-World War II capitalist development that ultimately doomed the independent corner groceries. It was the era when the South Side, as historian Robert Stepto writes, "burgeoned as thousands of African Americans, almost exclusively from the south, migrated to the city during the Great Migration of the World War II years."

Among the first black people to whom I was formally introduced — at about age five, one Sunday morning while accompanying my father to the store — was a plainclothes Chicago policeman named Two-Gun Pete. When we shook hands, his large paw engulfed my tiny one, and I noticed how the pink flesh of his palm contrasted against the dark brown skin on the back of his hand. Was I shown and allowed to touch the mother-of-pearl handle of one of his fabled guns, or was I merely told about them? My father impressed upon me Two-Gun Pete's prowess and fearlessness. He'd just as soon shoot a man as look at him, people said of Pete in tones of awe.

A couple of years ago, on television, I watched scenes of black "unrest" in Cincinnati, Ohio, in the wake of a police shooting of an unarmed African-American teenager, the latest in a string of similar killings over a number of years there. Like the other viewers, I was left with a few violent, familiar visuals: the plate glass window of a shop being smashed; a gaggle of young black men, several of them shirtless, running across a flame-licked urban landscape; a grainy video clip filmed at night, whose soundtrack carries an occasional police gunshot; the talking head of the sombre white mayor of Cincinnati declaring a curfew; a grieving mother. The succession of pictures provide a sort of check-list of scenes meant to prove that this "riot" is comparable to previous riots impressionistically stored in viewers' memory banks. Intentionally or not, the visuals successfully hinder any understanding of what might be going on.

"Race-relations" or, more properly, the impoverished, horizonless condition of masses of black people in blighted city cores across the United States, remains the great American internal political disgrace of the second half of the 20th century. But the bare declaration of the atrocity — and it is an undoubted atrocity, long drawn-out as well as punctuated by incidents such as those in Cincinnati — hardly conveys the horror of hundreds of thousands of slowly lost black lives in America.

When I look back on the time during which I grew up, the ubiquitous racism is now more apparent, even if it was only the muted version absorbed in my family, which, on my mother's side, included several small shopkeepers whose customers were mostly black. Then, African-Americans were known as Negroes, coloureds, or, among lower-middle-class Jews, the Yiddish term *schwartze*, derived from the German word for "black," was used.

(George Stanley recently observed how thoroughly and rapidly the term "black" succeeded "negro" in the 1960s; a brown-skinned woman of Caribbean descent with whom we were talking argued that the later "African-American" is a questionable usage arising from dubious aspects of contemporary "identity politics.")

Did my aunts utter the sentence, in reference to the impending arrival of a coloured cleaning woman, "Is the *schwartze* coming over today?" These relatives of mine, European-descended Jewish Caucasians, watched brutal scenes on TV of black civil rights protesters being menaced by police and dogs in Alabama or Mississippi in the mid-1950s. And they were probably appalled by the Southern practice of segregation — separate and unequal toilets, drinking fountains, and schools for Negroes and Whites. Yet their own unthinking references to blacks simply assumed them to be a separate and yes, inferior, people. Significantly, the contemporary white race riots of the early 1950s, against Negroes being apportioned a share of the newly-built public housing projects right there in Chicago, received far less attention than the televised barbarities in Georgia.

Apart from acquiring a liberal attitude in support of the black civil rights movement, as a teenager I was less absorbed by the politics of race than I was by the ontological mystery of the differences. How was it possible for human skin to be different colours? I'd encountered hundreds of black people — customers, workers, and people in the neighbourhoods on the South Side of Chicago where my father's successive failing stores were located. They included the young black men my father employed and trained in the skills of meat-cutting and clerking (valuable trades to acquire, given black unemployment rates), who in turn taught me to play basketball and instructed me in the rudiments of boxing in the alley behind the store during our breaks. I maintained a correspondence with one of them, Frank, a young man four or five years older than me, after he'd joined the army and was stationed in Alaska. With the ambition of a budding author (age thirteen), I proposed that I could "write up" his adventures in the wild.

Although it became conventional in the left-wing identity politics of the 1980s and 90s to intimate that sexual desire for the coloured "other" was also a form of imperialist racism (based on a judgment about white men sleeping with black women), it's a proposition I'm inclined to dispute as simplistic and partial. The mystery of skin colour wasn't fully impressed upon me until I became infatuated, around age 14 or 15, with someone I'll call Jesse Williams, a black schoolmate in my high school gym class.

I contrived to get the clothes locker next to Jesse's, and whenever I could, I lingered in the locker room. I sat next to where Jesse stood on the wooden bench, looking up in mute adoration. In the crowded change room, with the sound of showers hissing in the background, and the noisy horsing around of teenage boys banging locker doors and snapping towels, onlookers would hardly have noticed me, although I had the sense that Jesse himself was not unaware of my furtive glances at his groin as he stepped into his white jockstrap.

I couldn't have articulated my feelings then. I had barely thought about homosexuality yet; at most, I had a dim notion of the Freudian concept that boys passed through "a phase" of love for other boys. Yet, I felt a distinct difference between my desire for Jesse, and for others to whom I was attracted— pale blond Protestants, or the Irish and Jewish kids of my acquaintance. Having grown up with all of the latter, it seemed as if my attraction to them arose at least partially out of a shared cultural background in which I had gradually learned about the possibilities of beauty. Whereas, with Jesse the force of eros was startling, unprecedented, as if I had invented this particular recognition of desire all on my own (or as if it had invented me). Though it's hardly a cure for racism, desire and a healthy curiosity about others (a.k.a. xenophilia) seem like first steps away from it that are as plausible as any others. Equally, relationships between people of different races that create children of mixed skin colour deliver a small, more literal blow against racism (in the 1950s such relations were banned in the U.S. by so-called "miscegenation" laws).

A similar illumination on the intellectual side occurred when I walked into an algebra class on the first day of the semester and discovered that the teacher, Mr. Harris, was a black man. Clearly there was a dissonance between the slightly demeaning notion of *schwartzes* and the presence of an African-American man who would instruct us in the mysteries of mathematics, rendered alphabetical with mysterious x's and y's (e.g., $2x$ times $3y$ equals $4z$; what is x?).

The developing cognizances — erotic, intellectual — of actual black people I knew are more informative than the abstract political rhetoric of racism deplored. Recently, I happened upon Wayne Miller's book of photographs, *Chicago's South Side, 1946–1948*, gradually becoming pleasantly lost in the images of scenes I may have seen for myself as a boy.

There was no photograph of Two-Gun Pete in Miller's book, but I was intuitively certain I would find something. After looking at the pictures, I turned to Miller's introductory memoir of shooting those photographs and immediately found the passage I was seeking. Of the many hundreds of pictures he had taken a half-century before, Miller says, he remembers those "of Silvester Washington — a Chicago Juvenile Police Officer nicknamed 'Two-Gun Pete'; like the maverick General George Patton, he sported a pair of pearl-handled revolvers." There's a photo of a contemplative black teenager in a suit and tie who, according to the caption, is "at the Wabash Avenue police station presided over by Silvester 'Two Gun Pete' Washington." The boy appears to be listening to someone just outside the photo's frame, likely Two-Gun Pete himself, who also moves just outside the frame of my memory.

After Lorca

In the winter of 1958–59, Jack Spicer gave a poetry reading at San Francisco's Bread and Wine Mission, a proto-New Age storefront drop-in centre at the top of Grant Avenue in North Beach run by Father Pierre Delattre. I was in the U.S. Navy at the time, 18 years old, stationed at nearby Treasure Island in San Francisco Bay, my first posting after boot camp.

Had I already read about, or seen a picture — in *Life* magazine — of "Hube the Cube"? This improbable poster-person for the beatnik movement was a scruffy, thin man with a black beret whom I sometimes saw walking on Grant Avenue. What got him into *Life* magazine was the word "oblivion" tattooed on his right bicep, his unique way of declaring withdrawal from the "rat race" of conventional life in 1950s America.

When I went into the city, I searched out the "beatniks" and artists, and occasionally stopped by the Bread and Wine Mission for the free spaghetti dinner it offered once a week. That's likely where I heard about Spicer's reading.

I hadn't yet been introduced to Spicer, though I'd read a couple of his poems in the *Evergreen Review* a year or two earlier. But I was paying more attention to the stars of the burgeoning literary movement that would eventually become the "New American Poetry" — Allen Ginsberg, Jack Kerouac, Lawrence Ferlinghetti, and Gary Snyder.

In person, Spicer was an ungainly pear-shaped man in his early thirties, his thinning hair swept back from his sun-freckled forehead, garbed, the first time I saw him, in a rumpled sports jacket and ill-fitting black pants. While he read, he scrunched up his eyes, balled his chubby fists, and seemed to menacingly chew on the words of his poems.

I was soon to learn that Spicer, about a year or two before this reading, had experienced one of those extraordinary artistic breakthroughs that often determine a poet's career and shape the remainder of his life. That breakthrough is the subject of this passage.

Born in Los Angeles in 1925, and raised there, Spicer had come to the University of California at Berkeley at the end of World War II where he fell in with a group of young poets, the most prominent of whom — Robert Duncan, Robin Blaser and himself — formed a triumvirate at the forefront of a local poetry movement that became known as the "Berkeley Renaissance."

A decade later, while briefly and unhappily in New York and Boston, Spicer found himself at an artistic impasse. True, he had written several good poems in the past ten years, predominantly influenced, I think, by the work of W. B. Yeats and Wallace Stevens, but as he said in a poem commemorating the death of jazz musician Charlie Parker, "Song for Bird and Myself" (1956), "I am dissatisfied with my poetry, / I am dissatisfied with my sex life, / I am dissatisfied with the angels I believe in." In the opening chapter of an unfinished detective novel he subsequently attempted, Spicer offers a fictional self-portrait of himself as a stymied, "academic" poet, returning to San Francisco to seek new inspiration.

Just before his return to San Francisco, Spicer read a new edition of Federico Garcia Lorca's *Selected Poems* (1955), co-edited by Don Allen, a former Berkeley classmate working in the publishing business in New York. Toward the end of 1956, Spicer began dabbling in some translations of the work of the homosexual Spanish poet who had been murdered by the Fascists in 1936, at age 38. Spicer was attracted not only to Lorca's homoeroticism, but also by the Spanish poet's association with surrealism. Lorca had been in love with Salvador Dalí, and was a friend of the filmmaker Luis Buñuel. Spicer was also drawn to Lorca's Orphic theory of *duende*, and his interest in the 19th century American poet Walt Whitman. All of these were themes that resonated with Spicer's own poetic concerns. By Christmas 1956, back in San Francisco, Spicer had completed his translation of Lorca's angry "Ode to Walt Whitman," at which point he became stuck in this still undefined project.

It wasn't until summer 1957, after conducting a "Magic Workshop" for young poets and finishing a brief teaching stint at San Francisco State College, that his writer's block broke. When Don Allen arrived in San Francisco to spend the summer, Spicer had a new "Lorca" poem to show him practically every day when they met at Vesuvio's or The Place, two local North Beach bars. But the poems weren't simply translations. As Spicer wrote to Robin Blaser in Boston in June 1957, "Since school's been out (for me forever) I've been ignoring my unemployment and translating Lorca ... I enclose my eight latest 'translations.' Transformations might be a better word. Several are originals and most of the rest change the poem vitally. I can't seem to make anybody understand this or what I'm doing. They look blank or ask what the Spanish is for a word that isn't in Spanish or praise (like Duncan did) an original poem as typically Lorca. What I am trying to do is establish a tradition. When I'm through (although I'm sure no one will ever publish them) I'd like someone as good as I am to translate these translations into French (or Pushtu) adding more. Do you understand? No. Nobody does."

A year or so later, in 1958, in the middle of Spicer's next book, *Admonitions*, and as part of the text, there is another letter to Blaser. "You are right that I don't now need your criticisms of individual poems . . . Halfway through *After Lorca* I discovered that I was writing a book instead of a series of poems," Spicer says.

"That is why all my stuff from the past . . . looks foul to me. The poems belong nowhere. They are one night stands filled (the best of them) with their own emotions, but pointing nowhere, as meaningless as sex in a Turkish bath . . . Look at those other poems. Admire them if you like. They are beautiful but dumb," he laments.

"Poems should echo and reecho against each other. They should create resonances. They cannot live alone any more than we can . . . Things fit together. We knew that — it is the principle of magic. Two inconsequential things can combine together to become a consequence. This is true of poems too. A poem is never to be judged by itself alone. A poem is never by itself alone." Spicer tells Blaser, "This is the most important letter that you have ever received."

Allowing for a bit of vatic hyperbole in the claim that his earlier poems amount to no more than "one night stands," what's interesting is that Spicer's critical vocabulary uses the colloquial language of gay cruising to describe his dilemma, asserting that poetry, if not the poets who write it, is looking for love rather than sex. More important, in the midst of writing *After Lorca*, Spicer discovered the notion of what he and Blaser would subsequently call the "serial" poem, a form whose unit of composition is the "book" (using that word in a way slightly different from its conventional reference), and to be distinguished from the modern "epic," such as Ezra Pound's *Cantos*, or Charles Olson's *Maximus*, as well as other "long" poems, or poems in "parts." In the serial poem, each poem stands on its own, and yet integrally connects to the other poems that make up the "book." Furthermore, Spicer conjoins to the serial poem an Orphic theory that the poem is transmitted, from an unknown outside source, by a process of "dictation." For the remainder of his brief life — he died in 1965 — Spicer would write only dictated "books."

The first result of this breakthrough was *After Lorca* (1957), a thoroughly original work and a book unlike any other in American poetry in its era. Beyond the form of the serial poem, and the mixture of "transformations" and scrupulously accurate translations (the one of Lorca's "Ode to Whitman" is arguably superior to that of any preceding "professional" translation), Spicer gave the book an elegant and witty coherence by interweaving the poems with a series of letters to the dead Lorca that proclaimed Spicer's poetics and provided a sort of self-reflexive narrative of the writing of the poems. As well, there's an "introduction" to *After Lorca* written mock-posthumously by Lorca himself.

The assumption of the persona of Lorca is Spicer's first great invention in *After Lorca*, creating the trope that not only are the poems written in the manner of Lorca (hence, "after Lorca"), but that both Spicer and (the imaginary) Lorca are writing after the death of the Spanish poet. "Frankly I was quite surprised when Mr. Spicer asked me to write an introduction to this volume," Lorca begins, in a tone of dry, mild affront that Spicer sustains throughout the apparently reluctantly written preface. "My reaction to the manuscript he sent me (and to the series of letters that are now a part of it) was and is fundamentally unsympathetic. It seems to me the waste of a considerable talent on something which is not worth doing." However, Lorca adds, with grim wit, "I have been removed from all contact with poetry for the last twenty years. The younger generation of poets may view with pleasure Mr. Spicer's execution of what seems to me a difficult and unrewarding task."

The imaginary world that Spicer conjures up in this first paragraph is so smoothly and economically presented that its surreal metaphysics are almost imperceptible — a world in which living poets can communicate with dead ones by sending them letters through a celestial post office, and in which dead poets have enough of an afterlife to criticize the living one's efforts.

Lorca forcefully warns readers that the poems are not translations. "In even the most literal of them Mr. Spicer seems to derive pleasure in inserting or substituting one or two words which completely change the mood and often the meaning of the poem as I had written it." Moreover, there are hybrid poems, half-Lorca, half-Spicer, "giving rather the effect of an unwilling centaur (modesty forbids me to speculate which end of the animal is mine)," as well as an equal number of Spicer's own poems "executed in a somewhat fanciful imitation of my early style." Worse, there's "no indication of which of the poems belong to which category," and — in a final twist of the poetic knife — "I have further complicated the problem (with malice aforethought I must admit) by sending Mr. Spicer several poems written after my death which he has also translated and included here." As Lorca puts it, with gallows-humour, "Even the most faithful student of my work will be hard put to decide what is and what is not Garcia Lorca as, indeed, he would be if he were to look into my present resting place."

The letters to Lorca are "another problem," says the imaginary recipient of them. "When Mr. Spicer began sending them to me a few months ago, I recognized immediately the 'programmatic letter' — the letter one poet writes to another not in any effort to communicate with him, but rather as a young man whispers his secrets to a scarecrow, knowing that his young lady is in the distance listening." In this case, the young lady "may be a Muse, but the scarecrow nevertheless quite naturally resents the confidences." As for the reader of this odd amalgam, "who is not a party to this singular tryst," Lorca concedes that he "may be amused by what he overhears."

What follows are about thirty brief poems, each dedicated to a poet, friend, or lover of Spicer's acquaintance, two surrealist playlets featuring the silent movie comedian Buster Keaton (about whom Lorca had in fact written a playlet in his posthumously published *Poet in New York*), the famous polemical "Ode to Walt Whitman" in which Lorca — and Spicer — argue their uncompromising views on homosexual love, and the interleafed "programmatic" letters.

In the letters, Spicer propounds a poetics whose principal issues are the relation of language to poetry; the connections or "correspondences" of poems to each other despite their apparent disimilarities or distance in time, geography and language (a theory created in the 19th century by Rimbaud and Baudelaire); and necessarily, a metaphysics about art, life, love, and death — the latter realized through a metaphorical embodiment of "the dead," who, as Lorca says, "are notoriously hard to satisfy."

The poems in *After Lorca* are unassuming lyrics that nonetheless often carry the sting of the underlying poetics, but are far from the spectacular figures and romantic language that first attracted me to poetry (Allen Ginsberg's "angelheaded hipsters," say, "dragging themselves through the negro streets at dawn looking for an angry fix" — some of whom I would meet in San Francisco). Spicer's Lorca poems are stark, melancholy, disciplined, and cerebral. A characteristic one reads:

A Diamond

A Translation for Robert Jones

A diamond
Is there
At the heart of the moon or the branches or my nakedness
And there is nothing in the universe like diamond
Nothing in the whole mind.
The poem is a seagull resting on a pier at the end of the ocean

A dog howls at the moon
A dog howls at the branches
A dog howls at the nakedness
A dog howling with pure mind.

I ask for the poem to be as pure as a seagull's belly.

The universe falls apart and discloses a diamond
Two words called seagull are peacefully floating out where the
    waves are
The dog is dead there with the moon, with the branches, with
    my nakedness
And there is nothing in the universe like diamond
Nothing in the whole mind.

The complex metaphysics of "A Diamond" posit the merciless interrelationship of person to the world and perhaps something larger. The ordinary world of "branches," "a dog," "seagull," "the ocean," rendered in words — "two words called seagull are peacefully floating out where the waves are" — and the binary universe / "the whole mind," are offered as alternatives, mediated only by "the poem." The howling of Spicer's dog is far removed from the rhapsodic, Whitmanesque "Howl" that Ginsberg had written only a year or two before. In Spicer's vision, the universe "falls apart" to disclose "a diamond" at the heart of things — "the moon or the branches or my nakedness." The declaration is that "there is nothing in the universe like diamond / Nothing in the whole mind," and that the diamond is the poem.

The letters to Lorca make the poetics more explicit, despite a dialectical elusiveness. Spicer begins with a tactical feint, disclaiming the importance of the missives. "These letters are to be as temporary as our poetry is to be permanent," Spicer tells Lorca. "They will establish the bulk, the wastage that my sour-stomached contemporaries demand to help them swallow and digest the pure word. We will use up our rhetoric here so that it will not appear in our poems." Several times Spicer makes unfavourable comparisons of the prose of the letters to poetry. "See how weak prose is," he says. "These paragraphs could be translated, transformed by a chain of fifty poets in fifty languages, and they would still be temporary, untrue, unable to yield the substance of a single image. Prose invents — poetry discloses."

In the course of enunciating his stance, Spicer also provides, almost offhandedly, an autobiographical portrait of his own spare life. "A mad man is talking to himself in the room next to mine. He speaks in prose. Presently I shall go to a bar and there one or two poets will speak to me and I to them and we will try to destroy each other or attract each other or even listen to each other and nothing will happen because we will be speaking in prose. I will go home, drunken and dissatisfied, and sleep — and my dreams will be prose. Even the subconscious is not patient enough for poetry." Neither madness, dreams nor everyday discourse can take us beyond prose; only poetry can make something "happen." Spicer adds, almost by way of respite, "You are dead and the dead are very patient."

In a further letter, Spicer notes that although "a really perfect poem has an infinitely small vocabulary," there is a considerable difficulty embedded in language and reality. "We want to transfer the immediate object, the immediate emotion to the poem — and yet the immediate always has hundreds of its own words clinging to it, short-lived and tenacious as barnacles. And it is wrong to scrape them off and substitute others. A poet is a time mechanic not an embalmer. The words around the immediate shrivel and decay like flesh around the body ... Objects, words must be led across time not preserved against it."

Finally, on language: "Words are what sticks to the real. We use them to push the real, to drag the real into the poem. They are what we hold on with, nothing else. They are as valuable in themselves as rope with nothing to be tied to."

The difficult notion of "the real" and the problem of the "immediate object" or emotion are taken up in a subsequent letter, one that would attain some notice as Spicer's formal statement of poetics when it was published in editor Don Allen's *New American Poetry, 1945–60*. Although many of Spicer's contemporaries also made statements about poetics, the still-remarkable feature of *After Lorca*'s poetics, which are fully embedded in the work of art, is that no American poet had said precisely these things before, and no one had spoken in this intimate, confiding tone of voice about how poetry worked.

Spicer declares, "I would like to make poems out of real objects. The lemon to be a lemon that the reader could cut or squeeze or taste — a real lemon like a newspaper in a collage is a real newspaper." Immediately, and characteristically, Spicer invents a tantalizing dialectic between the impossibility of poems made out of real lemons and the reasonableness of a newspaper fragment pasted into a collaged artwork. "I would like the moon in my poems to be a real moon, one which could be suddenly covered with a cloud that has nothing to do with the poem — a moon utterly independent of images. The imagination pictures the real. I would like to point to the real," Spicer says.

If there is a dialectic between words and the real in poetry, there is something similar between mere images and "visibility" within a poem. "How easy it is in erotic musings or in the truer imagination of a dream to invent a beautiful boy. How difficult to take a boy in a blue bathing suit that I have watched as casually as a tree and to make him visible in a poem as a tree is visible, not as an image or a picture but as something alive — caught forever in the structure of words. Live moons, live lemons, live boys in bathing suits. The poem is a collage of the real."

But, as Spicer knows as well as the rest of us, "things decay . . . Real things become garbage. The piece of lemon you shellac to the canvas begins to develop a mold, the newspaper tells of incredibly ancient events in forgotten slang, the boy becomes a grandfather. Yes, but the garbage of the real still reaches out into the current world making its objects, in turn, visible — lemon calls to lemon, newspaper to newspaper, boy to boy. As things decay they bring their equivalent into being."

That is, "things do not connect; they correspond." It is the possibility of correspondence that gives meaning to the otherwise mysterious notion of "tradition" that Spicer mentions in both his letter to Blaser and the letters to Lorca. A poet "translates" real objects, "bring[s] them across language as easily as he can bring them across time." The corresponding objects are not at all identical — "that lemon may become this lemon, or it may even become this piece of seaweed, or this particular color of gray in this ocean. One does not need to imagine that lemon; one needs to discover it." Even the letters to Lorca "correspond with something (I don't know what) that you have written . . . and, in turn, some future poet will write something which corresponds to them. That is how we dead men write to each other."

At the end, after other letters and poems, Spicer announces that "this is the last letter." The connection between the two poets has faded away "with the summer. I turn in anger and dissatisfaction to the things of my life and you return, a disembodied but contagious spirit, to the printed page." The communion with the ghost of Garcia Lorca is over.

How was it ever able to happen? Spicer wonders. "It was a game, I shout to myself . . . There are no angels, ghosts, or even shadows. It was a game made out of summer and freedom and a need for poetry that would be more than the expression of my hatreds and desires." Yet, it was real. "The poems are there, the memory not of a vision but a kind of casual friendship with an undramatic ghost who occasionally looked through my eyes and whispered to me . . ."

In "Radar," a postscript dedicated to Marianne Moore, Spicer once more measures the uncertainty of the world in relation to the self, and the irreparable loss which shadows any such encounter:

No one exactly knows
Exactly how clouds look in the sky
Or the shape of the mountains below them
Or the direction in which fish swim.
No one exactly knows.
The eye is jealous of whatever moves
And the heart
Is too far buried in the sand
To tell.

At Spicer's reading that night in the winter of 1958-59, he read from his recent books, *Admonitions* and *A Book of Music*, two serial poems written in 1958. In about six months I would acquire an elementary understanding that permitted me to see why this poetry was more interesting than its spectacular, hip cousins, but at the time, what Spicer read went mostly over my head. Nonetheless, after the reading, I hung around anyway and fell into conversation with the poet. Somewhere in the course of talking — perhaps as a result of the talk, or simply because I was young and attractive, though I wasn't any more aware of my beauty than I was of his alleged ugliness — Spicer produced a rumpled brown paper bag, the kind you could get at any grocery store. He emphasised that although the books inside the bag normally sold for one dollar, on this occasion he was giving me a gift. At which point, he extracted from the paper bag a copy of *After Lorca* and handed it to me. Thus, I began my relationship with my mentor.

AIDS

I only have to re-open the pages of Paul Monette's *Borrowed Time: An AIDS Memoir*, as I did recently, and a lot of it comes back. From the chilling first sentence — "I don't know if I will live to finish this" — the aura of dread that for years permeated every minute of the time of that plague era returns in force, sending a shudder through my body. The memory leaves me off-centre, with a survivor's mixed feelings of guilt and gratitude, and also, a sense of being curiously obsolete for possessing personal recollections of what to others can only be an increasingly distant matter of history. Some 20 years after the inception of Acquired Immune Deficiency Syndrome (AIDS), and after or in the midst of subsequent, if lesser, epidemics (Ebola, West Nile and the SARS viruses), how can I explain what it was like then? Strange to have lived through — strictly by chance — a plague in my own lifetime. Strange that its location in people's minds, including my own, is now displaced, both temporally and geographically. Strange that in one sense AIDS is over, but hasn't at all ended, neither here, in North America and Europe, where it continues to afflict particular ethnic and sub-cultural groups, such as intravenous drug users, nor there. "There" is now Africa, where AIDS rages in catastrophic proportions, with literally millions of people on the verge of death, simply, as far as I can tell, because "we," the rich world, won't give "them," the poor world, the drugs they need and can't afford.

How to give an idea of what it was like then? Through our records of the plague, our dispatches from the front. There is, not surprisingly, a lot of very good writing about AIDS, from novelist Edmund White's fictionalized memoir, *The Farewell Symphony* to activist-scholar Douglas Crimp's militant essays, *Melancholia and Moralism*. The amount of good writing is not surprising in the sense that a sizeable number of talented, literate men, their minds "wonderfully concentrated," as Samuel Johnson put it, by the prospect of death, applied their intelligence to providing a description of the plague. Even works that are justifiably criticized — journalist Randy Shilts's best-selling *And the Band Played On* and Larry Kramer's shrilly-pitched *Reports from the Holocaust* come to mind — offer moments of legitimate illumination. But of all the books written in the midst of the plague, Paul Monette's *Borrowed Time* is the one that had the greatest impact on me.

I

The circumstances of Monette's grief-stricken tale are simple enough. Set in the mid-1980s, Monette and his friend, Roger Horwitz, lovers for a decade, are practically poster-boys for the joys of middle-aged gay domesticity. There's "a stucco 1930s cottage high in a box canyon above [Hollywood's] Sunset Strip" in which they live, "a view of the city lights through the coral tree out front and between the olive and eucalyptus across the way," while out back "is a garden court shaded by Chinese elms and a blue-bottom pool that catches the sun from eleven to three," and a terrace for dinners with friends down from San Francisco. There's a used, bawky, black Jaguar (upscale successor to a Mercedes), and holidays to Greece or the California foreshore at Big Sur. There are understanding parents with a house in swanky Palm Springs, fashionable restaurants, and an assortment of therapists and agents. They attend benefit dinners put on by the gay community, and Roger, a lawyer, and Paul can afford to sponsor a table. The occasional movie star, prominent producer, or famous writer passes through the scene of their domestic life.

But there's a darker side to this middle-class homosexual idyll. Monette, a once promising poet and novelist, the author of *Taking Care of Mrs. Carroll* (1978) and *The Gold Diggers* (1979), finds himself, five or six years later, at age 40, in something of a literary slide, stalled on a novel and reduced to writing sit-com movie scripts. There's a hint of recent past trouble in an otherwise monogamous relationship. And there is the rumour of the plague.

Monette recalls the "shadowy nonfacts," "the most fragmented of rumours" of the early 1980s. He remembers noting in his diary in December 1981, "ambiguous reports of a 'gay cancer,'" then adds, "but I know I didn't have the slightest picture of the thing. Cancer of the *what*? I would have asked, if anyone had known anything." A couple of months later, in early 1982, driving to Palm Springs to visit Roger's parents, Paul reads aloud from an article in the gay magazine *The Advocate*, an article titled "Is Sex Making Us Sick?" As Monette notes, "There was the slightest edge of irony in the query, an urban cool that seems almost bucolic now in its innocence. But the article didn't mince words," providing the first in-depth reporting he'd seen — it wasn't yet mentioned in the *Los Angeles Times* — of a mysterious — was it fatal? — disease that targetted gay men.

"I remember exactly what was going through my mind while I was reading," Monette writes a half-dozen years later. "I was simply relieved . . . because the article appeared to be saying that there was a grim progression toward this undefined catastrophe, a set of preconditions — chronic hepatitis, repeated bouts of syphilis, exotic parasites. No wonder my first baseline response was to feel safe. It was *them* — by which I meant the fast-lane Fire Island crowd, the Sutro Baths, the world of High Eros. Not us."

It wasn't "us," not yet. Nor was it yet known that the disease didn't present a neat set of preconditions. Not until a year and a half later, in autumn 1983, did Monette get a call from his best friend, Cesar, a teacher in San Francisco, who reported a swollen gland in his groin that he was going to get biopsied before the school semester began again. "AIDS didn't even cross my mind, though cancer did," Monette recalls. "Half joking, Cesar wondered aloud if he dared disturb our happy friendship with bad news. 'If it's bad,' I said, 'we'll handle it, okay?'" Paul and Roger were busy getting ready for their annual trip to Big Sur. Paul put the thought away. After all, "even though he went to the baths a couple of times a week, Cesar wasn't into anything *weird* — or that's how I might have put it at that stage of my own denial. No hepatitis, no history of VD, built tall and fierce — of course he was safe."

But days after their return from Big Sur, Paul arrived home one evening and "Roger met me gravely at the door. 'There's a message from Cesar,' he said. 'It's not good.' Numbly I played back the answering machine, where so much appalling misery would be left on tape over the years to come, as if a record were crying out to be kept. 'I have a little bit of bad news.' Cesar's voice sounded strained, almost embarrassed." Monette spends the evening working his way through a tangle of telephone calls, bracing himself for cancer news, before he reaches a mutual acquaintance named Tom. "The lymph nodes, of course — a hypocondriac knows all there is to know about the sites of malignancy. Already I was figuring what the treatments might be . . . I had Cesar practically cured by the time I reached Tom . . . But as usual with me in crisis, I was jabbering and wouldn't let Tom get a word in. Finally he broke through: 'He's got it.' 'Got what?'" Monette asks, but he knows at that instant that "it" is something other than a curable cancer.

The best thing about Monette's narrative is simply its accurate accumulation of mundane details. It is like a careful description of weather — a gathering storm — or a slowly advancing, but relentless, artillery barrage, closing in on your little foxhole. Though life will soon be as alien as "living on the moon," Monette's text respects the reality of his experience sufficiently that there is no vain striving to rise above it, to claim that he's anything more than a precise instance of something larger. Roger and Paul are ordinary, middle-class gay men, accustomed to the privileges available to them, not even necessarily the sort of gay men I especially like. They're politically liberal but not more than that, fussily self-absorbed (aren't we all?), "out" in homosexual terms, but not *too* out. All of that is part of the unheroic attraction of *Borrowed Time*.

Since Monette's book is a chronicle of a doom foretold, the inevitable happens: Cesar's condition deteriorates, Roger falls ill, is diagnosed with the deadly syndrome, and in turn, Paul tests positive for the virus. Among their circle of friends and acquaintances, more and more of them are struck down by what is clearly a plague. We know all this from the very beginning of Monette's book, as in a Greek tragedy where the chorus opens the drama with a recitation of the plot. Monette, looking back on the wreckage of life, ponders the difficulty of knowing where to start. "The world around me is defined now by its endings and its closures — the date on the grave that follows the hyphen. Roger Horwitz, my beloved friend, died of complications of AIDS on October 22, 1986 . . . That is the only real date anymore, casting its icy shadow over all the secular holidays lovers mark their calendars by," he says in the first pages.

Further, "the fact is, no one knows where to start with AIDS. Now, in the seventh year of the calamity" — the time at which *Borrowed Time* is being written — "my friends in L.A. can hardly recall what it felt like any longer, the time before the sickness. Yet we all watched the toll mount in New York, then in San Francisco, for years before it ever touched us here. It comes like a slowly dawning horror. At first you are equipped with a hundred different amulets to keep it far away. Then someone you know goes into the hospital, and suddenly you are at high noon in full battle gear."

Once Roger is hospitalized at the University of California at Los Angeles, their life together, with sporadic respites over the next year and a half, increasingly revolves around various rooms and wards at UCLA hospital. Henceforth, they live on time borrowed from the future they will not have. But there's more than one sense of time here. For gay men of their generation, there's the "lost time" of having been in the closet, the years before the declaration of public homosexuality in 1969. Making up for that lost time perhaps explains part of the gay sexual frenzy of the 1970s, a reaction to the recognition that what was once absolutely forbidden can be transformed into a state in which everything is permitted. Nor is time here only borrowed from the future. Recounting an earlier journey to Greece, Monette observes that "people who travel have dreamlike moments where they borrow time from the past, but it's not out-of-body at all. The echo of the ancient image, warrior or monk, is in you."

Finally, time borrowed from the past is the substance of writing. "I can see us so vividly side by side in bed—reading, dozing, roaming — always coming around again to that evening anchorage ... At the time I thought there were no more layers of innocence to peel ... I cannot say what pagan god it was, but I'd gotten in the habit, last thing at night, of praying: Thank you for this. I'd be tucked up against my little friend, perfectly still, and thanking the darkness for the time we'd had — the ten years, the house, the dog, the work. I did, I counted my blessings ... I knew what I had and what I stood to lose. I held it cradled in my arms, eyes open even as I slept. The night watch from the cliffs at Thera, clear along the moon all the way to Africa." Thera was the Greek island city they had visited, destroyed by a volcano in 1500 BCE, perhaps the source of Plato's myth of Atlantis. A couple of fresco paintings from its civilization survived, and like Monette, I've seen them in the museum in Athens. I have a postcard.

The rest of *Borrowed Time*, recounted in tones both measured and frenetic, is a mixture of inconsolable sorrow, political rage at governments and media slow to do what they could have done to reduce the ravages of the plague, moments of hyperventilating panic and claustrophobia, and eventually, exhaustion and "the desolate waking to life alone — this calamity that is all mine, that will not end till I do."

II

Living in Vancouver, I was on the periphery of AIDS, literally on the epidemiological margins of a fatal viral epidemic. It was transmitted mainly through sexual intercourse between gay men, and its epicentres were in New York, San Francisco, Los Angeles, and other North American cities that contained smaller but sizeable homosexual populations. But even being on the edge of the plague was close enough to feel the horror, to become hysterical in the middle of an afternoon, wake up in a sweat from nightmares (and wonder if it was those symptomatic "night sweats"), visit dying friends on the 8th floor of St. Paul's Hospital in Vancouver or in a bleak Berlin apartment, attend countless meetings that Monette describes as "boredom in a good cause," remember the dead at memorial services. Close enough to read *Borrowed Time* the first time, in 1988, with terror. Monette's account was not so different from the plagues referred to by Boccaccio in *The Decameron*, or described in Defoe's *Journal of the Plague Year* and Albert Camus's *The Plague*.

I remember calculating my degree of risk by means of a primitive equation I'd made up: acts plus number of sexual partners minus precautions taken, over geographical location multiplied by time, equalled risk of exposure. That is, if you were the recipient in acts of anal intercourse, and had had sex with many people without using condoms, and if you lived in one of the plague's epicentres at the time of the critical mass dissemination of the virus (the early 1970s), the odds were against you. I had lived in San Francisco for five years or so before moving to Vancouver in the mid-1960s, just before the main period of the virus' silent spread, so my comparative safety was simply a bio-geographical accident. The same was true of my bedroom behaviour. It was only at the insistence of a sensible friend in the early 1980s that I began to obey the protocols of a safer sex, so again, it was more a matter of chance than prescience that provided whatever protection I enjoyed.

The Human Immunodeficiency Virus (HIV) was attended by two particular cruelties. Its incubation period could be as long as a decade, so the "safer sex" procedures soon undertaken by gay communities (which successfully reduced new infections) would have no bearing on whether or not you had acquired the virus years before. Second, there were no available medications for AIDS other than those to alleviate the accompanying "opportunistic" infections that a deficient immune system invited. From the mid-80s — the time of Roger Horwitz's death — there were experimental drug protocols, and Monette, with his histrionic energy, chutzpah, and middle-class gay privilege, was quick to enroll his friend in available programs, but to no avail. Nothing worked. Retroviral inhibitor drugs, which don't cure AIDS but prolong life significantly, wouldn't be available for years.

In 1989, the year after Monette's *Borrowed Time* appeared and as a half-million mostly American gay men continued to die, I wrote, in a book called *Buddy's*, a fantasy about "How the Plague Ended": "It hadn't ended with a magic bullet, a cure, or even imperfect treatments." It ended, in gay communities, because self-education had dramatically reduced the rate of lethal transmission. "It ended, so it was said, because we had changed. And the change had changed us, in ways that were not yet apparent." And at the end, "we didn't even feel relief. Perhaps we permitted ourselves to take note of our exhaustion." But "what next?" We couldn't yet turn our attention back to everyday catastrophes. There were still committees to sit on, hotlines to staff, the dead to bury, memorials, demonstrations, and the rest. "Yet, we would continue to desire. We had not ceased grieving . . . we would continue to cry our eyes out. We would find ourselves numbly staring at the ocean on a muggy afternoon, then come to, recalling a dinner engagement. Gradually, it would become a memory, like the curling, yellow-edged pages of an old newspaper exposed to the air. But when it ended, we barely noticed." As it turned out, that effort to imagine an end of the plague, at least for the limited "us" that comprised gay men in North America — an attempt to provide a bit of somber political hope — was not that far off the mark. There were "imperfect treatments," but today, more than a decade after my fantasy of it ending, gay friends remark to each other on the eery disappearance of the mention of AIDS in the media, or even among ourselves.

Both the failure of governments and media to respond to AIDS and the inadequate efforts of scientists to develop effective medications sparked the politics of AIDS. There were two half-truths promulgated by gay activists, crucial to engendering support for a stricken community, but which can now be viewed in a more balanced retrospective light. The first was the slogan, AIDS is not a gay disease, but one that can strike anybody. That is of course true in a literal sense but, in reality, the virus was introduced into a primarily gay male population and, as epidemiologists learned, quickly and "efficiently" disseminated and contained within that aggregate, aided in part by that population's sexual practices at the time. What "leakage" there was of the virus (through blood transfusion, shared use of needles, and heterosexual transmission via bisexual men) was limited, and the grave anticipations of AIDS decimating the "heterosexual community" in North America never happened. Like others, I knew that at the time, but in the face of charges by evil Christian fundamentalists that "AIDS was God's punishment" of homosexuals, the claim that anyone could come down with AIDS was a useful political fiction.

The other half-truth concerned sites of transmission and "promiscuity," and became a point of contention within gay communities as well as outside, because it touched on one of the central premises of gay liberation. What public homosexuality proposed at the beginning of the 1970s was that the whole question of sexuality was up for grabs. Conventional — i.e., conservative heterosexual —- notions about who one slept with, how many sexual partners one had, the motives for sexual activity, and much more, were all subject to challenge. At the time, homosexuality was news from the front-lines of human relationships. The subtext of its challenge to conventional sexuality — especially to the shibboleth that sex was primarily reproductive or creational, rather than recreational — was a broader attack on institutional arrangements in bourgeois society. At least that was the case among radical adherents in Gay Liberation Front groups (I was one of the founders of the GLF Vancouver branch). As with other revolutionary proposals, there were excesses, in this case, of sexual activity, as became evident in mounting statistics of venereal diseases, hepatitis, and amoebic infections. When AIDS struck, a decade after public homosexuality, the response was often a barely disguised homophobia. "Promiscuity," it was claimed, violated a law of nature; homosexuals had brought the plague upon themselves.

In practical terms, gay bathhouses, which facilitated sexual encounters, were targetted as dangerous sites of AIDS transmission. Even some gay men themselves called for the temporary closure of such establishments. But for many gay activists, who had adopted the slogan "Silence=death," such proposals amounted to a betrayal of the principles of the gay movement. Hence, their insistence that the vital issue wasn't the number of partners or the circumstances of sexual encounters, but the practice of safer methods of sex. Again, while it is literally true that transmission of the virus could occur in a single act of "unprotected" sex, it was simply an epidemiological fact that the number of partners and the circumstances of the encounters were factors in the rate of transmission. Though insistence on prudence against accusations of promiscuity wasn't the whole truth, again, its political function was understandable.

If "Silence=death" was a call to act-up against delinquent authorities (Act-Up was the name of a prominent AIDS activist movement), then one form of acting out, namely, shouting at governments, media and even at each other equalled a kind of resistance. With respect to the latter, failure to toe the party line could get you labelled as a traitor. I remember one local incident, now almost comic in retrospect, in which I found myself on the wrong side of the line. Through my old friend John Dixon (he was also my colleague in the philosophy department at the college where we worked), I was a member of the board of the British Columbia Civil Liberties Association (BCCLA), over which Dixon presided, and which was actively engaged in issues involving people with AIDS. One of Dixon's contributions was a book, *Catastrophic Rights* (1990), arguing for the civil right to access to experimental drugs for those struck by catastrophic illness. I was also a member of the board of the local AIDS organization, one of those voluntary jobs that seemed to have more to do with bureaucracy, budgets and "boredom in a good cause" than the visible saving of lives. One simply signed up and, indeed, doing so did some good.

At one particularly untimely moment in the midst of the plague, the local conservative government of the day proposed a quarantine law. The proposal was in response to tuberculosis cases and had been innocently requested by the Vancouver public health officer, someone Dixon and I knew to be an intelligent and sensible medical official. The initial draft of the law, however, was so loosely written that it was reasonable for an already beleaguered gay community to see the spectre of concentration camps. The BCCLA, like other groups, opposed the initial draft, but rather than using the occasion to mount a political outcry against an insensitive regime, we successfully lobbied the government to redraft the bill to remove the threat to people with AIDS, which they did.

Of course, no good deed goes unpunished, as one of my friends wryly says. For supporting the redrafted measure, Dixon and I were called onto the carpet of a gay community meeting one evening and afforded the opportunity to be the target of a couple of hours of angry remonstrance. An intransigent slogan of "No quarantine" was obviously a simpler battlecry than the complexities of moderate legalese. As it turned out — BCCLA, as usual, formed a watchdog committee to monitor the effects of the legislation — no one with AIDS was ever threatened with quarantine. That minor fact didn't prevent the appearance of vitriolic, scurrilous articles in the gay press (even in gay newspapers that I wrote for), as much as five years after the fact, questioning the state of my soul. Few self-delusions are more convincing than righteous anger.

Meanwhile, the wounded continued to die. In outposts at the margins of the plague, unlike the blitzed epicenters, the deaths may have been epidemiologically proportional to location, but still, those dying were not strangers to us. Fred Gilbertson was a large man in his 30s, a friend of mine from writing groups and the gay newspaper for which we both wrote. His interests included politics, theology and a demimonde of sexuality with which I was also familiar. He had been a "character" in my book, *Buddy's*, and unlike some of the other friends I'd written about, he enjoyed his appearance as a semi-fictional figure, taking it, as intended, as a mark of respect for him. For him, the course of AIDS progressed swiftly. A year after his jovial appearance in my book, when I visited him at St. Paul's Hospital near the end, he was physically shrunken, breathing through an oxygen mask, and without illusions as to his fate. A few months later (I was writing an epilogue for the paperback edition of my book), he was dead.

Other people were acquaintances. Dixon and I spent some time with Kevin Brown, the president of the Vancouver Persons With Aids organization, working on medical and welfare issues for the disabled. Brown was one of the many people whose lives became more focused, as he told me when I interviewed him for a newspaper article, as a result of AIDS. Suddenly, because of the disease, he had become a spokesperson and discovered in himself a reasoned, gentle articulateness. Another person whom I slightly knew was Jon Gates, a social democratic activist. Even as he was dying, he had foreseen that the epicentre of AIDS would shift to Third World countries, and he campaigned to make drugs available to the destitute parts of the world years before the crisis in Africa was dimly perceived by the rest of us. A fellow member of the AIDS Vancouver board was a psychologist named David. On the last day of his life he held a farewell garden party for his friends and acquaintances. I was one of several people he had asked to provide drugs for his suicide, which he committed later that day among a circle of intimates. There were others, of course. I attended memorial ceremonies for Warren Knechtel, a faunlike photographer; for literature professor Rob Dunham; for political activist Maurice Flood. All people I knew. All gone. Now, as the poet Milosz says, "all they can do is make use of me . . . of my hand holding the pen, to return among the living for a brief moment."

Paul Monette did live to finish *Borrowed Time* and, as it turned out, quite a bit more. His memoir was accompanied by a suite of poems, *Love Alone*, in which he could rage against the dying of the light in another key. Two novels, *Afterlife* and *Halfway Home*, and an autobiography, *Becoming A Man*, followed. Finally, there was a volume of essays, *Last Watch of the Night*, published in 1995, the year of his death, at age 50.

Re-reading *Borrowed Time*, the terror of the first reading gives way to measured grief. Grief, as Monette says, "that will not end till I do."

Woody Allen

In a dream, I was having a conversation with the filmmaker and actor Woody Allen. We were in a busy university building, the foyer and staircase crowded with students on their way to classes. Allen and I were talking about Hegel. Yes, Allen was saying, Hegel on the subject of tragedy has been very important to me. But have you read Marulla? he asked, and was surprised when I said I hadn't. Oh, you have to, he urged, as he approached the staircase to walk upstairs to the seminar he was conducting. Just before the dream ended, he said, referring ironically to something earlier in the conversation, I have to buy a woman. You mean, I interjected, as he started up the stairs, you have to buy a *novel*! Several people around us who had been listening in as we talked burst out laughing at this, and so did Allen. I basked in the glow of having made a successful joke in the presence of the great comic.

Upon waking, I puzzled over the name of the book or author Allen had recommended, then quickly realized that there's frequently a verbal distortion or elision in dreams because of the vast distances they have to travel on their way from the unconscious. Marulla . . .? Mar . . . Mar . . .? Marcellus . . .? Then I got it. Allen wanted me to read the *Meditations* of Marcus Aurelius!

Allen is one of the great, if deliberately underappreciated, artists of our time. It became fashionable in recent years, among intellectualized elements of the middle classes, to display a sort of knowing contempt about Allen's films, citing their limitations, repetitiveness, and other imagined flaws. This critical scorn intersected with scandalous revelations about Allen's private life, namely, that he had an affair with his partner's adopted daughter, whom he subsequently married.

I've no objection to people criticising Allen's messy personal affairs, although I think they're probably irrelevant to the estimate of his work, or ought to be. But the criticisms of his art seem to me largely misdirected. One of the objections is a quasi-feminist, ideological complaint that the main character in many of his films (an obviously Woody Allen-like alter ego) is always chasing girls and women who are a zillion years younger than him. Leaving aside the political debate about whether intergenerational relationships are appropriate, one of the things I like about Allen's films is the tenacity of the erotic pursuits of his main Woody Allen-like character, even if they are self-admittedly neurotic. At least, Allen or his alter ego has a reasonably clear idea of the sort of young woman who attracts him and why, which is more than some people can say about their objects of desire.

Nor has he concealed his desires. In many of his films, he has investigated, in interesting ways, the source of his amorous obsessions. Further, the women he portrays in his movies are persons as complex, anxiety-stricken, and as "real" as the unvarnished self-portrait he offers of himself. In one of his funniest scenes, in *Deconstructing Harry* (1997), his therapist wife Joan (Kirstie Alley), who works out of their apartment, discovers that Harry (Woody Allen) has been screwing one of her clients. His character is portrayed as so ethically obtuse as to be almost endearing:

Alley: I knew when I married you that you were mentally ill, but I thought that because I was a professional that I could cure you.
Allen: Hey, the last thing you want to do is get down on yourself as a therapist.

A little later in their screaming match:

Alley: How could you sleep with one of my patients? Don't you realize that's a sacred trust?
Allen: We never go out. Where else am I going to find someone?

Which is to say, Allen gets the point about his supposed moral deficiencies, or minimally, his works of art are, like those of most artists, smarter than he is. More important than judgments about his moral life, Allen has made great films, creating them over a period of more than three decades with the regularity of the arrival of the seasons. The best-known ones, *Annie Hall*, *Manhattan*, or *Hannah and Her Sisters*, are self-mocking yet sympathetic portraits of elements of the New York intelligentsia and their risible contemplations of love and death. He also authored persuasive comic meditations on the nature of art in *The Purple Rose of Cairo* and *Bullets Over Broadway*.

In the latter, a mediocre playwright with a tin ear is forced, in order to secure financial backing for his play, to cast a talentless actress who is the girlfriend of a mobster. She's accompanied to the rehearsals by a hit man who serves as her bodyguard. The rehearsals are a disaster, the acting wooden, the play itself stilted. The hit man makes a small suggestion to the playwright for improving a couple of lines in the play. At first the artist is resistant, but in the face of impending catastrophe, he recognizes that the suggested lines have a certain versimilitude, are more like what the characters would really say. Gradually, the hit man — who, it becomes apparent, is the real artist here — makes more suggestions, until eventually he's rewriting and directing the whole thing. And when it becomes clear that the final sticking point of the production is the untalented girlfriend of his gangster boss, the artist-hit man unflinchingly uses the tools of his trade to hilariously solve the artistic impasse. Seldom has a comedy about art so sure-handedly hit the target.

At one point in Allen's career, sometime in the 1980s, he felt the need to make some films in the manner of his own master, Ingmar Bergman, but in *Stardust Memories*, a movie about a Woody Allen-like moviemaker attending a film festival in honour of himself, he had the wit to conjure up some aliens landing in a spaceship. After asking the space visitors what he should do with his life and art, their message to him was to return to the comic aesthetic of the films of his youth. "Tell funnier jokes," the little green men told Allen.

In my dream, when I delivered the punchline about having to buy a novel rather than a woman, I must have been thinking of Allen's story "The Kugelmass Episode" in his book *Side Effects*. Kugelmass is a professor at a New York university, his marriage is a disaster, and he's trying to persuade his psychotherapist that he needs to have an affair. When his therapist resists this plea for permission to embark on an erotic escapade, saying, You need a magician, Kugelmass dumps the therapist. A couple of weeks later, there's an unexpected phone call. The caller is a magician in Brooklyn who announces himself as "Persky," then adds his stagename, "The Great Persky." The magician's device is a box into which Kugelmass is placed, and the gimmick is that if you toss a novel into the magic box, you end up travelling through time and fiction to encounter the female protagonist of the book. Kugelmass chooses *Madame Bovary*, and the story goes on to comically detail Kugelmass's inevitable misadventures with the woman of his dreams. Since my name is Persky, I've always assumed that I am a version of The Great Persky.

Allen's critics regularly announce his decline and demise — he's lost it all, all that's left are one-liners and his pitiable sexual vanity, they confidently declare — but each year there's a "Spring Project" and a "Fall Project." Not everything works. No surprise there. Yet, as in the late masterpiece, *Deconstructing Harry*, Allen still occasionally succeeds in combining all the signature elements and themes of his work. He recreates his *meschugene* relations with his Jewish relatives. There's a send-up of his metaphysical preoccupations through a fully realized portrait of Hell (with fellow comic Billy Crystal doing a turn as the Devil). He offers reflections on making art and representations of desire. The hopeless tangle of all of it is endlessly, brilliantly inter-woven into his recognition of the temporality of being.

Near the end of the film, there's a great scene where Allen arrives at his small alma mater for a ceremony in his honour. Spilling out of the vehicle which he's precariously driven upstate from New York City are his "kidnapped" son from a previous marriage, a gargantuan but sensible black prostitute, the corpse of a man who has died en route, and Allen himself, harried as always. What Allen is saying here is that as absurd as both the voyage and the companions of the voyage may be, this is the truth of the matter. One does argue with one's ex-wife about how to raise the kid. One's desire takes the form of an Amazon, and yet she's interesting and tender as a person, more interesting than the stereotypes of such persons would make her out to be. One does have close friends, and sometimes they inexplicably die on you along the way. In the end, we appear at the obscure ceremony to receive a minor award, surrounded by the unexpected companions of the pres-ent moment of the journey as well as by all the ghosts of one's life, still chattering, shrieking, kibbitzing, exactly as they did when they were alive.

Alphabet

When I was four years old, my father, Morrie Persky, bought a blackboard on an easel for me. Across the top of the blackboard, the alphabet was printed in white letters. My father's method of instruction was to draw pictures I requested — a cowboy, say — and then to write the word on the blackboard, pointing out how the letters of the word related to the alphabet at the top of the board.

Once I'd mastered the basics, he drew me complicitously into a routine in which I demonstrated my rudimentary spelling ability to unsuspecting relatives. At a family gathering, he would show me off by innocently asking, "Now, Stan, can you spell 'cat'?"

"C-a-t," I replied.

"How about 'bat'?"

"B-a-t," I dutifully answered, to the silent chorus of adults nodding approval.

"Spell 'rat'," he commanded.

"R-a-t."

Then — just as boredom was about to set in among our familial audience — along came the punchline. "Spell 'idiosyncrasy'," my father said in a deadpan voice.

"I-d-i-o-s-y-n-c-r-a-s-y," I rattled off. My first parlour trick.

Now, much later, I'm tempted beyond the confines of the 26 letters of the English alphabet. I'm attracted to letters found in other languages: the Spanish "ñ" that gives us *niño* and *señor*, or the double "ll" for "llama" and "Mario Vargas Llosa." Also, the small diagonal slash across the letter "l" in Polish, pronounced as a "w," as in the name of the Polish labour leader, Lech Walesa, so that his last name is pronounced "Va-wen-sa" (the "n" sound comes from a cedilla under the "e"). I'm equally fond of the German double "s" in "Strasse," which has its own sign, ß, and the tongue-twisting "Schloßstraße" (Castle Street), two streets over from where I live part-time in Berlin. Finally, there are the various diacritical marks that can be placed above the letter "s" in Slavic languages to produce a "sh" sound, as in my childhood Polish nickname, "Staš."

Beyond that, other orthographies: Arabic, Cyrillic, Hebrew, Thai, Greek. I've always wondered why there's no equivalent in English to

Greek's sensible "theta" sign for the "th" sound. I guess it's just a matter of linguistic, um, idiosyncrasy. I suppose I should be grateful that my ABC's are not predicated on the thousands of characters in Chinese — then there would truly be no end.

Angkor Wat

I

I'm a more-than-reluctant traveller. I have no desire to go anywhere. I just want to sit at my desk in Vancouver and read and write. Walking up to my local supermarket on 4th Avenue is my idea of a big adventure.

Yet, again and again, I've gone to the ends of the earth, as if possessed by the ancestral gene of the Wandering Jew. I never intend to go, since, as I say, I have no desire to go anywhere. So, how to account for my presence at various times, over many years, in Gdansk, Berlin, Tirana, Vilnius, Naples, Mexico City, Managua, Shanghai, Bangkok, Angkor Wat?

I always seem to back into destinations. It is as if it's not me who wants to go to a particular place, but rather that the place is calling me to it. I know that is a romantic fantasy, but often that's the way it feels. Take Angkor Wat, an abandoned once-thriving Cambodian city-civilization from about 800–1450 CE, which surely meets the definition of the ends of the earth.

I was visiting Bangkok, Thailand, in early 2002 — not because I wanted to, of course, but because a friend of mine, Dan Gawthrop, was living there, and encouraged me to visit him. At the Malaysia Hotel where I was staying, I met a friendly middle-aged American from Kansas City named Larry who, one morning at breakfast, told me he wanted to go to Angkor Wat in Cambodia and was looking for a travelling companion.

It hadn't occurred to me to go there, but I saw when I located it on a map that Angkor Wat wasn't far, just across the Thai-Cambodian border. What's more, I'd vaguely heard it had recently been re-opened to tourists. This was after some three horrific decades in Cambodia: first, American invasion in the early 1970s, followed by civil war and the genocidal rule of the Khmer Rouge, then conquest by neighbouring Vietnam, and finally, a decade of "normalized" but bloody internecine politics. Now the situation was temporarily stable.

I was tempted, having heard of Angkor Wat as one of the fabled temple sites of Southeast Asia, one of the "seven wonders of the world." But for some minor reason — I think the airfare struck me as unreasonable — I held off. When Larry returned to Bangkok, just before heading home to the States, he gave me an enthusiastic account of his visit, and the idea of going there stayed in my mind.

A month later, in February 2002, I found myself at a Bangkok travel agency. It was just down the street from my hotel, a place I often passed on my way to the neighbourhood internet café in a narrow lane around the corner. The computer shop was a picturesque place filled with wall clocks, a large gloomy aquarium, and ten-year-old Thai kids playing Harry Potter video games. A rooster in a pen across the lane crowed regularly at an ear-splitting pitch. Passing the travel agency on the way back to the hotel, I thought nothing more profound than, Oh, what the hell, I'll just check the fares; it doesn't commit me to anything. So, I figuratively backed in. The overland fare was not only reasonable but ridiculously cheap.

A few days later, at 7 a.m., I was crammed into a mini-van with a half-dozen or so young foreign backpackers and we were on the highway to the border. I'm usually okay once I get to where I'm going but while in transit I assume the petrified posture of a frightened rabbit. The backpackers, dressed in shorts and floppies, were all in pairs, and at least thirty years younger than me, the only solitary traveller in the group. The American couple sitting next to me were "doing" Asia, a half-dozen destinations in two or three weeks, and seemed perfectly at home in the cramped vehicle, their feet propped up on their enormous rucksacks, eating junk food and mildly debating the comparative merits of the pop novelists whom they were respectively reading, John Grisham and Stephen King (they seemed to favour the literary merits of the horror writer King). They were slightly puzzled that I was staying in Bangkok for a couple of months — what could one possibly find to do there over such a long time? — and quickly turned their attention back to their thrilling paperbacks.

After five or six hours on the road, we reached the border. There's a Wild West frontier town, Popit (pronounced "Po-peet"), that you enter after going on foot through the usual complicated customs stations. Two things were immediately visible: gambling casinos and bread. The garish gambling palaces, built in the style of equivalent temples of chance in Las Vegas, are apparently for well-to-do Thai tourists. The bread, sold by kids who approach you as soon as you hit Cambodian customs, is a cultural vestige of French colonialism, since bread isn't a major feature of southeast Asia's rice-based cuisine. I bought a small loaf, which was crusty, delicious, and suddenly exotic after a couple of months of seldom seeing any bread except the toast that the hotel in Bangkok provided for Western breakfasts.

After getting our documents stamped, we were reassembled behind a corrugated metal fence in an empty lot that seemed to be a combination of garbage dump and informal bus depot, to wait for the vehicle taking us to Siem Reap, the Cambodian town closest to the Angkor Wat site. Through an arrangement between the Thai and Cambodian travel agencies, various tourists in the mini-vans are combined into a larger group and shifted onto a bus. While standing around, amid heaps of trash and various vehicles, waiting for our bus to appear, I reflected that the striking thing about travel is not just the landscapes but how you become familiar with an instant, if transient, group of people — backpackers, drivers, travel agents, vendors, guides and others just hanging about.

I was mainly and anxiously oriented to a young woman in her twenties named Ma, an obviously bright, efficient person who was in charge of the complicated business of ferrying the travellers across the border and recombining them onto the buses for the Cambodian stage of the trip. My anxiety about keeping her in sight diminished once we were at the assembly site and I was reasonably sure I wasn't going to become a lost straggler, abandoned in the middle of nowhere. We had to wait an hour or so. I fell into conversation — in a sort of pidgin made up of various languages — with a teenage boy who was a guide in Popit. He bought a couple of meat kebobs from a passing vendor and immediately offered me one of them. The friendliness of his unexpected gesture jolted me out of my uneasy anticipation of the future back to the present and, within a few minutes in that bedraggled garbage-strewn lot, in the afternoon sun, I began to fantasize a sort of life that I might lead in that border town. I could see a table in a motel room at which I would sit, reading and writing. I think that's the feature of travelling — in which we reconfigure our selves in an imaginary way — that changes us.

The vehicle was an ancient, unreliable-looking, battered school bus. The heat was 30-plus degrees outside and there was no air-conditioning. I sat up front, behind the driver. He kept the folding front door open to get some air circulating. At the last minute, as we were pulling out, a teenage boy hopped on, not the one I'd been talking with earlier.

The road on the Cambo side, in contrast to the smooth four-lane Thai highway, was unpaved, bumpy hard pan. It was the dry season and everything was coated in a layer of fine tan-coloured dust. Once the driver got the bus up to speed, he had to close the door to keep the dust out. It was hot inside, and there was nothing to do but settle in and gaze at the seemingly featureless landscape — seemingly featureless only because I didn't know what I was looking for — as the bus headed in a descending direction down the long ribbon of mostly traffic-free hard pan. The Cambodian teenager introduced himself. His name was Vonnie, he spoke English, and was an Angkor Wat guide from Siem Reap. He came up to Popit regularly and rode the bus back with the aim of securing some business from the travellers headed to Angkor.

Every once in a while, the bus passed through an inhabited place. As you got near a town, the view changed into agricultural landscape. The rice fields were dry at this time of the year, so you could see the banked-up borders of hard earth that enclosed them, and a system of what looked to be irrigation channels and reservoir pits. The earth-rimmed fields were designed to keep the rice partially submerged in water during the growing season. The towns were a sudden jumble of life, startling after the long stretch of desolate road between habitations. The houses were made of wood and set on stilts because of the flood season, there were groves of banana and other trees, now covered in dust, and there were children everywhere, along with the occasional tethered water buffalo, wandering chickens, and pigs nosing about. It was a quick blur of liveliness — kids playing, people washing clothes, a bit of a marketplace — and then we were back on the empty jostling road.

It wasn't until we passed through the third or fourth farming village that I realized that the whole point of going overland was to see precisely this: how the people lived. The noticeable feature of life was the enormous number of kids. I'd read somewhere that the population of Cambodia was 13 million now, about half again as many as the about 7 or 8 million it had been in the 1970s. And if more than half of them were under 15, that meant that the majority of the population hadn't been born at the time of the genocide in Cambodia. For teens like Vonnie, the gruesome image of "the killing fields" was just a piece of history, as it was for most of the backpackers aboard the bus. Only a middle-aged woman I glimpsed for an instant in one of the villages, or an elderly traveller might have the horror as a direct or indirect memory. So, this is a divided society: grandparents and parents who lived through hell, and their children for whom the horrors are stories.

It was a long ride, eight hours or more, with a late afternoon lunch break in the one sizeable town on the route, and a few rest stops along the way. As it was growing dark, something appeared in the distance that might be a city, but it was at least a couple of hours away. Vonnie had circulated among the backpackers, looking for business, and now dropped into the seat next to mine for the end of the haul. It was dark when we reached Siem Reap. I had tried to memorize the map of the town in my guide book, but I quickly lost track of where I was as we turned this way and that through the streets. Instead of anything like a sense of direction all I have is the sort of blurry visual field that 19th century French impressionist painters invented. I couldn't get any sense of the streets at night —

there were only shadowy buildings and the occasional patch of light provided by a flicker of neon or a string of coloured lightbulbs. The bus rolled into a compound behind a backpacker hostel.

Since I was a middle-class tourist rather than a backpacker, I asked Vonnie if he knew how to find the hotel noted in my guide book, the Golden Angkor. He'd take me there on his motorbike, he told me. First he had to help unload the rucksacks from the bus. I stood at the edge of the bustling crowd of backpackers, people from the hostel, and various kids with motorbikes in the warm, anxiety-tinged night. Then I was on the back of Vonnie's motorbike, clutching my satchel with one hand, and Vonnie with the other, weaving through the dark streets of Siem Reap.

My expectations of catastrophe, as almost always, were happily unfulfilled. We neither crashed nor was I abandoned in the middle of nowhere. The Golden Angkor, once we arrived, turned out to be a perfectly nice middle-class hotel, they had a room free, there was a Thai restaurant next door, and the room had a writing table. Angkor Wat, Vonnie explained, was about a half hour out of town. You could get there by motorbike — that's how he made his living, taking tourists out to the site — or rent a car and driver. I preferred the latter. He said he would arrange for me to be picked up at 10 o'clock the next morning. So, there I was, safe for the night in the middle of nowhere — but not nowhere for Vonnie and the other people of Siem Reap, a city of about 800,000 people. Safe, showered, fed, seated at my writing table, memorizing basic greetings and numbers in Cambodian, which uses a system based on the number five. So, ten is double-five.

II

In the morning there was no problem getting a little metal tankard of coffee from the Thai restaurant next door and bringing it up to my room. After my morning coffee and reading, I took a walk through the streets of Siem Reap. In the hazy, soft sunlight, the villa-like buildings still carried a trace of the town's French colonial provincial history, which had lasted until the mid-20th century. There were several construction sites with new hotels going up. The streets carried a surprising amount of traffic. Even though the map in my mind and the streets seemed to correlate, I wasn't very venturesome, going just far enough to identify various nearby restaurants, a place that sold postcards and stamps, a drugstore. At 10, the car and its elderly driver appeared as promised, along with Vonnie on his bike. I asked Vonnie how much he charged for a day's services, and hired him to walk me around the site, since the driver, who looked older than me and only

spoke Cambodian, didn't seem a likely guide. As a middle-class elderly foreigner who was only likely to see Angkor Wat once in his life,
I wasn't tempted to skimp.

The reason for this considerable narrative of utterly mundane travel
details and the self-portrait of a timorous narrator-traveller is to
make the contrast with the splendour of Angkor Wat as sharp as possible. Despite the fame of its great temple, Angkor isn't just the gigantic, moat-surrounded, five-towered 12th century building that is
mainly referred to by that name. Instead, Angkor is the name of a civilization that occupied a considerable interior region of Cambodia,
from the once fish-filled Great Lake at the south to the Kulen Plateau
in the north, all of it located partway between what would become
the modern Cambodian capital of Phnom Penh to the southeast (and
the Mekong River delta further south), and the Thai kingdom to the
northwest. So, when you go through the toll station at the entrance to
the Angkor grounds and pay the fee (in American dollars), you're
entering an area of a hundred square kilometres or more, with fifty or
so temples, and the remains of the towns and water reservoirs built
by successive dynasties over a 600-year period.

We drove along a fairly busy road for about ten minutes — already
at that hour there were busloads of tourists, people on bicycles and
motorbikes, pick-up trucks — until we were moving parallel to the
moat, on the other side of which was Angkor Wat. The driver pulled
into a large, dusty, tree-shaded parking lot opposite the temple.
Behind the lot was a row of open, barn-like sheds with restaurants
and souvenir stands. The tourists getting out of vehicles were quickly
surrounded by groups of kids hawking postcards, T-shirts, and other
items.

Vonnie took me to the low stone bridge across the moat that leads
directly to the main entrance of the temple. The first sense of the magnitude of the place is the scale of the moat surrounding Angkor Wat.
It is some 200 metres wide, and retained on both its inner and outer
banks by walls of laterite and huge blocks of sandstone, cut to fit one
against the next, all of which cover a distance of about 10 kilometres.
At the moment, rather than reflect on the precise facts of the size of
Angkor, I simply went on the impressions I had of the moat's vast
placid waters and the munificence of the bevelled towers ahead,
located behind the arcaded outer walls of the temple. I picked up the
details later on, reading Charles Higham, the leading Western archeological expert on the region, author of the rather dry but informative
The Civilization of Angkor.

From the inner edge of the moat there's a flat grassy expanse,
beyond which stand the outer walls, about 4 or 5 metres high. The
bridge across the moat is linked to the main entrance via a causeway

whose balustrades are in the form of sculpted mythical beasts, dragon-like animals known as *nagas*. Inside the walls, there are a series of galleries, lotus towers, and various side temples that comprise the heart of the complex. The walls of the outermost gallery are covered with bas-reliefs illustrating the life of the king and his court at Angkor in the 12th century. Accompanied by Vonnie, I wandered through the labyrinth of the temple for two or three hours, clambering over stone doorsteps, ascending the towers, meeting statues of gods, wandering through sunlight into dark inner chambers.

So, what am I seeing, I asked myself at some point — or maybe at every point — in the process of moving from scene to scene within the temple. How does the site of this once-upon-a-time civilization mesh with the tangle of individual memory and imagination constructed over a lifetime? First, all travel that's interesting is a kind of time-travel, or else it is merely two-dimensional. Here, it's 2002 and at the same time, roughly 1150 CE. Angkor is a faerie castle of childhood books, the Lost City in the jungle, the actual Magic Kingdom, as contrasted to kitschy, cartoon-based simulacra of various Disney theme parks around the world, safe holiday destinations for vacationing family ensembles.

There's an important, complex oppositional relationship between sprawling actual historical sites — Angkor, the Acropolis at Athens, the Egyptian Pyramids, those in Mexico, etc. — no matter how tarted up for tourists, and the carefully manufactured fakes. Nor are the theme parks only located in nations with relatively brief national histories like the United States, which might otherwise be a reason for their popularity there. They also appear in societies with millennia-long traditions, and have become a phenomena of globalization. Ian Buruma, a Western scholar of Asian culture, points out that one of the cultural conundrums of contemporary China, Japan, Singapore, and other parts of East Asia is the craze for theme parks, an extraordinary proliferation of which are woven into the new commercial urban landscapes. "They are to East Asian capitalism what folk dancing festivals were to communism," Buruma notes. They're all over Asia, and "are sometimes as quickly abandoned as they were built, or even before they were finished . . . What is curious is not just the insatiable taste for these fantasy places, but the fact that they often blur seamlessly into the 'real' urban landscape."

Buruma is primarily interested in figuring out the political relationship between the theme parks, as well as other replications and simulacra, and the ultimately similar communist and capitalist regimes of the region. "So why are Chinese officials prepared, or even eager, to tear down physical evidence of a real past and replace it with copies?" he wonders. "Why do they appear to be happier with virtual history? And what lies behind the ubiquitous taste for Western theme parks, for creating an ersatz version of abroad at home?"

Whether considering authoritarian Singapore, the dubious democracy of Japan, or the communist version of capitalism of China, Buruma believes "there is something inherently authoritarian about theme parks, and especially the men who create them. Every theme park is a controlled utopia, a miniature world where everything can be made to look perfect . . . [and] nothing is left to chance."

The theme parks, like globalized mega-malls, are themselves utopian models for the societies in which they're located, and which those societies are meant to increasingly resemble. As Buruma remarks, "Singapore, once likened to a Disneyland with the death penalty, is truly a place where nothing is left to chance." Everything is "subject to elaborate guidelines, more or less forcefully imposed." Among the uncertain political prospects of post-Maoist China, one of them, he suggests, is that the country, "as a continent-sized Singapore, will be the shining model of authoritarian capitalism, saluted by all illiberal regimes, corporate executives, and other PR men . . . the whole world as a gigantic theme park, where constant fun and games will make free thought redundant."

As-yet-undeveloped Cambodia, by contrast, has to make do with merely real history. Angkor Wat is relatively uncontrolled. There are a few paths marked off as not yet cleared of landmines, the occasional rope restraining barrier before the bas-reliefs on the walls of the galleries, and some uniformed official guides available for hire. Vonnie told me it was his ambition to ascend into their ranks one day. But the visitors were free to scramble around the site, skinning their knees on some precarious steep stairway up the side of a tower, free, in other words, to make whatever they can of the historical reality in which they find themselves. The first disjuncture, then, is one of ontology, of being in the presence of something real in a world whose character is increasingly virtual, not just by way of manufactured spectacle, but including all the digitalia of TV screens, computers, and relentless optics.

Second, as against the ahistorical contemporary theme parks, which can only be read as a set of signs of postmodernism, at places like Angkor, you're confronted with the half-solved historical puzzles of a vanished civilization. The story, albeit fragmentary, is put together by scholars like Higham, from the surviving stone or brick temples, archeological remains of the now dried-out great water reservoirs, and most important, scattered texts throughout the region. The "stone inscriptions set into these monuments," says Higham, "provide a vital social overlay to the skeletal archeological remains. These usually incorporate, in Sanskrit, the name or names of the founders, the presiding god and the date. Further information follows in Khmer. The names of the king or benefactor and the gods are repeated. Although Hindu gods are often named, with a preference for Shiva, local gods are also mentioned. We find reference to the god of the cloud, a tree, the old and the young god, and the god at the double pond . . . " The characteristic inscription lists the amount of land belonging to the temple, its boundaries, productive capacities, the names of people assigned to maintain the temple, and a royal warning against violating the rules of the establishment. The texts are absolutely specific. One, reports Higham, "records the assignment of 17 dancers or singers, 23 or 24 record keepers, 19 leaf sewers, 37 artisans including a potter, 11 weavers, 15 spinners and 59 rice field workers of whom 46 were female."

The textual records also attest to the power of the kingdom's rulers. About Indravarman, a late 9th century king, the inscription says that "the right hand of this prince, long and powerful, was terrible in combat when his sword fell on his enemies, scattering them to all points of the compass. Invincible, he was appeased only by his enemies who turned their backs in surrender." This claim was engraved on the foundation stone of a temple in 879 CE, followed by a pledge made on the king's accession: "Five days hence, I will begin digging." Indravarman lived up to his promise, constructing a huge reservoir of unprecedented size, 3800 metres long and 800 wide, which is recorded in another inscription: "He made the [reservoir], mirror of his glory, like the ocean."

Angkor Wat was built some 300 years later, the enduring temple of Suryavarman II, and without question, agree the scholars, the outstanding achievement of the civilization of Angkor. The foundation stone, mentioned by later visitors, is missing. What we know is that the temple was dedicated to the Hindu god Vishnu and opens onto the west, the god's quarter of the compass. For all its present splendour, Higham tells us, Angkor Wat today is but a grey reflection of its former state. Traces of gilded stucco remain on the central tower, and an early 17th century Japanese visitor reported gilding over the stone bas-relief panels. In the 12th century, it was literally a golden palace. The 4-metre-high statue of Vishnu remains, still venerated.

In the great illustrated galleries, I came upon the bas-relief panel of Suryavarman himself, sitting in state upon a wooden throne. He wears a pointed crown, heavy ear ornaments, a necklace, armlets, and bracelets. Straps crisscross his pectorals, and there are anklets above his feet, which are drawn up in a half-lotus posture. A forest of parasols, large fans, and fly whisks surrounds him as he receives his ministers, named in the inscriptions, offering scrolls and holding their hands over their hearts, signalling loyalty and deference.

Other sections of the gallery walls show scenes from the Hindu epics, massive battles with hand to hand combat; Yama, the god of death, sitting on a water buffalo, determining the fate of each person; a depiction of "the churning of the ocean of milk in search of the elixir of immortality."

But the specific purpose and symbolic meaning of Angkor remain elusive. A temple, sure, but also a mausoleum for Suryavarman? The central towers, the scholars think, represent the peaks of Mount Meru, home of the Hindu gods, while the moat possibly symbolizes the surrounding ocean, but even if Angkor and its counterparts are intended as earthly representations of Paradise — the temple as paradise theme park? — the explanations are thin and unsatisfactory. Did the outer wall enclose residential areas and the king's palace? Where did the rice-growing peasants live? What about burial rites?

If much of the history is patchy, one macro-feature of the civilization is clearer. In addition to its reality, and what we can piece together of its history, the third thing about Angkor civilization is, in a Marxist sense, its mode of production. What Angkor is founded on is rice, water, and labour — surplus rice, control of water, and the ability to organize, protect and exploit labour power. The mode of rice cultivation in the region is what's known as flood retreat agriculture. As the waters of the flood season subside, the rice grows in the half-submerged earth-banked fields. The point of the farming village fields I saw on the road to Siem Reap now becomes clear. The function of the giant reservoirs scattered throughout the region, however, remains something of a mystery, though one would immediately imagine some sort of irrigation system as the dry season sets in. Higham leads readers through an unresolved scholarly controversy about whether or not the reservoirs were for irrigation or other uses. But in the end, it is a surplus of rice, controlled by the warriors through force, that is the basis of dynastic power. Rice makes possible parasols, fans, fly whisks, kings on thrones, artists to make gilded stone bas-reliefs of the sinuous bejewelled body of Suryavarman.

III

Vonnie and I made our way back across the bridge over the moat, found our driver in the shaded parking lot, and I took both of them to lunch in one of the barn-like sheds that housed the restaurants. Then we got into the car again and drove along a winding, forested road, north to Angkor Thom, a city built by the regime succeeding the one that built Angkor Wat. At the entrance to the city is a stone gate about 25 metres high, a heap of columns forming a rough arch, topped by sculptures of giant, broad-faced, Buddha-like heads in elaborate headgear. In the centre of Angkor Thom is its main temple, with fifty or more of the same half-smiling, immense sandstone heads as the ones at the entrance gate. The heads are carved into the temple towers. I clambered over the stone slabs of the temple stairways, cracked and broken over time, crawling up onto a terrace a third of the way up the towers.

Angkor Thom is the creation of a king named Jayavarman VII, who was crowned in 1181, after a turbulent period of warfare in which he repulsed a water-borne invasion — up the Mekong and Tonle Sap rivers and across the Great Lake — by a rival kingdom to the east. During Jayavarman's reign, this great new city north of Angkor Wat was constructed, with the traditional moat, city walls about 3 kilometres long on all sides, pierced by the entrance gateways and their colossal heads, one of which we had passed through, and an array of temples and palaces.

On the walls of the principal temple, as at Angkor Wat, there are bas-reliefs providing a glimpse of life during Jayavarman's rule. In addition to the familiar battle scenes, the striking feature of the Angkor Thom bas-reliefs is scenes of domestic life that give us some visual sense of the everyday world of Angkor civilization. In one panel, a woman in labour is being helped by midwives. In another scene, two men are hunched over a game resembling chess. Workers are shaping building stones with chisels in another sculpted picture, and lifting them by means of a lever. Fishermen are casting nets and hauling in their catch, women are selling the fish in a marketplace. Crowds of onlookers watch a cockfight. A man carries a rice basket, another drives an ox-cart. For scholars and visitors alike, the domestic bas-reliefs are like a newsreel documentary of everyday life. They flesh out the details of the inscriptions, which record that 2740 officials and 2202 assistants lived and worked in Jayavarman's royal city, and 12,640 people had residential rights within the walls. To feed and clothe this population, there are scrupulously listed quantities of rice, honey, molasses, oil, fruit, sesame, millet, beans, butter, milk, and all clothing materials; "even the number of mosquito nets is set down," as Higham notes. Assigned to supply the temple were 66,265 men and women, a figure rising to 79,365 if you include foreign Burmese and Cham workers.

A century later, there's a final, unprecedented, remarkable text available for Angkor civilization. The king at the end of the 13th century is also named Jayavarman and the tangled politics of his regime are unclear, other than for the evidence that part of the ideological struggle involved religion. This Jayavarman, the eighth in the line of that name, was, as Higham reports, a worshipper of Shiva and an iconoclast who destroyed or modified every image of the Buddha that the two preceding regimes had created. If you really wanted to know anything about Angkor you'd have to sort out the ideas associated with Vishnu, Shiva, Buddha, and the rest. But the complex subject of the struggles between various belief systems promoting rival gods and philosophies can be left aside here. What's of interest during Jayavarman's regime is that there's an eyewitness, one who eventually sat at the equivalent of a writing table. He's the man with whom I identify.

He was Chinese and his name is Zhou Daguan. He arrived in August 1296 as a member of a diplomatic mission from the Chinese emperor to Cambodia, and he stayed as a guest in a house in Angkor Thom for eleven months, observing life at the court, in the capital, and in the countryside. After his return to China, Zhou wrote an account of his visit, which survived in the Chinese archives, and was first translated into French in the late 18th century.

Zhou describes the city, with its moat and walls, the gold-covered stone heads at the gates, which were closed each night and opened again in the morning, with only "dogs and criminals who had had their toes cut off ... barred entry." Angkor Thom's golden temples are recorded, along with the royal palace, the tile-roofed houses of the nobility and the homes of the lower classes, roofed with thatch. In the middle-class home in which Zhou lived for almost a year, the floor is covered by matting, but there is no furniture. Rice is husked in a mortar and cooked in ceramic vessels on a clay stove. Family members and Zhou sit on mats and eat from ceramic or copper plates. A half-coconut shell serves as a ladle, small cups made of woven leaves contain sauces. They drink wine made from honey and rice. At night, everyone sleeps on mats laid out on the floor, but it is so hot that people often get up during the night to bathe. Two or three families arrange for a ditch to be dug for use as a latrine, which is covered with leaves.

Zhou also provides an account of the life of the city, punctuated with religious festivals, fireworks, parades, martial art displays on elephants, and the twice daily royal audiences given by the king. But it is in that house where Zhou lived for a year that the human figures begin to move for us in the present tense, where those countless lives now utterly lost to memory have a momentary vividness.

IV

Just at the instant of exhaustion in the mid-afternoon sun, as the visual data blurred and I dreaded the prospect of a further excursion, Vonnie casually mentioned that we could drive back to Siem Reap for a mid-day break, and then return to Angkor Wat that evening to watch the sunset, apparently the custom of both tourists and local inhabitants. Back in the cool hotel room in Siem Reap, I showered, napped, sat at the writing table with my notebook, like Zhou Daguan.

In the early evening we drove back to the now recognizable great temple of Angkor Wat. The road was crowded with local people on bicycles and motorbikes who came out for picnic dinners along the grassy banks around the moat. I sat on the steps of one of the temple entrances, facing west, watching the sun slide below the tops of distant groves of trees.

Back in Siem Reap that night, I ate at one of the restaurants I'd noted on my morning walkabout, practiced my few phrases of Cambodian on the waiters, took an after dinner walk. On the edges of town were the shadowy hotel construction sites, not middle-class hotels, but luxury dwellings going up for a different class of tourist who would jet in from Phnom Penh, Bangkok, Tokyo. On the way back from Angkor, I had glimpsed a half-dozen giant gift emporia, temples for consumers. There was a current of uncertain excitement among the people I met, a kind of boom-town atmosphere. Those like Vonnie were quickly learning English. We'd run into some Japanese tourists at the site that afternoon, and I noticed that he'd already picked up enough Japanese for rudimentary conversations. The strangers who came to town were an opportunity, and it was all recent enough that the local Cambodians were still a little unsure about what these wealthy foreigners wanted, tentative about what should be offered, how flirtatious to be.

The next morning we drove out to the site and Vonnie walked me through various temples at a greater distance from Angkor Wat. The most energetic trek was to a temple atop a hill that you reached by scrambling up a long slope of broken rock. Once you reached the summit upon which the temple was perched, you could climb up its vertiginous staircases for a panoramic view of the countryside. The hike up the slope, however, was enough for me. I could see the towers of Angkor poking up in the forested distance. Noticing that I wasn't enthusiastic about the clamber down, Vonnie suggested that we could take the road at the back of the hill, a dirt path that wound gently downward. The main traffic consisted of elephants carrying tourists up and down, to and from the temple. When an elephant approached I pressed against the inner edge of the road to let the great swaying beast pass.

That was enough. I'd seen what it was possible for me to take in, unless I was planning to stay for a much longer time. We made a dutiful stop at one of the gift temples on the way back to Siem Reap, but

I'd already bought an Angkor Wat T-shirt from one of the kids hawking them in the parking lot, and there wasn't anything else I wanted. I'd seen it.

V

Angkor Wat was sacked in 1431 by the Thais, whose kingdom was based at Ayyuthaya, just north of Bangkok. It was then abandoned to the jungle. The subsequent history of Angkor is one of its "reception" — of how it was seen and understood — by explorers, colonial visitors, and now tourists like me.

In the late 16th century, some hundred and fifty years after it had been abandoned, Portuguese traders and missionaries became aware of a great city hidden deep in the wilds of Cambodia. The Portuguese had heard stories of a Cambodian king named Satha, who, while on an elephant hunt, with his retainers beating a path through the jungle undergrowth, was brought up short by stone giants and a massive wall. According to the account, Satha ordered a work-party of several thousand men to clear away the jungle, thus exposing the lost cities of Angkor civilization.

One of the first foreigners was a Capuchin friar, Antonio de Magdalena, who explored the ruined city in 1586. Three years later, shortly before the friar's death in a shipwreck, he gave an account of his visit to Diogo do Couto, official historian of the Portuguese Indies. "This city is square, with four principal gates, and a fifth which serves the royal palace," wrote do Couto, setting down the friar's recollections. "The city is surrounded by a moat, crossed by five bridges ... The stone blocks of the bridges are of astonishing size. The stones of the wall are also of an extraordinary size and so joined together that they look as if they are made of just one stone ... the source of which is, amazingly, over 20 leagues away ... "

The 16th century account goes on to record that "half a league from this city is a temple called Angar. It is of such extraordinary construction that it is not possible to describe it with a pen, particularly since it is like no other building in the world. It has towers and decoration and all the refinements which the human genius can conceive of ... The temple is surrounded by a moat, and access is by a single bridge, protected by two stone tigers so grand and fearsome as to strike terror into the visitor."

Two decades later, in 1609, Bartolomé de Argensola wrote, "One finds in the interior within inaccessible forests, a city of 6,000 homes, called Angon. The monuments and roads are made of marble, and are intact. The sculptures are also intact, as if they were modern. There is a strong wall. The moat, stone-lined, can admit boats ... There are epitaphs, inscriptions, which have not been deciphered. And in all this city—the natives discovered it—there were no people, no animals, nothing living. I confess I hesitate to write this, it appears as fantastic as the Atlantis of Plato." I too hesitate.

French missionaries entered the region in the 17th century; at the end of the next century Zhou Daguan's memoir was published in Paris; and in the mid-19th century, with Cambodia now a French protectorate, a steady flow of mostly French explorer-naturalists, photographers, and archeological scholars began the study and restoration of the monuments. The obscure volumes of the memoirs of the often strange, wandering, fever-wracked men — I later read one by Henri Mouhot — can be found occasionally in Bangkok bookstores.

The next morning, I sat on a bench in front of the Golden Angkor, along with some local drivers, anxiously wondering whether the bus bound for Bangkok would actually appear. The desk clerk had assured me more than once that he had been in contact with Ma, the woman who handled the travel arrangements. I saw it as a problem in logistics equivalent to the provisioning of Napoleon's army in Russia, and likely to have the same doomed outcome. Well, that overstates it, but only a little, at least from the viewpoint of the reluctant traveller. The bus arrived, the backpackers were aboard, and we pulled out of Siem Reap, back onto the highway towards Popit, the border station, and then onto Bangkok. A young French couple was sitting alongside me. "How did you like Angkor?" I asked. The woman said, "Oh, the temples are all right, but we're more interested in, you know, the people."

That night the bus pulled into the driveway of the Malaysia Hotel in Bangkok. There was an odd rush of feeling as I recognized and was greeted by the familiar faces of the desk clerks, the bellman by the elevator, the waitresses standing at the entrance to the hotel coffee shop. Did you have a good trip, they asked. "Yes," I said, "it was astonishing," then added, as do all returning travellers, "but it's good to be home." In time-travel, what you learn is that home is in the middle of nowhere, as are we all.

Animals

The answer to the titular question of Clive Wynne's *Do Animals Think?* (2004) is: Not very much. I mention this not only to dispel unnecessary suspense but because the students in the first-year university philosophy classes that I teach often believe that their dogs, cats, budgies, and goldfish are thinking pretty much the same thoughts they are. Unfortunately, some of them are right, I point out — but I point it out only when I'm in a snide and grumpy mood.

Wynne, a peripatetic academic who grew up on the British Isle of Wight and is, at last report on his book jacket, a psychology professor at the University of Florida, asks, "Are we human beings alone on this planet in our consciously thinking minds, or are we surrounded by knowers whose thoughts are just too alien for us to understand?" As the philosopher Ludwig Wittgenstein famously suggested, If a lion were to speak, we would not understand what it said. Although there is a lot of popular mysticism about animal minds, the answer Wynne comes to in his book is that we humans are alone in the kind of thinking we do, at least until some recognizable artificial intelligence comes along. Yet the urban and jungle myths persist. "If I had a penny for every time I have been told that chimpanzees are genetically as nearly identical to us as makes no difference and, given appropriate training, can communicate in human language," Wynne says, "I would have a great pile of small change." Ditto for tales about dolphins using "an elaborate language among themselves that we are not smart enough to decode," to say nothing of whale songs, weeping elephants, and loyal hounds.

Of course, animals are wonderful, and Wynne devotes a large part of his book to writing charmingly about the behaviour of honeybees, bats, pigeons and dolphins. Each species has unique sensory capabilities, from the sonar of bats and dolphins, to the ability to see ultraviolet light possessed by birds, and the sensitivity to electric and magnetic fields experienced by some fish. "The obscure Australian duck-billed platypus can tell if a battery has any current left in it," Wynne notes in one of dozens of oddball factoids he provides, then deadpans, "though there are easier methods of testing batteries." At the same time that there is tremendous diversity in the animal kingdom, there are shared "basic psychological processes like learning and some kinds of memory, along with simple forms of concept formation, such as identifying objects as being the same or different from other objects ... All of these seem to be common to a wide range of species and to operate in similar ways in animals as diverse as chicks and chimpanzees."

But there's a difference that makes a difference. "After forty years of trying we can say definitively that no nonhuman primate (or any other species) has ever developed anything equivalent to human language," Wynne reports. Though humans are distinct, if not utterly unique, Wynne is not at all suggesting that some "divine intervention separates us humans from all the rest of creation. In denying human-style language to any other species, I am not trying to lift humans up from the beasts and closer to God ... To admit that humans are different does not return them to the centre of the universe." That is, Wynne is a straightforward Darwinian who argues that evolutionary development is the best explanation of human intelligence and communication capacities.

For most of the animal kingdom and nature, "red in tooth and claw," it looks like instinct, or hardwiring with some adaptive capacities, handles most of what in humans involves thinking. And conversely, a lot of what humans think about doesn't occur in the brains of non-human animals. In case there's any doubt about nature being red in tooth and claw, Wynne provides lots of grisly details about the lives of digger wasps, who paralyze beetles or locusts and deposit them in their birthing burrows, so that when the baby wasps emerge from their eggs, they'll have something to munch on before digging out into the big world. But if you interrupt the digger wasp's birthing routine, it'll go back and perform the whole routine over and over, no matter how many times you interrupt it. The wasp never figures it out; it is hardwired to do it one way.

Students in the philosophy classes I teach are only momentarily persuaded by such examples. Invariably, they return to the question, "But how do you know that Fido and Felix aren't thinking just like us?" Well, I say, they give no evidence of such thinking in their behaviour or in their communications, presumably because they don't have the kinds of brains that have evolved to do that sort of thing. "But maybe they're thinking thoughts, anyway," they insist, perhaps thinking of oppressed people under dictatorial regimes who have thoughts they don't utter. "And maybe they have their own way of communicating them," the students add, as prepared to entertain the notion of animal psychic powers as they are to consider human psychics. Even my concession that their pets are sort of thinking about their student owners' arrival home from school, and are happy to see them, and are sort of thinking about food, walks, taking a pee, or digging up a well-remembered bone, doesn't appear to satisfy the students. They think me rather cruel and close-minded for denying that their dogs and cats are pondering the prospects of the local hockey team winning the league championship, just as they are.

The crux of all this, and "the critical question to bear in mind is, Has any animal succeeded in learning an open-ended language system like our own, or have other species only mastered communication in a more closed manner . . .?" The notion of chimpanzee speech acquisition achieved a breakthrough in 1970 when Allen and Beatrice Gardner taught a chimp named Washoe to use about 125 Ameslan, or deaf language, signs. "Prior to the Gardners' research," Wynne observes, "the prevailing position was that chimps were incapable of learning human language because they lacked the specialized brain structures that underpin its comprehension and production. With the publication of Washoe's feats, the new received wisdom became that chimpanzees only lacked the ability to speak." What happened after that was curious. The story of Washoe passed into educated popular wisdom and became a staple of urban legend.

While the signing chimp achieved popular currency, other researchers were discovering the limits of chimp language acquisition. Herbert Terrace of Columbia University published *Nim* in 1979, an account of his work with a chimpanzee he named Nim Chimpsky, with a little intended malice towards linguist Noam Chomsky. Terrace began with a predisposition favouring environmental factors in language learning as opposed to the innate language acquisition mechanisms proposed by Chomsky. At the end of several years' work with Nim, Terrace concluded, according to Wynne, "that what Nim was doing had little to do with language as we normally understand it. Instead . . . the chimp had achieved a simpler form of learning: that making certain signs led to certain consequences. The chimp had learned to produce certain arm and hand movements to demand things he wanted: 'I do this; I get that.'"

Terrace also noted several other limits to chimp learning. The vocabulary acquired by apes, about 250 words over three or four years, is pretty modest compared to human infant acquisition rates. The chimps never experienced the "spurt" of language learning that occurs in humans at about age two. Although there is a bit of controversy about particular primates and their vocabularies, Wynne reminds readers that "though it is always fashionable to bemoan the limited vocabulary of contemporary youth, the average U.S. high school graduate knows about 40,000 words." I'm not sure I've observed 40,000 word vocabularies in most of my students, but even a half or a quarter of that puts it beyond mere quantitative comparison with Nim. Of course, the argument about vocabulary size in relation to chimps is subject to the objection of the irrelevance of criticizing dancing dogs, since the wonder is that they can dance at all.

But while humans are stringing together little sentences at age three, "this never happened to Nim. The average length of his utterances remained stuck at only a little over one word throughout his training period." Even more important, neither Nim nor any of the subsequent language-acquiring chimps of the 1980s and 90s ever demonstrated anything close to a minimal grasp of grammar. "And grammar," argues Wynne, "is what makes the difference between being able to express a number of ideas equal to the number of words you know and being able to express any idea whatsoever." Grammar is what turns lexicons into open-ended systems, and without it, you don't develop what we call thinking. Yes, there's some thinking going on in other primate species, but not much. Wynne comes to similar conclusions about non-human primate tool-use, self-identification and "culture." Yes, there's a bit of it, "but on the other hand— how slight this culture is." (By the way, none of these limitations is an argument for treating animals badly.)

"For all the excitement and all the TV documentaries," Wynne concludes, "the so-called 'language-trained' apes have not learned language . . . They sign or press buttons because doing so gets them what they want. They can be drilled to string a couple of signs together but usually can't be bothered. Although some of them have been in training for decades, there is nothing to suggest that any of them ever comprehend grammar. Grammar is the crucial lubricant that opens language up from being limited by our vocabulary to being completely infinite in its expressive possibilities." As Wynne says at another point, "Without grammar there is no language." And maybe, without language, there isn't much thinking.

And then: Just as I finished writing a review of Wynne's book and posted it on the website magazine I write for, I suddenly remembered a book in my home library that I hadn't thought about in years. I went to my bookshelves, and there it was: *Animal Friends*, and inside the cover (a picture of horses and colts on a farm) there was a filled-in form noting that the book had been presented to me by my Uncle Docky on my third birthday, January 19, 1944. It was the first book in my library, and 60 years later, I still had it. The children's book that brought me closer to the world of animals would also, through its use of language, take me irrevocably further from them.

Apartheid

One day in the 1980s, when apartheid still existed in South Africa, I saw scenes of rioting in the sprawling black African township of Soweto on the evening television news. The visuals featured menacing armoured vehicles that were more tank than truck, rumbling through the racially segregated encampment of more than a million people, spewing tear gas and bullets.

The next day, I was visiting my friend Tom Sandborn. He'd seen the news, too. As we sat at a picnic table in his sunny Vancouver backyard, I said, "Tom, we've got to do something."

This was one of those rare occasions when the famous political question, "What is to be done?", had an obvious answer. The black leadership in South Africa had called for international sanctions against the country's white apartheid government, sanctions that ought to take the form, they advised, of a boycott of products imported from South Africa. The call for sanctions received the support of the United Nations and the boycott was being enforced, albeit haphazardly, by various countries around the world.

One of the few exceptions to the boycott was occurring where Tom and I lived, in British Columbia, on the west coast of faraway Canada. Practically every other province in Canada had implemented a boycott against South African liquor products, but not the conservative provincial government of British Columbia. Even as people in Soweto were being shot before our televisual eyes, the beefy minister for liquor sales in British Columbia was justifying the continuing sale of South African liquor products on the grounds of the sanctity of consumer rights in a free market. Consumers, he argued, have the right to individually choose whether or not to support the apartheid government of South Africa by buying or not buying its products.

Tom didn't bat an eye. He didn't engage me in theoretical arguments about the efficacy of the sanctions strategy or about the inconvenience of engaging in acts of civil disobedience, topics that were the subject of extended hand-wringing in newspaper columns and among political activists. Instead, we went straight to his basement and began rehearsals. Our first task was to learn how to smash a bottle without cutting our hands. There's nothing worse than political *klutzes* who can't get the champagne bottle to smash against the about-to-be-launched ship or who end up a bloody mess themselves. Since this was to be a symbolic act for the eyes of television cameras, and since television cameras are easily distracted, we wanted to be sure that their eyes stayed focused on the bottle rather than any fumbling slapstick of ours. Soon, armed with ordinary gardening gloves and a small hammer, we had progressed to the ranks of journeyman bottle smashers.

A couple of days later, accompanied by a gaggle of TV cameras and print reporters whom Tom had alerted, the two of us appeared on the premises of the B.C. government liquor store at the corner of 18th and Cambie in Vancouver. Among Tom's many virtues are his organizational thoroughness and tidiness. He had already cased the store, and we were able to go directly to the South African wines section. Furthermore, Tom had phoned the union, informing them of our intentions, and asking them to tell the workers in the store so that they wouldn't be overly alarmed by our criminal act. Finally, Tom had brought along plastic bags, so that the broken glass and spilled wine wouldn't make a mess for the store's employees.

We each selected a bottle of South African wine, donned our gardening gloves and wielded our hammer while the cameras duly recorded our minor protest against apartheid and the policies of the government of British Columbia. There was a bit of a hitch with the authorities. While Tom borrowed a mop and bucket to tidy up the floor, I had to remind the store manager that it was his job to call the police. Then we had to stand around for a while until they showed up. When they did, there were a half dozen of them, two constables and four senior members. They took us into the back room of the liquor store for questioning. At the end of the questioning, the constable said, "Okay, we'll send you a summons in the mail if we decide to charge you." Tom and I shared a bemused glance. As everybody knows, the last shot in a televised story of this sort has the police car pulling away from the curb after the miscreants had been ushered into the back seat.

I should include a political philosophy note here about civil disobedience since it's a topic not well understood by many people, even by some civil disobedients. They often detract from the focus of their action by whining about whatever small punishment they may receive or protesting that they're really innocent because of the greater good they're doing. In protesting against apartheid, or whatever other evil, by breaking the public mischief law, you're not claiming that the minor law being violated is wrong, unless you're some kind of anarchist. Instead, you're saying that evil is wrong, and you're prepared to accept whatever punishment is necessary in order for you to appeal to the public, a public of which you're a normally law-abiding member in good standing. It's theoretically pretty simple. Practically speaking, it's only complicated in countries like China where civil disobedients are still thrown in jail for ten years.

I said, "Constable, I have to inform you that if you don't apprehend us, it's our intention to return to the store and do further damage." The officer said, "I'll have to consult with my superiors." The police huddled. Perhaps they imagined that once we got done with South African wine, we might move on to vodka from the neighbouring province of Alberta. In due course, if a bit grumpily — I think it was lunch hour for them — Tom and I were packed into the police cruiser, and driven down to the police lockup at 222 Main Street. The cameramen had their concluding shot.

Since the media is a player in this drama, something should be said about its informational/disinformational roles in relation to political acts. While Tom and I were awaiting our trial, one local newspaper columnist worked himself up into an incensed state, devoting an entire column to denouncing our "attention-seeking media stunt." This otherwise unremarkable and noxious bit of journalism stays in mind because it's both typical of the subtextual silences of much journalism and it raises questions about the ability to engage in political action in nominal democracies where the media and most other forums are dominated by the ideas of ruling-class corporations.

What I mean by "subtextual silences" is this. First, there's nothing "natural" about any "news." While there's a history, and even a professional ethos, of how journalists decide that something is newsworthy, there's also a strong sense in which all of the news is a "media stunt," i.e., a decision by journalists to feature some aspect of everyday life that may or may not deserve such attention. Two of the best bad examples of this are: 1) the media's overemphasis on sporadic violence, giving sensationalised attention to empathy-provoking murders while in fact violent crime is statistically declining, and 2) treating practically all business decisions as implicitly rational and good.

Second, even given the colloquial usage of "media stunt," it's not clear why our citizenly action was any more of a manipulation of the media than the ceaseless parade of political "photo-ops," indirect corporate advertising and governmental press conferences announcing or defending some policy, such as the liquor minister's defence of apartheid. That is, the columnist in this case is subtextually silent about why he's so irked by us, a silence that makes me suspect that he thinks the media should have the right to determine who is or isn't a legitimate political actor in the public forum. Apparently, not all media stunts are created equal.

Finally, the one other interesting thing about this newspaper column, as we now know from the ideas of deconstructionist reading, centres around the trope of innocence and guilt. The columnist is making the flimsy claim that Tom and I are "seeking attention" for ourselves, rather than seeking to bring attention to the evil of apartheid. The claim is flimsy because we're not obvious crazies ranting in formulaic jargon, but adults in our forties who speak in sentences. At the same time, while chastising the protesters for illegitimate attention-seeking, the column is silent, either willfully or naively, about the columnist's own attention-seeking self-portrait as a tough-minded critic willing to blow the whistle on self-indulgent, ineffective political activists. The column implicitly pretends that the columnist isn't a guy who has to come up with something three times a week if he wants to continue to receive the attention of having his name at the top of the column, not to mention his paycheque. More important, the column is silent about the evil of apartheid, suggesting, again implicitly, that it's possible for one to be innocent, to not be complicit, whereas the protesters are saying that everyone is implicated, everyone could do what the protesters have done in order to concretely resist that particular evil.

I've gone on about this topic at some length because the widely observed passivity of the citizenry in nominally democratic societies usually goes unexplained by the very institutions that are partially responsible for reinforcing that passivity. How hard it was to imagine distant South Africa, notwithstanding its brutal televised availability, how hard it was to conceive of oneself as having the right, if not the responsibility, to alleviate the suffering of people living far away whom we did not know. Perhaps one definition of politics is caring about strangers, a uniquely human ability. I consoled myself that this neurotic column helped, in some small way, to increase public awareness of the fact of apartheid.

While awaiting trial, the political problem of South African wine and spirits in Canada was solved when the federal government announced a national policy of boycotting South African products in compliance with the United Nations' anti-apartheid program, thus taking the matter out of the hands of the free-market enthusiasts running the government of British Columbia.

The judge I appeared before some weeks later, a charming eccentric named Wally Craig — I later got to know him at the local YMCA health club where I play squash — gave me an absolute discharge in exchange for forbidding me from making a speech in the courtroom. Like most other directors of courtroom theatres, he preferred to reserve the speechifying for himself.

These days, on television, I observe large groups of youthful demonstrators in the streets of cities from Seattle to Genoa, protesting against capitalism. Apartheid has at long last ceased to exist in South Africa. The strangest after-effect of apartheid for me is its amnesiac absence in the present world, especially when I happen to mention South Africa while talking with students in college classes I teach. I'll casually refer to, say, Nelson Mandela, the black former president of South Africa and, feeling a sudden gap in the psychic space of the classroom, I'll glance up and recognize from the looks on the students' faces, that although these nineteen-year-olds were alive when black people were racially denied any political existence whatsoever during the apartheid regime, that for them what I'm talking about is history while for me it's memory. For me, it's real, for them it's abstract, and a frisson of despair snakes down my back, as I imagine a dystopia in which almost everything has been forgotten.

Arcadia

Arcadia, like the Garden of Eden or El Dorado, is one of the many images of utopia that human beings have imagined over the centuries. The Argentine-born writer Alberto Manguel gave me a copy of his friend Tomás Eloy Martínez's book, *The Peron Novel*, and inscribed on its flyleaf, "et in Arcadia ego," a phrase popularised in the Renaissance (and sometimes credited to Virgil). It means, "And (even) in Arcadia, I am." "I" is the figure of death, and the phrase is a stark reminder that death is everywhere present — yes, even in the earthly paradise of that region of the Greek Pelopponesian peninsula, Arcadia, where amorous shepherds engaged in pastoral dialogues.

In summer 1992, at a gathering of writers held in the Banff Centre for the Arts — a rather Arcadian place itself, located amid the alpine forests of the Rocky Mountains in Alberta, Canada — I met Martínez, whom Alberto, as the host of the occasion, had invited as a guest. I often jokingly refer to Manguel, who is a Canadian citizen but frequently lives elsewhere, as "Civilization's ambassador to Canada," but it's no joke. Alberto's choice of Martínez as a visitor was perfect. Martínez was working on a new novel, *Santa Evita*, a true story about the fate of the corpse of Evita Peron, and the story he told us of writing it was more precise and intimate than any writer's tale I'd ever heard. When I asked Martínez to autograph my copy of his Peron novel, he wrote, along with expressions of friendship, "Scripta manet," "the writing remains" — beyond our mortality. I've long had the sense that writing, puny as it often seems, is our weapon against time, yet at the same time, it always recalls us to our human fate.

In Nicolas Poussin's 17th century painting, *Et in Arcadia ego*, the phrase is discovered on a tombstone by a group of shepherds. Arcadia is inextricably linked to the homoerotic desire proclaimed in the shepherds' love for each other, recorded in the poems of the old bards. The linkage is found in contemporary texts, too. The first part of Evelyn Waugh's homoerotic novel, *Brideshead Revisited*, is titled "Et in Arcadia ego." In Gore Vidal's memoir, *Palimpsest*, he describes his boyhood love affair in the early 1940s with 17-year-old Jimmy Trimble as one in which "there was no guilt, no sense of taboo." Vidal adds, with characteristic arch wit, "But then we were in Arcadia, not diabolic Eden." Eden is read as a site of original sin; Arcadia renders homosexual love almost innocent.

Perhaps a year or so after reading Vidal's book, in summer 1996, Thomas Marquard (a friend of mine from Berlin) and I rode on an afternoon bus along the twisting, mountainous road that threads through Arcadia. Not many shepherds in sight but, as we drove along the main streets of the villages of Arkady, old men in black clothes sitting at tables in their roadside cafés, watching the infrequent passing traffic. Former shepherds, ex-loves?

Art aphorisms

Normal art: I've lately begun to entertain the perverse idea that making art, or meaning, or trying to understand the world, are, contrary to popular notions, normal activities of human beings, even an evolutionary feature of our survival. It is the failure to do so that should be seen as abnormal, odd, demented, and not the other way around.

Art and politics: While there's no requirement for art to be political, art today ought to see itself as an active cultural politics against "entertainment," which is the capitalist replacement of art and culture (for example, the replacement of books by "reality" TV).

Reasons to write: The writer Brian Fawcett gave a talk on "reasons to write," offering such reasonable motives as money, ideology, keeping a record, healthy curiosity, and serving the Muse. The poet Lisa Robertson wittily added love and revenge to the list. When I mentioned the subject to Robin Blaser, he immediately said, "Because of life." That is, the condition of our existence is sufficient reason to interrogate it.

I'd say the same thing. What I mean by "life" is not a definition or abstraction, but the sense conveyed by an Arthur Rimbaud poem, *c.* 1870, translated by Charles Olson:

... (O saisons, o chateaux!
Délires!

      What soul
is without fault?

Nobody studies
happiness

Every time the cock crows
I salute him

I have no longer any excuse
for envy. My life

has been given its orders: the seasons
seize

the soul and the body, and make mock
of any dispersed effort. The hour of death

is the only trespass

Art and Auschwitz: Theodor Adorno sternly declared in the wake of
the Holocaust that lyric poetry is impossible after Auschwitz. I think
that the best way to interpret that remark is not that good poetry
can't be written after Auschwitz, but that good writing now requires
an understanding of the Holocaust.

Charles Olson's dictum: "Art is life's *only* twin." That's the banner
under which we ride into the fray.

Art, Life, and Imitation: Equally, there's John Berger's assertion, "Art
does not imitate nature, it imitates a creation, sometimes to propose
an alternative world, sometimes simply to amplify, to confirm, to
make social the brief hope offered by nature."

The Anxious Asp

Memory, quick as a stolen kiss at midnight: for a year, age 24-25, 1965-66, in San Francisco, I worked in Arlene Arbuckle's bars in North Beach. There were two of them. On Grant Avenue, near Green St., was her "respectable," mostly-gay bar, the Capri, run by the bartender-lieutenant of her little fiefdom, a prissy, lean, but hard-nosed guy named Lee. The other establishment, a tiny beer-and-wine bar called the Anxious Asp, was around the corner, on Green St., between the Green Valley Restaurant and Gino and Carlo's, Jack Spicer's literary headquarters.

On a crowded Saturday night in Gino's, sitting at Jack's table, during a lull in the evening, or maybe just needing a breath of foggy fresh air, somebody — George Stanley or Lew Ellingham or I — would get up and announce, "I'm going to take a look at the Asp for a minute."

Inside the Asp it was even more crowded, and the jukebox, even louder than in Gino's, was playing the same Beatles songs, "She's A Woman," and "I Wanna Hold Your Hand," over and over. The atmosphere was, compared to the sedately drunken Gino's, more frenzied, erotic, given to abandon. Although there wasn't any room to dance, there was a kind of dancing in the Asp. Gino's was the old world: Italian leftists breaking out into an occasional chorus of "Bandera Rossa"; the alcoholic longshore foreman Tom, our Roman centurion, pounding his fist against an imaginary warrior's breastplate; poetry in the person of the hunched figure of Jack Spicer. The Asp was the new world, the world of the Beatles, rock'n'roll, cool images rather than feeling, as Spicer complained. It was just after the 1964 American presidential election — the first since John F. Kennedy's assassination — and George Stanley had compaigned for Lyndon Johnson against the right-wing Republican candidate, Barry Goldwater. "In your heart, you know he's right," went Goldwater's slogan. "And in your guts, you know he's nuts," his opponents replied. It was the beginning of the U.S. war in Vietnam, and in a sense, the beginning of the Sixties.

I'd been working in the warehouses south of Market Street. Getting a job at the Asp, and eventually at the Capri as well, introduced me to the lesbian subculture of North Beach. Don't remember how I got the job, maybe through Armando, a bartender friend of George's, who had worked for Arlene at various times. Arlene was a slim, curly-haired, butch woman in her late 30s, who usually had a fem girlfriend in tow. Occasionally one or the other of them would turn up in the morning at the Capri, sporting a black eye, as I was setting up, slicing the limes, peeling the lemons, putting the coffee on, while the morning drinkers sat stiffly at the bar, awaiting their first hit of coffee and brandy. Arlene's best friend was a tall, masculine woman named Sherman who ran an artist's supply shop on Grant. Sometimes, after work, Sherman would join Arlene and her girlfriend and a couple of the other women in their circle for an early evening cocktail. Arlene was a discreet presence, who seemed to leave the running of her businesses to her lieges. Or maybe, since I was an innocent, I didn't really notice much of what went on. I simply reported to Lee, who laid down the rules, which mainly had to do with not stealing and keeping a certain decorum, a tone that Lee liked to maintain, an idea of classiness.

If Gino's was the Greek war camp, and the Capri was doomed Troy, the Asp was mere "roistering in Thessaly," as Socrates put it. The shift ran from six in the evening to two in the morning. By midnight, the Asp was in Bacchanalian dishevelment. A baseball bat was kept under the bar in case of trouble. A nice neighbourhood character, a nearly seven-foot-tall black man named Big Jim, took a liking to me, and turned up periodically to keep an eye on the place. In return I provided free beer. The poets trickled down from Gino's during the course of the evening, usually for a brief visit, but the Asp wasn't their kind of poetry, unless, like Lew or George, they'd gotten very drunk. The Beatles warbled on. Sometimes the Asp was so crowded, the party spilled out onto the sidewalk.

One midnight, I slipped into the john for a quick pee, and found Doc Salter there, looking into the mirror. He was an attractive young man, the same age as me. Something clicked — what? whatever — and we stole a kiss at midnight. "Stick around for closing?" I asked. "Sure," he said, though he wasn't really gay, as I learned when we bedded down later in the Swiss-American Hotel on Broadway. He was just high on the excitement and his own desirability. "Do what you want," said that San Francisco Narcissus.

They're all gone now, I'm pretty sure. I have a vague memory of being told, maybe by George, of Arlene's passing. Lee, Sherman, Big Jim, Doc. Only the shades are dancing.

Athens

At the centre of modern Athens is Omonia Square, a vast inferno of roaring, polluting traffic. At the time, in July 1996, it was undergoing infrastructural redevelopment, so that ragged wooden hoardings and the pounding of pile drivers and jackhammers were added to its usual chaos. The square is surrounded on all four sides by shops, newspaper and cigarette kiosks, eateries, and slowly-moving glutinous crowds of people. But Thomas Marquard, my travelling companion, and I, who were staying at a cheap hotel behind Omonia Square, weren't looking for modern Athens.

Perhaps some other time we would seek out present-day Athenians, look up its artists, or attempt to figure out the politics of this southernmost great metropolis of Europe, a city of some three million people. Instead, we were treating contemporary Athens, apart from casual contacts with waiters, taxi drivers, desk clerks and the like, as merely a translucent palimpsest through which to peer down its many historical strata to the *polis* that existed around the 5th century BCE

Looking south along one of the narrow, traffic-clogged commercial streets — we were standing in front of a grocery where we'd stopped to buy plastic bottles of water to rehydrate ourselves in the July heat — we could see at the horizon the 90-metre-high gleaming Acropolis, a big stone plateau covered with the columned facades of the ruins of its temples. Thomas, a thorough and indefatigable traveller, saved me from my usual lethargy upon arrival in a new city, and we set off immediately for the winding, circular trek up to the heights.

We paused at the Theatre of Dionysus, a stone amphitheatre carved into the back side of the rock, resting for a moment in the seats once occupied by theatre-going citizens who had seen the tragedies and comedies of Euripedes and Aristophanes on opening nights in the 5th century BCE. Thomas, a drama teacher and theatre director at a Berlin high school, explained some of it to me.

We made it to the top, dutifully touring its most famous temple, the Parthenon, whose construction began in 447 BCE, when the city's eventual greatest philosopher, Socrates, was a young man in his early twenties. But Socrates — who, allegedly a stonemason in his youth, may have even worked on the project — though conventionally observant, was never really interested in the Greek gods nor, I suspect, the temples atop the Acropolis where they were worshipped. From the Areopagos, a nearby hill of slithery russet-coloured marble, it was possible to find a perch and look down over its rim to a patch of rubble far below.

That was our destination, the Agora or marketplace of ancient Athens, once the centre of the known world. Here, amid its streets and shops, baths, schools, gymnasia and public spaces, Socrates had entered into those teasing, probing conversations in which modern discourse has its roots. What's striking about the dialogues preserved (and half-invented) by Plato — I was re-reading his *Symposium* during this trip — are precisely how recognizable they are to us. That is, between the end of ancient Rome around 500 CE and, say, the 15th century Renaissance, almost a thousand years later, there is no talk so understandable to us, either in terms of subject matter — how to self-consciously live a good, or at least examined, life — or method, namely, secular arguments about definition, meaning, categories. So much of the intervening discourse really is phantasmal chatter about how many angels can dance on the head of a pin.

I was introduced to that talk in my mid-twenties when I studied political philosophy with Bob Rowan at the University of British Columbia. We read the *Apology*, in which Socrates, charged with corruption of the young and worshipping false gods, pleads and loses his case before an Athenian jury that sentences him to death. Then the *Crito*, set in the Athens jail, where Socrates rejects his wealthy friend Crito's offer to arrange his escape. Can you imagine me, at my age, roistering in Thessaly? Socrates asks. No thanks, he says, declining the offer of escape, in the *polis* we have our second birth, after being born of our parents, and it is the City that raises and nurtures us. Should I reject its laws now, simply because of a decision that goes against me? And finally, the *Phaedo*, and the last conversation between Socrates and his friends before he drinks the fatal hemlock, and feels the cold chill of death move up his limbs. Now, once again, on our travels in Greece, I was reading the *Symposium*, where Socrates, Aristophanes and their friends spend the night talking about the nature of love.

What's more, the appearance of such talk in Athens in 400 BCE is a surprise in human history. In contradistinction, the warrior society talk of Troy or Sparta is of a piece with the kingdoms of Mesopotamia and Egypt or the stateless warlord regimes of contemporary Africa or central Asia. The ritual language about the gods atop the Acropolis has its equivalent everywhere. You can find great temples and palaces all over the world. Nor is the marvellous Greek theatre entirely unexpected. Its stories of the legendary heroes, the pity and terror of implacable fate, arise from the ritual search for right conduct in the relations between humans and the gods. And while the talk of commerce and human desire is trans-temporal, before Athens there was no talk like this, no semi-abstract argumentation that sought meaning. This Greek discourse does not replace poetry, the basic mode of story-telling that begins with *Gilgamesh* (although Plato inveighs against poetry in his *Republic*), but is another way of knowing, another attempt, as the philosopher Wilfred Sellars once put it, "to see how things, in the broadest possible sense of the term, hang together, in the broadest possible sense of the term."

While I'd feel as estranged from the Jews in dusty Jerusalem at the time of Jesus as I am from the ravings of contemporary born-again Christians, and as distant from medieval courts as we are from the ziggurats of our digitalized bankers, I have the sense of utterly knowing these Athenians, from their philosophic ponderings to their young adults who remain erotically alive for us in the suspended desire of their sculptures or the late-night talk of the *Symposium*. I'm astonished that the talk of the Greeks is conversant with the latest developments in postmodern theory. Socrates would not be baffled by Richard Rorty.

Thomas and I ambled along the sun-baked streets of the Agora. What remain are the stumps of the foundations of buildings. Here are the outlines of the gym where naked youths stretched their bodies; here at the north end of the Agora is the prison where Socrates was executed; here's the broad ramp leading to the procession road up to the Acropolis. Almost impossible to imagine it, even with Thomas's reading of the maps, were it not for the adjacent reconstructed Stoa, the colonnaded trading hall that now houses the Agora museum. In a dusty glass case, we found some eggcup-sized drinking thimbles, allegedly the kind used for administering the hemlock that Socrates drank. Outside, in the blistering heat again, a tortoise emerged from the rubble of the foundations, like a figure from Zeno's paradox.

And that is all that's left, this patch of ground in contemporary, debased Athens. That, and a few similar ruins scattered about the city. Outside of Athens, once we were on the road, across the Corinthian isthmus into the Pelopponeses, there were other old places — Olympia, Mycenae, Arcady, seaside Navplion on the Bay of Argos.

In each place, in the morning, before we went out to see the ancient world, I read Plato's *Symposium*. Each of us who reads has such landmark books, re-read again and again in the course of a lifetime. The symposium is an evening drinking party, held at the house of the young and handsome playwright Agathon, whose work has just been performed and won the first prize at the theatre of Dionysus, in whose seats Thomas and I had sat. The subject of the *Symposium* is the nature of Eros. The dialogue contains three and a half great speeches. The most practical talk is that of Pausanias who, in specific detail, explains the rules and motives for courting boys, and how those of Athens differ from Sparta, other Greek cities, and the Persian kingdom, where men are not as devoted to conversation as in Athens.

The greatest speech, aesthetically, is that of the comic playwright Aristophanes, who declares that love is "the desire and pursuit of the whole," and tells the story of how the gods divided us into two parts so that we go through life seeking our other half, and warns that if we continue in our errant ways, the gods will split us again, cutting us into quarters the way a hair is used to slice a hard-boiled egg. Socrates's speech is metaphysical, and attempts to link the desire for a particular beautiful boy with larger and larger forms of love, up a ladder of desire, until we contemplate the nature of the beautiful itself.

The half-great speech is provided by Alcibiades, a drunken young warrior and politician in his late 20s, who tells the story of how, years ago, when he was the most beautiful youth in Athens, he offered himself to Socrates, crawling into the philosopher's bed and wrapping a blanket around the two of them, but that Socrates rejected this offer of beauty, not satisfied that Alcibiades was interested in the pursuit of truth, which would be one of the appropriate motives for entering into a relationship with someone. The chaste night they spent together is the source of the mistaken notion of "platonic love." But reading the banter between Alcibiades and Socrates once more, at the seaside port of Navplion, it was clear to me that of course they had had sex together, on other occasions, many times, though in the end, Alcibiades proved a moral disappointment to his would-be teacher.

Of all the places we saw, the most beautiful was Delphi. It's a temple north of the Pelopponesian peninsula, up in the mountains. The Athenians came there by boat to question the Delphic oracle. We spent half a day wandering through its ruins, looking out from the mountain on whose slope it is set, down the throat of a long valley to the small port, Itea, on an inlet of the Ionion waters, where the Athenians landed. That evening we ate dinner at a terrace restaurant, which had a similar view of the valley. The night sky was a pure black that neither Thomas nor I, we both noted with some amazement, had ever seen before. The black heavens were marked by a constellation of stars just at the horizon — Scorpio, Thomas told me. As we left the restaurant terrace, we gazed down the valley under its black sky a last time. For an instant, it seemed all of a piece: magical Delphi, where the Athenians learned from the Delphic oracle that no one among them was wiser than Socrates, who alone knew how little he knew.

B

Bald

My father was bald, and I inherited, along with much else from him, his standard male pattern baldness. I fretted about it, mainly worried, I suppose, about its potential effects on my sex life. For years, I fought a losing battle by arranging my hair in a desperate "comb-over," attempting to disguise the obvious. What an extraordinary waste of time, of mirror gazing, of brilliantine and gels.

Although there is no limit to human self-delusion (much less vanity), at long last I decided to get a haircut. My friend Tom Sandborn, who doubles as my lifelong therapist, accompanied me to a barbershop on Main St. in Vancouver, and the woman who ran it left me with less hair and one less self-delusion. I re-entered the world with a perfectly unremarkable bald pate. The new me, as far as I can tell, suffered no ill sex-life effects, proving once more that desire fashions a niche for almost everyone. It even became briefly fashionable, in the 1990s, for men with hair to shave all of it off and go around bald. I'll leave it to the semioticians to explain what it all meant.

Occasionally, walking around the streets, when a breeze comes up and riffles through my fringe, I forget that I'm bald, and like people who have lost an arm or a leg are said to experience a phantom limb, I experience some imaginary hair. Then I run my hand over my crystal-ball-shaped dome, and move on.

Bangkok

I

At about 8 o'clock in the evening in Twilight Alley, there's a suspended moment of languid nothingness mixed with tremulous expectation — and that moment is at the centre of my idea of Bangkok. Twilight Alley, named after the Twilight nightclub at its mouth, is a short, mostly pedestrian lane off Surawong Road, which is one of the two main thoroughfares (the other one is Silom Avenue) of the Patpong tourist and sex district. At night both of these streets are filled with continuously moving two-way bumper-to-bumper traffic through which one precariously dashes to get to the other side. To make matters more congested, the sidewalks are narrowed to nearly single-file width by canvas-covered stalls selling every kind of object imaginable, from ordinary tourist-item T-shirts to honey-coated fried insects, and are packed with meandering hordes of visitors. The air is a blast-oven mixture of sultry heat, bus and motorbike exhaust fumes, and the cooking oils and spices of crammed open-air sidewalk eateries.

At 8 o'clock in the evening, Twilight Alley is an oasis of temporary calm compared to the traffic-clogged main streets. The mostly "go-go boy" bars along Twilight Alley are just opening. The doors are ajar, the bartenders are setting up, the various bar-captains and their lieutenants, in dark, loose, silky suits, are performing the last of their preparatory chores before the evening begins, and the young men from the bars are often sitting out front, enjoying a final moment of leisure before a night of work. Since the bars advertise the young men with the English word "boy" — and since there's a great deal of publicity about child sex in Thailand — I should immediately make clear that the young men are all 18 or older.

In addition to the dozen or so bars in Twilight Alley, there are also a couple of restaurants, one of which is called Dick's Café, whose waiters, rather indistinguishable from the guys in the bars, are standing in front of their workplace. As well, there are two or three seedy hotels and several beauty salons filled with both male and female customers and hairdressers. A few vendors are pushing carts with fruits and other foods, or selling watches, cigarette lighters, and assorted geegaws. It's December, and there's even one kid trying to peddle Santa Claus hats with battery-powered blinking lights, though it's far too early in the evening for anyone to be drunk enough to think that buying one might be a good idea. The occasional puttering motorbike or delivery truck wends through a thin trickle of early evening tourists. You can sit in a rattan chair on the patio of Dick's Café, about halfway up the lane, have a cold Singha beer or a glass of fizzy mineral water — always welcome in the constant plus-30-degree sweltering air — and maybe strike up a conversation with another foreigner at the next table, or flirt with one of the waiters, all of whom have time on their hands at this hour.

Then at some imperceptible instant during the next hour, Twilight Alley transforms itself into a spectacle of desire, one of the dialectical poles at whose distant other end is the notion of the cessation of suffering that pervades the Buddhist philosophy of Thailand. Parties of diners replace the solitary drinkers of apertifs in the restaurants, the coiffeured customers leave the hairdressers' salons, hosts in front of the bars now tout the pleasures of their particular club, the music is turned up, spilling out into the lane, and the trickle of sex tourists thickens into a steady stream. Because the change is gradual, when what begins as a sleepy scene blossoms into a full-blown spectacle, the effect seems sudden and surprising. Inside the Classic Club, some way up Twilight Alley, just where it makes a little dogleg and soon gives out onto a dark boulevard behind it, the place begins to fill and young men in body-hugging white wrestling singlets take their place on stage.

II

The Patpong district, with its honeycomb of narrow lanes and dozens of bars (mostly heterosexual, of course, though I've little knowledge of that side of things), occupies only a tiny patch of the vast sprawl of Bangkok, with its ten million inhabitants. When I arrived at the airport one midnight in early December 2000, I was rescued by my journalist pal Dan Gawthrop and a Thai friend of his, Daeng. Dan was living and working in Bangkok as a copy-editor at an English-language newspaper. He spotted me as I pushed my luggage cart through the sultry night air of the airport lobby. My first impression, even in my dazed traveller's condition, was of being in a place that, for all its hyper-modernity, was rapidly regressing into ruins.

As the taxi took us into the city, Dan pointed out a several-kilometre-long set of cement stanchions along the dark freeway. They were meant to support an additional raised highway, but the project had been precipitously abandoned in the fiscal collapse of 1997, three years before. Only Y-shaped blocks of concrete were left standing, like mysterious Stonehenge plinths.

The intimation of decline was confirmed in subsequent days. In the neighbourhood of the Malaysia Hotel, where I was staying, there were numerous contemporary ruins — an abandoned, now over-grown villa, a modernist art gallery that had failed, and a three-storey gay bathhouse, the Babylon, which had moved to a nearby new location, leaving behind an empty building full of sexual ghosts remembered only by its former patrons. Even the occasional bits of infrastructural repair work I saw barely appeared to keep pace with the rate of deterioration. Though the shiny towers of luxury hotels, corporations, and shopping centres, some of them done in a fanciful pastiche of classical Thai architecture, were manifestly functioning, I could easily picture them slowly rotting in the equatorial heat, thickly-polluted atmosphere, and periodic meltdowns of globalisation. In time these future ruins would come to resemble the ancient remains of temples that I'd looked at in guidebooks and that I'd eventually see in the old 15th century capital of Ayutthaya, a couple hours north of the city.

The original Bangkok or Krung Thep (as it's known in Thai), founded in the late 18th century, was built on both sides of the Chao Phraya River, now displaced to the city's western edge, as burgeoning Bangkok sprawled eastward over the decades. Though it was no longer central to Bangkok, I was repeatedly drawn to the river's choppy mass of muddy brown water. Whenever I was there, aboard one of the dozens of pitching, flat-bottomed ferries that churned up the Chao Phraya's surface, I could feel the energy of the river, its cool relief, the life carried by its currents, as a sort of natural antidote to the inevitable decay of human things.

Though I paid minimal attention to the politics of the capital, Dan's work at an English-language newspaper made him an avid observer of the tides of power, and I absorbed a certain amount of political information through conversations with him. Everywhere you went — in places dotting the riverbank, at the corner 7-11 convenience store, along wealthy Sathorn Boulevard (halfway between my hotel and the Patpong district) — there were various-sized photographs of Thailand's 75-year-old king, on display in shrine-like settings. The kingdom had been a constitutional monarchy since the 1930s, but although Thailand was a nominal democracy, its actual recent history was one of rule by political bosses and ex-army generals, interspersed with periodic military coups. Even now, in the midst of a general election that saw every tree and lamppost along the main streets festooned with the posters of various candidates, newspapers could blandly and credibly run headlines proclaiming, "Threat of coup lurking in the wings."

Perhaps it was more accurate to say that Thailand's nascent democracy had come under the control not only of corrupt local politicians and warlords, but of international capital. Although Thailand was distinguished from many of its neighbours in never having been subjected to direct colonial rule, it had lately been colonised by consumerism. The results were uneven. If the first wave of globalisation in the 1980s and early 1990s had produced a conspicuous middle class, the subsequent fiscal crash had once more revealed the bare-bones structure of poverty underlying everything. Now, in the wake of the crash, the local business elites again mimicked the latest global dictates on prosperity, dutifully prattling on in the financial pages about "computerization," "venture capital," and the other money-see-money-do catchphrases of the day.

The other immediately notable feature of the city, in addition to its perilous politics and precarious commercialism, is a visible and varied spiritualism. First, there's Buddhism, the official faith of the country. In referring to Buddhism, I'm not talking about a hazy mysticism meant to soften the contours of poverty, or its North American transformation into one more form of Western self-therapy. I simply mean its physical visibility in Bangkok: temples, ubiquitous orange-robed monks, a certain cultural style. (Eventually, I became acquainted with a monk and accepted his invitation to visit him at his monastery barracks, where we sat on the concrete floor in his sparsely furnished cell, almost bare except for a desk with a computer on it.) But beyond the institutionalization of Buddhism in Thai society, it is also a philosophical body of thought, and I often puzzled over its possible meanings.

Beyond Buddhism, there's a more pervasive and historically deeper observance of spirits, a kind of animism. Outside every sizeable building, establishment and residence, there are ornate "spirit houses" and shrines, often miniature temples placed on small columns, to which offerings are daily made. In the garden restaurant next door to the hotel where I was staying, two large trees were swathed in cloth, and the waiters at the restaurant put a tray at their feet, amid the roots, with offerings of food, drink, and incense, with the same regularity that they swept the terraces clean of leaves in the afternoon, or covered the tables with cloths in the early evening.

Given my situation — a general ignorance of the culture and the limited time available in what I thought of as a first foray — I kept base and field narrowly circumscribed. "Base" was the Malaysia Hotel and the immediate neighbourhood; "field" was the twilight zone of the Patpong district. My routine was organized within this restricted space, except for periodic ventures to temples, museums, bookstores, the suburban newspaper where Dan worked and the nearby gated housing estate where he lived.

III

What most intrigued me were the doings of the sex tourists at the Malaysia and in Twilight Alley. At the hotel, I saw them in the restaurant, around the swimming pool, or sitting in the lobby, reading newspapers or occasionally dropping off for a little snooze, unperturbed by the bustle of the reception desk where people were arriving and departing. They were often in groups of three and four at tables in the restaurant, some in their forties, but mostly in their fifties, sixties, even seventies, dressed in child-like shorts and T-shirts, having breakfast and planning their day. Or sometimes, one of them was sharing a morning table with one of the several young men who frequented the hotel, presumably after the two of them had spent the night together.

The sex tourists were the subjects of my imaginary anthropological research. Though I'd studied anthropology at school, and conducted some actual urban field work while I was a grad student, this of course wasn't actual research, but more of a game to help me think about where I was.

I'd initially learned anthropology from a great teacher named Michael Kew at the University of British Columbia, where I'd taken a degree in the subject in the late 1960s, but my main influence came from the writings of the anthropologist Hugh Brody, who worked in British Columbia in the 1970s and 1980s, and with whom I'd had a couple of friendly meetings.

The book of his I particularly learned from was *The People's Land*, a study he had made of Canada's eastern Arctic. Unlike anthropologists who solely studied the native people of a place, Brody gave equal attention to the inevitable community of white administrators, teachers and businessmen who now colonized every indigenous culture on the planet. So, for example, although much is made in the popular press about drinking problems among native people, Brody shrewdly turned his attention to the drinking problems of the whites, describing them with the same sense of the exotic that conventional anthropology normally accords only to indigenous hunters and gatherers. His point, which I quickly adopted for my informal Bangkok research about sex tourists, is that there is no possible description of the native inhabitants that doesn't include a description of the non-natives who so often dominate and alter local life now.

I should make it clear that, even as a metaphoric anthropologist, I'm not at all a detached, objective witness of these scenes but, as the social science phrase has it, a full-fledged "participant-observer." If there were a group photo of all of us sex tourists at the Malaysia Hotel, I would be rather indistinguishable from the rest, other than for refusing, as do a minority of the other guests, to wear the child-like clothes, opting for short-sleeved shirts and long trousers (the costume that the guidebooks advise is approved by Thai people for foreigners).

The main but imperceptible difference between me and the other participants in the scene is that I write about our lives. I have the odd notion that writing redeems some of whatever it is we do in the world that might otherwise be seen as private, idiosyncratic, or merely self-serving. I'm using "redeems" in a sense that is close to the phrase "moral redemption," but maybe all I mean is that writing gives us a second chance to make sense of what we do, to enlarge our existence in the direction of shared human experience. Though I see writing as morally redemptive, I'm not in the least tempted to engage in moralising about what I'm describing, even if it seems to invite moralising, given that it touches on homosexual prostitution, public displays of sex, inter-generational affairs, etc. Here, I take it that my readers are smart enough to supply their own moral perspectives to the portrait I'm drawing. But I am frankly puzzled by people who don't "double" their lives, as I call it, by writing about them.

Even though the men I saw at the Malaysia Hotel didn't, as far as I know, do anything more with their experiences than contribute accounts of them to the ongoing and interesting fraternal flow of gossip, I nonetheless rather admired them. They had the ability to spend their days hanging around with the young men, watching television, lingering at table or around the pool, not a great deal pressing on their minds. They were unlike me in not needing great stretches of solitary time. They were casually indifferent to language or Thai history, politics, and art, only going off to look at some tourist attraction as simply something interesting to see rather than as an attempt to understand the context. I mean, I'm horrified by the illiteracy of such a stance while at the same time I see its lure.

A coda to the issue of writing, especially about sex: though I'm writing about the sex tourists and what goes on publicly in the go-go boy bars of Twilight Alley, as well as about other topics concerning Bangkok, you won't find much here about my personal sex experiences. There are a couple of reasons for this. One is historical. When the disingenuous question, "But what do you homosexuals do in bed?" was a live issue in the 1970s, it was informative to say precisely what gays did do in bed, and I did so, drawing on my autobiographical experiences.

I no longer think it's so informative. Most people now know or can know what anybody does in bed. Homosexual bedroom gymnastics are no longer news. Now, homosexuals are pretty much in the same position as heterosexuals when it comes to describing sex: unless you have something of specific interest to relate, usually of a psychological nature, that reveals something about us all, sex descriptions tend to be either self-indulgent, schoolyard boasting, or pornography. In saying this, I'm not in any way dismissing such descriptions, and in fact I think that carefully described sexual encounters can almost always yield something interesting, but I'm also saying that such descriptions have to be really accurate these days if they're to be revelatory. Second, my particular sex experiences in this instance are so unremarkable that I would regard insisting on them as, at worst, vanity, and at the very least as an intrusion on readers who might otherwise be interested in the larger portrait.

IV

In an airport, in early January, 2001, at the end of my first three-week trip to Bangkok, while waiting for a connecting flight from Taipai back to Vancouver, I ran into one of the men I'd seen napping in the lobby of the Malaysia and we struck up a conversation. Neil Philpott (not his real name) — tall and portly, in his early seventies — was a retired businessman from Toronto. When I expressed my novice's enthusiasm for Bangkok, Neil quickly warmed up, offering me the benefits of a veteran visitor's anecdotes as we passed a half-hour or so in one of those geographically indistinguishable global airport lounges.

Neil had been seasonally migrating to Bangkok for a decade or more, and had a relationship of several years' duration there with a Thai man in his late-twenties. While this companionship had its benefits, he readily admitted that it had its amusing restrictive side as well, such as when Neil wandered off for the odd extracurricular sexual adventure. "Oh, he gets very angry," Neil chuckled about his boyfriend, in the discreet, mock-naughty style characteristic of an older generation of gay men.

"So, this looks like something one can do," I said after listening to Neil's accounts, meaning that Bangkok might be a viable choice for one's later years. "It's possible to go on with your life."

"Oh yes," Neil said. "I'm 73 — semi-retired of course." He still kept a hand in his former business dealings, he told me. "Why, you," he said to me appraisingly, though I was only a decade or so his junior, "you're still a young fella."

I liked Neil's matter-of-fact, phlegmatic view of things. No obfuscating moralising, or self-defensiveness, simply the recognition that Bangkok satisfied certain desires, without any corollary claim that its cornucopia of sexual offerings was a natural order that one could take for granted. What's more, Neil struck me as relatively typical of the men I'd seen at the hotel.

But if Neil seemed to me clearly non-malevolent, a more ambiguous case was the Irish television producer, a friend of Dan's who was visiting Bangkok while I was there. Since it was established early on that this was an Irishman who hadn't read James Joyce, I'll call him Kinch, in honour of the nickname given to Stephen Dedalus, one of the protagonists of Joyce's *Ulysses*, a moniker which appears on page one of that epic.

Although you could stay in a perfectly acceptable hotel like the Malaysia for a pittance, Kinch had opted for a place on Convent Road, just off the Patpong district, costing five times the rates at the Malaysia, primarily, Dan told me, because it was right next door to one of those fake Irish pubs that you can now find in almost any big city in the world. By chance, I'd been in Dublin the summer before and had been taken to actual Irish pubs, so I had some idea of the difference between them and the tourist version. Still, the Bangkok Irish pub — it was called Shenanigans — was certainly pleasant enough, if not, as Kinch appeared to regard it, a necessity.

The first time I saw Kinch, I was at Dick's Café in Twilight Alley. I was with Robin Ringold, an English freelance journalist in his late twenties, another friend of Dan's I'd been introduced to, and with whom I played tennis once or twice a week. Dan and Daeng said they would bring Kinch from his hotel to join us for dinner, but they were a half-hour late. Robin and I were just starting to wonder if there had been a misunderstanding when Kinch, who I only recognised by the fact that he was with Dan and Daeng, sailed into view. He was a short man in his fifties, of colossal girth, 125 centimetres or more (for those unfamiliar with the metric system, that's a 50-inch waist), sporting a tentlike pink T-shirt, worn outside his trousers.

He was in a jolly mood. As if there weren't enough young men on hand, Kinch apparently prearranged meetings with various of them through the Internet, so as not to lose a moment's time. He saw himself as "auditioning" them for some role in his life. During dinner, where he predictably dripped sauce onto his pink T-shirt, Kinch, a practised raconteur, entertained us with accounts of two assignations he'd already had on his first day in town.

"Dan tells me you've just had quite a success with a television series," I said, changing the subject.

"A year-long program about 20th century Irish history," Kinch replied. I expressed admiration for the magnitude of the project and asked how frequently the programs aired. "Oh, t'was on every day," Kinch said, "just before the 6 o'clock news." I was slightly puzzled. A whole program every day for a year? "Yes, every day. Well, two-and-a-half minutes," Kinch amended. I vaguely remembered something similar on TV at home, called "Canadian Moments," little snippets of dramatised patriotic kitsch. I made a non-committal murmuring sound. It was a positively heroic effort, Kinch assured me, what with having to cram at least ten stories into every segment. Ten stories? I exclaimed. Out of the corner of my eye, I saw Dan wince, knowing what I was making of this cultural recital. "Sometimes eleven," Kinch said blandly. While I was trying to calculate the average number of seconds per item, Kinch had gone on to declare what a success it had been. "Yes, many letters from parents saying it'd gotten their kids interested in Irish history."

By now, grasping at conversational straws, I mentioned that I'd been in Dublin the summer before. I could see that the names of his literate countrymen and their watering holes only dimly registered with Kinch. "And we had lunch in the restaurant where Leopold Bloom ate his gorgonzola sandwich . . .what was it called?" I prattled on, trying to remember the name of the place — Davy Byrnes? — in which Bloom, Joyce's main protagonist in *Ulysses*, had dined. That's when Kinch said, "I haven't read Joyce," in a tone of perverse pride, as if not doing so was something of an accomplishment on that Joyce-ridden emerald isle. Instead, Kinch went on to discuss his next opus, an abridgement of the history of forty years of Irish television.

Another night, Dan and I met Kinch in Shenanigan's, his favoured location. He was, I noticed, a bit difficult to turn off or cut into once launched on a tale of sexual accomplishment. Kinch professed modest puzzlement at the eagerness with which his auditioning young men pursued him. "Me," he said in self-deprecating wonder, "just a fat little fooker."

Daeng was visiting his family upcountry that week, and when Dan sighed with relief at being permitted a night out without him along, Kinch was quick to pounce. Though he'd only met Daeng once for a couple of hours, he was prompt with elaborate advice, analysis of the relationship, and repeated offers. "I'll be glad to take him off your hands," Kinch said to Dan, more than once. But it wasn't just a compliment about Dan's choice of boyfriend. Soon Kinch was fantasizing opening a Thai restaurant in Dublin that Daeng could run, moving Dan's boyfriend in, leaving his house to Daeng in his will. The vulgarity of Kinch in this little incident was that he seemed blissfully unaware that he was both passive-aggressively threatening to steal Dan's boyfriend and boasting that he was capable of doing so.

The last I heard of Kinch was some time later, after I was back in Vancouver. Dan sent me a message recounting a trip on which he and Daeng had guided the Irishman about. When Dan proposed a tour of some temple, Kinch had declined, saying, "If you've seen one temple, you've seen'm all." Perhaps the remark was meant as an ironic parody of the typical sex tourist's barbaric indifference to sights other than the obvious, but perhaps not.

It might be reasonably wondered why, if Kinch is such a fool, he's a friend of Dan's in the first place, or why I'm being civil to him. There's no big mystery to that. First, Kinch was a long-standing friend of a friend and Dan's hosting of him was part of a more complex web of social and sociable relationships. Second, there's an obligation to help out newcomers who are sent your way, whether you particularly like them or not. Third, Kinch isn't a complete fool. Far from it. In addition to whatever else, I also saw him as rather generous as well as an oddly intrepid soul. His charm grew on me. From a writer's perspective, Kinch's saving grace is that he's a great character. Writers collect monsters.

Another evening, around eight, I was sitting at Dick's Café, when I noticed a man at the adjoining table. He was an athletic-looking guy with dark, curly hair, in his late thirties. A noticeable tension exuded from his body, the tendons in his wrist and forearm were taut as he clutched a glass of beer, and he appeared to be periodically muttering to himself.

We introduced ourselves — I'll call him David Roth — and gradually fell into conversation, though he was distracted through most of it. An American from Florida, Roth now lived in Japan where he taught English, had been to Bangkok as a sex tourist many times, had an interest in Buddhism, and was, like me, a Jew. In fact, there were enough similarities between us that I immediately saw him as my younger, more anxious, *Doppelgänger*. I've seldom encountered a man in a more extreme condition of metaphysical agony. The cause of his torment, he blurted out with the directness of someone near madness, was his addiction to the young men in the bars. He hated himself for his unsatisfiable desire, judging it, as a Buddhist, to be both spiritually bad for himself and for the young men, whom he saw himself as "using." "It's like fuckin' cocaine, man," Roth said.

Even as he was telling me this — and though he'd mentioned he had a date for later that evening with one of the go-go guys in the club next door — more than half of Roth's attention was fixated on a tall, handsome young man, about twenty, with dark-brown skin characteristic of people from northeastern Thailand, wearing a red vest over his otherwise bare chest, who was sitting on a stool in front of the bar across the lane, obviously waiting for the evening to get underway. In the middle of a sentence, Roth got up and dashed over to the guy's side of Twilight Alley, where they engaged in a brief, animated conversation during which Roth pressed a bill into the young man's hand.

"What was that all about?" I asked when Roth returned to his table. "Tomorrow night," he muttered, gulping the beer whose glass I thought he might crush in his unconsciously furious grip. "Man, it's a fuckin' fantasyland here," Roth said.

V

If Roth and Kinch were striking exceptions to the untroubled, rather bovine placidity of most of the sex tourists I saw in the Malaysia Hotel, there were, besides the paying customers, two other categories of gay foreigners I also, if more superficially, identified in Bangkok. The first group I thought of as "adventurers" — young, relatively attractive men in their late-twenties and thirties, like Dan or Robin Ringold, who were in Bangkok for six months or a year or more, their plans rather open-ended. They found various jobs, in journalism or teaching English, and struck up relationships, both casual and more complex, with gay Thai guys they'd met in the discos and baths.

I was drawn to Dan's earnestness in dealing with all of this new material — trying to write, learn, love. At least, he'd had the nerve to go off on an adventure, unlike many of his agemates, and he was basically attentive to things or, as the Buddhists say, mindful.

Robin was also likeable. He was a wiry adult in his late twenties, English, with close-cropped blond hair, and a somewhat gruff, taciturn manner (a look and style currently fashionable among younger gay men). We'd meet at the nearby courts for an afternoon set or two of mad-foreigners-in-the-midday-December-sun tennis. The Thai middle class, more sensibly, only came out to play under the lights at night.

Other adventurers offered variations on the basic model. A guy from Quebec named Marcel was teaching Thai students questionable business techniques (some form of public relations, I think), and one evening at dinner he gave me an extended account of his present life, which struck me as half-fantasy, half-real. Marcel represented himself as an attractive boy-toy foreigner, even though he was in his thirties, who was regularly picked up and occasionally half-kept by wealthy middle-aged Thai men. We were eating in the garden restaurant next door to the Malaysia, and long Christmas-strings of tiny electric bulbs threaded the tall trees, illuminating Marcel's prim face and trendy wire-rim glasses, as I tried to imagine the penthouses and yachts owned by the men of whom he spoke. Marcel seemed to like this version of his desirability. Of course, it was possible to see another version of him as a vain, spoiled rich kid who was deluding himself, but since I knew him so slightly, it didn't seem worth the bother to really try to decide between the alternatives.

The other category of foreigners that included gays was permanent expatriates, people who had, in some fashion and for different reasons, gone native. One evening after work ended at his newspaper, Dan took me to a nearby party where I met several of these old hands. The party was an easy mixture of people of various preferences and nationalities, Thais and foreigners. The ex-pats, a few of whom were gay, had been in Thailand for a decade or more, had adopted some of the local customs and, unlike most of the adventurers, spoke considerable Thai. The style at the party was to directly approach people whom you hadn't seen before (visitors like me) and engage them in conversation. So, I heard some of their stories. But again, as with Marcel, since I knew them so superficially, I got little more than the idea that it was possible to settle here long-term. Any serious judgment of their choices was out of the question.

When I visited Dan at his newspaper office that evening, he had introduced me to Pravit, an Oxford-educated young Thai editor, who later turned up at the party with his wife. Pravit had an impressively nuanced, if melancholy, sense that something had gone historically wrong in the relation of Thai culture to the current dominance of Western business practices. In the course of an hour's conversation, in which I expressed a desire to learn more, he mentioned a man he regarded as a sort of mentor — his name was Sulak — with whom I might make an appointment. If I wanted, I could phone Pravit at home the next day and he would give me Sulak's phone number.

For the most part, I spent my days in study, reading Thai history and literature, and picking up some of the language. The initial stage of Thai struck me as relatively easy, since the language doesn't require conjugations or declensions, has few complexities in terms of plurals or tenses and, although tonal, isn't too demanding at the outset. An Australian language student I'd met in the hotel restaurant assured me that it became difficult once you got to the next level and started using Thai orthography. I quickly learned for myself how hard it was to pronounce the language's phonemes with sufficient accuracy to make yourself even minimally intelligible.

Occasionally, I went off to one of the temples and sat contemplatively in front of a Buddha statue, or took meandering neighbourhood walks in the afternoon heat. I socialized regularly with Dan and Daeng, who joined Robin and me at the tennis courts a couple of times. Attached to the courts was a place that advertised itself as a tennis school, and there'd be a young man or two — I had the idea that they worked in the evenings as ballboys for the middle-class patrons — skillfully stroking a ball against the practice wall. I thought then that if I ever came back to Bangkok, I might take a few lessons to improve my groundstrokes, and in fact, when I returned the following year, at the end of 2001, my centre of gravity quickly shifted from the hotels and bars to the courts.

Just as the tennis courts were located about midway between the Malaysia Hotel and the Patpong district, I saw the game of tennis itself as halfway between desire and meditation. In the dead calm of afternoon the only sound was the familiar plonk of the ball hitting the racket; one's attention was narrowly focussed on the ball's movement, and the rest of the world fell away. When I hit the ball into the net and glanced up, I was surprised to discover the pale hazy sky, a bird diving into the shell of an abandoned, unfinished office building next door, the dusty greenery around the mesh enclosure of the courts. I was surprised to find myself in Bangkok.

Often my meditations simply took the form of gazing down from the fourth floor window of my hotel room into the fenced-in back compound behind the Malaysia. There was a cement-paved parking area flanked by two white concrete apartment buildings. Near the back fence adjacent to the street leading to the tennis courts, there was a narrow inverted T-shaped strip of grass. On the T itself was a jagged little tree, with bright green, large oval leaves that provided a bit of shade, and during the day various people from the apartment buildings, mostly women and their children, gathered under it to chat while doing small chores. I liked to imagine the tree as a cousin to the legendary Bo tree Buddha was sitting under when he attained enlightenment. But more realistically, looking at those human figures from a distance, I felt the distance between our lives and theirs, especially the economic disparity between middle-class tourists who could afford to jet around the world in pursuit of pleasure and those barely scraping by on a couple of hundred dollars a month, a difference not just arithmetical but exponential.

VI

In the evenings, I went to Twilight Alley. Each bar has its own logistics, but in the Classic Club, the customers are seated and served drinks on a long tier of bleachers facing a stage where about half the young men working there are arrayed; the others are scattered in a group of chairs at the end of the bleachers, waiting their turns. As recorded music plays, they pose in their white wrestling singlets (in other bars, they just wear underwear or swimming briefs), to each of which is appended a number on a button. If a customer would like the company of one of the young men on stage, he signals to one of the bar captains, who arranges the introduction. In other bars, the procedure is somewhat more informal, with the young men approaching the customers directly. The behaviour of the young men on stage varies as well, ranging from blatant displays of masturbatory activity to the more demure style favoured at the Classic. In either case, a customer, identifying a young man by the number on his button, can take him off the premises, paying a stipulated "off-fee" to the bar, and then paying the young man whatever might be agreed to afterwards at the hotel.

Later in the evening, there's a sex show on stage. Again, depending on the bar, the acts and configurations vary, as do the props — bubble machines, shower stalls, gleaming oils, soap suds, even a human aquarium. The denouement is a scene of anal intercourse, which has its own rather strict protocols (including use of condoms). The active partner tends to be somewhat exaggeratedly masculine while the bottom is markedly effeminate, and is further feminised by having his genitals covered. All of this reflects an older Thai tradition of homosexuality in which gender roles are sharply demarcated, even though in the last quarter-century a Thai gay scene of relatively undifferentiated partners has replaced the classic pairing of straight-appearing man and transgendered "boy-girl" (the word for this category in Thai is *kathoey*).

In the version at the Classic Club, there were four people on stage: the macho top who penetrated the passive partner in a series of rapidly-shifting acrobatic positions, a young man who was fellated by the bottom, and a rather beefy guy in a leather costume who provided simulated sadomasochism with a foam baton.

Even for those who have seen such shows frequently enough to be partially desensitized to the spectacle, there can still be the occasional glimpse or flash that reveals the enormity of the taboo that's being broken. Notwithstanding the sexualization of Western culture, including the widespread availability of visual pornography, the public or semi-public display of sex — since this is taking place in a closed bar before a self-selected clientele — remains a rare event. It violates the notion of sexual privacy and intimacy, brings into play a more elaborate social arrangement of actors and spectators who mutually affect each other, and promises the acquisition of a kind of knowledge otherwise unavailable. Just as theatre has the advantage of "life" over films, the sex show offers an immediacy for which pornographic videos are only a substitute.

Whether homo- or heterosexual, sexual intercourse is constructed for us as one of the great human mysteries. By constructed, I'm referring to the history of the ideological web by which the meaning of sexual intercourse is presented to us. It includes everything from its mandated scarcity in the economic transactions of traditional marriages between families at various historical moments, to the mundane sexual smirking and boasting of classmates at school as they enforce preferred sexual styles of manhood. The result of all this ideological discourse is to both mystify sex and present it to us as a holy mystery.

The experience of seeing actual sexual intercourse is "interesting" — a word I often use in a semi-technical, ideologically neutral sense, meaning that the event seen is simply phenomenologically engaging for some specific reason. That other people also find the viewing of sexual intercourse interesting is attested to by the enormous market for pornography. The sex show, even when it occurs in circumstances that make it a sleazy exhibition wrapped in what many observers see as exploitation and humiliation, is a challenge to our privatization of sexuality, a transformation of mystery into a multifaceted game of power and fun. But "fun" for the performers, the critics will be quick to ask, or just exploitation of them? Having talked to some of the sex performers, I only know that the answer is more complicated than many of the critics would make it out to be. And the answer in this instance is further complicated by homosexuality, which makes the situation different from similar heterosexual scenes, which raise the question of the role of women under sexism. I don't have a simple account of what's going on or an exact answer to the moral quandary. Still, I'm not talking about heterosexual relations and how they affect women, and I think it's accurate to insist that homosexual descriptions of male-male sexual scenes must not be assimilated to the heterosexual paradigm.

Once, at a bar less demure than the Classic, during a sex show in which the "top" caught my eye and exchanged mutual complicitous glances with me, he slowly maneuvered the "bottom" across the room toward me until the pair were literally at the arm of my chair, and drops of sweat splashed from their bodies onto my forearm. The guy taking the active role in this sex performance all the while looked at me, straight in the eye, gleefully, naughtily, suggesting he could do the same to me. Later, after the show, I ran into him in the bar's bathroom and we had a friendly chat in which I praised the performance. Between us now: the knowledge that I had seen him, his knowledge that he had seen me seeing him.

The primary business of the bar, apart from dispensing drinks, is the organization of pairings of young men with customers. It would be presumptuous to think one could in any significant way know those young men, apart from the uncertain, if intense, information picked up during one's erotic encounters with them. Nor did I have any realistic idea of how they might see us. For instance, appearances to the contrary, Thai culture generally disapproved of homosexual behaviour, but at the same time didn't provide sanctions against it. In addition to the cultural gaps, there was the simple fact of linguistic barriers. That's why I spent a lot of my time learning rudimentary Thai. Most of the young men, many of them recently arrived in Bangkok from farming villages, spoke only Thai, apart from a few stylized phrases — "What your name?", "Where you from?", "How long you stay?" — that had been learned for conversations at work. (Once, I saw the notebook of one of the young men who worked in a bar, in which these introductory sentences were written in several languages.)

I could only begin to know these young men if, like Dan or Robin, I had more extended relationships with them and, even then, as I saw with Dan and Robin's relationships, large ambiguities remained. But the one obvious sociological fact of the situation is that such relationships, casual or enduring, were predicated on the poverty that produced such an excess of services of all kinds to foreigners. It is here that the dialectic of desire and its cessation becomes pertinent, even though it may have been of little concern to most of the sex tourists, the occasional David Roth excepted. Here, though, I think Roth's perspective, which I share, if not in such an agonized way, is better. That is, I think it's preferable to keep both desire and poverty simultaneously in view, rather than being indifferent to the latter in order to pursue the former.

The widespread poverty generated a sea of suffering, from the extremes of legless beggars on rolling platforms snaking through the nighttime tides of shoppers on the single-file cramped sidewalks of Surawong and Silom avenues to the more benign morning-after scenes of patrons and young men at the breakfast tables of the Malaysia Hotel. In Buddhist politics, the goal is the cessation of suffering. The cause of suffering, according to Buddhist thought, is desire in all its forms, not just the sexual. At the time, I was reading commentaries on the Buddhist *sutras* — which are primarily narrative accounts of the teachings of the Buddha. While not emphasising sexual desire as a special evil, I noticed that Buddhist writing tended to be slightly more puritanical about such matters than first appeared on the surface of its texts. Finally, the source of desire — although this is a radical oversimplification — is to be found in the illusion of self. Seeing through the illusion of self and world, even the appearance of good and evil, and consequently ceasing to cling to those illusions was the aim of the meditative practices of Buddhism, the path to enlightenment.

VII

On the day before my departure from Bangkok — shortly after the turn of the New Year, which I'd raucously spent with Dan, Robin, and Kinch in a bar where the midnight show of anal intercourse was interspersed with lip-synching drag queens — I had arranged to see Sulak, the mentor Pravit had told me about. In the interim, through reading some books and articles by and about him, I learned that Sulak, far from being merely the nice, old knowledgeable guy suggested by the image of Pravit's "mentor," was in fact the most famous dissident intellectual in the country. A key figure in the International Network of Engaged Buddhists, Sulak, for some four decades, had been bluntly denouncing military dictatorships, the "religion of consumerism," as he called it, and the spiritual passivity of the temples, which had turned monkhood into a mere profession. The price for speaking out had included both appearances in the courtroom docket and extended periods of exile.

That afternoon, I took a taxi across the Chao Phraya river to the Thonburi side, as it's known, and was deposited on a broad, busy boulevard. Between two buildings housing a motorcycle repair shop and other similar businesses, there was a narrow, garbage-strewn gravel path and a sign with the street number I'd been given. The dank pathway produced an instant of trepidation in me. Quickly enough, however, it opened out into a small, pleasant compound that included some trees, a pond, a couple of skinny dogs, a chicken coop, and a good-sized main building and some out-buildings, linked by a metal-roofed social space that contained some tables and chairs and a ping-pong table. Seeing various sets of sandals on the steps of the entrance to the main building, I placed my shoes there, and then went in to sit in the waiting area I'd been directed to by a secretary. If I thought to attain a preparatory moment of calm while waiting for my visit with Sulak, my efforts were interrupted by one of the small dogs who went straight to the fresh scent of my shoes, gripped one of them in its jaws and began making off with it in the direction of the pond. There was an instant of un-Buddhist panic on my part as I chased the creature down a slope of lawn until it lost interest and dropped the shoe on the grass, allowing me to retrieve it.

Sulak was a slightly heavy-set, brown, smooth-skinned man in his sixties, wearing a traditional long white shirt over his trousers. He invited me into a spacious, cool office in which floor-level chair-cushions were placed around a low table, and poured me a cup of tea from a metal pot. I remarked on the house, now the headquarters of his Spiritual Education Movement, or SEM. Sulak was a great inventor of a series of overlapping and interlinked non-governmental organizations and their acronyms. He told me, in the accents he had acquired at law school in England, that it had belonged to his mother. It dated back to the days when such houses near the river had been at the centre of the elegant, canal-crossed city then known as the "Venice of the East."

When I began with a sort of pro-forma question, asking him if he had any interest in the current election campaign, then in its final days, Sulak readily admitted, "Not really." He regarded most of the parties, including the one leading the polls and headed by a media mogul, as money-wasting entities, one step removed from political gangsterism. While they mouthed the slogans of globalisation, development and consumerism, he said, there was nothing in their programs that addressed the real issues of poverty, environmental destruction or spiritual emptiness. "Still, it's better than dictatorship," he wryly added.

His remark about spiritual poverty provided an opening to ask about what was mainly on my mind, the state of Buddhism and the relationship between its goal of the cessation of striving and his own notion of a socially active, "engaged" version of it. "Buddhism has been fairly successful in simple agrarian societies," he said, "but I don't think we know how to apply it to a complex industrial society. I think that's true of most religions." Instead, countries like Thailand had been overtaken by "the religion of consumerism." (He called Thailand by the older name of "Siam," eschewing the now standard usage on the grounds that it had been invented by fascist-leaning Thai generals in the 1930s, in imitation of Nazi Deutschland.) As Sulak had written in one of his essays, "Today Bangkok is a third-rate Western city. The department stores have become our shrines. For young people, these stores have replaced the Buddhist temples as centres of social life ... Although Siam was never colonized by a Western power, in many ways we have been more devastated by this insidious force than those who were." Now, in our conversation, he reiterated various of these ideas.

We spoke for about an hour or so. Near the end, I asked Sulak one of the theoretical questions on my mind about Buddhist philosophy. "Is reincarnation a necessary doctrine of Buddhist belief?"

"No, it is not necessary," he replied without hesitation, slightly emphasising the word "necessary," as if to suggest that no doctrine was necessary, either to Buddhism or anything else. Sulak added, "Buddha said, Don't believe in anything unless it is helpful." Being a Western ironist, I naturally also heard in Sulak's remark the parodic echo of scenes in which the spiritual seeker makes his visit to the wise man, but in this instance, Sulak's neatly turned reply seemed to me reasonable enough.

Outside, before plunging back into the city, I paused in the garden a moment. A skinny dog lapped at the edge of the pond (I couldn't tell if it was the one who had stolen my shoe), a household rooster squawked, and a transparent red butterfly floated amid the leaves of a tree, a reminder of the famed Buddhist suggestion of the impermanence of all things.

In Twilight Alley, between the Classic Club and an open-sided restaurant at the dogleg of the lane, there was a neighbourhood shrine. Despite the official dominant status of Thai Buddhism, the spiritual culture was crosscut with remnants of Hinduism, acquired from the earlier sweep of Indian thought across southeast Asia, as well as royalist cult worship and even more deeply, with local animism. I wasn't clear about the relation of these shrines to Buddhism, or the meaning of the small statuettes of different figures along with various trinkets housed in glass containers, or the elaborate miniature houses. But the shrines, I had noticed, are regularly tended by people from the establishment responsible for them — in this case, the Classic bar.

I was waiting in the adjacent outdoor restaurant just after 8 o'clock for a young man whom I was seeing named Joe. He came out of the bar, but before we went off, he walked over to the shrine or spirit house. He removed his shoes, stepped onto the low platform before the altar, laid a yellow flower garland on a corner of it, and lighted a handful of incense sticks, which he placed in a vase-like container. Then he knelt before it, brought his hands together, and bowed low.

Joe got up, joined me, and we walked down Twilight Alley toward Surawong Road, to get a taxi that would take us to the Malaysia Hotel.

Lawrence Bantleman

Memory, quick as a flash of intelligence: on many evenings, in the 1970s, the four of us — Lawrence Bantleman, Bob Rippon, Michael Steele, and I — gathered around a terrycloth-covered table in the Ambassador, a Vancouver gay pub. Bantleman, whom we called Larry or Lolo, was a heavy-set, dark-skinned, saturnine man, family origins in India, who spoke with a charming Anglo-Indian accent. He was, I suppose, a failed poet, and he no doubt drank too much, which led to an early death. But he had some practical success developing housing for poor people in Vancouver's Downtown Eastside, and he had a wonderful, mostly literary, intelligence. He often chided the rest of us for wasting our time gossiping about sex and politics. One evening at the pub, he described to us in considerable detail a novel he was writing that would criticize gay sado-masochistic lifestyles. The punchline of the description was the novel's proposed title: *Intimate Nazi Dining*. Every once in a while, over the years, that title, unbidden, pops up in my mind and brings with it a smile, and a nostalgic longing for Bantleman's now departed intelligence, for his voice, for his elegant grumpiness. I've often imagined the pleasure of reading that imaginary book, *Intimate Nazi Dining* by Lawrence Bantleman.

Bar mitzvah

I'm a non-bar mitzvah'd, or unconfirmed, Jew. I never went to the after-school Jewish school where boys were instructed in the religion and learned Hebrew, or at least enough bits of it to participate in the confirmation ceremony at age 13. At one point around that age, my father Morrie casually asked me if I wanted to have a bar mitzvah, and I said equally casually, No, I don't think so. That was good enough for him.

The great point of contention between my father and his father, my grandfather Jacob, had been over religion. My father as a boy had opposed religious observance on rationalistic grounds, while his father had defended the doctrine, somewhat hypocritically, not on grounds of belief, but for reasons of tradition. My own reasons for not wanting a bar mitzvah were considerably less intellectual: I saw Hebrew school as cutting into my time for playing baseball with the kids in the neighbourhood. My father had determined, as a result of the experiences with his father, that he would never impose beliefs upon me, especially ones he didn't believe in, and would do every-thing in his power to protect my intellectual freedom. The news that I wasn't going to have a bar mitzvah created considerable consterna-tion in some parts of the family. But when various relatives voiced their objections to my sacrilege, my father settled all arguments with the pronouncement, "He doesn't want to."

So, no bar mitzvah. No Hebrew school. I don't think I was in a syn-agogue more than a handful of times during my youth, most likely to attend bar mitzvahs of cousins and friends. Vague memories of an occasional dinner table ceremony at some kinsman's home during a Jewish holiday. But that's it.

How strange it is, then, to find, among all the thousands of things in my mind, decades after I last heard the words uttered, the Hebrew words, *Baruch ata Adonai, Eloheynu melech ha-olam*, "Blessed are you, O Lord our God, King of the Universe." That's the first line of the Jewish sabbath prayers blessing the wine, the bread, children, and the lighting of candles. Let the believers be comforted. I suspect, however, that my retention of that Hebrew blessing is less a testament to the enduring power of divinity and more an indication that memory doesn't care about belief, but about music, the intoned melody of a few words.

Dave Barrett

Dave Barrett was the first social democratic premier of the western Canadian province where I've lived for 40 years. The province is British Columbia, a huge, coastal, mountainous, forested tract of territory stretching from Washington State to Alaska. Barrett was the premier of the province from 1972-75. His New Democratic Party government had been preceded for more than two decades by that of a regional conservative party known as Social Credit, headed by a small town hardware store owner named W.A.C. ("Wacky") Bennett, who presided over the resource-rich region during its boom years of the 1950s and 1960s. Wacky's favourite slogan was, "The finest sound in the land is the ringing of cash registers." Barrett's brief tenure was followed by another decade of Social Credit conservatism (contracted to "Socred" in popular parlance), led by Wacky's son, Bill Bennett, a dour real estate entrepreneur.

Barrett was a boisterous, somewhat rotund figure, with a booming if high-pitched voice. He was a former social worker who had made his reputation by blowing the whistle on various mistreatments of the poor and disadvantaged, displaying a passionate sympathy that may have been rooted in his Jewish heritage. I knew Barrett only casually, but well enough that he once proposed that I might ghost-write his political memoirs. "I'll do the talking, you do the writing," he laughed. Though the project never came off, Barrett remains emblematic for me of the period and of my flirtation with mainstream, left-of-centre politics. It's a subject I've never addressed seriously before.

The story will have to be roundabout. At the end of summer 1975, in Vancouver, I got a telephone call on a Friday afternoon from Leonard Minsky. He was a former English professor at Simon Fraser University whom I'd known for several years, from literary and radical student political circles. "How would you like to teach at a college?" Minsky asked in his instantly recognizable Brooklyn accent.

"Teach what?" I asked. "A college where?"

Minsky skipped the first question. "In Terrace," he said.

"Where's that?" I asked.

Terrace, it turned out, was a small town of 10,000 people on the Skeena River in northwestern British Columbia, about 600 kilometres, as the crow flies, north of Vancouver. Minsky had been hired as the organizer of one of four instant, regional colleges that the Dave Barrett provincial government had recently authorized as part of its program to make post-secondary education more accessible to citizens in British Columbia's outback. The college was to open almost immediately, with classes beginning that fall. One of Minsky's several chores was to round up a faculty for the school.

"Where are you calling from?"

"Terrace," Minsky said, a little impatiently, as if this, and much more, ought to be obvious to me.

"But what would I teach?" I persisted.

"Anything you want," Minsky replied. When I pointed out that colleges were normally organized into departments and disciplines, he grudgingly allowed that I might teach sociology, a subject in which I had a degree. But it was clear that teaching wasn't Minsky's first priority.

"Gee, Leonard, I don't know."

I was, at the moment, working as a story editor for a morning radio news program broadcast in Vancouver by the publicly-owned Canadian Broadcasting Corporation's station there. The program was produced by a man I liked named David Cayley, whose soft-spoken demeanour belied the program's radical reputation. In local media circles, Cayley's show was known as "Radio Peking." The CBC's offices and studios were located in a slightly shabby hotel in downtown Vancouver, which is where I was sitting, in my slightly shabby cubbyhole, when Minsky phoned.

"Listen," Minsky said, closing the deal, "why don't you fly up here and take a look?"

That weekend Minsky met me at the Terrace Airport, and we drove over to nearby Lakelse Lake, which had a restaurant and lodge on its shores. That's where we were to meet Peter Burton, a mutual friend of ours who had become a labour leader at the Alcan Aluminum plant in the neighbouring town of Kitimat. While waiting for Burton to drive in from Kitimat, Minsky and I walked along the shore of the lake and he told me about his plans for the college. Minsky was a remarkably animated figure in his early 40s, with a corolla of greying, curly hair, and a cackling, distinctive laugh that sounded as if he was just about to put something over on the world. He was a Chaucer scholar, whose students reported that he was the only English prof they knew who was able to relate Chaucer to the recently-ended Vietnam War, which may have had something to do with Minsky not getting a tenured professorship at Simon Fraser. This time around, in his new role as a college organizer, he really was planning to put something over on the world.

As I'd intuited, Minsky's first priority wasn't teaching. It was revolution. Teaching literature, sociology, psychology, and history were the least of Minsky's plans. The big idea was that the college would be a base from which to organize the community for a great and democratic people-controlled future. The academic stuff was just window dressing. Groups had already been lined up, Minsky told me, to put on community-controlled programs in aboriginal, labour and women's studies. As well, Minsky had hired another mutual friend of ours, Jeff Marvin, and armed him with a Land Rover to penetrate distant native villages and organize the masses. The chairman of the local labour council, a Danish-born carpenter named John Jensen, was onboard. Key figures had been identified in the neighbouring towns of Kitimat (like Peter Burton), Prince Rupert, Smithers, and other habitations along the Skeena.

As we peered out across Lakelse Lake, looking at the distant mountainous backdrop, Minsky cited some tidbit of Maoist wisdom that went, more or less: the mountains surround the countryside, the countryside surrounds the cities, etc. Capture the mountains and the countryside, and you'll conquer the cities. He came down to earth long enough to also try to persuade me of the sublime pleasures of canoeing on Lakelse Lake. I was wary of the surrounding mountains — you could easily get lost — and I definitely wasn't going to get into some flimsy canoe and paddle around the lake, in which you could easily drown.

By now, I was having doubts about whether the college existed or if it was just Minsky's fevered fantasy. But he assured me that it actually had some buildings on the uplands at the edge of town, which now housed a provincial vocational school whose administration and staff we would have no trouble taking over.

Back in Vancouver, just as the autumn rainy season was beginning, two things convinced me to take the job. First, one morning at about 6:30 (the show ran from 6-9), I was at my post at the radio station lining up the guests slated to appear on that day's edition. The show consisted of a half-dozen telephone interviews, along with breaks for news, weather, stock market and traffic reports. It was raining. I was standing at the window, looking at the rain falling onto an ugly fountain below in front of the city courthouse. I had two telephones to my ears. My job was to keep the about-to-be-heard guests entertained and to check the pre-interview material for any last-minute glitches. On one phone was Herman Kahn of the Hudson Institute, who was a sort of futurologist and enthusiast for World War III. On the other phone was a worm farmer who had a ranch somewhere west of Prince George, B.C. I'd just said to one of them, "Now, Dr. Kahn, what are the two major problems facing the world?" and he was launched onto a rapid-fire answer in a heavy New York accent, when I interrupted to say, "Can you hold that thought for a sec?" and I turned to the phone with the worm farmer to check on just how far west of Prince George the wiggling worms were located. That was the moment — holding the two phones to my two ears and gazing at the dreary rain — when I thought to myself, This is crazy.

The second reason for taking the college teaching job was that the 1960s, unbeknowst to most of us, had just ended in April 1975 with the conclusion of the Vietnam War, and the volunteer newspaper collective I was a member of was breaking up. The paper was a weekly called the *Western Voice* and was subtitled "a newspaper of working class struggle." When the war ended, the paper held a celebration and fund-raiser for the reconstruction of Vietnam in a local hall, which we decorated with slogans on large pieces of red paper, in the Chinese "big-character poster" style. I made a pass-the-hat speech.

The *Voice* had evolved from a series of local counter-culture newspapers, starting with the *Georgia Straight*, a weekly founded in the late 1960s by a local poet named Dan McLeod, whose staff I had joined early on. It was sundered by a political squabble. The feminists on the paper became aggrieved at their treatment, occupied the paper's offices, and were only cleared out when McLeod, a heretofore mild-mannered defender of hippies and free speech, obtained an injunction from the courts. At that point, I went with the new, more radical group that started a rival paper called the *Grape*. That's where I became friends with Peter Burton, who later became a union leader in Kitimat. Eventually, the *Grape* also split, which gave birth to the pro-proletarian *Voice*. Then the *Voice* embarked on its own political travails, which took the form of what was then known as a "two-line struggle." One "line" was discovered to be reactionary, while the other line, the "correct" line, was properly revolutionary.

My political ideas were a mish-mash whose only coherence was, as a line in a Robert Creeley poem has it, "a small boy's idea of doing good." My understanding of politics ranged from Socrates, whose wisdom I had imbibed in Bob Rowan's philosophy classes at the University of British Columbia, to the latest New Left works of the German-born thinker, Herbert Marcuse. A few tidbits of Marx, social contract theory, and anarchism were sprinkled in. On the whole it was not an altogether bad mish-mash and when it was threatened by the madness of the moment, such as the internal debates at the *Voice*, it was leavened by a temperamental core of reasonableness I'd inherited from my father.

Meanwhile, in the real world, in British Columbia, *circa* 1975, there was a social democratic government about which we radicals were too contemptuous, even when, like me, we were card-carrying on and off members of the governing party. And in a dark basement staff meeting, the "correct line" of the *Voice*, rather than the fact that it only had about 600 readers, required the paper's "liquidation." A final, fat issue of the paper, crammed with "position papers" and turgid analyses of the present political moment, brought our journalistic enterprise to a conclusion. Most of the members of the collective then went on to several years of attempting to build a revolutionary Marxist-Leninist political organization, an effort that petered out only in the 1980s. But by the time the last issue of the *Voice* rolled off the presses, I was on the road — to Terrace.

While Terrace is 600 kilometres north of Vancouver as the crow flies, as the road rolls it's 1200 kilometres plus. I was in a small Honda Civic, crammed to the gunnels with books and belongings. The road from Vancouver goes east for about 150 kilometres to a town called Hope, then north up through the daunting Fraser River Canyon until you reach Prince George six or seven hours later, then you turn left onto the Yellowhead Highway, heading west along the Skeena River, which runs out to the coast at Prince Rupert. Terrace is on the river, 135 kilometres inland from the Pacific Ocean. The whole journey is an enormous geographical zig-zag.

Minsky was living in an apartment in a motel-like building on Loen Avenue, a place I would soon inherit as Leonard moved into a large, rambling house to accommodate his wife and kids, who were arriving shortly. I pulled into the driveway and was greeted by Minsky's grin. My arrival was clearly part of what Leonard was putting over on the world, as he marshalled his troops. Inside, in the kitchen, Jeff Marvin was there, and a heavy-set, dark-haired man named Ray Jones, one of the leaders of the nearby Gitksan native band, through whose territory I'd just driven. Jones's first words to me were, "Not another Jew!" It was true. Minsky, Marvin, and me. Leonard cackled with pleasure, and began whipping up a lunch of fried chicken, while Jeff poured the drinks from a bottle of Minsky's brand of choice, Cato's Scotch.

Eventually, I was taken up to the college which, I was happy to see, actually existed. It mostly consisted of workshops, where students learned to become welders, auto mechanics, electricians and heavy equipment operators, along with a few classrooms in which to teach accounting and office management. The vocational staff, who were justifiably suspicious of the T-shirt-garbed mad conspirators who had arrived in their midst, were dressed in shirts, ties, and shop coats. I was introduced to the administrators, who were mostly former business managers from town. Across the road from the school's undistinguished architecture was a fallow expanse of land known as Frank's Field, where migrating geese pulled in for a pit stop on their way south. By early October, the field was already covered by a light dusting of snow.

The semester began, and the hastily assembled staff — an English teacher, a psychologist, an anthropologist, a chemist, myself, and an early childhood education instructor I became friends with named Larissa Tarwick — began doing what college instructors everywhere do, and a sufficient number of the children of the local middle classes turned up to fill the classrooms. We were peripatetic teachers — imagining ourselves, on the Maoist model, to be travelling "barefoot doctors" — who drove through logged valleys to teach classes in Kitimat, Prince Rupert and other towns along the Skeena. There was also a lot of extracurricular, "revolutionary" activity. The special programs in aboriginal, feminist, and labour studies were launched with democratically-controlled boards staffed by community representatives. Jeff Marvin wandered through the countryside and remote valleys, doing something called "community development." And there was a good deal of strategizing and plotting, as the old vocational school principal was eased out and plans were made to install a more politically astute college president. The rhetoric of Minsky's revolution was over-dramatic, but the idea, which was really straightforward social democratic doctrine, was sensible. Despite the fashionable sloganeering, the idea was simply to make education available to more people, on the theory that a better-educated society would be more sensitive to human suffering. The idea was really old-fashioned 19th century liberalism, modernised in a social democratic way to ensure public funding, government oversight, democratic control, and a commitment to previously marginalised groups of people.

I rode up and down the highway with John Jensen, to labour halls in places like Smithers and the small mill-town of Houston, where I gave amateurish talks about labour history in the evenings to gatherings of trade union members. We drove home in the middle of the night, the highway following the course of the great, dark Skeena River, which I thought of as the god or spirit of the region.

Jensen was the most interesting person I got to know in the years I was there. He was a master carpenter, about 15 years my senior, a wiry, compact man with a greying brush mustache and sparkling eyes that signalled his amusement at the follies of his fellow humans. Most of all, Jensen was a man of impeccable integrity with a wry sense of humour, and a range of experiences that he had fashioned into a sort of immediately recognizable wisdom.

One summer, before the semester began, I was permitted to serve as his carpenter's helper as he built a new house for himself and Larissa Tarwick in a sparsely inhabited area outside of Terrace called Jackpine Flats (which we instantly dubbed Jackass Flats). My job mainly was to carry things around, and Jensen let me hammer in a few nails, presumably in places where I could do the least amount of damage. I once asked him where the plans for the house were, since I knew houses had plans. We were in the midst of lifting massive railroad ties by means of a pulley that Jensen had rigged up, installing them as ceiling beams. Jensen paused, pulled out his carpenter's pencil, used for marking off measurements, and drew the entire thing for me on a 2x4 plank. The house was in his head. I was in awe.

Another year — this was after the "revolution" — I suggested that we begin a regional monthly newspaper. Jensen took about a second to think about it, and said, "Okay, let's do it." He didn't ask what would be in it, how it would get written, or where the money would come from. The answers, by the way, were: a) stories about the world from the perspective of an imaginary pro-native, pro-feminist, pro-labour reader; b) I would write it; and c) Jensen would finance it through the various regional labour councils who provided the funds simply on Jensen's word that it was "okay." For a year, then, every one of the 15,000 or so households in the region received the paper, delivered by the postal workers' union.

Most of the revolution took place at Minsky's sprawling house, taking the form of wonderful, large parties of Minsky's closest conspirators (consuming sufficient quantities of Cato's Scotch), and consisted primarily of Chairman Minsky fuming, fretting, plotting, and imagining the counterplots of his many mortal enemies and the betrayals of his loyal friends. As revolutions go, it was a pretty benign affair, and we even had some fun, an unusual accomplishment in the annals of changing the world.

Obviously, it was too good to last. Minsky's "revolution" ended on December 10, 1975, the date of a provincial election that Premier Dave Barrett had prematurely called, a little over three years into his term. The campaign that autumn, long before the invention of modern "negative" or "attack" political advertising, was as vicious as electoral politics could provide. Barrett, a social democratic populist, was portrayed as a raving socialist. British Columbia's owning classes weighed in with all the third-party anti-government advertising that could be purchased. "Thanks for the memories," warbled the mocking farewell of the insurance industry, aggrieved by Barrett's establishment of public auto insurance. The logging and mining industries plastered bumper stickers on vehicles all over the province to warn voters that resource-based jobs were doomed under the rule of the socialists and their trade union toadies. Real estate developers, landlords, and farmers declared their opposition to social democratic schemes to control rents and protect agricultural land. And for good measure, everybody charged the social democrats with "tax and spend" policies and pandering to fraudulent welfare recipients. The media wasn't subtle about its preference for Barrett's opponent, Wacky Bennett's tight-lipped son, Bill.

That evening I was in the basement rec room of chemistry instructor Norm Webster's house, watching the election returns on TV with others from the college. Outside, the snow was banked up two metres high. Inside our bunker, the gloom settled over the soon-to-be-former revolutionaries. It was over in a few minutes. There were scenes from NDP headquarters, where Barrett made the ritual concession speech, calling, rather sentimentally, for "love" in the face of his enemies' rancour. We shook our heads in bewilderment and trooped out into the snow.

Practically the first act of the new provincial government was to fire the college board, dismissing the little group of feminists, natives and trade unionists appointed by the social democrats, and replacing them with more suitable business managers. Minsky was doomed. But there was a final comic epilogue.

The board was in the midst of appointing a new college president to replace the departed vocational school principal. The candidate of the "revolutionaries" was a socialist economics professor from Winnipeg, Cy Gonick, who also ran a leftist magazine, *Canadian Dimension*, and whose academic credentials were sufficiently impressive that he made the short list of even the new college board. Minsky was in his final moments of glory, lobbying various middle-of-the-road board members, on the phone to Gonick in Winnipeg, plotting with his minions, making us at least half-believe one more time.

At the board meeting to decide on the president that winter evening, it was close. At the last minute, Minsky stiffened a wavering board member, and the vote went 6-5 for Gonick. There was only one little hitch. Gonick, on the other end of the telephone, wasn't sure he wanted to come. His wife, imagining the differences between outback Terrace and relatively civilized big city Winnipeg, was against it. But you only have to do it for a year, Minsky pleaded with him. The revolution was in his hands. Gonick sighed. No, he thought not. Minsky sagged. Gonick's refusal was relayed to the board and he was dropped from their list. The phone rang. It was Gonick. He'd talked it over with his wife again and, on second thought, maybe he would come. Too late, too late. In due course, a very non-revolutionary college president was installed.

After that, the college was fated to become a more or less normal community institution. Minsky was unceremoniously dumped. Later, he and his lively clan turned up in Washington, D.C., where he got a job working for the anti-corporate Ralph Nader organization, a place where he could plot to his heart's content. Jeff Marvin remained for a while. Years later, I ran into him in Vancouver. He was on his way to South America to climb mountains. A year or two later, I heard he'd fallen off a mountain in Ecuador, plunging into a crevasse. His body was never recovered. And John Jensen, the man I'd taken for my unofficial mentor in Terrace, remained in Jackpine Flats, settling into his role as a community elder. As for Dave Barrett, he returned to electoral politics for a while, winning a seat as a federal member of parliament, and eventually became one of the senior statesmen of the social democratic party.

Those of us with teaching contracts were legally protected and could stay on. The revolution was over, but not the college. A lot of small, good things happened. My friend, the poet George Stanley, joined the English department, and soon developed an affection for the place and the people, as evidenced in his many poems about the region, especially in a series called "Terrace Landscapes" in his book *Gentle Northern Summer*. I notice that I've adopted a self-mocking tone for this bit of social democratic memoir, but when I read Stanley's poems about Terrace, I remember that it's a real place — if not the centre of the universe, not Hicksville, either — and that many of us had a dream about its possibilities. I suppose the self-mockery is to protect the dream from getting too bruised.

One year, as I mentioned, we had the newspaper. Another year, in spring 1977, just after the death of Chairman Mao Zedong, Jeff Marvin wangled a spot for me on a tour group to China. The visit was disillusioning in terms of politics — that is, "people's democracy" was not all it was cracked up to be — but China wasn't disillusioning in terms of a place whose images entered my permanent memory.

There were personal events, too, unconnected to our grandiose political struggles. One autumn, I arrived back in Terrace from summer holidays with a companion in tow, Martin Bell, a young man I'd met in the Vancouver bars. He became a welding student at the school, and we carried on a bumpy, fond domestic relationship for a year or so. Somewhere in the wreckage of books and boxes that piles up in the wake of our lives, there's a photograph, taken by Jeff Marvin, of Martin and me grinning happily over a birthday cake at a party for me that Jeff and his girlfriend had put on in his house in Thornhill, a mostly trailer-park encampment just outside of Terrace. So that, too, remains.

But I wanted out. In 1978-79, I took a leave from the college and returned to Vancouver. It was nearing the end of the first term of Bill Bennett's government. That summer I began writing a book about the unfortunate defeat of Dave Barrett and the ill-judged policies of his successors, a sort of election run-up warning. I'd written poetry and stories when younger (a volume of those writings had been published as *Wrestling the Angel* in 1976), and I'd discovered a flair for journalism ever since I'd been at university in the mid-1960s, but I'd never written a book-length work of popular journalism about contemporary politics. It was mostly a matter of re-writing, gathering up the news clips from the last several years of British Columbia provincial politics, and turning them into a coherent narrative that attempted to make a mild social democratic sense of those events. The book, *Son of Socred*, came out in the spring and became a surprising regional success. I was soon a minor figure of punditry, called on to provide instant quotes and soundbites to the omniverous media.

The book had no discernible impact on the election, held in May 1979, in which the conservative government was handily re-elected, and in fall I returned to teaching in Terrace. But something important had happened personally, namely, I had learned how to write books. I'd discovered the pleasure of telling stories, and equally important, the pleasure of writing. In the midst of bookwriting, a lot of existential anxieties disappear. Bookwriting answers the ever-present questions, Where am I? and, What am I doing? I'm in the book, and I'm writing it, it confidently replies. I wasn't quite a writer yet — that would come a few years later, along with another kind of book — but I was learning the skills of writing, which weren't all that different from carpentry. Like John Jensen and his house, I had the book in my head. Having written one book, I quickly saw that I could write others, and did. But the stories of how I became a writer, and how I became a teacher, are different from this one. This one is about politics.

My local notoriety as a political writer and commentator, plus my history as a radical student leader in the '60s, gave some people the idea that I might do as a political candidate. It was a couple of years later, the early 1980s. I'd gotten out of Terrace and found a job teaching political science (and eventually, philosophy) at Capilano College in a suburb just outside of Vancouver. My flirtation with electoral politics was launched when a couple I knew slightly, Bill and Sandra Bruneau (he was a prominent professor in the University of British Columbia's education faculty), suggested that I seek the New Democratic Party nomination for the upcoming provincial election in the neighbourhood where I lived. Sandra, a long-time NDP stalwart, volunteered to be my campaign manager.

I quickly discovered that I wasn't really cut out for electoral politics; I had neither the elbowing ambition required, nor was I sufficiently disciplined not to see the humour in it. The inevitable moment of craziness — something like the time when I was holding two phones to my ears at the radio station — came when one of the local members, trying to decide who he would vote for as our candidate, asked me, "What's your position on hiking trails?" Hiking trails? I had no position on hiking trails. I had positions on education, women's rights, public ownership, the universe, but on hiking trails, I drew a blank. I was the last person in the world you'd find on a hiking trail in the wilderness, where you could easily get lost or eaten by a bear. But nonetheless, there I was, babbling away in favour of hiking trails, prepared to discuss K-Tels fabrics or Frye boots or whatever it is that's relevant to hiking. At the same time, I was thinking to myself, "Gee, I've only been in politics for five minutes, and already I'm lying."

Still, I gamely gave my speech — another talent I'd discovered back in university when I was on the student council. The political columnist for the *Vancouver Sun*, Vaughn Palmer, an old acquaintance from university days, said it was a good speech in his column the next morning. He also added, Unfortunately, good speeches don't win nominations. They only get you to a second ballot, at best. The riding association wisely chose a more appropriate candidate, who was duly defeated in the subsequent election, as the conservatives, led by Bill Bennett, were handily re-elected. I contented myself with writing another book.

All of that — the "revolution" in the British Columbia outback, the flirtation with running for office, the life of what came to be called "the public intellectual" — took place in conservative times some two decades ago. It was the era of President Ronald Reagan in the United States and Conservative Prime Minister Brian Mulroney in Canada (and, on one emblematic occasion, the two of them, arm in arm, singing, "When Irish Eyes Are Smiling"). It was the period of the dismantling of the post-World War II welfare state. I remained active in public affairs — the old habit of wanting to throw one's two cents into the conversation dies hard — but privately I resigned myself to a mild political despair.

One of the books I haven't written — one of my "imaginary books," as I describe them — is called *What Is Social Democracy?* This isn't the place to write it, but I'll say something, briefly (very briefly), about why I'm neither a revolutionary nor a neo-conservative, but a mild-mannered social democrat, even at this late date.

Social democracy is among the most scorned of political ideologies, reviled by both left and right. Within its own political ranks, it is subject to a constant tension between those who want it to be more socialist and those who think its policies should be tempered in the cause of gaining power. As it happens, the country of my citizenship, Canada, is pretty much a social democratic country, even if its social democracy appears under various labels, including "liberalism" and even "progressive conservatism." Only in the last decade has a full-fledged American-style conservatism, favouring unregulated capitalism, appeared in Canada.

Part of the reason that Canada tends to be social democratic is a matter of accident, both historical and geographical. In a country so physically large — 7,000 or so kilometres coast to coast — and mainly populated along a narrow strip just north of the U.S. border, there's an almost deterministic tendency to recognize that certain activities — health care, communications, education and the like — need to be collectively organized. But another part of the reason is conscious. As social pollster Michael Adams shows in *Fire and Ice* (2003), the notion that values and beliefs in the United States and Canada are converging is a myth. Instead, Canadians, at least in the last decade, tend to be more tolerant, less violent, more socially-minded than their neighbours to the south. Of course, since Canada is not a world power, it is spared the inevitable corruption of imperial power, if not the corruption of self-righteousness. Canadians differ from Americans on questions of health care, gun control, public broadcasting, the environment, gay marriage, abortion, and the use of recreational drugs, among many other things.

I think social democracy, as an ideology, can be pinpointed in three or four tenets. First, though it recognizes, however grudgingly, the dominance of the capitalist marketplace, it holds the view that capitalism ought to take a regulated rather than an unregulated form, as much as possible. It's not entirely clear what that means, or how possible it is in the face of globalized capitalism, but it does include the recognition that certain human activities are better organized publicly rather than privately, and that social values should not be suborned to the dictates of the mall.

One minor concrete example of this is publicly-administered auto insurance, the policy Dave Barrett introduced in B.C. a quarter of a century ago. Though there was vigorous, even histrionic, opposition to the policy, mainly from the powerful insurance industry, it has proven over time to be the most sensible, fairest, and safest way of dealing with one aspect of the necessary evil of private transportation. In one Canadian province after another, as private insurance rates have increased and provided only selective coverage, public auto insurance has gained public support. The examples of such policies can easily be multiplied, but public auto insurance provides a representative example of actual social democracy.

Second, social democracy is committed to care for the welfare of the poorest, weakest members of society. I'm always astonished by the rage of people against the "not truly deserving" recipients of public aid, who are often contemptuously portrayed as lazy cheaters. First, the poor are a tiny percentage of the citizenry, and not a terribly expensive budget item in a country of enormous wealth. But second, why would anyone think that welfare recipients would willfully choose the marginal lives they suffer? What stands in need of explanation is the resentment against alleviating their conditions, not the impulse to do so. As Robert Creeley said in a poem called "The Immoral Proposition," "If you never do anything for anyone else / You are spared the tragedy of human relation- / ships."

Third, there's the current debate about taxation, which reflects a wider range of views about how people ought to live together. The sole governmental promise of more barbarous forms of conservatism is the reduction of public expenditure, and government itself, through reduced taxation. It's an almost ironic policy, given the condition of wealth in which the majority of us live. Opposition to collective goods and social programs — the existence of which also serve to protect the rich from the rage of the dispossessed — is self-destructive, even for the ruling classes. While I'm as aware of government mismanagement, petty corruption, and wrongheaded expenditures as the next viewer of our alarmist media, I remain among the most cheerful of taxpayers. The reduction of taxes inevitably means the cutback of public services in health, welfare, education, culture, environmental protection, and a host of other aspects of collective life.

Finally, social democrats, under whatever label, are for the protection of constitutional rights and the rule of law. In Canada, the advances in a generation for the equality of women, ethnic groups, and people of diverse tastes and abilities have been largely the result of social democratic advocacy. Unsurprisingly, such gains are accompanied by occasional excesses, self-righteousness, and at worst, a tribalist clamour. Perhaps the crucial aspect of constitutional equality ought to be reflected in educational policy, although admittedly social democracy in recent decades has probably been less than intellectually adequate in making that case. There's been increased access to education, true, but most of the expansion has been narrowly oriented to occupational training rather than to the shared vocation of being citizens.

Well, that's the short version of what I began thinking about as I drove alongside the winding route of the Skeena River for the first time, long ago. Now, I suppose I'm thinking more about the river and where it goes than I did then, but I haven't altogether forgotten the communities along the road.

Roland Barthes

The book by Roland Barthes that changed my idea of writing is titled *Roland Barthes* by Roland Barthes. Here's how I became interested in it and him.

In the early 1980s, I frequently spent my weekend evenings in a Vancouver gay bar called Buddy's. I quickly recognized that Buddy's was for me and other of its patrons a potent site — puns intended — that regularly generated not only adventures in cruising and sex, but also all sorts of scenes, stories, glimpses, thoughts, aphorisms, moments and meditative arias as I watched and sometimes participated in the passing parade.

If you're a writer, your life tends to bifurcate. On the one hand, there are your personal problems, and how you do or don't solve them is pretty much your private affair. On the other hand, there are your problems as a writer, which may or may not include as subject matter your personal problems and how you solve them. But how you solve your writing problems isn't a private affair because it affects not only you, but your readers and the world in which you and they live. My problem as a writer was how to get at least some of the stuff that was happening in Buddy's, and in my mind and life at the time — I'd recently turned 40 — into my writing.

Up until then, I had the idea that there were two ways to do it. Either you could write poems or else you could write conventional, sustained narrative. Poems have the advantage of dispensing with narrative continuity to more accurately reflect the imagistic, intermittent quality of phenomena, but poems also have the disadvantage of sacrificing narrative. In any case, I didn't want to write poems about Buddy's. Narrative has the advantage of recognizing that life often presents us with experience in story-form. Even dreams come in narrative shapes, though they don't in principle have to — it would be conceivable to have purely abstract dreams — thus attesting to the depth of the notion of story in the human psyche. But narrative also has the drawback that it distorts the fragmented character of reality, and often dispenses with discursive or theoretical modes — ways of thinking that are at times more important than the unfolding of a story. And anyway, whatever was happening in Buddy's was not happening in the form of a story, or at least not simply in story-form.

That's when I encountered the oddly-titled *Roland Barthes* by Roland Barthes. I'd heard of Barthes, of course, since he was a famous French intellectual who had died a couple of years earlier, but I hadn't read him. I'll presently say something about Barthes and the contents of his book, but first here's the short version of what I got from it: 1. There are no predefined rules for what goes into a work of art, or how it is constructed. 2. Forget genre. It is okay, in a single book, to mix narrative, discourse, prose poems, theory (with or without a capital T), and what-have-you, as long as the accumulating whole amounts to more than the sum of its disparate parts. 3. "Theorising" yourself — or, as Barthes puts it in the epigraph to *Roland Barthes*, "Everything here must be considered as if spoken by a character in a novel" — is a way of getting some distance on your experiences and thus is one more tool in avoiding the traps and tropes of subjectivity, or mere self-expressiveness. Or, to put it in the jargon of post-modernity, the "I" should always be a contested site. In retrospect, those insights, some of which I already knew but had forgotten, all seem pretty obvious, if not outright simplistic, but at the time, as far as I knew, nobody had said exactly those things or shown that such a book could be written. Roland Barthes's self-titled book did, and reading it was an indelibly liberating experience. Here, I mean "indelible" in the same way that a tattoo permanently stains the skin.

Roland Barthes by Roland Barthes is, by any standard, a pretty curious work of art. There had been a series of books published in France since the 1950s in which autobiographical writings by prominent writers and intellectuals were strung together, usually by an editor, to produce a brief photo-illustrated volume titled, even though the book was in a sense "unauthored," with the name of the author and the phrase, "by himself" — for instance, *Jean-Paul Sartre par lui-meme*. Roland Barthes's book was a take-off on this model. One further twist: technically, the title really is *Roland Barthes by Roland Barthes*, i.e., the usual author credit is incorporated into the title, and the author credit is dispensed with, rendering the book "unauthored." It is as if we have a book about a fictional character named "Roland Barthes" written by a fictional author of the same name, a book which just happens to be written by a person who has the same name as the character and the author.

Even before I began reading it, I was seduced by the very idea of a book whose title was its author's own name, since it implied that any writer could do it. I could imagine a book called *Stan Persky* by Stan Persky.

Published in 1975, five years before his death, and arranged in alphabetically-ordered passages, *Roland Barthes* begins with a "reward": a series of photographs chosen by Barthes, images from his life, which he presents as "the author's treat to himself, for finishing his book." The first time I read *Roland Barthes*, I didn't pay much attention to this series of more than 40 photos and Barthes's accompanying captions and annotations. I assumed they were simply the conventional "signature" of photographs one usually finds in the middle of any biographical or autobiographical volume. I flipped through them quickly, impatient to get to the text itself. It was only upon subsequent re-readings that it occurred to me that the photographs and their captions contained not only more autobiography than almost anything else in the book, but that this sheaf of images was Barthes's first move in disrupting the genre of conventional autobiography by interrogating the conventions themselves.

The series of photos (which Barthes admits to including for his private pleasure) plunges us into the streets of Bayonne, the small riverine city in the southwestern corner of France, just above the Basque Coast on the Atlantic. That's where Barthes, born in 1915, was raised by his widowed mother during and just after World War I, his father having perished early in the war. The first photo is of a cobbled, narrow, curving street in Bayonne, *circa* 1920, hemmed in on both sides by four- and five-storey apartment buildings with louvred shutters on the windows and wrought-iron balconies. The buildings lean over the narrow ancient lane, lurching toward each other like old people walking. As well, there are a few barely discernible figures and objects in the picture: a woman in a long white hooped dress on the sidewalk, holding the hand of a small child standing in the street (is it Barthes and his mother?), a horse and carriage parked just beyond them, a shopkeeper or clerk standing in a doorway under a sunwashed awning, a couple of empty tables edging onto the sidewalk from the open front of a neighbourhood café. The cobblestone street slowly ascends in the direction of the twin spires of a cathedral in the distance. Here, in a single image, is an entire bygone world.

The intense feeling of loss that I experience upon gazing at such pictures derives, I think, from my own weird sense of the past. I'm immersed in the permanent project of imagining the world, including places and people now dead, as a way of simultaneously creating myself and engaging the world. But I'm also assailed by an irrational feeling that the past never existed, simply because its people and ways of life are no longer around. I half-believe that everything has come into being only insofar as I can see, imagine, or remember it. This is no doubt reflective of the fear that I don't exist, an anticipation of the moment when in fact I won't exist. Even though my thought is irrational, I have the illusion that time itself is a violation of the rational, that it is impossible that someone could have once existed and now no longer does, that only buildings or books from that time remain as traces of their existence. Looking at the photo of a street in Bayonne, France, *circa* 1920, its placid stability is contradicted by my fearful uncertainty about existence.

Mostly, the pictures in *Roland Barthes* are of childhood scenes and urbanscapes, for "these images alone, upon inspection, fail to make me regret the time which has vanished," Barthes says. That's because childhood is the time of timelessness, when you have no idea that human fate is destined for mortality. "So it is not a nostalgia for happy times which rivets me to these photographs, but something more complicated." Elsewhere in his work, Barthes declares, "I have no biography. Or, rather, since the time of the first line I wrote, I no longer see myself." As one commentator on Barthes, Jonathan Culler, puts it, "He can and does recall his childhood and recounts his adolescence, but since then, 'everything happens through writing.'" Barthes's self, after the narrative of youth, is simply the series of his texts. The reader isn't required to agree with this idiosyncratic theory, merely to consider it as an interesting possibility for constructing one's subjectivity.

In addition to the photos of parents and grandparents, and sites in Bayonne during the 1920s — a world of *temps perdu* for us as viewers — there are also snapshots of the adult Barthes, appearing among his students and friends, or at the lectern, or looking bored during a panel discussion. The last photo in the series shows Barthes in his early sixties, white-haired, rather handsome even with his long nose, in a light-coloured raincoat, holding a lighter to his cigarette. The caption, provided by the author, tersely says, "Left-handed," drawing our attention to a heretofore unnoticed "sign" that he unexpectedly points to as central to that portrait of himself. Later, in the text itself, Barthes has a passage titled "Left-handed," in which he asks, "To be left-handed — what does it mean?" After noting the minor inconveniences of dealing with table settings, telephone grips, and scissors, he says, "In school, years ago, you had to struggle to be like the others, you had to normalize your body, sacrifice your good hand to the little society of the *lycée* (I was constrained to draw with my right hand ...)." In short, left-handedness was "a modest, inconsequential exclusion, socially tolerated, that marked adolescence with a tenuous and persistent crease: you got used to it, adapted to it, and went on."

Even when I was growing up, a generation after Barthes, left-handedness was still something to be remarked upon, a mild worry for my parents. Reading Barthes, I now saw my left-handedness as my first perversion in what would be an escalating series of social dissents: atheism, homosexuality, bookishness, political radicalism.

The notions of pleasures, gifts, rewards, and the diminuitive "treat" within a literary text, as well as life, are characteristic of Barthes who, after all, made the phrase "the pleasure of the text" (it's also the title of one of his brief, fragmented books) a catchphrase among post-modernist intellectuals. What I like about Barthes is his contrarian intelligence. *Roland Barthes* is the precise opposite of a self-indulgent, nostalgic, anecdotal autobiography. Yet, in it Barthes takes the stance that characteristics that are roundly disapproved of by his peers, such as self-indulgence, an interest in everyday trivialities, or passivity in the face of political struggle, ought to be occasionally embraced, and heretically investigated for their virtues. They were traits that were sneeringly, and not a little self-righteously, denounced in the 1970s by one's Marxist colleagues as "petit-bourgeois" sins. What did the prohibition on self-indulgence conceal? And what could be more self-indulgent than giving yourself the "treat" of some photos to accompany the text as a reward for finishing your book? Or admitting that you wanted a treat? Did the insistent disapproval of lazing about, ease, irresponsibility, or writing-as-pleasure, mask the social face of industrious efficiency, even among the self-declared opponents of capitalism? If French intellectuals were applauded for their brilliance, Barthes was interested in his stupidity. The intellectually forbidden, as far as Barthes is concerned, is not a sealed gate but an entrance.

Barthes sees his intellectual life as a succession of "reactive formations." In a key passage of *Roland Barthes*, he says, "A popular opinion is posited," such as the taken-for-granted denunciation of petit-bourgeois traits. "Intolerable," Barthes declares. "To free myself from it, I postulate a paradox; then this paradox turns bad, becomes a new concretion, itself becomes a new Doxa, and I must seek further for a new paradox." Barthes traces the trajectory of his entire writing life through this formulation, from his first book, *Writing Degree Zero* (1953), a reaction to Sartre's *What Is Literature?* (1948), to his later inventions of "semiology" and *The Pleasure of the Text* (1973).

"At the work's source," he says, "the opacity of social relations, a false Nature; the first thrust, then, is to demystify." *Mythologies* (1957) began as a series of newspaper columns about popular culture. Barthes wrote about the underlying meaning of such familiar things as wrestling matches, the Eiffel Tower, soap powders, the Tour de France bicycle race, pop songs, that year's model of the Citroën, always undercutting the assumption that such things simply were themselves and nothing more. "Then, when the demystification is immobilized in repetition, it must be displaced; semiological science tries to stir, to vivify, to arm the mythological gesture or pose, by endowing it with a method." But the whole project of semiotics — the systematic, structuralist reading of cultural signs — which Barthes introduced into cultural criticism in the 1960s, "is replaced by the (often very grim) science of the semiologists; hence, one must sever oneself from that, must introduce into this rational image-repertoire the texture of desire, the claims of the body; this, then, is the Text, the theory of the Text. But again the Text risks paralysis: it repeats iself, counterfeits itself in lustreless texts, testimonies to a demand for readers, not for a desire to please: the Text tends to degenerate into prattle." Barthes asks himself in *Roland Barthes*, "Where to go next? That is where I am now."

Where Barthes goes next is to *A Lover's Discourse* (1977), a book that comes out of the language, complaints, and reflections of lovers. This language, critic Jonathan Culler observes, is now unfashionable as a topic of serious analysis. "Though it is spoken by millions of people, diffused in our popular romances and television programs as well as in serious literature, there is no institution that explores . . . and otherwise assumes responsibility for this discourse," Culler says. He adds that Barthes, taking on this role of monitor of amorous discourse, "finds in it a way of producing 'the novelistic': the novel minus plot and characters." I don't mean to suggest disingenuously that Barthes's writing is anything less than complex, dense, and of enormous velocity, but however hermetic his prose was, *A Lover's Discourse* found an audience, becoming the surprise best-seller of the season, with a hundred thousand copies snapped up in short order.

Readers saw themselves in the "figures of love" that Barthes delineated, such as "waiting" for the telephone to ring or the tardy beloved to show up. Or the physical delight of the slightest bodily contact — "a knee which doesn't move away, an arm extended, as if quite naturally, along the back of a sofa and against which the other's head gradually comes to rest — this is the paradisiac realm of subtle and clandestine signs," Barthes declares. And the multiple meanings of the "gift," a mere "little something," but nonetheless something, for nothing involving the beloved is without meaning for the lover. Here, Barthes reclaims from everyday life things normally dismissed with a gesture, insisting that the meanings of love's "discourse" is what gives love its texture.

The photos collected in *Roland Barthes* seem to presage his final book, *Camera Lucida* (1980), which is about photography and death. Barthes was one of those writers, like E.M. Forster and Constantine Cavafy, who spent much of his life living with his mother. Four or five photos of her appear sporadically in the series in *Roland Barthes*. There's a frontspiece photo in the English edition (translated by the poet Richard Howard) of this all-important personage in

Barthes's life. She's in her 30s, wearing a sleeveless white dress, walking along what appears to be a beach or sandy field — there's a blurry horse and dray-wagon in the background. The resemblance between mother and son is striking.

In *Camera Lucida*, written shortly after his mother's death, the 65-year-old Barthes, representing himself as no more than an amateur viewer of this ambiguous documentary art, seeks to "derive all photography" from one photograph of his mother that he stumbles upon while rummaging through her effects. It is a photo that represents her "changed into herself," that eclipses all those images that "don't really look like you." In photography's connections with love and what-has-been, Barthes sees that "what I have lost is not a Figure (the Mother), but a being, and not a being but a *quality* (a soul): not the indispensable, but the irreplaceable. I could live without the Mother (as we all do, sooner or later); but what life remained would be absolutely and entirely *unqualifiable*."

Like Barthes in *Camera Lucida*, I, too, have frequently noticed the pleasure of writing descriptions of photos, or about photographic images. I find myself trying to see into the photograph, as if my looking will animate a tale about to begin: "One morning, on a narrow street in Bayonne in 1920, a mother and her small son . . ." There's also something attractively easy about writing about photographs, like the one of the street in Bayonne, compared to essayistic or narrative writings that one has to "make up." Does my attraction to easy writing advertise laziness on my part? But why shouldn't this alleged vice also have its place in the utopian act that writing is? Isn't laziness akin to the playfulness of composition that grim-visaged censors forbid?

Roland Barthes by Roland Barthes is an intentionally strange kind of autobiography, at once impersonal, and yet personally theoretical. If Barthes provides only minimal snippets of conventional autobiography — mostly glancing or casual remarks, or an expression of some trivial taste, offered variously in the third or first person — his theorising about how the subject of an autobiography might be constituted undermines the potential solipsism that endangers the autobiographical project.

It would be a mistake, I think, to see Barthes's strategy as a failed attempt to make what is personal and idiosyncratic into something that is theoretical and objective. Barthes's stance is always provisional: what would it be like to see it this way? he recurrently asks, without clinging to the provisionally inverted perspective. What if our personal idiosyncrasies were momentarily thought of as objects about which one could construct a theory? There are those who think such procedures inevitably end up with the would-be theorist's head buried in his own navel, or stuck up some other portion of his anatomy, but the way I see it is that Barthes's method — a preoccupation of French writing since Montaigne and Descartes — puts him into the world, one object among many, no more, no less.

Barthes became famous in the 1960s and 1970s for introducing semiology, linguistics and psychoanalytical theory into literary and cultural studies, and he was, along with Michel Foucault, Jacques Derrida, and Jacques Lacan, among the most prominent French intellectuals in the generation following Jean-Paul Sartre and Albert Camus. He was an indefatigable inventor of neologisms and founder of disciplines in the humanities. Yet, as Culler notes, this characterization, too, "proves somewhat awkward. Each time Barthes urged the merits of some new ambitious project — a science of literature, a semiology, a science of contemporary myths, a narratology ... a typology of textual pleasure — he swiftly passed on to something else. Abandoning what he had set in motion, he often wrote wryly or disparagingly about his prior preoccupations. Barthes is a seminal thinker, but ... when his projects flourish, they do so without him and despite him."

If accused of dilettantism, Barthes would invent a defensible theory of the dilettante. It is more accurate to say that Barthes displaced his successive world-views without abandoning them. He left behind Marxism at the moment when it was a heresy to do so, yet he continued to utilize a decentered Marxism to make sense of economic reality. Although French structuralist thought of the period was fixated on the analysis of binary pairs, Barthes's dialectic was ultimately not an arbitrary settling on two poles, but an attention to the dynamic relationship of the multiple alternatives for meaning and action that the world contains. The dialectics of language itself is attention to the inter-relationship of a hundred thousand lexical and referential items in a vocabulary that resembles a cosmos. Nor is Barthes merely a mechanical and abstract practitioner who excludes half the real world for the sake of a theory: he talked about soap powder and soap-operas as easily as he ventured into the laboratory of a "pure science" of language, even as he recognized that much of what he wrote would appear arcane and disarticulate to many.

One thing that distinguished Barthes from his contemporaries, increasingly so as he got older, is that he was passionate about the relation between the content of his intelligence and its form. However interesting Michel Foucault's ideas about the interplay of power/knowledge are, no one would suppose that he was trying to create a work of art in writing any of his books, from *Madness and Civilization* to *The Use of Pleasure*. Whereas, when Barthes reflects on his work in *Roland Barthes*, he sees himself not only as a critic or semiologist, but also as a writer. Perhaps he was a failed writer, given that he never achieved the uninterrupted narrative he occasionally longed for, even as he penned another preface to support someone else's book, but he was a writer nonetheless. His fondness for beginnings, and hence for fragments, puts him in the company of Borges, Pessoa, and Italo Calvino, other writers who inspire misplaced rage among some readers who don't like "that sort of thing."

Barthes not only weighs, and usually finds wanting, the validity of his past concepts, but also sees their use as tactics of writing, to "make the text go," or to "permit him to say something." Barthes's vocation is not simply analyzing particular phenomena, but also writing. In *Roland Barthes*, he says, "I do not say: 'I am going to describe myself' but: 'I am writing a text and I call it R.B.'" I read him, as do others, not just for a dazzling mind that illuminates the world, but also for his beautiful sentences, his experimental literary structures, for the pleasure of his text.

Barthes traces his propensity to write in fragments — highly condensed firecrackers of thought — to the dictation exercises of the French *lycée* he attended in Paris as an adolescent. That's where "Monsier B., on Saturday afternoons, by way of amusement, would ask a student to suggest a subject for reflection, anything at all, and no matter how preposterous, he would always manage to turn it into a little dictation exercise, which he improvised as he strolled around the classroom." Those recited paragraphs, spontaneous or not, which schoolboys were required to take down as a test of their command of the written language, left Barthes with a wry sense of the "parodic affinity" of the fragment and the obligatory school composition.

The fragmentary form goes back to Barthes's earliest published writings, an article about Andre Gide's *Journals*. "His first, or nearly first text (1942) consists of fragments," Barthes writes about himself. "This choice is then justified in the Gidean manner 'because incoherence is preferable to a distorting order.' Since then, as a matter of fact, he has never stopped writing in brief bursts."

I don't know if Barthes's theory that the initial writing provides an ur-text for the author one becomes is true, but his remark has a personal resonance for me. My first writing, at about age 16, titled *How the Night Comes to Me*, was a manuscript of bits and pieces — prose poems, passages, sketches, little narrative essays. Though I've since written many other books, often in the form of a sustained narrative or discourse, I inevitably circle back to that original experimental work. As Culler says of Barthes, "Against the 'readable' — works that conform to traditional codes and models of intelligibility — he set the 'writable' — experimental works that we don't yet know how to read but can only write and must in effect write as we read them."

But there's something deeper than the origin of fragments, namely the origin of one's imagination of oneself as a writer. "Can one," asks Barthes, "begin to write without taking oneself for another? For the history of sources, we should substitute the history of figures: the origin of the work is not the first instance, it is the first posture: one copies a role, then, by metonymy, an art."

Of all the things in *Roland Barthes*, the passages that most fascinate and delight me are Barthes's recurrent reflections on the strangely active operations of language itself. In a passage called "Amphibologies," Barthes writes, "The word 'intelligence' can designate a faculty of intellection or a complicity *(to have intelligence that . . .)*; in general, the context forces us to choose one of the two meanings and to forget the other."

But each time Barthes encounters one of these double words, he "insists on keeping both meanings, as if one were winking at the other and as if the word's meaning were in that wink, so that *one and the same word*, in *one and the same sentence*, means at *one and the same time* two different things, and so one delights, semantically, in the one by the other. That is why such words are said to be 'preciously ambiguous': . . . because . . . I can *actualize* their amphibology, can say 'intelligence' and appear to be referring chiefly to the intellective meaning, but letting the meaning of 'complicity' be *understood*." I suppose some people read Barthes's fantasy of words "winking" at each other as merely another instance of intellectual insiderdom, exclusionary obscurantism. But such resentment is misplaced. Rather, Barthes is saying that the world reveals its portentousness even in the minuscule workings of language, the medium which is inseparable from our understanding of reality, which in turn suggests the permanent mystery of the larger dimension. It's the constant reminder of that interplay that strikes me every time I open one of Barthes's books and read a few sentences of his writing.

Recently, an acquaintance complained that a writer whom I liked, Edmund White, was too "precious" — a criticism that could no doubt also be made of Barthes — but instead, I heard the amphibology, the other sense in which "precious" means "of great value, beloved." More than most writers, Barthes is supremely sensitive to philosopher Hilary Putnam's notion that "elements of what we call 'language' or 'mind' penetrate so deeply into what we call 'reality' that the very project of representing ourselves as being 'mappers' of something 'language-independent' is fatally compromised from the start."

I'm puzzled by the hostility of otherwise sensible people to writers like Barthes, Borges, even Proust. The best explanation I've encountered for this misunderstanding is offered by philosopher Richard Rorty, who divides writers — pardon the dualism — into two groups. In one group, "the desire for self-creation, for private autonomy, dominates"; in the other group, "the desire for a more just and free human community dominates." Rorty urges that "we not try to choose between them but, rather, give them equal weight and then use them for different purposes." As Rorty says, "We shall only think of these two kinds of writers as opposed if we think that a more comprehensive philosophical outlook would let us hold self-creation and justice, private perfection and human solidarity, in a single vision." Like Rorty, once I sought absolutism. Now, I think pluralism will do.

Sitting in Buddy's, occasionally scribbling a note on a scrap of paper, I was becoming, although I wasn't fully conscious of what was happening, a writer, something I now see that despite much writing I hadn't really been. In playfully imagining what it might be like to be Barthes and yet write something more sexually "out" than he had, while employing his aesthetic, I began to write a book inspired by my readings of *Roland Barthes*. Of course, I wasn't Barthes and what I eventually had to say was different from what he would've said, but in the five years or so that it took me to write that brief book, Barthes was the ghostly companion who, as Jack Spicer put it in another context, "occasionally looked through my eyes and whispered to me." The work that began as an effort to find "correspondences" in Barthes was published as *Buddy's: Meditations on Desire* — my homage to Barthes's memory.

At the end of *Roland Barthes* by Roland Barthes, the author asks, "And afterwards?"

The terse auto-dialogue that ensues goes, "What to write now? Can you still write anything?" Those are every writer's questions, every day.

To which Barthes replies, "One writes with one's desire, and I am not through desiring."

Lanny Beckman

In the first image I have of Lanny Beckman, we're at a crowded party in a house at 2249 York Avenue in Vancouver in spring 1968. We're all in our mid-twenties, graduate students at the University of British Columbia, and I'm just about to move into the house. The party is a sort of farewell to one of the students who lives there, Vernon Kabrinsky, whose place I'm taking. He's in anthropology and has just gotten a teaching job elsewhere in Canada. The other inhabitants of the house are Lanny, a psychology student, and Dick Woodsworth, a young man from a well-known Canadian political family, who is getting a degree in the Asian Studies department.

The house is in a row of three similar, squat beach houses, with dark wood panelling and low-ceilinged A-frame attics. They're owned by a man named Bill Bailey, who lives a couple of houses away, and works as a taxi driver. The street is just a block or two up the slope from Kitsilano Beach. A couple of years later, our group, now expanded into a "commune" rather than just students sharing a house, will move three blocks west, to 2504 York, and Lanny and I will continue as housemates. Coincidentally, when I first came to Vancouver from San Francisco a couple of years earlier, I'd almost rented this exact house, but just missed it. Now, needing a place to live, I'd heard from Ralph Maud, I think it was, a prof at Simon Fraser University and a mutual acquaintance of Lanny's and mine, that someone was moving out of 2249 York and they were looking for someone to move in. I had a little interview with Lanny, and he must have invited me to the party that weekend.

Lanny was a lean, agile, energetic guy, Jewish, who was writing his doctoral thesis. His longish hair frizzed out around his head. From the beginning, I was taken by his mixture of gentle good sense and quick wit. He was politically intelligent, but not given to rhetoric. His good sense was practical and notably non-malevolent. He had an almost instinctual compassion for the wounded, whether immediate acquaintances or distant peoples. Both physically and temperamentally, he slightly resembled the young comic and movie maker, Woody Allen. He also skilfully played a guitar — songs by the Beatles, Phil Ochs and the biting satires of Tom Lehrer ("'Once the rockets go up, who cares where they come down?/ That's not my department,' says Wernher von Braun"). He and I were both naturals at the kind of quick back-and-forth repartee of young intellectuals. We were mockers of convention, ironists, the life of the party.

The music of the times is playing on the stereo — Beatles, Rolling Stones dirges, Bob Dylan — there are empty beer bottles left on the window ledges, overflowing ashtrays, people are sitting out on the deep front porch, and crammed into the kitchen, but it's not rowdy. Across the crowded rooms, I spot Lanny, talking to a girlfriend, having a good time, and we exchange a glance of mutual recognition, at the beginning of friendship.

About thirty-five years later, still housemates, but neither of us any longer the life of the party, Lanny and I were at a baseball game in Vancouver's Nat Bailey stadium. On the way into the dusty parking lot, Lanny had recalled that the park next door, which also contained a baseball field, was where he had played Little League baseball as a kid. Inside the stadium, there were about three or four thousand fans, a respectable crowd on a perfect summer afternoon.

Vancouver had fallen on hard times in the world of minor league professional baseball. For many years, Vancouver had been home to a "Triple A" team, just one notch below major league baseball, but its fortunes had declined in recent seasons and now the city was down to a single "A" league team owned by the San Francisco Giants.

We had box seats along the third-base line. Although the players were young, just at the beginning of their careers, it was a surprisingly well-played game with decent pitching and solid error-free fielding. But most of all, it was the way baseball should be played: under a cloudless blue sky rather than in a domed stadium, on real grass rather than on artificial turf, no TV, and by skilled youngsters anxious to make their mark rather than by the pampered millionaires of major league baseball. The wonderful thing about the game of baseball is that its slowness turns time into a gentle temporary eternity. Down in the front rows of box seats, businessmen who had taken their clients out for a lazy afternoon were ordering rounds of beer in large plastic cups. Now, Lanny and I were just two elderly guys, kibbitzing about the game.

In the eighth inning, the batter hit a high pop foul ball in our direction. I'd been going to baseball games, very occasionally, most of my life, and I'd never caught a foul ball, never ended up with "a souvenir of the game," as the radio announcer in my childhood described this gift of the gods. We watched the arc of the foul rise over our heads and in its final rush of descent, an audible *whoosh*, I saw it was going to land closer to us than I'd expected. In fact it hit the concrete a row in front of us, next to an empty seat, took a little hop, and dropped right at my feet. I picked it up, vaguely aware that we were the momentary centre of attention of the cluster of fans around us.

"Now what do I do with it?" I asked Lanny, as I held the baseball in my hand. As if he had been expecting my question, and in the same reasonable, practical, gentle way he had responded to questions about politics, art, sex and the cosmos over the years, he said, "Well, you can either keep it or you can give it to a kid." At exactly that moment, standing in the aisle a couple of seats away, there appeared one of the unloveliest kids in the world, a pudgy ten-year-old, sporting a baseball glove and a needy look in his eyes. I tossed the ball over to him and he caught it. Suddenly, there was a round of applause in our section of the crowd, directed at the nice old guy who had given the kid the ball. I was still admiring the good sense of Lanny's suggestion even as I became aware that I had become the crowd's momentary hero. The whole thing took about 10 seconds.

Then the game went on. I guess that's the point. The crowd's attention returned to the field and the instant of local celebrity dissolved back into anonymity, just like life. In the bottom of the ninth, with the home team Giants trailing 1-0, one man on base, the batter whacked one over the left field fence, providing a perfectly satisfactory story-book ending. We won, 2-1.

Then we were out in the chaotic parking lot; cars that had been baking in the sun all afternoon now had their windows rolled down, and were churning up the dust and gravel. In the thirty-five years between the party and the ballgame, we had lived a part of our lives, housemates. I could tell you the story of Lanny's life, but as with the baseball and the kid, it seems much more sensible to simply dedicate this book to him.

Wilder Bentley and Walt Whitman

The first college course I took, at San Francisco State College in the early 1960s, was a survey of American literature taught by Wilder Bentley. Although in my naïveté I had no idea of who Bentley was, he was well-known in the college, if not beyond it, as one of those professors who is an inspiring catalyst for receptive students.

Going to college reflected a shift in my intellectual allegiances towards the views of the poet Robin Blaser, who was then working as an acquisitions librarian at SF State, and who thought it a good idea to become educated. Conversely, taking classes was a slight turning away from Jack Spicer, who regularly offered us young poets dire warnings against going to university. Spicer especially admonished us — as we sat at what was known as the "poets' table" in Gino and Carlo's bar in San Francisco's North Beach district — not to study in the "good, grey, dead" English department, on the grounds that it would surely destroy one's ability to write anything beyond the deadening academic verse that the English department approved of and fostered. I was also influenced in my decision to go to college by Jim Herndon, a former classmate of Spicer's and Blaser's when they were all at the University of California, Berkeley. Jim, an elementary school-teacher and writer, pointed out to me with common-sense amusement, "Oh, sure, Jack's against university education — he's got one."

The two things that happened in that college course at San Francisco State were, first, I encountered Bentley, a white-haired, elderly, enthusiastic expositor of the beauty and significance of American writing and, second, under Bentley's tutelage, I read the poetry of Walt Whitman. The first point, about the presence and acquisition of teachers in one's life, is more interesting than the second one. But I'll also say something about what I got from reading Whitman.

In the matter of teachers — in schools and elsewhere — I was both exceptionally lucky and a good student, that is, I was a "quick study" who also makes his own luck. In the course of eventually studying anthropology, sociology, and philosophy — Spicer's admonitions against the English department had their effect — I would discover a series of professors like Bentley, men and women who were both competent and inspiring, and who disinterestedly — without prejudice or favour — shared their understanding of the world and provoked my interest in it.

My first teacher was my father, whom I loved almost unreservedly. As a result of my trust in his pedagogy, I had little of the neurotic resistance to education that one often observes. Instead I possessed an openness to schooling and a talent for recognizing what Jim Herndon, in his book *Notes from a Schoolteacher*, called "good schools," taught by good father-figures (and mother-figures) against whom I had no impulse to rebel. As a later teacher of mine, Joseph Tussman, would point out, docility in a student, paradoxically, is a sign of health. It is a recognition that necessary submission to the more knowledgeable minds of others is not oppression, whereas rebellion often means that the student is trying to learn something other than what the teacher can teach. Almost everyone I've met who has never had a real teacher in his or her life has struck me as slightly warped.

I was in no hurry to go to college. As a 16-year-old high school student in Chicago, I'd received an invitation from the University of Chicago to quit secondary school and enter its "accelerated" program, a course of action urged upon me by most of my family, aspiring first generation immigrants for whom university was an ultimate sign of achievement. Despite being flattered by the invitation — which meant you were "bright" — I was drawn to adventure rather than university and, protected by my father's approval, joined the U.S. Navy, first entering the world-at-large instead of the world of the classroom. It wasn't until my early twenties that I was ready for college.

Going to school a couple of times a week, riding the trolley-car out to the SF State campus at the edge of the city, was a pleasant enough change from the waterfront warehouses and North Beach bars where I worked. I may have taken other courses — I think I did — but it was only Bentley's course that filled me with anticipation. At the same time, there's an embarrassing lacuna in my memory. I'm chagrined at how little I actually remember of Bentley. How often did I see him? Twice a week, I suppose, for at least three or four months, and yet I recall, at this great remove in time, little more than a faint physical image of Bentley, his slightly bowed shoulders, longish white locks. I hardly remember a word he said, except for one remark about me that I'll relate in a bit.

When, much later, I became a teacher myself, I recognized the ways in which students do or don't take you into their lives. In my own classrooms today, I often observe the difference between students for whom something important is happening (and for whom I'm someone significant) and those who are so self-absorbed or distracted that I'm little more for them than the anonymous clerk in a convenience store.

The faintness of my memory of Bentley, to whom I wasn't at all indifferent, hints at something deeper that retrospectively strikes me about my younger self. I'm disturbed by how little I retain of people who were significant to me, though I could plead in this instance that I really only knew Bentley peripherally. The broader point, however, is that again and again, when I revisit past scenes (or am revisited by them), the striking feature of the scene is how unconscious I was, how inattentive I was to anything except myself. I thought the world was all *for me*, barely aware that I was a bit player *in it*, nothing more. And in the case of Bentley I only remember something he said about me. "Me," that's the problem. To put it another way, I was too full of myself, that is, full of shit. Or, to use a standard phrase from school that students remorsefully invoke before "finals," as they're called, "I should've taken notes." That's especially to the point now, when I really am faced with the final exam. Now, I'm ashamed — before the shade of Wilder Bentley — that I was so unmindful of him.

Still, mindful or not, under Bentley's tutelage, I read Walt Whitman, which is to say, I learned something about both poetry and the history of American thought, especially its phase of Transcendentalism. It was through Bentley that I was formally introduced to that great mid-19th century moment in American letters when Emerson, Whitman, Thoreau, Melville and Hawthorne were contemporaries. I'd already picked up bits and pieces about them from Spicer and others — my father had given me Melville's *Moby Dick* to read when I was ten — but the haphazard manner of instruction that Spicer favoured was now complemented by a more systematic approach.

Both temperamentally and intellectually, I felt closer to Henry David Thoreau and his book, *Walden*, whereas my initial interest in Whitman, I now think, was a superficial attraction connected to matters of style.

I have to untangle another bit of confused memory here. It's likely that I had read Allen Ginsberg's *Howl*, whose poetic line and political vision is derived from Whitman, before I read Whitman's "I Sing the Body Electric" or any of the other poems in his *Leaves of Grass*. When I encountered Whitman's long poetic line, his colloquial language, and mixture of bardic prophecy and conversational intimacy, I recognized the work as "modern" because I was reading Whitman, in a sense, through Ginsberg, whose rhapsodic vision and contemporary subject matter (those "angel-headed hipsters dragging themselves through the negro streets at dawn") seemed to me the epitome of "cool" romanticism.

The critic Harold Bloom cites Whitman's canonical "originality" as the feature that makes him central to American writing and, indeed, his exuberant invocations of self in a new national context seem unprecedented. Whitman's poems teem with life, and are filled with catalogues of jostling people, objects, crowded streets. Nothing before Whitman in American poetry is like him, just as there's nothing quite like Whitman's younger contemporary, Rimbaud, in earlier French poetry. Only William Blake, among Whitman's immediate predecessors, strives for such an expansive vision, though Whitman's compatriot, Thoreau, offers a comparable, if far more critical, exposition of American life. Bloom grandly claims that "we have never got Whitman right," because Whitman is really a difficult, even hermetic poet. If so, I missed it. My partial revulsion to Whitman, like that of my discomfort with Ginsberg, is that he too often just lets it all hang out, undercutting or "getting in the way" of the poem, as Spicer would say, with his own self-expressive gush.

Maybe I didn't get Whitman right, way back then, but I did get excited. Understandably — given my own sensual inclinations and the desire, in my early twenties, to not only experience but to understand those inclinations — the aspect of Whitman to which I was first drawn was one of the least important, namely, the homosexuality that appeared to be blatantly and unprecedently evident in Whitman's poems.

I'd already learned, from Spicer, Ginsberg, and Blaser, of some of the long roll-call of homosexually-inclined writers, from Rimbaud to Lorca, Hart Crane, Cavafy, and many of the contemporary poets of the "New American Poetry", including my immediate mentors in the art. Today, in the period of what I see as post-homosexuality (i.e., gay is not such a big deal these days), Whitman's sexual proclivities merely assume their place as an historical fact of some minor relevance, but at the beginning of the 1960s, the contested matter of Whitman's sexuality was a cogent political issue.

Whitman spoke in his poetry of "comradely love" and "adhesion," a curious 19th century word that Whitman turned into a reference to same-sex affections. But when directly asked, late in life, about his sexual tastes by such avowed homosexualists as Edward Carpenter and John Addington Symonds, he professed shock, adamantly denied his interlocutors' lurid imaginings, and cobbled together an implausible cover story about heterosexual affairs and the fathering of children.

Harold Bloom argues that Whitman was primarily auto-sexual. "One of the many current ironies of Whitman's reception is that he is acclaimed as a gay poet. Beyond doubt, his deepest drive was homo-erotic, and his poems of heterosexual passion have convinced no one. Including Whitman himself." However, "there is very little evidence that Whitman ever had sexual relations with anyone except himself ... For whatever reason, in his poetry as probably in his life, his erotic orientation was onanistic ... More even than sadomasochism, autoeroticism appears to be the last Western taboo." While it's nice to have Bloom put in a good word for wanking, his theory about Whitman's desire is just plain silly.

Bloom's view mistakenly implies that homosexuality must mean homosexual sex, which isn't true. Bloom allows Whitman but "one abortive attempt at relationship, presumably homosexual, in the winter of 1859-60," out of which were written the indubitably erotic "Calamus" poems. Yet, what are we to make of such a line as, "How you settled your head athwart my hips and gently turned over upon me," or any other of a dozen similar descriptions? If there was only one "abortive attempt," Whitman certainly got a lot of poetry out of a small amount of experience.

At the time of my reading, just about a century after Whitman wrote, and many years before Gay Liberation, although poets like Ginsberg could urge the American bard to "put your queer shoulder to the wheel, Walt Whitman," among literary scholars there was still widespread denial that Whitman might be referring literally to homosexual encounters. At most, there were discreet, embarrassed suggestions of Whitman's inclinations. Even the most prominent of the scholars of the period, F.O. Matthiessen (himself gay), maintained a judicious neutrality. But I read Whitman's texts, including the emendations —where he erased a "he" and replaced it with a "she" — as well as the clues in the sanitized biographies and critical analysis. In short, I put it together for myself — with some help from Blaser and Bentley, no doubt — and the resulting essay that I submitted to Wilder Bentley was, for the time, a daring bit of original if limited scholarship.

Bentley read it with his characteristic admirable disinterestedness. By the way, I knew nothing then or subsequently of Bentley's private life or of his views on the topic of homosexuality. A week or two later, he returned my essay to me with the highest possible grade, and enthusiastic scrawled comments. I remember the emphatic phrase, "Great work, Stan!" As I say, I'm embarrassed that those are the only words of Bentley's I retain. Now, I write similar comments on student papers myself, some of which are comparably encouraging. Perhaps that writing, the often-unread teacher's comments and marginalia involved in "paper-marking" — about the drudgery of which we teachers endlessly complain — is the most fitting tribute to Bentley's memory I'm capable of offering.

As for Whitman, the details of his sexuality, whether Bloom's version or mine, matter far less than Whitman's insistence on the presence of living bodies within the vision of an American space. In the long run, who-slept-with-whom amounts to little more than a skeleton humping a fossil. In a passage cited by Bloom — one that I also like — Whitman moves quietly among the wounded young men in a military hospital during the American Civil War:

> I wander all night in my vision,
> Stepping with light feet, swiftly and noiselessly stepping and
>   stopping,
> Bending with open eyes over the shut eyes of sleepers,
> Wandering and confused, lost to myself, ill-assorted, contradictory,
> Pausing, gazing, bending, and stopping.
> I stand in the dark with dropping eyes by the worst-suffering and
>   the most restless,
> I pass my hands soothingly to and fro a few inches from them,
> The restless sink in their beds, they fitfully sleep.

That's the image of Whitman — with its unintentionally humourous portent of New Age "touch therapy" — that stands before me in the flux of time. When I was in the Navy, on night-watch, I also walked through the barracks of sleeping young men, with similar feelings: maternal, comradely, incestuous.

David Berg

Fritz Perls, one of the founders of Gestalt therapy, came to Vancouver around 1970, a couple of years before his death there. Gestalt, unlike protracted Freudian analysis, emphasised the existential "here and now." It proposed a psycho-dramatic technique for "getting in touch" with one's suppressed feelings, and enacting the divided elements of self in an effort to create a more integrated or whole person. Perls, a rambunctious man in his seventies — possibly a lascivious old fraud, but possibly a legitimate guru — quickly gathered around him a corps of students whom he trained in the particular techniques of this latest manifestation of the "talking cure."

The most brilliant of Perls's young adepts in Vancouver was a junior philosophy professor at nearby Simon Fraser University, David Berg, a friendly bearish man in his early thirties. Berg was bored with the dryness of academic philosophy, and its distance from both ultimate questions about how to live and the immediate turmoils of the social politics of the late 1960s. That disaffection drove him toward the personal authenticity promised by Gestalt therapy. Soon, with Perls's imprimatur, Berg gave up his teaching post and set up shop as a therapist in a studio space in Vancouver's Gastown district, an older part of the city that had recently been refurbished in a redevelopment scheme then typical of North American urban centres.

Many of the factors that led Berg to becoming a therapist brought many of us to "group," as the activity of attending sessions with Berg and other practitioners was called. We, in this instance, were a collection of mostly university students and artists living together in communal housing circumstances. At group, we discovered others with similar interests. It was at Berg's, for instance, that I first met Tom Sandborn, who quickly became one of the half-dozen intimate permanent friends in my life.

The underlying question about any therapy, I think, is whether it really works. Once we're formed — whether in infancy, childhood or adolescence — can we, as deeply habituated adults, significantly change ourselves? The argument against the possibility of change is evidenced, to take an easy example, in the failure of dietary progams

— half of North America, at any given moment, is on a diet (including me) and yet the population just gets fatter and heavier.

But if there was a counter-example of refashioning oneself, it was Tom. At the time that he arrived at Berg's group, Tom — as he later described himself when we reminisced about all of this — was a half-formed pup, who had come to Vancouver from a redneck small-town California trailer park to evade the American draft board and to sort out the doomed tangles of an early marriage. In short order, there was a remarkable and lasting transformation. Tom revealed himself to be an astutely sensitive intelligence, enormously trustworthy, and committed to changing the world, a political project for which he had unusual organizational talents. Perhaps it wasn't so much a characterological change as simply the revelation of something nascently present in him, but certainly Berg was a catalyst for Tom. In any case, as Berg was Perls's star student, Tom would become Berg's most talented therapist-trainee.

Gestalt therapy was very much of a piece with the late 1960s — a period subsequently much maligned by conservative critics and historians — in which we experimented with a wide range of aspects of our lives. Politics, art, sexuality, domestic arrangements, and even our identities and minds came under intense scrutiny. In psychology, books like R.D. Laing's *The Divided Self* and Perls's own *Gestalt Therapy* (written with Paul Goodman and Ralph Hefferline) challenged the reigning shibboleths of a seemingly insipid social science. If Rimbaud's 19th century call for "a systematic derangement of the senses" was ever heeded, it was in this period of 20th century North American life. For those of us engaged in radical politics, on campus or in the city, Gestalt promised humanising relief from the sterility of sloganeering and the rigidity of a renascent Marxism.

Gestalt, under Berg's perceptive tutelage, was magic, certainly at the outset. After one particular moment of tearful personal illumination in group, Berg asked the woman who had just "worked," a characteristic therapist's query, "What are you experiencing now?" Having just produced an intense half-hour or so of interpersonal pyrotechnics, she paused, and then said, with some wonder, "The room seems brighter now." The rest of us burst out laughing, and that utterance became a kind of catchphrase about emerging from our shadowy, repressed inner world, like baby chicks newly hatched from the egg.

Therapy, as near as I could tell, was more art than science. It was dependent on the therapist's intuition and a comedian's sense of timing, and refined through the accumulation of experience. Once, there was a young man in group, a slim, attractive blond of Russian extraction named Mischa, who was obviously distressed, and during a particularly strained session in which he slowly worked up his courage, he finally blurted out that he was a homosexual. I was surprised, since my radar hadn't picked up the slightest hint of his secret. When he made his "round" of rather defiantly telling each of us of his sexual orientation and got to Berg, the most authoritative figure in the room to whom to make this declaration, "I'm a homosexual," David leaned back in his chair, very faintly smiling, and said, with his exquisite sense of timing, "Do you want me to be for you or against you?"

There was a moment of puzzled silence in the room — as with "the room's brighter now" remark — and then, as we simultaneously got the point, we all erupted into laughter. Although Berg wasn't conventionally political, he had astutely cut to the core of the "coming out" dilemma. Beneath the resistance to coming out as a homosexual, there was the anticipation of not only the hostility of others but, as well, the loss of affection among friends, family, and even strangers. What Berg's remark pointed to was that the act of coming out wasn't merely a declaration of identification, but a challenge to other people, a challenge in which the person revealing himself was not a helpless subject of others' acceptance or rejection, but someone making a demand: "I'm gay, and I want you to be for me." Part of the feeling of illumination in this analysis was Berg's brilliant condensation of it into a single, seemingly offhand, remark.

He did something similar in working with a woman named Joan, whose mother had committed suicide when she was a girl. Berg suggested that she make a "round," beginning her contact with each person with the phrase, "My mother killed herself when I was twelve, and . . ." As she worked her way around the room, one could almost see the waves of grief, rage and fear roll over her. By the time she got to Berg, she was in full throat. "Oh, god, David, she killed herself and I never got over it." Berg leaned back in the big armchair he occupied, looked directly into Joan's eyes, smiled his particular version of the Mona Lisa smile, and said, "Well, Joan, don't let it come between us." Two beats of silence later, Joan threw back her head and began to roar with a laughter that appeared healing. She seemed to let go of the frozen posture of grief and grievance she'd built up around her sorrow, and melted into genuine adult amusement at how much she had let herself harden into a mask of loss. Once more, Berg's point wasn't that one wasn't haunted by such tragedies, but that one needn't be necessarily immobilized by those events, that there might be at least some degree of self-determination in how much the suicide of even your own mother affected your actual, individual relations with others.

Although there remain questions about the enduring effect of such momentary enlightenment, there was no denying the power of those dramatic moments. In working with Tom and me, Berg examined figurations he saw us as having internalized. For me, there was the discovery of an inner beast, a creature who thought it was more useful to be wary than aware, and who could be reached not through my characteristic deployment of language, but by growling and roaring in the voice of this creature with enough force to truly alarm those among whom I was doing my round. If this frightened beast could talk, he would say, I want to frighten you enough that you won't hurt me.

With Tom, on the other hand, Berg encouraged him to externalize his pained relations with his father — what Tom later called one of "the usual run of *Long Day's Journey into Night* family legacies" — into imaginary, "here and now" conversations with the image that he had stored of that tortured and torturing parent. Although such exercises, by definition, change nothing in one's actual past encounters, the theory is that what's relevant, and alterable, is the introjected, imaginary figure who now affects one's present-day behaviours. Whether or not it's true that the figures (even inanimate objects) of memory or dream "inside" oneself are best conceptualized as "splits" of the self, the notion provided, at the very least, an interesting heuristic device for thinking about oneself.

One summer afternoon, Berg was sitting on the upstairs back balcony of our house, along with me and my housemate, Lanny Beckman. A woman, walking in the lane, was berating her six- or seven-year-old son for some minor misbehaviour, and suddenly Berg intervened from our second-storey perch, loudly chastising her for possibly traumatising her kid forever. The embarrassed mother quickly scuttled down the lane, her child in tow. Again, while this instant, public intervention in family relations hardly settled anything, it pointed toward a utopia of more transparent interpersonal encounters. I encouraged Berg to write about some of what he had learned and he dutifully produced a short, but interesting, mimeographed book called *White Gestalt, Black Gestalt*.

And then Berg collapsed. I don't know very much about the process of his falling apart, because I had drifted away from group, partially, I suppose because the novelty had worn off, and we now recognised the predictable stages of "human growth potential" as almost therapeutic clichés, and partly for other practical reasons — new jobs, political engagements, etc. I heard that Berg had had a breakdown and was now a patient in the psychiatric ward of Vancouver General Hospital. Lanny and I went to visit, and found David in the "occupational therapy" room, obediently working on some small craft project. A shocking transformation had occurred — this large, jolly, confident guru had shrunk into a fragile, depressed, broken man. We offered him a place to live at our communal house, but Berg mentioned that another friend had made available a rural cabin and that he was thinking of going there for a while.

Later, I thought of Berg's breakdown as possibly a result of cracking up on the reef of certain philosophical questions, but I may be wrong, and I don't really know the cause. However, there are questions in philosophy about the meaning of life that take you to the limits of possible understanding, and they can drive you crazy. The modern exemplar of confronting such issues is Wittgenstein, who avoided shipwreck by deciding that "what cannot be spoken of must be passed over in silence." What made me think that Berg had reached an absolute intellectual impasse were the rumours I'd heard of his flailing about in search of some framework that might save him — he apparently tried everything from Scientology to various New Age mysticisms.

But it may have had more to do with his private life. I knew little about it, though I'd been at his house — a spacious place with large rooms, broad staircases and solid oak beams — and had met his wife, Marie, and some of his children. Like other therapists at the time, Berg had had affairs with various of his woman clients — then, such sexual activity between therapist and group member wasn't seen as the reprehensible relationship it is today — and I don't know what effect that had on his family or himself.

The injunction, "Physician, heal thyself," utterly failed. One day, there was a phone call from Tom. David had killed himself. Along with my predictable, shocked, "Oh, no," I asked the inevitable question, "How?", as if knowing the method of suicide will tell us something about its cause. Marie had come home one afternoon, and found David hanging by a rope attached to a beam in the broad stairwell. In our speculations, it seemed to us a cruel means of declaring to his immediate intimates, You can't save me — from myself. It is as if the self was making a final, futile assertion of narcissistic power, but then, what idea did we have of his desperation at the end?

The funeral ceremonies were a blur. I was, with others, at Berg's house. I looked at the stairwell in which he had hung himself. I was at the gravesite in a North Vancouver cemetery. A fine drizzle was falling. I smelled the woodsmoke from neighbouring houses perched on the slopes of the first ridges of the nearby mountains. Much later, I would work at the college located next door to the cemetery.

Where are you now? the therapist might ask in group. I'm with the Hanged Man — as on a Tarot card — who is an imaginary figure in the gallery of the people in my life. The suicide accuses us of our ultimate failure to save him, although the echo of that accusation grows fainter. If I said, "Oh god, David, you killed yourself," would the therapist lean back in his chair, wistfully smile, and say, "Well, don't let that come between us"?

Out of order

No sooner do I create or adopt an ordering of something, in writing or most anything else — in this instance, an alphabetical order for an ABC book — than I want to be "out of order," in both senses of that phrase. I want to disturb the order I've proposed — with, for example, crosscutting entries that are numerical or chronologically-based (today is March 19, 2002, or it was when I began writing this passage). In the other sense of out-of-order, I give in to my desire to be unruly, as on those occasions governed by "Robert's Rules of Order," when the chairperson of the meeting declares a disruptive speaker "out of order," because what needs to be said violates the grid in which the occasion has been organized. The disorderly remark reveals the constrictions created by the order itself. Although I don't like political anarchists, I recognize a spark of anarchy in myself.

Alphabetical order in writing is okay for showing the arbitrariness of "order" as an idea. Basically, I prefer the chronological to any other ordering of writing because it most easily displays the development of the thoughts in a given work. As it happens, the first entries in this book, "ABC Books" and "Aboutism," were the first entries both chronologically and alphabetically.

What being "out of order" represents for me is the incursion of the unexpected event that disrupts the plan of the text. You see something, in a flash, that's so "true to life," that it demands inclusion in the otherwise orderly procession of a writing that suddenly seems falsely magisterial, pompous, contrived for posterity.

A sparrow crashed through the balcony doors of my apartment in Berlin one day, and scuttled across the floor to the far side of the room, finding a refuge under the big sideboard cabinet I'd inherited from Aunt Nanni. No sooner do I mention Aunt Nanni's sideboard — a large, heavy, black cabinet with two tall linen cupboards flanking a glass-doored section of bookshelves that sit above two convex bay-drawers, the whole thing resting on ball-shaped feet — than I see that I'll have to explain who she is. Immediately, what's exhibited is the principle of storytelling — that one thing leads or, more accurately, digresses, to another, and then to another, but not necessarily in an orderly way.

Aunt Nanni was Thomas's aunt — Thomas is my friend and upstairs neighbour who's married to Ilonka — on his father's side, I think. I remember seeing her some years ago at the post-funeral lunch for Thomas's father, Johannes Marquard, which was held at Thomas's and Ilonka's flat. Already in her eighties, she trudged up the six flights of stairs to their place — Thomas had rushed down to place chairs on each of the landings in case she needed to rest — but once she was ensconced at the table among the other mourners, I noticed how heartily she tucked into the spread of Brie, sausage and bread that had been laid out for the guests. A few years later, Aunt Nanni died, and when I arrived at my apartment in Berlin that spring, I discovered that I'd "inherited" the sideboard and her TV.

Now the bird was under the sideboard. I was terrified in the way we are when any creature that belongs outside — in the back courtyard onto which my apartment faces, amid the two maples and one ash tree where the birds hang out — is suddenly inside. Even in my fright, as I was trying to figure out what to do, another part of my mind glimpsed the way in which "outside" and "inside" are arbitrary notions, as evidenced by the sparrow's intrusion. I cautiously got down on my hands and knees and peered under the sideboard. The sparrow had wedged itself into the far corner and was still. Either it had knocked itself out as it hit the balcony door and instinctively scuttled under the sideboard before losing bird-consciousness, or else it was frozen in fear, which I dimly recalled reading is what animals did in uncertain situations. Or maybe it was dead.

In any case, I had a problem on my hands. If it was dead, I'd have to figure out how to dislodge it from under the sideboard, get it swept into a dustpan, and deposit its corpse downstairs in one of the garbage bins. Or, if it wasn't dead, and regained consciousness, it would probably start flying around the apartment, since it probably had no idea of the human division between outside and inside, and I'd be trapped with a bird in my flat, roosting on high ledges, shitting everywhere. As I often do in uncertain situations, I decided to do nothing and went back to my desk and continued reading a history of moral philosophy from the 16th to 18th centuries. I vaguely thought about calling Thomas or Ilonka, since both of them, especially Ilonka, seemed to know a lot about birds.

After about ten minutes, I decided to have another look. The sparrow hadn't moved. I imagined its eyes were closed. I went to the kitchen to look for a dustpan, but all I could find was a long-handled broom. I didn't want a dead bird stinking up the house. (Do dead birds stink up houses? I realized that my ignorance about the subject of birds was almost total.) On my hands and knees again, I maneuvered the broom handle towards the sparrow.

At exactly that instant, the bird woke up, shook its head, took a couple of tottering take-off steps, and flew from out under the sideboard, straight across the room and right through the open balcony doors, as if it understood inside and outside as well as anybody else. Soon the sparrow was among the other birds in the leafy maples, indistinguishable, to my eyes anyway, from the rest of the sparrows. I got up feeling I'd lived through a complete true-to-life adventure. Maybe the sparrow felt the same way.

John Berger

In one of the thirty or so stories in John Berger's *Photocopies* (1997), the then seventy-year-old author, who lives in a French alpine village, visits an old friend in Paris, the photographer Henri Cartier-Bresson, at the time in his eighties. The two men have a rambling and suggestive conversation about "the instant of taking a picture . . . 'the decisive moment,' " as the photographer had once put it.

Later that afternoon, in the Paris Metro, Berger says, "I find a seat in a coach which is more than half full." He notices that "at the end of the coach, a man in his early forties makes a short speech about his handicapped wife whom he is leading by the hand and who follows him with her eyes shut. They've been turned out of their lodgings, he says, and they risk to be separated if they apply to any institution."

> You don't know, the man tells the coach, what it's like loving a handicapped woman — I love her most of the time, I love her at least as much as you love your wives and husbands.
>
> Some passengers give him money. To each one the man says: *Merçi pour votre sensibilité.*
>
> At a certain moment during this scene I suddenly glanced towards the door, expecting [Cartier-Bresson] to be there with his Leica. This gesture of mine was instantaneous and without reflection.
>
> Photography, [Cartier-Bresson] once wrote in his maternal handwriting, is a spontaneous impulse which comes from perpetually looking, and which seizes the instant and its eternity.

Berger's vignette of a person literally forced to declare his love to the world in order to survive, as well as his "snapshot" or "photocopy" of it, is titled, "A Man Begging in the Metro." Most of the other pieces in *Photocopies* have similarly simple labels: "A Woman and Man Standing by a Plum Tree," "A Young Woman with Hand to Her Chin," "A Bunch of Flowers in a Glass." They're the sort of titles usually attached to photos or paintings.

Like much of Berger's other work — from his cultural criticism in *Ways of Seeing* to his periodically collected volumes of essays, such as *The Sense of Sight*, to his novels (*A Painter of Our Time*, *G.*, and the later trilogy, *Into Their Labours*) — the compact narrative about Cartier-Bresson and the man begging in the Metro courts the danger of sentimentality or of the portentous turning into the merely pretentious. After all, the subways of Europe are filled with people begging, selling street newspapers, telling public tales of woe. Who knows if the begging man and his blind wife are who they claim to be? Does it matter? Aren't we allowed to give in to "compassion fatigue" and stop looking? Berger asserts that the condition of perpetually looking — in his case, looking from a political perspective of human solidarity — is what gives rise to the spontaneous impulse that occasionally permits us to "seize the instant and its eternity." While there are innumerable snapshots that can record the instant, it is those works which also point to the instant's eternity that provide a succinct definition of art. For an artist, to arrive at the unexpected consideration of the eternity of an instant is what justifies running the risk of failure.

During the course of Berger's conversation with Cartier-Bresson, the photographer periodically fingers his camera, even though he's officially given up photography some two decades ago. He's turned to drawing, something Berger also does. But Cartier-Bresson still has his camera at hand, and occasionally picks it up, glances through the viewfinder without clicking, puts it down again. Then, at some point, holding the camera, looking at Berger, he clicks the button. Now, on the back jacket of Berger's *Photocopies*, I'm looking at Cartier-Bresson's photo of Berger, taken that day. The picture is shot from above, so that Berger's face, with its wavy white hair, is tilted upwards, imploringly, urgently alive. One of his hands juts forward, magnified by its proximity to the camera lens, the fingers spread as though forcefully making a point.

I once heard Berger give a reading in Berlin. It was at the Literature House, a villa on Fasanenstrasse in downtown Berlin that now contains a basement bookshop, a garden restaurant, and the various rooms of the building where readings and exhibitions are held. The walls of the upstairs room in which Berger was appearing, along with several other rooms in the villa, were covered with his framed drawings, so that we were surrounded by his work as well as being in his presence. I recognised him from Cartier-Bresson's photo, as he entered from a side door and walked across the room to take his place behind a table on a platform at the front.

He had recently published a book called *King*, written from the point of view of a dog living among an encampment of homeless people alongside a busy English motorway. He took the persona of the stray dog seriously enough to give samples of its barking — and momentarily Berger's face took on the lineaments of a rather fierce terrier — which he interpreted as proclamations of "I'm here! I'm here!" When the host of the reading, in conversation with Berger, offhandedly referred to the characters in the book as "drop-outs," Berger interrupted him, banging his hand on the table, to insist that the homeless and the poor were not marginal, but central, since they constitute the most numerous proportion of the global population. Berger's anger struck me as refreshingly vigorous and healthy, a rude insistence in the middle of a polite literary evening that the world is imperative, that, as he'd written, "we live in a world of suffering in which evil is rampant, a world whose events do not confirm our Being, a world that has to be resisted. It is in this situation that the aesthetic moment offers hope."

After the reading, and before the obligatory autographing session, I ran into Berger downstairs — he had gone there in search of an ashtray — and we had a brief conversation. When I mentioned that I came from Vancouver, he immediately asked me if I knew Hugh Brody, an anthropologist who had once lived there for some time. I liked Berger's characteristic impulse to make even our fleeting exchange specific and, as it happened, I did in fact know Brody, and admired the stories he told.

Berger's stories are invariably about ultimate subjects — death, love, art. The dead — in Homer and Ezra Pound's *Cantos* — come to the trenchlike fosse, demanding blood. Because they prey upon my mind these days, it is John Berger's preoccupation with mortality that immediately calls to me. As he remarks, "Sometimes it seems that, like an ancient Greek, I write mostly about the dead and death. If this is so, I can only add that it is done with a sense of urgency which belongs uniquely to life."

Recurrently, Berger offers a requiem to those who are no longer with us. Whether telling the story of how the Austrian philosopher Ernst Fischer died, almost literally in Berger's arms, or puzzling out the mystery of the revolutionary Russian poet Mayakovsky's suicide, or presenting a triptych portrait of the deaths of three of his neighbours from the peasant village where he lives, Berger ponders the relationship between the death recounted and the storyteller who tells the tale.

Writing of a close friend who, shockingly, "the day before yesterday ... killed himself by blowing his brains out," Berger recognizes — as the friend's death "assembles a thousand memories of his life" — that a "certain kind of story is told to contest the opportunism" of life's tendency toward simplifications. "In one sense a story does not go anywhere, it just is — as my departed friend now is in my imagination." A moment's reflection "shows that any story drawn from life begins, for the storyteller, with its end," Berger says. "It is in this sense that one can say that storytellers are Death's secretaries. It is

Death who hands them the file. The file is full of sheets of uniformly black paper but they have eyes for reading them and from this file they construct a story for the living ... We Death's secretaries all carry the same sense of duty, the same oblique shame, and the same obscure pride which belongs to us personally no more than do the stories we tell."

If many dead bodies and their stories lie before me, Berger also reminds me that he and I are not indifferent to living flesh. On the Greek island of Sifnos, a harsh place of marble, goats, olive trees, bitter laurel, hibiscus, and cacti, Berger asks himself, as he looks beyond the church cemetery to the sea, "What can flesh mean here? *Sarka* in Greek. All over the world women and men picture their bodies to themselves differently, for this picturing is influenced by the local terrain ... the surrounding natural risks ... Flesh here is the only soft thing, the only substance that can suggest a caress; everything else visible is sharp or mineral, shattered or gnarled ...

"Consequently the body is aware of a cruelty even before it is aware of pleasure ... Thus for everybody, not just philosophers and theologians, the physical lurches constantly towards the metaphysical. The lurch doesn't require words, a glance is sufficient. There's nobody here who isn't an expert in longing, in the long drawn-out desire for a life a fraction less cruel. And oddly, this co-exists with the beauty and is part of it."

At the end of *Photocopies*, sitting on a bench outside a public swimming pool in a Parisian suburb, "my towel drying in the sun, I open a book that has just been sent to me from New York," a collection of letters and communiques written by Subcommandante Marcos of the Mexican Zapatista insurgent movement. Berger notes that the style of this revolutionary's writing "combines modesty with unflinching excess ... The excess is not that of political extremism ... The excess comes from their conviction (which personally I accept completely) that they also represent the dead, all the maltreated dead — the dead who are less forgotten in Mexico than anywhere else in the world."

Here, in a Paris suburb, where kids are clowning around on the edge of the swimming pool, and where the local Lebanese shopkeeper has given an elderly homeless man "a bag of black bananas because they are far too overripe to sell," Berger reflects on the briefly headlined, quickly forgotten, half-a-world-away "ideological struggle between a few thousand faceless but true men and women, hidden in the sheltering mountains, and the triumphant World Order. How is such an unequal duel possible, if 'only for a moment'?"

Berger observes that "everywhere these days more and more people knock their heads against the fact that the future of our planet and what it will offer or deny to its inhabitants, is being decided by boards of men who control more money than all the governments of the world, who never stand for election, whose sole criterion [is profit]. Deep down people know, when they wake up at 4 a.m., that, one day, the system is going to crack. At dawn they bow their heads once again and obediently try not to go under. But the doubts are beginning. And at 4 a.m. the Subcommandante talks to us."

But at the very end, it isn't only politics on Berger's mind, but also language. He quotes a passage in which Subcommandante Marcos explains why he is addicted to postscripts when he writes letters. Marcos says, "It happens that one feels that something has remained between the fingers, that there are still some words that want to find their way into sentences, that one has not finished emptying the pockets of the soul. But it is useless, there never will be a postscript that can contain so many nightmares . . . and so many dreams."

Berger, too, leaves us with the image of words stuck between the fingers like crumbs, and the sense that he hasn't finished emptying his own pockets yet. Both the stylistic "excess" that comes from the conviction of "representing" the dead, and the modesty of "Death's secretaries" are stances that serve the narratives we make about those who are now only here in us, rather than among us. Both Berger, with an "urgency which belongs uniquely to life," and Commandante Marcos, with his postscripts, recognize that what they have to say is not "the last word." There are words to be written "after writing."

Berlin

I. *My Berlin*

"Now I want to recall those who introduced me to the city," is the way Walter Benjamin, the German thinker and literary critic of the 1920s and 30s, begins "A Berlin Chronicle" (1932). So do I. "For although the child, in his solitary games, grows up in closest proximity to the city," Benjamin says, "he needs and seeks guides to its wider expanses . . ." As does the stranger to the city.

The first of my guides to Berlin was the Canadian painter Michael Morris. It was a mid-March afternoon in 1990, a day or two before the first election in East Germany since the fall of the Berlin Wall on November 9, 1989. Michael was waiting at a bus stop on the Ku'-damm, the tree-lined main boulevard of West Berlin, when my travelling companion Tom Sandborn and I piled off a city bus with our heap of luggage. We had just ridden in from the airport after the long flight from Vancouver, at the beginning of a six-week tour of the capitals of Central and Eastern Europe in the wake of the fall of communism.

Even from the first glimpses through a bus window, Berlin is hardly a beautiful city in the conventional sense. Half or more of it had been destroyed some fifty years ago during World War II. As I soon learned, the rubble was cleared away in the following decades and the gaps between surviving buildings filled in with brown and gray five-storey stucco dwellings through a civic construction program in West Berlin launched at the beginning of the 1950s. The East Berlin rebuilding program was comparable, but favoured massive, desolate, Soviet-style apartment tower complexes.

The city's famous historical topography is pictured in the postcards that I sent home from Berlin. There's the totemic Brandenburg Gate that marked the city limits at its imperialistic height in the 1870s, and at the other extreme the intentionally unaltered war-damaged remains of the Memorial Church steeple at the east end of the Ku'-damm, which registers the nadir of the Nazi defeat. Berlin is a city of resurrections. They extend from the restored 300-year-old summer palace in Charlottenburg to the post-Wall phoenix of the Sony-Daimler building complex at Potsdamer Platz. So, the face of Berlin presents an historical cycle of triumph, destruction, and renewal all at once. For those who know something about architecture, that is part of its interest.

But in the luxurious Charlottenburg neighbourhood where Michael met us, dozens of Art Nouveau or Jugendstil edifices from the turn of the 20th century had survived the war. That period, *circa* 1880-1910, is when newly consolidated bourgeois wealth was expressed in elegant five-storey apartment buildings, with deep loge-like balconies held up by caryatids and atlantids, elaborate roof façades, and bas-reliefs of women with flowing tresses draped over ornate doorways. These richly-decorated stone heaps exuded their owners' sense of a satisfactory place in the social structure, a bourgeois eternity. As Benjamin says, there "reigned a species of thing that, no matter how compliantly it bowed to the minor whims of fashion, was in the main so wholly convinced of itself and its permanence that it took no account of wear, inheritance, or moves, remaining forever equally near to and far from its ending, which seemed the ending of all things." It was an eternity that, ironically, would last barely half a century.

On that first day, Tom and I dragged our suitcases along Mommsenstrasse, following our portly guide, who chatted away in the faintly-tinged English accent that he'd retained from his boyhood in England, until we arrived at the building where he had lived since the beginning of the 1980s. A second set of doors opened onto a courtyard (in German, a *Hof*) at the centre of which was a four-storey-high chestnut tree. On the far side of the *Hof* a turret staircase led to Michael's third-floor apartment and studio. Once inside, we could at last drop our bags, and settle around the kitchen table, having reached that moment of safety for which all travellers long, while Michael lit the stove and put on a kettle of water for tea. The kitchen window offered a view of the bare branches of the chestnut in the courtyard, giving the place something of the feeling of a tree house; the walls of the kitchen were crowded with various pictures, both Michael's and those of artist friends. Tom and I emerged from the airlock of time-travel into the famous free atmosphere of Berlin.

Now, after more than a decade of living part of my life in Berlin, that moment of entry has a magical double quality. From one point of view, it simply moves on, as if I released the pause button on a recorder, and watched the mundane moments of my arrival. Michael bustles around the kitchen, keeps up a steady reassuring patter which, being the skillful host he is, he knows will help orient us. He disappears for a moment and then returns to bring us a photo album with which we can amuse ourselves while he prepares the tea. I'm looking at snapshots of the people Michael knows in Berlin, people I might conceivably meet, while Michael tells us anecdotes about them in a style I'll come to think of as his "illustrated conversations."

Later, Michael takes us downstairs again, leads us along nearby Schlüterstrasse to the Hotel Bogota where we can check in for a couple of nights. Afterwards, he guides us to an upscale restaurant that he likes on the Ku'damm, and in the evening the three of us go to the funky Kleine Philharmonie bar, just off Joachimsthaler Strasse, presided over by a small elderly woman (now deceased) named Wanda. The next morning, Tom and I make our way to East Berlin, passing through a checkpoint of the remnants of the Wall, where gates ominously clang shut and border personnel still stamp the passports of foreigners, until we eventually emerge into the forbidding open space of Alexanderplatz, and turn ourselves into unofficial observers of the East German election.

But in its other aspect, I see the moment of entry as a moment of destiny. It's a freeze-frame that offers a panorama of my future. Though "destiny" is almost too grand a word for the accretion of such accidents of biography, it's the moment when, unconsciously, I decided that I would return to Berlin, again and again. It is the moment when I decided that the next phase of my life (I was about 50 then) would unfold in Berlin, with its nightmarish resonances of the Holocaust and its uncertain prospects as the centre of an enlarged and unified Europe. People who know I live part-time in Berlin often ask, "Why Berlin?" The answer isn't simple. It includes elements of biographical accident, a preference for big (European) cities, a romantic idea of how to live my life, erotic tastes, the famous Kultur of Berlin, and a sense of history and irony (what's a Jew doing in Berlin?). So, yes, why not? Destiny — as both obedience to an injunction and the choice of free will.

"I have long, indeed for years, played with the idea of setting out the sphere of life — *bios* — graphically on a map," Benjamin says. "I have evolved a system of signs, and on the gray background of such maps they would make a colourful show if I clearly marked the houses of my friends and girlfriends, the assembly halls of various collectives . . . the hotel and brothel rooms I knew for one night, the decisive benches in the Tiergarten, the ways to different schools and the graves that I saw filled, the sites of prestigious cafés whose long forgotten names daily crossed our lips . . ."

Equally, my Berlin, though steeped in the public acts and figures that claim the attention of anyone even minimally interested in history, is made up of similar personal sites, routes, routines. My own labyrinthine map of the city is curiously removed from such recent events as the unification of the former East and West Berlins, the return of the German capital from Bonn to Berlin in the early 1990s, or even the decade-long building projects in the wasteland occupied by the Berlin Wall for nearly thirty years. Rather, it is typified by the different ways — like the "ways" in Proust's *Swann's Way* — to walk from my current apartment near Charlottenburg castle, to Savigny-platz, just north of Michael Morris's former studio on Mommsen-strasse.

Savignyplatz is a patch of urban green with bowers, lawns, gardens, and trees, divided by busy Kantstrasse and bordered on the south end by the S-Bahn. At its north end, where three streets converge on the traffic circle, there is a sculpture by August Kraus, done in 1930, of two naked boys tugging at equally recalcitrant goats, their pedestals facing each other under large shade trees. Savignyplatz was one of the first places in the city with which I became familiar when I returned to Berlin in 1991 and stayed at Michael's apartment the summer after my first brief visit.

One of the three streets emptying into the square, Carmerstrasse, is where Benjamin lived as a child. Each weekday in the first decade of the 1900s he crossed Savignyplatz, fearful of being late, on his way to the "sad, spinsterish primness" of Kaiser Friedrich School, a red brick Gothic building (still) located in nearby Bleibtreustrasse, within sight of the elevated tracks of the S-Bahn.

Today, the square is surrounded by sidewalk restaurants and cafés. Among them, also on the north side, with a view of the goatboys, is my favourite, the Zwiebelfisch, an establishment founded in the 1960s, where, mockingly posted over the front door, is Dante's line, taken from the entrance to the Inferno, "Abandon all hope, ye who enter here." Many of the clientele at the Zwiebelfisch look like they've taken the injunction literally, and give off the air of the now fading "generation of '68ers," as they're known, caught in the time-warp of outmoded hairstyles and clothes.

It was during the spring and summer in 1991, when I returned to Berlin, that I really took Michael as my avuncular mentor, more so than in the previous year when he had been accidentally and briefly pressed into service as Tom's and my initial guide to the city. It was not so much the physical, present-day Berlin to which Michael now led me, although there was inevitably a good deal of that too — occasions where we went to an art exhibition, a party, or simply took a walk through a park to observe the burgeoning signs of spring — but rather to the historical "mind" of a culture. The process was imperceptible, casually offhand, and sometimes didn't require so much as my leaving the large high-ceilinged room in his apartment in which he had installed me.

The very day of my return to Berlin, jet-lagged, while I was plunked down in that room in a modernist chair of tubular steel and suspended black leather located next to a desk illuminated by a table lamp with a milky-white cupola and a base of green glass, Michael handed me an oversized coffee-table book. It was a volume of the pictures of Herbert List, a homoerotic photographer of the Weimar period, who had grown up in Hamburg, an hour or two north of Berlin by train. With his characteristic discretion, Michael left me to my own travel-dazed devices, and went off to attend to household and neighbourhood chores. My eyes gradually settled into List's images, and I inadvertently meditated on the now long-dead or long-lost objects of the photographer's — and my own — attention. There was an introduction to the book by the English writer Stephen Spender, whom I'd once met, decades ago, in San Francisco. The introduction was in German, which I attempted to piece out in my rudimentary knowledge of the language.

Adjacent to the desk was a narrow monk-like bed where I would sleep, and in the small bookshelf alongside it, I noticed a copy of Spender's long-suppressed homosexual novel, *The Temple*, in which List and his young friends in Hamburg appear as characters. The cover photograph — which I'd previously noticed in bookstores and been attracted to without perusing the book — was of a young man in a white bathing suit standing in the shallow water of a lake, with a handsome face innocent of the catastrophes that would soon befall him. I recognized that the photo was by List. This otherwise minor novel now acquired an urgency, and I began reading it that night.

Timeless hours passed, whole days, "sorrowless times" (as the title of one of my friend Jim Herndon's books has it), while I looked at those photos that afternoon, and simultaneously located myself in a Berlin composed of fragmented strata of various intellectual histories. The room in which I sat was full of gradually emergent treasures. The chair and the lamp, I learned from Michael, were Bauhaus designs of the 1920s, furniture which also appeared in Spender's novel. So, I was no longer sitting in a chair that had surprisingly retained its sleek modernity some three-quarters of a century after its creation, but a "Marcel Breuer" chair; the cozy lighting fixture was now a "Wagenfeld" lamp. And the chair and lamp were also connected to a larger world of architecture, design, and ideas about domestic life, examples of which I would find scattered throughout Berlin. When I expressed an interest in all this, Michael immediately produced an illustrated Bauhaus history by Hans Wingler for me to thumb through. Gradually a little library piled up on the desk.

Above the desk was a contemporary "word-painting" by Michael's friend and artistic collaborator, Vincent Trasov, a large 2-metre by 2-metre glass-framed work containing 16 pieces of grey construction paper, each bearing the stenciled word *Knabe* (the old-fashioned German word for "boy"). It referred, in a post-modern conceptualist way — again, this was Michael's explanation in response to a question I'd asked about the painting — to a sentimental German tradition of glorifying and eroticizing adolescent males. It was a tradition that extended from early 19th century German Romanticism to the *Wandervogel* youth movement at the beginning of the 20th century, a movement that loosely included List, Benjamin and even the goatboy statue in Savignyplatz. In its most horrific moment, the tradition could be found in the "purified" Hitler Youth corps, and later, more benignly, among the long-haired teenaged German draft-evaders who settled in West Berlin during the 1970s, or the young men whose snapshots Michael had taken and which were in the photo albums he had shown me. Each object or idea — photos, furniture, paintings, historical references, gossip about the figures in the albums — contributed to a complicated, dense, intellectual portrait of an exfoliating larger realm, whose parts I absorbed, via Michael, and then joined to my own experiences, in a gradually developing sense of "my Berlin."

I dwell on the subtlety and generosity of Michael's guidance because the notion of the guide is a persistently recurrent personage in my life. This figure ranges from my beloved father, teachers, and other mentors to the seamiest of pimps and dealers. Even the stranger on a streetcorner from whom I receive directions to the next street is numbered among their ranks. The classic figure of Hermes is the one who leads you from one world to the next and, in doing so, reveals to you the multiplicity of worlds.

That evening, after Michael had fed me (he was, almost inevitably, a superb cook), he took me out for a flaneur's stroll down the Ku'-damm. It was the same Ku'damm I'd previously seen, and it was a perfectly ordinary after-dinner walk past the expensive shops with their well-known names, lighted display cases of goods set in the middle of the sidewalk, shadowy trees that lined the median, public toilets, and well-lit cafés (the Möhring, Kempinski Corner, Kranzler's) whose crowds spilled out onto the sidewalk tables. But it was also now a boulevard transformed from my previous idea of it, one that was suddenly dense with intimations of a city I was about to discover.

My Berlin includes the numerous castles and parks around the outskirts of the city, spaces mostly designed by the great 19th century landscape gardener, Peter Lenné. They're the sites of regular Sunday walks with my friend Mark Johnson, the second of my guides to Berlin. We met in a bar in 1993, and soon this computer technician — in his early forties, with salt and pepper hair, and a conservative, wry sense of humour and politics — was showing me the places, known to Berliners but mostly hidden from strangers, where one can stroll on summer days, arguing about current events or falling into a meditative state of mind that is inseparable from my idea of writing. I, too, came to know the places Benjamin recalls: "The orchard at Glienicke, the broad ceremonious promenade of Schloss Babelsberg ... the shadowy ways through the foliage leading down to Lake Griebnitz at the places where there were jetties."

Despite Berlin's bucolic core, it's possible, as various civic historians and travellers demonstrate, to barely notice, as one more observant writer, Anton Gill, puts it, "the wooded parks which cover half the city's acreage and which are, with the lakes," and the serpentine Spree River, "the reason for the city's good air." In more obtuse descriptions of the city, there's seldom a moment in which the observer sits at the lakeside café next to Köpenick Castle in the southeast corner of Berlin, or finds the "beer-meadow" across the water from Babelsberg park at the city's western edge. Even in the city proper, most passers-through don't have time to watch the swans floating in the Lietzensee on a summer afternoon, or dawdle at one of Benjamin's "decisive benches" in the central Tiergarten park. I prefer more modest historians who notice that "the grey city alone on its plain has a necklace of countryside and parkland."

My own private Berlin takes in, as do Benjamin's "hotel rooms and brothels I knew for one night" from his "Berlin Chronicle," various geographic zones of desire, beginning with the intersection of Eisenacher and Fuggerstrasse, just off Nollendorfplatz, southeast of the Ku'damm. That's where gay rent-bars and other homosexually-oriented drinking establishments have been clustered for more than three-quarters of a century. Though stretches of Eisenacher Strasse were reduced to heaps of rubble during World War II (I'd seen post-war photos of the street by another German photographer, Herbert Tobias), the turn-of-the-century patch of elegant buildings at the corner of Fuggerstrasse survived. .

On the ground floor of one of them is a small bar named Pinocchio's. On a summer afternoon, I can sit at one of the tables outside the bar and watch the street traffic, chat inconsequentially with one of the regular customers or the bartender, or simply gaze at the pale blue stone walls of the apartment buildings across the street and the flowerboxes on their deep balconies spilling over with the fierce brightness of geraniums. Next door is a similar but larger bar, Tabasco's, and around the corner, Blue Boy. At the corner there's a small, scruffy, fenced-in playground that contains a soccer cage, some trees and benches, and a ping-pong table where I often see some of the young men who hang around the bar playing table tennis. I like the way a patina of the utterly mundane overlays the erotic currents, the way contentless eternity and the urgent particularity of desire merge.

From the first time I walked down Fuggerstrasse, in 1991, I sensed the power of the countless stories that its bars, restaurants and buildings contained, stories of love affairs, breathless encounters, disasters of the heart. One night, in the shoebox-sized Pinocchio's, its few barstools and half-dozen tables crowded with both the grotesque and the beautiful, someone I knew, sitting at a corner table and playing a dice game with some of his pals, hailed me as I made my way through the mob, and then made a place for me to squeeze in on a stool next to someone he knew I was attracted to. At that moment, absorbing the flow of information circulating throughout the bar and at the same time the specificity of the person against whose thigh my own was pressed, I had the sense of being inside. Wherever we are, there's a nominal sense in which we're "inside," whether it's a city, a building or a room. But at the same time, we can know ourselves to be "outside," outside of a culture, a history or even a group of people. At that moment, in a tiny bar that felt like a galley sailing through the sky, I was inside for the first time — *inside* Berlin, *inside* Pinocchio's. And inside is my idea of Paradise.

Benjamin, too, recalls "an afternoon . . . to which I owe insights into my life that came in a flash, with the force of an illumination. It was on this very afternoon that my biographical relationships to people, my friendships and comradeships, were revealed to me in their most vivid and hidden intertwinings." At that moment he attempted to make a diagram of his life; subsequently the sheet of paper, to his chagrin, was irretrievably lost. But in remembering the labyrinth it sketched out, Benjamin says, "I am concerned not with what is installed in the chamber at its enigmatic centre, ego or fate, but all the more with the many entrances leading into the interior . . . entrances I call 'primal acquaintances' . . . So many primal relationships, so many entrances to the maze."

The entrances to Schlossstrasse (Castle Street), the street I like best in Berlin, are often roundabout. Thomas Marquard and Ilonka Opitz, a married couple who are friends of mine as well as my upstairs neighbours in the building in Berlin where I live, are the third of my guides to the city. They were the ones who first took me to Schlossstrasse one evening in the mid-1990s, while we were out walking their golden retriever, Kimba. The "secret way," as Thomas once called it, to Schlossstrasse leads from our building on busy Kaiser-Friedrich-Strasse, past the Little Europe food stand where various neighbourhood characters hang out, and by an inexplicably but always failing café at the corner, down a little side-street to where Haubachstrasse and Hebbelstrasse make a V. Nearby, there is an obscure entrance path into a sunken rectangle of green lawn, with a few trees, park benches, and cobbled paths, lit at night by imitation gas-lamps.

The first evening I entered Schustehrus Park, I had the feeling not only of entering the maze, but of stepping into a previous century, its gas-light illumination marking out dark anthropomorphic shapes of bushes and trees, a faint mist hovering over the lawn. Emerging from the far end of the park, it is a brief walk down Schustehrusstrasse to the corner of Schlossstrasse, where the bower garden of the Bohemian restaurant is located. Thomas, Ilonka, and I occasionally stop there for a drink beneath its tangle of vines. For me, all the names of streets and sites of cafés and restaurants, either taken for granted by long-time residents or merely exotic words in a foreign language for distant strangers, have a particular resonance. These markers literally mark the place and, once entered into a vocabulary of experiences, function like computer hypertext markings that instantly call up particular stretches of urban landscape.

Schlossstrasse is partially paved with traffic-slowing bricks, and divided by a parkway. The edges of the median are lined with linden trees, and in the center is a broad, sandy path, where local people gather to play boules, the small metal orbs clicking against each other when they hit. The path, several blocks in length, leads directly to the gates of Charlottenburg Castle, whose aqua cupola is illuminated at night, rising over the low, French-style, early 18th century building, once a summer stopover for Prussian royalty on their way between Köpenick Schloss in the east and Frederick the Great's San Souci Palace in Potsdam. Schlossstrasse itself is lined with sombre, former bourgeois villas, now transformed into apartment buildings, a couple of museums, and some ground-floor cafés; its cobbled sidewalks, shaded by lindens, become sticky in the summer from aphids' secretions in the trees. On the far side of the street, towards its south end — I get there a different way, along Zillestrasse, walking past the green carpeted soccer field — is my neighbourhood café, the Kastanie, where I go to drink coffee and read in the afternoons at a table in the back of the café. As Benjamin says, "So many entrances to the maze."

In a 1927 review of his friend Franz Hessel's novel, *Unknown Berlin*, Benjamin remarks, "What is 'unknown,' secret, about this Berlin is no windy whispering, no tiresome flirting, but simply this strict classical image-being of a city . . . that holds within itself the yardstick . . . for the figures in a dance."

Berlin is also a city of texts, a city of its authors, both those who lived and wrote here, like Benjamin and his friend Hessel, and those who come to write its history. A little more than a block from Pinocchio's, at 17 Nollendorfstrasse — my friend Mark's apartment is located in the same block — is a peach-coloured five-storey apartment building on whose wall is a plaque that records that the English author Christopher Isherwood (1904-86) lived in this building, where he wrote the stories of *Goodbye to Berlin*.

Other than the natural growth of the trees that shade Nollendorfstrasse, little has changed from the description Isherwood offers in the first lines of "A Berlin Diary, Autumn 1930," where he says, "From my window, the deep solemn massive street. Cellar-shops where the lamps burn all day, under the shadow of top-heavy balconied facades, dirty plaster frontages embossed with scroll-work and heraldic devices. The whole district is like this: street leading into street of houses like shabby monumental safes crammed with the tarnished valuables and second-hand furniture of a bankrupt middle class."

From that window overlooking Nollendorfstrasse, Isherwood announced himself to the world: "I am a camera with its shutter open, quite passive, recording, not thinking. Recording the man shaving at the window opposite and the woman in the kimono washing her hair. Some day, all this will have to be developed, carefully printed, fixed."

A fresh coat of pastel paint has been laid on some of the "dirty plaster frontages," and one of the cellar-shops that now sells sex toys and videos has been brightened up and sports a rainbow flag outside its entrance. But the street itself, "the little hotel on the corner, where you can hire a room by the hour," and the nearby gay bars and the young men in them are not much different from when Isherwood "passively recorded" the scene some three-quarters of a century ago.

The evening I discovered Isherwood's lodgings, I stood across the street, transfixed, looking at the narrow wooden and glass door of number 17, half-expecting Isherwood himself to emerge and join me on the walk to the bar. I knew at that moment that ghosts can also be guides.

"Soon the whistling will begin," Isherwood wrote. "Young men are calling their girls. Standing down there in the cold, they whistle up at the lighted windows of warm rooms where the beds are already turned down for the night. They want to be let in." He tries not to listen to the whistles. "But soon a call is sure to sound, so piercing, so insistent, so despairingly human, that at last I have to get up and peep through the slats of the Venetian blind to make quite sure that it is not — as I know very well it could not possibly be — for me." Isherwood, writing about himself at a time before homosexuality could be openly discussed, is being a little coy. Some of the whistles were for him. Today the young men no longer whistle; they all have cellphones.

On Chausseestrasse, the northern continuation of Friedrichstrasse, the main commercial street in east Berlin, I visit the house where Bertolt Brecht lived at the end of his life in the mid-1950s; his writing table is still in place. Brecht, and his wife, Helene Weigel, are buried next door in the Dorotheen Cemetery, along with dozens of other writers, artists and thinkers of the past two centuries, from Fichte to Anna Seghers and Heiner Müller. In that sense, the city is crowded with writers, past and present — Alfred Döblin, author of *Berlin Alexanderplatz*, Heinrich Mann, Arthur Koestler, Vladimir Nabokov, Stefan Heym, as well as elder contemporaries like Günter Grass, Christa Wolf, and Günter de Bruyn, right up to the present generation in their cafés in fashionable Berlin Mitte and Prenzlauer Berg. The presence of the writers, both ghosts and living, whose habitations are often marked by ceramic plaques, is another of the reasons I feel at home in Berlin.

And then there's Walter Benjamin himself, my primary guide in this account of the city, who was also the author of various urban portraits, of Moscow, Berlin, Paris, Naples and Marseilles. A few years ago, while in Chicago, the city of my birth, I met Lisa Fittko, then 89 years old, the woman who led Benjamin through the Pyrenees Mountains on his fatal flight from Hitler in 1940. For her, Benjamin was but another of the many left-wing Jewish refugees who appeared at her door in Port-Vendres in southern France, seeking assistance from the small Jewish resistance group she led. "I took him over the mountains, not because he was the [posthumously] famous philosopher," she told me, "but just because he was one of us."

In Fittko's own account, she recalls the morning Benjamin appeared. "My dear lady," he said to her, "please forgive the intrusion — I hope this is not an inopportune time." Fittko adds, "The world is falling to pieces, I thought, but Benjamin's courtesy is unshakeable." Sitting in her apartment, located on the South Side between the University of Chicago and Lake Michigan, and gazing at this elderly heroic woman, whose sight, she tells me, has grown somewhat fainter with the years, I was conscious of looking into eyes that had looked upon both Benjamin and Hitler.

In the Berlin of the new millennium, Benjamin's shade remains to instruct me, as do his words. Walking down Leibnizstrasse one day, I noticed that what had been a construction-site excavation hole for many years was now the site of two facing grey stone buildings (designed by the Berlin architect Hans Kollhoff), with a large plaza space and a geyser-like fountain in between them. The ground floors of the pair of buildings are lined with pillars, giving them an arcade effect, a nod toward Benjamin's long-standing interest in the arcades, or passages, of 19th century Paris, and the subject of his unfinished book, *Passagen-Werk* (in English, *The Arcades Project*). Glancing up, I saw that a new street sign named this space: Walter-Benjamin-Platz.

Benjamin translated Proust into German. In Benjamin's "Berlin Chronicle," the Proustian project is always at the margins of his consciousness. "He who has once begun to open the fan of memory never comes to the end of its segments," he says. "No image satisfies him, for he has seen that it can be unfolded, and only in its folds does the truth reside — that image, that taste, that touch for whose sake all this has been unfurled and dissected; and now remembrance progresses from small to smallest details, from the smallest to the infinitesimal, while that which it encounters in these microcosms grows ever larger."

The infinitesimal details of my Berlin emphasise an unexpectedly romantic side of the city. That doesn't mean I'm unaware of what Benjamin calls "noisy, matter-of-fact Berlin, the city of work and the metropolis of business," or its shabbier faces, and the brusque interpersonal style of its inhabitants known by the almost untranslatable term, *Schnauze* (the word means, among other things, "muzzle" or "snout"). Frequently enough, in various parts of the city, especially on cold, wet days, I see Berlin stripped of my illusions and most of its own. Then it's a place of run-down neighbourhood "brown bars," dying game arcades, and empty shops for rent, with overflowing garbage, reeking sewers, and dogshit on the sidewalks, populated by spitting young thugs and hobbled ancient people who seem to be made of human spare parts. Who knows what thoughts crossed their once innocent faces during the Nazi era, or what they did during the War, or what the young ones like them will do during the next one?

On the whole, though, the romance prevails. The young adults, born of parents themselves born after the Third Reich, are, with more frequency than in most places I know, so sensuously striking that they have made Berlin one of my cities of desire. But the shrunken old woman, who sits on a chair before a florist's on Bismarckstrasse, wrapped in a tattered fur stole, reminds me that even the young beauties are subject to time and mortality.

One night, in early May, some friends and I were having dinner with Thomas and Ilonka at their apartment. We had lingered at table until almost midnight and someone remarked on the sounds of the birds echoing in the back courtyard. "They're the nightingales," Thomas said, and Ilonka, who identifies with birds above all other creatures, explained it was the time of year when they sang to mark out their mating territories.

"But you really have to hear them," Thomas insisted and, despite the hour, he led us downstairs, packed us into his car and drove us to a wooded, nearly deserted part of Berlin, one of those numerous places that make you forget you're in a city of three-and-a-half-million people. There, past midnight, we cocked our ears toward a patch of fuzzy trees to hear the distinctive territorial and mating songs of the nightingales, miniature operatic arias, duets of property negotiations. The nightingales weren't the only birds out on the town. Later, as we straggled along a path bordering the Spree River, in the darkness, floating down the river, there appeared a white swan. "On his way to a swan bar," I said.

The "microcosms of the infinitesimal" unfold even beneath my feet. Though I now take them for granted, one of my earliest fascinations was with Berlin's sidewalks, or what George Stanley refers to in one of his poems as "the precious pavement" — a phrase that sees the magic of cities even in what's underfoot.

The walkways of Berlin are a hand-made kaleidoscope of stones. Although there are some poured concrete slabs, unlike the homogenous sidewalks of North America, those in Berlin are mostly unique arrangements of multi-coloured stones: paving stones, flagstones arranged in diamond patterns, cobbles, red-tinged bricks that mark the bicycle lanes, interlocking pre-cast blocks, and especially small "argument stones" — so-named because they could be pulled up and thrown at the authorities during episodes of civil unrest. Each stone is tapped with a mallet into the sandy marsh on which the city is built. The fact that the ground under Berlin shifts so much is probably the main reason for the hand-made walks, since conventional sidewalks would break up. Also, the mosaic of small stones is easier to pull apart to gain access to the subterranian infrastructure, and cheaper to restore than cement slabs.

Still, what's unusual about all of this at the beginning of the 21st-century is the maintenance of a 19th-century hand-work craft. The persistence of a seemingly obsolescent mode of production is even stranger in the midst of a self-proclaimed decade-long "Construction-Site Berlin" (in German it's *Baustelle Berlin*), filled with a tangle of towering yellow building cranes and dozens of recently-erected post-modern skyscrapers. What's more, these workers from the past, almost ghost-workers, contradict the civic bureaucracy's obsessive drive to dehumanize the city — replacing public toilets with privatized automated bathroom machines, extending store shopping hours, threatening to eliminate the old honour system of payment on public transportation with mandatory computerized fares, etc. I expect an enterprising civic official, any day now, to suggest making the stone-workers redundant, and replacing them with money-saving poured-cement sidewalks.

On my desk in Berlin, facing windows that look onto the maple and ash trees in the back courtyard, I keep a paving-stone paperweight. Mark got it for me from a heap outside the recently built Scandinavian Embassies. It's an irregular squarish chunk of granite, flecked with mica, that I keep as an anticipatory relic of the days when citizens thought that even the precious pavement of the city mattered.

II. *Berlin and the Angel of History*

The most memorable image in Walter Benjamin's writing, "the angel of history," appears in his "Theses on the Concept of History," a late schematic essay written in 1940, a few months before he died. Benjamin portrays the angel as a witness to the ongoing disaster of history:

> His face is turned toward the past. Where we perceive a chain of events, he sees one single catastrophe which keeps piling wreckage upon wreckage and hurls it at his feet. The angel would like to stay, awaken the dead, and make whole what has been smashed. But a storm is blowing from Paradise; it has got caught in his wings with such violence that the angel can no longer close them. This storm irresistibly propels him into the future to which his back is turned, while the pile of debris before him grows skyward. The storm is what we call progress.

If any city can claim to lie under the gaze of the angel of history, it must be Berlin. Nowhere has the wreckage of the past been piled higher — sometimes literally, as in the mountainous accretion of World War II rubble known as Devil's Mountain, or Teufelberg, heaped up and greened over in the nearby woods of Berlin — and nowhere has the storm of "progress" blown more ferociously. Beyond "my Berlin," then, there's the Berlin of history, an imaginary personage, one whose objectivity is open to the varying interpretive perspectives of its urban biographers.

In reading that Berlin — that is, reading the numerous books about the city — one confronts the theoretical problem of the genre of such urban histories and civic portraits. The notion of the imaginary personage derivable from the city's evolving material facts and its historical events is itself dubious. As one critic, Peter Paret, puts it, "For dramatic effect, a city's history is sometimes called a biography, but cities are living organisms only by courtesy . . . the personality of a city is a doubtful explanatory device." Still, most of the recent and arguably definitive histories of Berlin make use of the conceit. Anthony Read and David Fisher's *Berlin: The Biography of a City*, David Clay Large's *Berlin* (which is subtitled *Biographie einer Stadt* in its German edition), and even Alexandra Richie's monumental *Faust's Metropolis* all suggest this phantasmal aspect, and it's an idea to which I'm drawn.

The problem is how to render the likeness of the personality that emerges from an assemblage of people, physical structures and institutional arrangements over time. Many historians often produce ungrounded sentences of the form, e.g., "Berlin wanted . . ." or "Berlin thinks . . ." where the Berlin personified in the sentence may amount to little more than the wishes and thoughts of a particular class, or worse, the public relations rhetoric of the local tourist bureau.

The case of Berlin poses the added difficulty of being an unusual national capital. It is distinguishable from such long-standing big city capitals as London and Paris in that its role as a capital has been more violently interrupted by events than anywhere else. Berlin, the principal, if sleepy, garrison city of Frederick the Great's "enlightened" and militarized Prussia in the 18th century, was the capital of Germany from the unification of the country in 1871 to the Nazi-provoked devastation of both the city and the nation in 1945. Then the eastern part of the city was the capital of East Germany from 1949 to 1990, while the provincial town of Bonn served as West Germany's always provisional capital. It was a city divided from 1961 to 1989 by the Berlin Wall, which was magnified into the symbol of the "Cold War" of that period, and now, in the wake of German reunification in October 1990, Berlin has subsequently resumed its position as the capital of unified Germany.

The challenge of telling Berlin's story no doubt accounts for the numerous books written about the city in recent years. I've read most of those in English, and although I'm not going to critique them individually or in detail, I've found them, almost without exception, to be unsatisfactory. I should note, by the way, that although there's a vast field of German historiography, urban histories are not a popular genre in German, hence my attention to English-language histories of Berlin.

The books about Berlin that I've read go wrong in different ways. One way to go wrong is to view Berlin through the prism of German history, and vice-versa, to the mutual disadvantage of both, but especially to the disadvantage of the city. The point of the title of a recent German movie, *Berlin is in Germany*, is that it's meant as an ironic counter to the often-uttered dictum that "Berlin is not in Germany," that it's something else, somewhere else. And in my experience it is not like the rest of Germany, as both Berliners and non-Berliner Germans are quick to reassure or warn visitors. The decision to write a history of Berlin through the prism of German history is fatal, especially when one of the striking features of Berlin is its difference from and resistance to that national history.

Another way to go wrong is through simple hostility. It seems odd to write a book about a city you don't particularly like, but I've read books in which the central thesis emerges as a tendentious emphasis on debunking the "myths" and "legends" of Berlin and its unusual record of political resistance. These myths can be presented as self-serving, self-promoting and self-deluded rhetorical tropes of its inhabitants and boosters. But the conceptual strategy of demystifying Berlin requires the writer to deconstruct or simply diminish a vast amount of prima facie evidence of civic resistance. That evident resistance ranges from the politics of "Red Berlin" at the beginning of the 20th century, to the legendary Weimar culture of the 1920s, to the fate of the city under the Nazis and beyond. If one is in a merely debunking frame of mind, it's often accompanied by a tendency to disdain everything in the city's recent past, from the chaotic social experimentation of the 1960s and 70s, right on down to the city's contemporary reputation as a European centre of *Toleranz.*

The cultural history of Berlin is frequently, in such wrong-headed books, written off as dazzling, but superficial and decadent. Perhaps the biggest distortion of such accounts is a portrait of Berlin as a typical site of Nazism. Here, in order to portray Berliners as mindless "good Germans," authors obscure the fact that Berlin, unlike many other places in Germany, was remarkable in never having voted for the Nazis. Further, the reality of the situation was that after free elections were suspended in the mid-1930s, Berlin's opposition forces — social democrats, communists, liberals of various classes, trade unionists, artists, and segments of Berlin's liberal Jewish community — were all either exiled, murdered, or forcibly interned in concentration camps. That left only a "purified" population of Berliners most likely to be acquiescent to or supportive of Hitler's regime.

A rather different way of going wrong in portraying Berlin is through affable blandness. Such books are not distorted through the imposition of an ideological agenda, but through a failure to adequately conceptualize the themes for a civic history. This process of conceptualization is the crux of any urban biography. It's possible to emphasize the city's uncertain self-esteem as a late-arriving national capital, or its difficult relations with the rest of Germany, and the corollary tension between its own governance and that of the rulers of the nations, from kaisers to the Nazis, most of whom distrusted and disliked the sprawling capital on the Spree River. Finally, in terms of thematics, it's possible to see Berlin as merely a city of constant self-reinvention, but one that always confronts its transformations with the regret of nostalgia. All of these concepts are true enough in a mundane fashion, but such a conceptualization as a whole suffers from a blandness that diminishes the epic quality of the disasters that have befallen Berlin.

My own response to dissatisfaction as a reader of Berlin history, one that's characteristic of me, is the invention of an imaginary unwritten book that gets it right, or is at least more adequate than the books I don't like. The book I imagine is called *Berlin and the Angel of History*, and in part is an answer to the question that, as I mentioned before, I'm frequently asked: "Why Berlin?"

I'm attracted to Berlin, first, by its shattered history, which I see as emblematic of 20th century Western history. Second, as the city where the international homosexual rights movement was founded by Magnus Hirschfeld in the late 19th century, the city's century-long, uninterrupted gay social history is bound to be of interest to anyone with my erotic preferences. Equally, as a Jew, as faint as that identification may be for me, Berlin is the magnetic ground zero of one of the most horrific historical processes of the last century, the murder and attempted genocide of European Jewry. Wherever I walk in Berlin, in old Jewish neighbourhoods or in the ghostly Jewish cemetery in Weissensee, there is an historical resonance. Whenever I listen to public conversations between Berlin's contemporary Jewish community and the city's rather philo-semitic government, or even when I pick up a passing, possibly anti-semitic remark ("That building used to be owned by Jews"), I sense a living debate unlike anywhere else. Fourth, as a writer, I'm interested in Berlin's cultural history, which at various historical moments was as vibrant and distinct as those of any of the great cities of Europe and America. Finally, Berlin's reputation as a city of tolerance promises a possibility for the future as a centre of the new 21st century Europe.

The text of my imaginary book is governed by three principal themes. The first is Walter Benjamin's "angel of history," who presides over the successive cataclysms that shape the temporal story of the city of Berlin. It regards the catastrophes that have hit Berlin as irreparable. Berlin is a city where history is repeatedly broken, where there are historical breaks that cities like London, Paris and Rome haven't known. The wreckage fades but is never transcended.

Rather than a strategy of viewing Berlin through the prism of German history, and vice-versa, the narrative recognizes that German history is partially separable from that of Berlin. Such an urban history would locate not only the city's indigenous story, but also distinguish the "intersections" where German and world history is visited upon the city and those where the events in Berlin, while shaping German history, are integral to the chronicle of the city.

To take a single example: the diplomatic blundering of Kaiser Wilhelm II in the second decade of the 20th century which leads to Germany's fatal involvement in World War I is an intersection dominated by myopic German history and the kaiser's erratic foreign policy. The war, envisaged as one to be brought to a speedy, triumphant conclusion by Christmas 1914 (when the victorious troops would come marching home through Brandenburg Gate, from which they had set out in summer), instead turned catastrophic for Germany, and everyday life in Berlin became a matter of unceasing, prolonged hardship. Daily life in Berlin during the war is part of the city's experience, as much as its fevered industrial proletarianization from the 1880s on. The Kaiser's wrong-headed politics, on the other hand, belongs primarily to German history.

By contrast, the events of the 1919 civil war in the streets of Berlin, though an "intersection" that shapes Germany, since it eventuated in the Weimar Republic, can be largely viewed in terms of the city itself, where the struggle took place. The new Social Democratic government of Friedrich Ebert, in collusion with conservative forces — a collusion that is a persistent problem of social democracy generally — included in its ranks all-important military and paramilitary troops. This coalition shot it out with a fragmented left that included "independent" Social Democrats, the recently-formed German Communist Party, and its ultra-left fraction, the Spartacists, led by Rosa Luxemburg and Karl Liebknecht. Both Luxemburg and Liebknecht were murdered in the course of the failed revolution. We're left with the image of the bloated corpse of the once-brilliant Luxemburg surfacing in the canal in the Tiergarten where she was dumped by her executioners. Simultaneously, the scenes of anarchy in the streets of the city are mixed with vignettes of ebullient night life recorded in the diaries of Count Harry Kessler.

While the demarcation of the intersections between Berlin/Germany is obviously not hard and fast, decisions about what to emphasize would be an integral feature of the narrative. A history that chooses as its overarching image the metaphor of a Faustian bargain, with its implications of the city making a deal with the devil or selling its soul in return for eminence, strikes me as historically wrong-headed. Benjamin's angel of history, with its neutral but empathetic gaze, is an image that makes more sense of the series of developments and cataclysms in relation to the mind and personality of the city. Measured against the "wreckage upon wreckage" hurled at the angel's feet, or the "storm from Paradise" caught in its wings, notions of mere constant self-reinvention seem trivial and reductive.

The second theme of *Berlin and the Angel of History* is that the cultural history of Berlin can be read as a collective intelligence. If one takes up the metaphor of the imaginary personage of the city, then there's a tendency to see cultural history as the mind of the city. In any case, Berlin's cultural history, from its popular cabaret tradition to its avant-garde experiments, is not simply something that occurs in Berlin but, in a sense, is integral to the city, *is* Berlin.

The imaginary mind of Berlin consists of everything written, painted, danced, built, composed and thought in Berlin over a period of about two centuries. Just to glance at its literary aspect, such a personified mind is fascinatingly complex and includes the varied contents of the works of E.T.A. Hoffman, Theodor Fontane, Alfred Döblin, Benjamin, Isherwood, Musil, Kafka, Nabokov, Brecht and dozens of others, right to the present moment of Thomas Brussig's comedic account of the fall of the Berlin Wall in *Heroes Like Us* or Günter Grass's imagination of a contemporary Fontane in the reunified Berlin of *Too Far Afield*.

The city's thought places its 18th century Jewish philosopher Moses Mendelssohn in the precincts of the Prussian Academy, Hegel in the university classroom, and Isherwood in a rent-bar. It is sustained all the way to a Sunday morning colloquium I attended at the Theatre am Lehniner Platz in which the American cultural theorist Judith Butler was in conversation with Berlin choreographer Sascha Waltz, discussing the latter's latest dance performance, *Körper* (Body). While works set in Berlin, such as Döblin's *Berlin Alexanderplatz*, Isherwood's *Goodbye to Berlin* or Brussig's *Heroes Like Us* have a certain natural priority, the point is that every book written in Berlin, whether or not it takes the city as its subject, is part of a unique civic mind. I imagine a history of Berlin that makes extensive use of the texts of its writers, slowly weaving together a civic portrait based on their descriptions and preoccupations. It is less a guided tour of literary landmarks than a treatment of literary work as entrances into the hidden city.

The handling of the history of the city's intelligence is an enormously complicated matter and here I can offer just one example I'm personally interested in to indicate the contrasting treatment of a moment of Berlin social history. In 1997 I visited a massive exhibition at Berlin's Academy of Art commemorating the one hundredth anniversary of the international gay movement. That movement had its origins in Berlin in 1897 with the founding, by Magnus Hirschfeld, of the Scientific-Humanitarian Committee, a political group that had, among its objectives, the repeal of the country's anti-homosexual statute. Hirschfeld, a member of Freud's Berlin Psychoanalytic Society and a precursor of sexologist Alfred Kinsey, was prominent in Berlin history for some three decades, but especially during the Weimar period in the 1920s as the founder-director of an institute for sexual research. For visiting artists like W.H. Auden, Christopher Isherwood and Stephen Spender, Hirschfeld's headquarters, located at the edge of the Tiergarten, was one of the first stops on the tour. At the Nazi book-burning in Bebelplatz in 1933, Hirschfeld's works as well as a bust of him were among the first objects thrown into the flaming pile, and the sacking and closure of his institute followed by his exile were of a piece with that conflagration.

Even by this brief thumbnail sketch, it's clear that Hirschfeld is an inescapable figure of modern Berlin social thought. Yet, in the histories of Berlin I've read, the presence of Hirschfeld is a hit-and-miss affair. While in some texts, he's accorded a reasonable discussion, in most others he merits no more than a passing reference, and at the extreme, he receives not so much as a mention. If a Berlin history doesn't notice Hirschfeld, one has to wonder what else has been missed.

In such works, it's unsurprising to find that not much is said about homosexuality in general, though Berlin has a major place in the history of modern homosexual life. Where homosexuality is discussed at all, it's often relegated to the notion of a naughty, decadent Berlin. But homosexual life and thought are also something other and more than that, especially in Berlin, where they have been part of the city's social and mental life for a century. I don't want to make more of this topic than it deserves. It's a thread in the weave, no more than that. Nor am I arguing for some multicultural recognition, some ethnic flavour of the month. In any case, that recognition is more than satisfied by the city's annual Christopher Street Day gay parade, which draws up to a half-million participants. Rather, what I'm suggesting is that if you start by taking Hirschfeld seriously, I think a case can be made that the place of homosexual life in Berlin, rather than simply of a piece with the mystique of Berlin *noir*, is closer to the historical experience of the city's Jewish community, both in its periodic victimization as a scapegoat, and in its sporadically successful quest for tolerance and integration.

One of the reasons I'm drawn to the metaphor of the mind of Berlin is that in most histories only minimal attention is paid to the city's thinkers. An adequate cultural history of Berlin would have to examine what those thinkers thought. From Mendelssohn, Hegel and Schopenhauer in the 18th and 19th centuries, to the 20th century minds of Albert Einstein, Rosa Luxemburg, Eduard Bernstein, Benjamin and comparable figures of the Berlin intelligentsia, Berlin is a city of ideas, a city with something on its mind.

A third and final thematic, one that stands out for me, is that Berlin is a left-wing city. Some histories of Berlin present most of the facts for this claim but fail to explicitly draw those facts together, while others treat it as a motif for debunking. But the historical evidence is massive, consistent, and incontrovertible. Berlin is the centre of the naissance of the German Social Democratic movement — led by August Bebel in the 1870s and 80s — the political formation instrumental in creating the image of "Red Berlin" by the turn of the century. The city provided the thinker's study for Eduard Bernstein, a still-underappreciated social democratic theorist at the beginning of the 20th century, and a precursor of contemporary European social democratic thought. Berlin was the site of, simultaneously, a civil war and a bloody internecine struggle among leftist parties in 1919, as well as the place where a workers' general strike defeated an attempted right-wing coup, the Kapp putsch of 1920.

The striking, seldom-noted feature of Berlin's relation to the Nazis, as I mentioned, is that the city never voted for Hitler's party. Throughout the rise of Nazism and the tragic failure of the Weimar Republic, Berlin's vote for the Nazis was always proportionally less than in Germany as a whole, and even in the various elections of the 1930s, at the time of and after Hitler's ascension to the chancellorship, the Nazi vote in Berlin never amounted to more than slightly over a third of the city's electorate, while a more than fifty per cent majority supported left-wing parties. After the Nazi debacle and the division of the country, while West Germany opted for the Christian Democratic regime of Konrad Adenauer, the city of West Berlin elected a post-war socialist mayor, Ernst Reuter. In the late 1950s, Berlin provided the base for the political career of Willy Brandt, one of Germany's most interesting left-wing civic and federal icons.

One would be hard-pressed to make any sense of the various anarchist, "autonomous," student radical, "squatter," and green political activities of the 1960s through to the mid-1980s without placing them in the context of the history of Berlin as a left-wing city. In East Germany's first free election in 1990, while the newly post-communist East Germans elected a Christian Democratic Union government (lured by the economic prospects offered by Chancellor Helmut Kohl's West German CDU regime), East Berlin gave fully two thirds of its vote to the Social Democrats, the Party of Democratic Socialism (the moderate successor party to East Germany's Communists), and other left-of-centre formations. Finally, and most recently, after a fifteen-year Christian Democratic city administration led by a popular if bland mayor, post-millennial Berlin voted into office a "Red-Red" coalition government of the SPD and PDS, headed by a social democratic mayor who, shortly before the election, casually announced that, by the way, he was gay "and it's okay."

The reason I point to all of this in some detail is because of the historian's problem I flagged earlier about the difficulty of locating the voice of the imaginary personage that is a city. If anything stands out in trying to determine what "Berlin thinks," it is the actual behaviour of its citizens at the polls on a series of occasions that extend more than a century. One could argue that the support for the left at the polls is merely a sort of rhetorical posturing rather than a reflection of the civic popular mentality, but I think that's a hard case to make. While voting is hardly the only measure of what a city thinks, the strikingly consistent pattern of Berlin's voting, and its contrast to the national pattern, certainly makes it a candidate for one of the foundational themes upon which to build the story of the city's history.

As Benjamin's angel of history knows, nothing can "awaken the dead, and make whole what has been smashed." But our stories ought to at least make sense of the swirling storm of progress that propels the angel into the future, while the wreckage of the catastrophe piles up at its feet.

Bibliography

I'm an inveterate reader of bibliographies and often, after reading just a few introductory pages of a book, I find myself turning to the bibliographical listings. Mostly, the bibliography is simply a handy list that shows what other and related works there are about a given subject. It's a place for scholarly rummaging. But sometimes, the bibliography is like an ocean in which one can not only survey the depth of sources from which the author has drawn, but upon which one can embark on a voyage of further reading.

I have fierce bibliographic preferences, as do other bibliography readers. In the case of multiple entries for an author, should the author's name be repeated, or is once enough, with subsequent entries indicating the author's name by a set of dashes? (Repeated, I say.) What if the date of writing is markedly different from date of publication? What to do about editors, translators, introducers? And how wonderful to have the rare luxury of an "annotated bibliography."

For a writer like me, there's a more practical relation to bibliographies. I notice that over the years my writing has become increasingly a tangled skein of bits and pieces of other authors' writing, a Talmudic interweaving of my own and others' commentaries, a text filled with quotes from and references to other texts. My books, like late-medieval chrestomathies, are a patchwork of books. So, here's a bibliography of the books and articles I cite or make use of in this book. Where the date of composition significantly differs from the publication cited, the date of writing is parenthetically noted first, followed by a semi-colon, and the standard publisher and date of publication notation. Occasionally, where they are germane, translators, editors, and introductions are noted. Many older titles cited are in the public domain and easily found online at http://onlinebooks.library.upenn.edu.

Michael Adams, *Fire and Ice* (Penguin, 2003)
Adonis, *The Pages of Day and Night* (tr. Samuel Hazo, Northwestern, 2000)
Adonis, *An Introduction to Arab Poetics* (Saqi, 2003)
Theodor Adorno, *Minima Moralia* (1951; Verso, 1974)
Giorgio Agamben, *Stanzas: Word and Phantasm in Western Culture* (1973; Minnesota, 1993)

Nelson Algren, *The Man With the Golden Arm* (1949; Seven Stories, 1999)

Don Allen (ed.), *The New American Poetry 1945-60* (Grove, 1960)

Woody Allen, *Side Effects* (Random House, 1980)

Hannah Arendt, *The Origins of Totalitarianism* (Meridian, 1958)

Marcus Aurelius, *Meditations* (c. 170 CE; Penguin, 1964)

Honoré de Balzac, *Pere Goriot* (1835; Oxford, 1999)

Benjamin Barber, *Jihad vs. McWorld* (Ballantine, 1996)

John Barber, "The Richard Brautigan Bibliography plus," www.brautigan.net

Roland Barthes, *Writing Degree Zero* (1953; Cape, 1967)

Roland Barthes, *Mythologies* (1957; Hill and Wang, 1972)

Roland Barthes, *The Pleasure of the Text* (Cape, 1976)

Roland Barthes, *Roland Barthes* (tr. Richard Howard, Hill and Wang, 1977)

Roland Barthes, *A Lover's Discourse* (tr. Richard Howard, Hill and Wang, 1979)

Roland Barthes, *Camera Lucida* (tr. Richard Howard, Hill and Wang, 1981)

L. Frank Baum, *The Wizard of Oz* (1900; Ann Arbor Media, 2003)

Simone de Beauvoir, *The Second Sex* (1949; Vintage, 1974)

Saul Bellow, *The Adventures of Augie March* (1953; Penguin, 1996)

Saul Bellow, *Ravelstein* (Viking, 2000)

Walter Benjamin, *Illuminations* (ed. Hannah Arendt, Schocken, 1969)

Walter Benjamin, *Reflections* (ed. Peter Demetz, Schocken, 1986)

Walter Benjamin, *The Arcades Project* (Harvard, 1999)

David Berg, *White Gestalt, Black Gestalt* (n.p., n.d.)

John Berger, *Ways of Seeing* (Penguin, 1972)

John Berger, *A Painter of Our Time* (1958; Random House, 1996)

John Berger, *G.* (Viking, 1972)

John Berger, *The Sense of Sight* (Pantheon, 1985)

John Berger, *Into Their Labours* (Penguin, 1992)

John Berger, *Photocopies* (Pantheon, 1997)

John Berger, *King* (Bloomsbury, 1999)

Eduard Bernstein, *Evolutionary Socialism* (1899; Schocken, 1963)

Robin Blaser, *The Holy Forest* (intro. Robert Creeley, Coach House, 1993)

Robin Blaser, *The Last Supper* (Boosey and Hawkes, 2000)

Harold Bloom, *The Western Canon* (Riverhead, 1994)

Boccaccio, *The Decameron* (c. 1350; Penguin, 2003)

George Bowering, *Burning Water* (Musson, 1980)

George Bowering, *Blondes on Bikes* (Talonbooks, 1997)

Jorge Luis Borges, *El hacedor* (Alianza, 1960)

Jorge Luis Borges, *The Total Library* (ed. Eliot Weinberger, Penguin, 2001)

Robert Brandom (ed.), *Rorty and His Critics* (Blackwell, 2000)

Richard Brautigan, *Trout Fishing in America* (1962; Dell, 1967)

Hugh Brody, *The People's Land* (Penguin, 1983)

Thomas Brussig, *Heroes Like Us* (Harvill, 1997)
Ian Buruma, "AsiaWorld," *New York Review of Books*, June 12, 2003

Italo Calvino, *Invisible Cities* (1972; tr. William Weaver, Minerva, 1997)
Italo Calvino, *If on a winter's night a traveller* (1979; Vintage, 2002)
Italo Calvino, *Mr. Palomar* (1983; Vintage, 1999)
Italo Calvino, *Six Memos for the Next Millennium* (1985; Vintage, 1996)
Italo Calvino, *Hermit in Paris* (Vintage, 2004)
Albert Camus, *The Plague* (Knopf, 1948)
Constantine Cavafy, *The Complete Poems* (tr. Rae Dalvan, intro. W.H. Auden, Harvest, 1976)
Adam Cohen and Elizabeth Taylor, *American Pharoah* (Little, Brown, 2000)
Robert Creeley, *For Love: Poems 1950-1960* (Scribner, 1962)
Douglas Crimp, *Melancholia and Moralism* (MIT, 2002)
Jonathan Culler, *Barthes* (Fontana, 1983)

Richard Henry Dana, *Two Years Before the Mast* (1840; Modern Library, 2001)
Dante Alighieri, *The Divine Comedy* (c. 1321; tr. C.H. Sisson, Oxford, 1998)
Daniel Defoe, *Journal of the Plague Year* (1722; Oxford, 1990)
Jacques Derrida, *The Work of Mourning* (ed. Pascale-Anne Brault and Michael Naas, University of Chicago, 2001)
Denis Diderot, *Jacques the Fatalist* (c. 1770; Oxford, 1999)
John Dixon, *Catastrophic Rights* (New Star, 1990)
Alfred Döblin, *Berlin Alexanderplatz* (1929; Ungar, 1983)
David Dollenmayer, *The Berlin Novels of Alfred Döblin* (University of California, 1988)
Robert Duncan, *The Opening of the Field* (1960; New Directions, 1973)
Marguerite Duras, *Practicalities* (HarperCollins, 1990)
Marguerite Duras, *The Lover* (Pantheon, 1985)

Laird Easton, *The Red Count: The Life and Times of Harry Kessler* (University of California, 2002)
Alan Ehrenhalt, *The Lost City* (Basic, 1995)
Lewis Ellingham and Kevin Killian, *Poet, Be Like God: Jack Spicer and the San Francisco Renaissance* (Wesleyan, 1998)
Clayton Eshleman, "The Lorca Working," *Boundary 2*, Fall 1977

Walter Farley, *The Black Stallion* (Random House, 1941)
Brian Fawcett, *The Secret Journal of Alexander Mackenzie* (Talonbooks, 1985)
Brian Fawcett, *Virtual Clearcut* (Thomas Allen, 2003)

Lisa Fittko, *Escape Through the Pyrenees* (Northwestern, 1991)
Gustave Flaubert, *Madame Bovary* (1857; Penguin, 2003)
E.M. Forster, *Maurice* (1913; Penguin, 2000)
E.M. Forster, *Pharos and Pharillon* (1923; Hogarth, 1967)
E.M. Forster, *Alexandria: A History and a Guide* (1938; Peter Smith, 2003)
Michel Foucault, *Madness and Civilization* (1961; Vintage, 1988)
Michel Foucault, *The Use of Pleasure* (1984; Vintage, 1990)
Ruth Franklin, "The Lost," *New Yorker*, Dec. 16, 2002
Sigmund Freud, *On Narcissism* (1914; Yale, 1991)
Milton Friedman, *Capitalism and Freedom* (University of Chicago, 1962)
Milton Friedman and Rose Friedman, *Free to Choose* (Harcourt, 1990)

Jean Genet, *Our Lady of the Flowers* (1943; Olympia, 1960)
André Gide, *Journals* (Northwestern, 1987)
Gilgamesh (tr. Stephen Mitchell, Free Press, 2004)
Anton Gill, *A Dance Between Flames* (John Murray, 1994)
Allen Ginsberg, *Howl* (City Lights, 1956)
Jacques Godbout, *Les Têtes à Papineau* (Seuil, 1981)
Günter Grass, *Too Far Afield* (Harvest, 2001)

James Herndon, *Sorrowless Times* (Simon and Schuster, 1981)
James Herndon, *Notes From a Schoolteacher* (Simon and Schuster, 1985)
Franz Hessel, *Unknown Berlin* (Rowohlt, 1927)
Charles Higham, *The Civilization of Angkor* (University of California, 2001)
Thomas Hobbes, *Leviathan* (1651; Penguin, 1982)

Christopher Isherwood, *Goodbye to Berlin* (1939; Minerva, 1989)
Christopher Isherwood, *Down There on a Visit* (1961; Minnesota, 1999)
Christopher Isherwood, *Christopher and His Kind* (1976; Minnesota, 2001)

James Joyce, *Ulysses* (1922; Penguin, 1992)

Jack Kerouac, *On The Road* (Viking, 1957)
Harry Kessler, *In the Twenties: The Diaries of Harry Kessler* (University of California, 1999)
August Kleinzahler, "No Light on in the House," *London Review of Books*, Dec. 14, 2000
Arthur Koestler, *Darkness at Noon* (1940; Bantam, 1984)
Tadeusz Konwicki, *A Minor Apocalypse* (Farrar, Straus and Giroux, 1983)
Larry Kramer, *Reports from the Holocaust* (St. Martin's, 1989)

R.D. Laing, *The Divided Self* (Tavistock, 1960)
David Clay Large, *Berlin* (Allen Lane, 2001; published in German as *Berlin: Biographie einer Stadt*, Beck, 2002)

Christopher Lasch, *The Culture of Narcissism* (Norton, 1974)
Primo Levi, *Survival in Auschwitz* (Free Press, 1961)
Primo Levi, *The Search for Roots* (1981; afterword Italo Calvino, Penguin, 2001)
Robert Liddell, *Cavafy* (Duckworth, 1974)
Herbert List, *Junge Männer* (intro. Stephen Spender, Twin Palms, 1988)
Jack London, *Call of the Wild* (1903; Penguin, 2004)
Jack London, *The Sea Wolf* (1904; Booksurge, 2004)
Jack London, *White Fang* (1905; Penguin, 2004)
Jack London, *The Iron Heel* (1908; Lawrence Hill, 1981)
Federico Garcia Lorca, *Selected Poems* (eds. Francisco Garcia Lorca and Donald Allen, New Directions, 1955)
Federico Garcia Lorca, *Poet in New York* (1930; Farrar, Straus and Giroux, 1998)

Alexander Mackenzie, *First Man West* (ed. Walter Sheppe, University of California 1962; Dover, 1996)
Subcommandante Marcos, *Our Weapon Is Our Word* (Seven Stories, 2000)
Tomás Eloy Martínez, *The Peron Novel* (Random House, 1989)
Tomás Eloy Martínez, *Santa Evita* (Doubleday, 1997)
Karl Marx and Friedrich Engels, *The Communist Manifesto* (1848; Signet, 1998)
Herman Melville, *Typee* (1846; Kessinger, 2004)
Herman Melville, *Moby Dick* (1851; Bantam 1981)
Wayne Miller, *Chicago's South Side, 1946-48* (University of California, 2000)
Czeslaw Milosz, *The Captive Mind* (Knopf, 1953)
Czeslaw Milosz, *A Treatise on Poetry* (1956; Ecco, 2001)
Czeslaw Milosz, *Native Realm* (1968; Farrar, Straus and Giroux, 2002)
Czeslaw Milosz, *Bells in Winter* (1978; Norton, 1996)
Czeslaw Milosz, *Road-side Dog* (Farrar, Straus and Giroux, 1998)
Czeslaw Milosz, *Milosz's ABC's* (Farrar, Straus and Giroux, 2001)
Czeslaw Milosz, *Collected Poems 1931-2001* (Ecco, 2003)
Paul Monette, *Borrowed Time: An AIDS Memoir* (Avon, 1988)
Paul Monette, *Love Alone* (St. Martin's, 1988)
Paul Monette, *Last Watch of the Night* (Harvest, 1995)
Mother Goose's Nursery Rhymes (1781; Everyman, 1993)

Thomas Nagel, *What Does It All Mean?* (Oxford, 1987)
Miriam Nichols (ed.), *Even on Sunday* (National Poetry Foundation, 2002)
Frank Norris, *The Pit* (1903; North, 2003)

Charles Olson, *The Maximus Poems* (University of California, 1995)
Charles Olson, *Selected Poems* (University of California, 1997)

George Orwell, *Homage to Catalonia* (1938; Penguin, 2003)
George Orwell, *Nineteen Eighty-Four* (1949; Penguin, 1990)
Ovid, *Metamorphoses* (1st century CE; Oxford, 1998)

Peter Paret, "Unter den Linden," *New York Times*, April 26, 1998
Bob Perelman, *The Marginalization of Poetry* (Princeton, 1996)
Fritz Perls, Paul Goodman, Ralph Hefferline, *Gestalt Therapy* (Bantam, 1977)
Stan Persky, *Wrestling the Angel* (Talonbooks, 1976)
Stan Persky, *Son of Socred* (New Star, 1979)
Stan Persky, *Buddy's: Meditations on Desire* (New Star, 1989, 1991)
Stan Persky, *Then We Take Berlin* (Knopf Canada, 1995)
Stan Persky, *Autobiography of a Tattoo* (New Star, 1997)
Fernando Pessoa, *Book of Disquiet* (1935; Serpent's Tail, 1991)
Plato, *The Symposium* (4th century BCE; Penguin, 1951)
Plato, *Apology*, in *Five Dialogues* (4th century BCE; Hackett, 2002)
Plato, *Crito*, in *Five Dialogues* (4th century BCE; Hackett, 2002)
Plato, *Phaedo* in *Five Dialogues* (4th century BCE; Hackett, 2002)
Plato, *Philebus* (4th century BCE; Penguin, 1982)
Plato, *The Republic* (4th century BCE; Penguin, 2003)
Ezra Pound, *The Cantos* (Norton, 1996)
Marcel Proust, *Swann's Way* (1913; Penguin 1957)
Marcel Proust, *Within a Budding Grove* (1913; Vintage, 1996)
Hilary Putnam, *Realism With A Human Face* (Harvard, 1990)

Anthony Read and David Fisher, *Berlin: The Biography of a City* (Pimlico, 1994)
Alexandra Richie, *Faust's Metropolis: A History of Berlin* (Carroll and Graf, 1998)
Richard Rorty, *Philosophy and the Mirror of Nature* (Princeton, 1981)
Richard Rorty, *Contingency, Irony, and Solidarity* (Cambridge, 1989)
Richard Rorty, *Truth and Progress* (Cambridge, 1998)
Richard Rorty, *Philosophy and Social Hope* (Penguin, 1999)
Philip Roth, *American Pastoral* (Vintage, 1998)
Jean-Jacques Rousseau, *The Social Contract* (1762; Penguin, 2004)
Mike Royko, *Boss* (Dutton, 1971)

William Saroyan, *The Daring Young Man on the Flying Trapeze* (1934; Norton, 1997)
Jean-Paul Sartre, *What Is Literature?* (1948; Routledge, 2001)
Jean-Paul Sartre, *Jean-Paul Sartre par lui-meme* (Seuil, 1959)
John Ralston Saul, *The Unconscious Civilization* (Anansi, 1995)
John Ralston Saul, *Reflections of a Siamese Twin* (Penguin, 1997)
Adam Schatz, "An Arab Poet Who Dares to Differ," *New York Times*, July 13, 2002

Bruno Schulz, *The Street of Crocodiles* (1934; Penguin, 1995)
Bruno Schulz, *Sanitorium Under the Sign of the Hourglass* (1937; Penguin, 1988)
Jorge Semprun, *Life or Literature* (Viking, 1997)
Randy Shilts, *And the Band Played On* (St. Martin's, 1987)
Charles Shively, ed., *Calamus Lovers: Walt Whitman's Working Class Camerados* (Gay Sunshine, 1987)
Upton Sinclair, *The Jungle* (1906; Bantam, 1990)
Sulak Sivaraksa, *Seeds of Peace* (Parallax, 1992)
Adam Smith, *The Wealth of Nations* (1776; Bantam, 2003)
Alexander Solzhenitsyn, *The Gulag Archipelago* (HarperCollins, 1974)
Stephen Spender, *The Temple* (1936; Grove, 1988)
Edmund Spenser, *The Faerie Queene* (c. 1590; Longman, 1980)
Jack Spicer, *After Lorca* (White Rabbit, 1957)
Jack Spicer, *Admonitions*, in *The Collected Books of Jack Spicer* (ed. Robin Blaser, Black Sparrow, 1975)
Jack Spicer, *A Book of Music*, in *The Collected Books of Jack Spicer* (ed. Robin Blaser, Black Sparrow, 1975)
Jack Spicer, *The Tower of Babel* (Talisman, 1994)
Duncan Sprott, "The Naked Civil Servant," *Guardian*, Aug. 14, 2004
George Stanley, *Opening Day* (Oolichan, 1983)
George Stanley, *Gentle Northern Summer* (New Star, 1995)
George Stanley, *At Andy's* (New Star, 2000)
George Steiner, *Grammars of Creation* (Yale, 2001)
Eugène Sue, *The Mysteries of Paris* (1843; Kessinger, 2004)

Herbert Terrace, *Nim* (Eyre Methuen, 1980)
Henry David Thoreau, *Walden* (1854; Princeton, 2004)
Jacobo Timerman, *The Longest War* (Knopf, 1982)
Herbert Tobias, *Fotografien 1950-1980* (Janssen, 1996)
John R. Tunis, *The Kid from Tomkinsville* (1940; Odyssey, 1989)
Joseph Tussman, *Obligation and the Body Politic* (Oxford, 1960)
Joseph Tussman, *Government and the Mind* (Oxford, 1978)

George Vancouver, *A Voyage of Discovery to the North Pacific Ocean and Round the World, 1791-1795* (1798; Hakluyt Society, 1999)
Jules Verne, *Twenty Thousand Leagues Under the Sea* (1870; Penguin, 1994)
Gore Vidal, "Calvino's Death," *New York Review of Books*, Nov. 21, 1985)
Gore Vidal, *Palimpsest* (Random House, 1995)
Voltaire, *Candide*, in *The Portable Voltaire* (1759; Penguin, 1977)

Charles Watts and Edward Byrne, eds., *The Recovery of the Public World: Essays on Poetics in Honour of Robin Blaser* (Talon, 1999)

Evelyn Waugh, *Brideshead Revisited* (Penguin, 1945)
Tom Wayman, *Selected Poems 1973-1993* (Harbour, 1993)
Edmund White, *The Farewell Symphony* (Random House, 1997)
Walt Whitman, *Leaves of Grass* (1855; Oxford, 1998)
Christa Wolf, *Accident* (Farrar, Straus and Giroux, 1989)
Clive Wynne, *Do Animals Think?* (Princeton, 2004)

Zhou Daguan, *The Customs of Cambodia* (c. 1297; Siam Society, 1993)

Birth

I *was born in Chicago in 1941*. A quarter-century later, a group of white Chicago musicians, the Paul Butterfield Blues Band, recorded a song, "Born in Chicago," in which that sentence, "I was born in Chicago in 1941," repeated twice, provides the opening lines of their blues anthem.

I was born in Chicago, in 1941, on January 19, a Sunday morning at about 3 a.m., into the hands of the attending physician at Lutheran Deaconess Hospital, Dr. Nathan Kane, my Uncle Docky. Actually, he was my mother Ida's uncle, and therefore my great-uncle; his wife, Dora, a sister of my mother's mother, was my great-aunt. Before she became Dora Kane, she and my maternal grandmother had shared the family name of Alpert — I eventually saw photos of the patriarch, Sam Alpert — but my mother's maiden name, acquired from her mother's married name, was Malis, itself probably an immigrant's abbreviation of something like Malinowski. This gradually exfoliating genealogy seemed to me more a tangled vineyard than a family tree.

It was a horrendously long labour for my mother, some forty hours. The story of my prolonged birth, occurring only after my mother had endured three previous miscarriages, and told to me variously by several relatives, is the founding episode of the legend of my life. "You almost killed your mother," they would say, laughing because the story had a happy outcome.

By the year of my birth, France had already fallen to the Nazis in World War II; by the end of the year, the Japanese attacked Pearl Harbour. One side-effect of my arrival — again, this is a vaguely recalled family tale — is that it may have exempted my father, Morrie, who was almost forty, from military service in the war, thanks to a regulation by which men of a certain age who were parents couldn't be drafted. Though I was my father's son, my birth belonged solely to my mother.

Yet, she was but an affectionate stranger to me through my childhood. She was an utter paragon of the virtues recorded on the gravestones I saw when we made periodic Sunday visits to the cemetery to pay homage to the family dead: dutiful daughter, loving wife, devoted mother. And the next day, during her regular round of telephone calls to her sisters-in-law — Rose, Lily and Pearl, the wives of her three brothers — I'd hear her reporting that "we were at the cemetery yesterday."

I was puzzled by her and by most of her family. Not by Uncle Docky and Aunt Dora, though. He was a lean, severe, ramrod-straight man with silver hair, politically a left-winger. Often, before the Friday (or occasionally Saturday) night dinners at their house, sitting in the living room and listening to the sonorous bass voice of radio newscaster H.V. Kaltenborn, intoning, "There's gooood news tonight," or gravely announcing "bad news tonight," some item in the broadcast would provoke an escalating, angry discussion that centred around my Uncle Docky and ended with someone, his son Herbie or his daughter Marge's husband, Harry, shouting, "Well, if you think it's so great there, then go back to Russia!"

On some Saturday afternoons, my mother and I went to Aunt Dora's to join her and her daughter as they prepared the meal for that evening. The radio brought us music from the Metropolitan Opera in New York, and during a lull in the cooking, the women would repair to the dining room table for a few hands of canasta. Among the treats that Aunt Dora prepared were *gribinets*, as they were called in Yiddish, the bits of crusted chicken skin left from rendering the chicken fat to make *schmaltz*, and a sweetroll she baked in the oven, *kickels*, an airy, crisp, tan-coloured confection covered with speckles of sugar.

Aunt Dora is the one who is clearest in my mind. I see the pouches under her melancholy eyes as she dries her hands on her apron (do people still wear aprons at home when they're cooking?) while going to answer the doorbell. One night, just before dinner, was it in 1945?, when the bell rang — Marge's husband Harry or my father were expected, back "from work" — I announced presciently, "It's Herbie." The genius of four-year-old babes was confirmed when it turned out that Uncle Docky's and Aunt Dora's son Herbie had been discharged from the Army a couple of days early, and was now at last home from the War, a big stolid man still dressed in his military uniform. I glimpsed Aunt Dora, as she rushed from the kitchen toward the apartment foyer, closed off from both the dining room and the living room by doors with small glass panels, drying her hands on her apron, her eyes welling with tears as her medal-decorated son came up the stairs.

After dinner and the clearing away of plates, the family would remain around the table for a friendly but loud game of penny-ante poker. Noticing her reluctance, while they played, to enjoy the pleasure of a cigarette — for obscure reasons of economy, connected to memories of the Depression of the 1930s — Marge or Herbie would press upon Aunt Dora one of their own. And when she reluctantly accepted a long Pall Mall from one of them, she would cut it in half with a scissors, saving one half and announcing, "I'll smoke it later," pronouncing the word, with a Yiddish accent, as *schmoke*. While they slapped their cards on the table, and impatiently urged each other to, "Play, play already," I crawled amid the animal-claw legs of the mahogany table, and fell asleep at their feet, only to briefly half-awaken in my father's arms later as he and my mother walked to the car for the ride home.

But the rest of my mother's family, her brothers and sisters-in-law and their children, and my mother herself, were a puzzle to me. Her family bored me, and I quickly learned that I didn't have much capacity for that kind of boredom. I didn't understand their interests or passions — mostly connected to businesses like currency exchanges, insurance companies, accounting, and grocery stores — and instead identified with the many brothers, sisters, and offspring of my father's side of the family, who were raucous bohemians, or at least interested in books, conversation, stories, tall-tales. My mother's stories, on the other hand, came from the radio soap-operas during the day, and the occasional *True Romance* magazine. Who were these people? I wondered about her and her family. At one point I must have actually voiced that question to my father, who gently explained to me that all of her relatives were part of the package that came with my mother, whom he after all loved, and who loved us. The important thing, he indicated, was to navigate these relations with a sort of social courtesy or, as he put it, "Even if you don't like them, at least you can be a *mensch*, and have a drink with them."

It was from my father that I tacitly learned a lesson about love, a rather terrible lesson: that *for love* (to recall the title of Robert Creeley's book), I might have to become intellectually discreet, that I might love someone with whom I couldn't fully share my thoughts, with whom I couldn't talk about certain things because they wouldn't understand them.

My father was an intellectual. He read books, thought about the cosmos, engaged me in serious conversation. On his rare holidays from work, he would spend his free time reading. With the autodidact's eccentric sense of selection, he read anything from Eugène Sue's *Mysteries of Paris* to the six-volume official history of the Mormon Church that he'd bought in Salt Lake City during our trip to the West Coast when I was thirteen. In the mornings, as I was getting ready for school, I'd find him at the dining room table, head on his arms, asleep after a night of reading, surrounded by books, an overflowing ashtray, and the little tin coffee percolator with its cut-glass knob that showed you when the coffee had fully perked.

Something traumatic had happened to him before my birth. I only have a sketchy version of the story. It had happened during the Depression, which was the always recurrent, and for me mysterious, reference point upon which were founded all economic warnings of the present. ("Money doesn't grow on trees, you know," someone would intone, and then launch into a tale of the unimaginable deprivations of the Depression.) The Depression, which was the great issue of my parents' generation, is now almost completely forgotten — as are issues that were contentious during most of my lifetime — but in my childhood its resonance was immense.

During the Depression of the 1930s, when my father was in his twenties, he had been on the road, riding the boxcars, living in hobo camps, bumming around. The road had led to youthful trouble, and the trouble — something about safecracking (the story was kept from me until my twenties) — involved a several-year stretch in jail. When he returned home, he made a decision, essentially to save his life. The decision was his compromise with society. The package included marriage to the unmarried, late 20-something niece of Uncle Docky and Aunt Dora, and help into small business from her family, some of whom were the owners of prosperous wartime grocery and meat markets. The prosperity, I recall from family anecdotes to which I inattentively listened, was dependent on access to fresh meat supplies beyond the officially rationed quotas.

That decision provided my father with social stability, however economically shaky, but more importantly, with love, which was a mystery to me. Love, I learned, entailed intellectual sacrifices. My father was interested in the abstract questions and aesthetics I was interested in, but he couldn't talk about them with my mother, or with her family. His learning, insofar as it involved them, was reserved for something like parlour-trick displays of bits of knowledge. This disjunction between what was on his mind and real life was connected to the need for love. Or at least this is the way I perceived it. Although I wasn't conscious of how deeply I absorbed this model of affection while an adolescent, as soon as I entered into similar relations of my own, I saw that in some (neo-Freudian) fashion, I tended to reproduce the model of my father's idea of love. More often than not the beloved other was someone "simpler" than myself, someone whose reciprocal love for me included the loving respect for my intellectual complexity, a prowess they could recognize but not fully participate in.

It is that experience of love, I think, that makes me recognize (and resist) the partial truth in the more contemporary feminist demand for egalitarian love relationships, a demand I've always felt a trace of guilt about ever since I first heard it. We should love and be loved only by those who are our social, generational, economic, and intellectual equals, the feminists propose. But that is not the world I was given.

My mother had another, final miscarriage when I was four, after which she was told, by my Uncle Docky, that any further pregnancy would be life-threatening. While she was in the hospital and even after she came home to recuperate, Alice, a black cleaning woman, was hired to come every day to keep house, cook, and babysit me. After my mother recovered sufficiently to resume her domestic duties, Alice was kept on to help with the housecleaning on a weekly basis.

Her great effect upon my life was based upon an innocent lie she told that instilled in me a perpetual anticipation. One afternoon, after finishing her work, perhaps in response to a desire I'd voiced, Alice told me, "Child, next week I'm going to bring you a puppy dog." The next week, I awaited her arrival with unbearable expectation. But there was no puppy dog. The puppy was still in transit, the puppy was getting its shots, the puppy would surely arrive the following week. The amazing thing is that I never figured it out. Every week I awaited Alice's arrival with puppy-like enthusiasm, expecting her to bring the dog.

After her miscarriage, my mother increasingly retreated from my view, a semi-invalid wracked by severe diabetes and associated ailments. She died in her mid-fifties, in 1965. I was living in San Francisco and flew home to be with my father for the funeral and the period of several days that followed of the Jewish ceremony of sitting *shiva* for the dead. It was the year that the Paul Butterfield Blues Band recorded "Born in Chicago," but on the airplane to Chicago, a current sentimental ditty that went, "Mrs. Brown, you've got a lovely daughter" turned in my mind. I thought of my mother, with her enclosed, blameless, physically-painful life now over, as Mrs. Brown's lovely daughter.

So, I didn't really know the woman from whose body I was born. But if I didn't know her, I retained the songs I learned, so to speak, at my mother's knee. They were mostly tunes by Sophie Tucker, a hefty nightclub singer then in the waning days of her career, but who was still billed as the "Last of the Red Hot Mamas." My mother also crooned snippets of Yiddish tunes that had filtered into the American culture of middle-class Jews. Among the songs my mother sang were *Bei Mir bist Du Schön* ("To Me, You're Beautiful"), Tucker's version of "St. Louis Woman," and "The Anniversary Waltz" ("Oh, how we danced / On the night / we were wed . . ."). But the one that most often comes to mind — perhaps her muted call for recognition, valorization — was "Some of These Days," which went, "Some of these days / You're gonna miss me, honey."

That's the word I was looking for in looking for my mother among my vocabularies: "Honey."

Robin Blaser

I

My first encounter with Robin Blaser's poetry was in 1960. I was a 19-year-old sailor stationed at the American naval air base at Capodichino, Italy, a few kilometres outside of Naples. Harold and Dora Dull, a couple from the San Francisco poetry scene, whom I'd met the year before at Sunday afternoon poets' meetings there, had arrived for a sojourn in Europe. They were staying at a small fishing village, Amalfitano, along the Amalfi coast just south of the bay of Naples. On Friday afternoons, I left the military base and took the bus from Naples to spend the weekend with them. Later, in easy stages, they made their way north, to Rome, Florence, Paris, with me tagging along in their wake, and eventually they temporarily settled on the island of Ibiza, where Dora gave birth to twin girls.

Harold and Dora were six or seven years older than me, old enough for me to adopt them as putative modernist parents or elder siblings. They introduced me to music, paintings, museums, churches, books, thought — in short, civilization — in all the places I visited them. Amalfitano, on the Mediterranean Sea, consisted of narrow lanes and jumbled houses clinging to the vertiginous cliffs just back of the beaches, where fishermen mended their nets and sorted the catch.

The first weekend I arrived at the eyrie they'd rented above the sea, Harold handed me a mimeographed copy of a recently-written sequence of poems that he'd brought from San Francisco. It was by Robin Blaser, a San Francisco poet who had been living in Boston and working as a librarian at Harvard. I knew of him only from talk in San Francisco that placed him as one of a literary threesome that included Jack Spicer and Robert Duncan. They had all been classmates at the University of California in Berkeley at the end of World War II.

The booklet Harold handed me was called *Cups* and contained the breakthrough poem Blaser had written almost immediately upon his return to San Francisco. It was also his first "serial" poem, the form Jack Spicer had invented a couple of years earlier in his book *After Lorca*. Like Spicer's book, *Cups* marked a crucial stage of transition in a poet's life. It is the moment when you go from being someone who writes poems, quite good poems even, to being a poet.

Right at the outset of *Cups*, Blaser introduces one of the poem's predominant themes, the art of poetry itself. It's a familiar theme in poetry, but in this case it's an art made in oppositional friendship:

> There were two.
> Their posture
> taken out of the wall-
> paper (a ghost story)
> Jack talked.   His
> determined privacy against
> My public face.   The poem
> by dictation . . .

The relationship of the "two" is encoded in a kind of shorthand, bearing traces and notations of private biographical references, such as the wallpaper at a communal house where they had lived as students. But there's an immediate opposition in their "posture." One's "determined privacy" against the other's "public face," is resolved, however, in the agreement on "The poem / by dictation." The idea is the Orphic notion that the poem is transmitted from some unidentified outside source through the poet, and although it makes use of the poet's own vocabulary, biographical details, etc. (what Spicer called "the furniture in the room"), the poet is not permitted to interfere with the "dictation." Whether this theory of poetry is true, I quickly learned, matters less than the fact that Spicer and Blaser used it as their working procedure, as their "myth."

The first part of *Cups*, like most of the succeeding ones in the serial, ends in a semi-rhymed, musical language:

> The clown of dignity sits in a tree.
> The clown of games hangs there too.
> Which is which or where they go —
> the point is to make others see
> that two men in a tree is clearly
> the same thing as poetry.

The two men are Jack Spicer and Blaser himself, and the poem traces the narrative of their art. They appear in their respective, characteristic guises, Blaser with his notion of dignity, Spicer with his love of games, both of them clowns, but more importantly, both of them in the tree, which is "clearly / the same thing as poetry."

The other themes of *Cups*, the title of which refers to one of the suits in a pack of Tarot cards, include the shifting figure of Amor, under whose sign the poets work. As well, the poem is about erotic desire itself — ". . . the comical physical union / their arms like briars / wrapped around" — and the sources of the poet's vocabulary. In Blaser's case, the sources were the scenes of his boyhood, the arid landscapes of rural Idaho in the 1930s, with its sere gullies and desolate railroad tracks.

In Blaser's poetry, I quickly learned, it is characteristic that some sight from the mundane world is seen as a "marvel," or some object, like a cup, is looked into until it spills out: "This / time I saw the god / offer with out-stretched hand / the heart to be devoured. The / lake flowed into my hands. / Dante would say the lake / of the heart." But throughout, the ballad-like passages, reminiscent of rhymes in a children's book, are subverted by an unsentimental realism. The romance of desire becomes the "comical physical union" of actual sex. Our behaviour, as poets and lovers, is farcical: "Two men sit in a tree / and wink and spit." Yet ". . . this is the tree / where Amor sits," and it is gift-giving Amor who lays down the "rules" of the game.

Both the landscape and memory of Blaser's childhood emerge from the metric narrative. The "shadow of the sagebrush / turns the hill blue . . ." in the place where Blaser grew up. Robin's Uncle Mitch writes Westerns and whistles between fragmented sentences, invoking an older history of the American frontier, its aboriginal inhabitants, and the rider-scout-guide "who leads us out." Even as Blaser is riding a bus in present day San Francisco, casually aware of the passing sexual desire aroused in a crosstown trip, his awareness is crosscut by the memory of amorous beginnings. In the sexual darkness of youth in the Idaho outback, there is the "effort to untie the strings / of the loins. The lips endure / the semen of strangers." Although the poem assumes homoeroticism, it doesn't insist on sexual preference. More important is the relation between Amor, the body, and poetry. "Where Amor sits," the poem says, "the body renews itself, / twists / inhabits the rights of poetry." Throughout it all:

Two men sit in a tree.
How ugly they are
in the bright eye
of this pageantry.
In service to love
is dignity, one cried,
1, 2, 3, the other replied,
you're out
when the dew falls from imagination's dark.

Amor turned geometer,
briefly, of course,

and cut their bodies into triangular parts.
When reassembled
they hung in that tree,
their genitals placed
where their heads should be.

If poetry is the "pageantry," the poets are ugly, which is to say,
merely human, as they spout their maxims about our undignified
efforts to maintain our dignity in desire or recite the rule in baseball
about three strikes and "you're out." For their trouble, the self-decep-
tions of desire leave them with their genitals placed "where their
heads should be." Images of incestuous desire, sexual mutilation, and
jokes about bestiality and the like, all of which turn up in *Cups*, are
the turnings back and forth of language and desire. The children's
rhymes function as metamorphoses: so, "The dew fell from imagination's dark / on to our hands where it stuck like bark," and later,

What falls from the tree
renews itself in the guise
of poetry.
        The guide
rides out of the dark
with a body shaped
from the sluffing bark.

I'd learned to "read" poetry only the year before, at the poets' Sunday afternoon meetings in San Francisco presided over by my teacher,
Jack Spicer. Through listening to and observing what excited the
poets' interest, I quickly got an idea of what poetry was about, and
soon I was writing some poems of my own. Now, above the Mediterranean, with Harold and Dora vicariously sharing my pleasure, I
immediately recognized Blaser's shape-shifting poem about the intersections of myth and memory, of poetry and desire. I got it, and I also
got the point of it as a serial poem, as I had with Spicer's *After Lorca*.
    The idea of the serial poem came, I'm pretty sure, from the serials
shown before the main feature at the movies that I'd seen as a kid in
the 1940s and 50s. They were often Westerns, and each episode
advanced the narrative, but ended in a "cliffhanger," so you had to
come back the following week to see what happened next. Similarly,
each poem in the serial has to stand on its own, and yet integrally
connect to the other poems that make up the "book." The individual
poems are at once independent episodes but, as Spicer had put it, they
"should echo and reecho against each other. They should create resonances." This unusual definition of a book and the insistence on the

coherence of the basic unit of composition was one of the things that marked off the San Francisco poets both from the so-called academic poetry of the period, and from other groups in the emerging movement known as the "New American Poetry." At the moment of reading *Cups*, though, what I principally got was the excitement of the poems, and the echo of Harold and Dora's approval of my being excited.

Cups may have initiated my interest in Dante, or perhaps I found the Italian master through Harold, who had considerable facility with language and was learning to read the 14th century poet's *Commedia* in the original. In any case, I, too, soon encountered Dante's *lago del cuore*, "the lake of the heart" that appeared in Blaser's *Cups*. But thinking of the fishermen at Amalfitano, I wrote,

It was not *the lake of the heart*
it was the load
taken from the sea
and the seen is not enough
to know the poetry. For that
you have to go
into the poet's country
which is a darkling wood . . .

thus, echoing, as so many poets have, Dante's *mi retrovai in una selva oscura* ("I found myself in a dark wood") in the first canto of *The Inferno*.

II

When I returned to San Francisco in January 1962, I found Jack Spicer sitting on a barstool at Gino and Carlo's on Green Street in North Beach, and brought him my poem, "Lake," upon which he promptly placed his imprimatur. He shyly clapped me on the back and proclaimed it "the best poem anyone around here has written in two years," a double-edged compliment in that it was also meant to chastise those poets who had been lazing about not writing the best poem in the last two years. Though I was pleased by my master's approval, sitting in the half-deserted bar on a chilly January night, it looked like a long winter ahead.

Spicer mentioned that Robin Blaser was in town, back from Boston. As much to relieve Spicer's boredom and to forestall his complaints that "no one was coming around to the bar," I suggested that we call Blaser up and get him to join us in Gino's.

"Oh no, Robin never comes out to the bar," Spicer groused.

"He will if I call him," the arrogance of youth replied.

Spicer bet me a quarter I couldn't get Blaser down to the bar, and even supplied me with the nickel for the telephone call.

"Hi," I said to Blaser, giving my name and announcing, "I'm 21 years old, I've just come back from the Navy, and I'm here in Gino's with Jack Spicer. Jack says you don't come out to the bar, but I told him he's wrong. So why don't you come down here and have a drink with us like a regular guy?" Utterly shameless. But what does youth have to trade on but youth? That, and the fact that, after all, "regular guys" got together for drinks, didn't they?

In about half an hour Blaser appeared in the doorway of Gino's. Jack paid off his bet, which he no doubt considered a bargain, given the entertainment value of having Blaser in the bar. For his part, Blaser acted as though, on the one hand, he'd been invited to a chic cocktail party which he was longing to attend, and on the other, that having a drink in Gino's is what regular guys did all the time.

Blaser was a trim man, in his mid-thirties, with an aquiline nose, high cheekbones, and a careful brush-cut. He was one of those people who, while gawky as a youth, becomes strikingly handsome as an adult, and distinguished-looking as an elder. There was a slightly fey edge to him, but he was unlike full-fledged homosexual queens I'd met who enacted the wounded bitterness found in much of camp behaviour. Rather, Blaser's manner derived from an older connection to the world of faerie, as he called it in a subsequent poem he'd written that played on Edmund Spenser's *Faerie Queene*. In any case, Spicer had the satisfaction of an entertaining evening in an otherwise desolate bar, I got to meet the author of *Cups*, and we had our drinks. Robin walked me home.

Blaser and I soon began a relationship, and we lived together for about five years, eventually moving from San Francisco to Vancouver in 1966, the year after Spicer's death, where Blaser became a professor at Simon Fraser University. I intend to draw the proverbial curtain around our private life, treating it as simply that, private. I have no intimate and/or scandalous gossip to retail here. If there are any personal details to reveal, they'll be relevant to my main subject, Blaser's poetry. I can say of my part of the relationship that I was often thoughtless in the way people in their twenties can be, but didn't cause, I think, any lasting damage. More important, more than thirty years later, Blaser and I remain intimate friends, who happen to live less than a block from each other in Vancouver. In various book inscriptions, dedications, and notes from him, I'm always regarded as a *companion du voyage*, attended by "love, of course."

What remains, from the clutter of the personal and the orders of the places where we lived, are the poems. While I would turn out to be something of a loner, Blaser was by temperament inclined toward the domestic. His ideal working condition as a poet included the rustle of the other person, or even the roar of the televised crowd as I sprawled in the next room watching a Sunday afternoon football game while he "fumed," as he described it, over a poem at the book-cluttered kitchen table. Both the companion and the house — a series of friends and apartments and houses, on Baker Street, Bernal Heights, and Allen Street in San Francisco, and on 1st Avenue, then Trafalgar Street in Vancouver — were central to his way of life. While my basic mode of habitation is the more or less anonymous hotel room, something close to Jack Spicer's shabby rented rooms, Blaser introduced me to the magic of the household.

As visitors to all of Blaser's domiciles immediately remark, sometimes jokingly referring to them as "museums," the house for him is an order of objects, art, furniture, carpets, books, each deliberately chosen and arranged, so that their inter-relations set up a sort of field of activity. The old notion of household gods is treated literally.

The house is connected to the outside by way of the garden, whose trees and flowers Blaser tends, and from which he brings into the house buds of willow, blue irises, branches of pepper tree and other blossoms that appear in his work. In one poem, Blaser refers to a blue bottle in the shape of a goddess, into whose open head he inserted a stalk of daphne one day. The unmistakeable sweet scent of the daphne plant had filled the house by the time we returned late that night, an event which Blaser reads in a poem as "giving power" over the house to the goddess. Again, whether or not such magic is "true" in a conventional sense, it should, like "the poem / by dictation," be regarded as a working procedure.

Finally, beyond the garden, which is the domestic representation of nature and part of the larger entity Blaser calls "the holy forest," there is the city. With its buildings looming out of the fog of San Francisco, or its downtown towers perched on a peninsula amid the "burning water" of Vancouver's Burrard Inlet, the "city" is connected to notions of community and the public realm, the political themes of Blaser's poetry. The actual city is shadowed by the historical notion of the Greek *polis*, an urban space defined by the active engagement of its *polites* or citizens. In fact, all of these — house, garden and city, sometimes the whole of it a holy forest — have to be seen as both specifics and categories in Blaser's ordering of the world.

It was a strange event in the house that inspired Blaser's book, *The Moth Poem*. One day in 1962, in his Baker Street apartment in San Francisco, he heard an eerie sound emanating from the baby grand piano, as if the instrument itself was playing. When he lifted the lid of the piano, he discovered the source of the sound, a moth trapped in the piano strings. The moth was duly rescued and the poem began. Once the first moth appeared, so did others, over a year or more, inexplicably turning up in the most unexpected ways, to provide the images or metaphors upon which successive poems in the serial were predicated.

If the appearances of the moths were a kind of "magic," as Spicer and Blaser used that term, nonetheless, Blaser insisted on identifying himself as a "literalist," as the titles of the first two poems in the series put it. I.e., it really happened.

> the moth in the piano
> will play on
> frightened wings brush
> the wired interior
> of that machine

> I said, 'master'

One of the differences between poetry and prose is that the lines of poetry function as "doubles," bearing the meaning contained in the line — the moth in the piano "will play on," that is, will continue to play, whether one reads the moth as simply a literal creature or a representation of the poet — as well as the meanings extended by succeeding lines. The moth in the piano "will play on / frightened wings ..." And "frightened wings brush / the wired interior / of that machine." This fleeting reminder of why poems have lines is the most fundamental element of the art, yet it's a point seldom made in schools, leaving students puzzled about how the poem tells multiple stories.

The story of *The Moth Poem* is of a man and his episodic encounters with the emphemeral meaning of the world, embodied in the figure of moths. At its core is the narrative of the "medium" in a world of language, moth-wings, house, holy forest, and the politics of the city. Blaser says in "The Medium,"

> it is essentially reluctance   the language
> a darkness, a friendship, tying to the real
> but it is unreal

> the clarity desired, a wish for true sight,
> all tangling

> 'you' tried me, the everyday which
> caught me, turning the house

in the wind, a lovecraft   the political
was not my business   I could not look

without seeing the decay, the shit poured
on most things, by indifference, the personal

power which is simply that, ...

Poetry's language, Blaser asserts, is essentially a "reluctance"; the art of it is neither easy nor simple. The language is a "darkness," yet it is also a "friendship," tying us to the "real" world, but as throughout this dialectic of assertion and denial, the real is also "unreal." The desire for clarity and "true sight" is tangled, and we are "tried," tested, by the forces, both literal and metaphoric, that shape our lives.

In "The Medium," Blaser makes one of his first uses of a pronominal figure, the second person singular placed in single quote-marks, 'you', which will reappear throughout his life's work. While the word *you* (without quotes) is used in conventional ways to address another person or to reflexively refer to oneself, 'you' in single quotes becomes a god or spirit of otherness. Like other figures in Blaser's poetry, 'you' is a shape-shifting entity, whose apparitions range from simply the other person in the sense of his or her separateness from ourselves, to an embodied figure in one of Blaser's late works, an opera libretto called *The Last Supper* (2000), where the 'you' is a woman who is the ghost of the 20th century addressing the audience:

I am the ghost of you,
of your century,
of your courage,
in the fragments
of our paradise
I can see myself in your eyes.

While Blaser is a poet who envisions a fragmented paradise, embodied in the marvels of literal objects and events, this possibility is consistently juxtaposed against the actual political world. As the ghost says to the public of *The Last Supper*, "... each of us, / a bare thing, swims / against the brutality and terror / of our century." Although Blaser's poetry is remarkable for its beauty, even its "poetical" qualities, the magic of the real always appears within the context of a 20th century of war, genocide, and exclusions. It is not at all inconsistent when the Christ in Blaser's libretto declares, "The Holocaust shattered my heart," offering the naked apology that the Roman Catholic Church, which claims to operate in Christ's name, was unable to pronounce, even a half-century after the murder of European Jewry.

"The Medium" was written one weekend while we were staying at a friend's summer cabin on the Russian River, north of San Francisco. That night, says the poem,

                              . . . I slept
in a fire   on my book bag, one dried wing

of a white moth   the story is of a man
who lost his way in the holy wood

"Lost," the poem says, "because the way had never been taken without / at least two friends, one on each side," an oblique reference to Spicer and Robert Duncan, their long friendship now strained by quarrels over poetry and flare-ups of personality. Friendship gone astray, so that Blaser is

    . . . now left to acknowledge

he can't breathe, the darkness bled
the white wing,   one   of the body

of the moth that moved him, of the other
wing,   the language is bereft

Repeatedly, in a poem that argues that art and intelligence are as perilous as the lives of moths, these creatures reappear, tapping against a window with the sound of "it it it it," and evoking immediate scenes as well as a childhood past replete with remembered grandmothers. As a moth "tacked with the wind's changes, / careened, then, taking flight, hid / in the fig tree" of the garden, it is encircled by the larger cosmos, "the moon, the stars, the / planets and below, under the earth"; equally, the sound of the moth in the piano becomes "a tone / beyond that, the lyre," until the mind of the poet-priest is "nearly destroyed by the presences, the fine / points which have no beginning." The moments caught by *The Moth Poem* are precise miniatures, the poems of modest size, but the poetry is large.

At the end, in a sort of epilogue called "The Translator: A Tale," Blaser is translating Catullus's "Attis" one morning. He notices that

last night's coffee spoon sticks to the drainboard
under it the clear print of a brown moth, made of sugar,

cream, coffee with chicory, and a Mexican spoon of blue
and white enamel

The ashtray is full and should be emptied before working that translation, *Attis ran to the wooded pastures ...*

Instead, the ashtray is neglected while the poet translates from the
Latin of Catullus's gender-shifting poem, only to produce a final
epiphany:

the mound of cigarette butts moves,   the ashes shift,
fall back on themselves like sand,   startle   out of
the ashes, awakened by my burning cigarette, a brown
moth noses its way,   takes flight

Even as he was concluding *The Moth Poem* with a last magical
appearance of a moth rising from the full ashtray, a virtual phoenix,
Blaser had already embarked upon a new, but different kind of serial
poem. *Image-Nations*, the first of which were written in the midst of
the previous composition, is an intermittent, rather than consecutive
poem, one that would continue, concurrent with other poems, over
the next three and a half decades. This kind of serial poem was not
without its precursors in San Francisco. In Robert Duncan's book,
The Opening of the Field, which had appeared in 1960, a similar
serial, "The Structure of Rime," begins with eloquent bravado:

I ask the unyielding Sentence that shows Itself forth in the
language as I make it,

Speak! For I name myself your master, who come to
serve.
Writing is first a search in obedience.

For all the disputes of local friendship — the bitchiness, bitter gossip, the feuds — the San Francisco poets of the early 1960s were
indisputably engaged in a community of poetry. If the poems within a
given serial poem resonated against each other, it can be equally said
that the poems and books, the work of various poets — Duncan,
Blaser, Spicer, but others such as George Stanley, Harold Dull, Joanne
Kyger and Ebbe Borregard as well — also resonated with and against
each other in this West Coast city that was easily seen as a double-
city. There was the visible one whose streets, hills, and business
canyons we walked, and the invisible city that bound us both to con-

temporary poets across the country — Charles Olson, Robert Creeley, Allen Ginsberg, Frank O'Hara and others — who were part of
the "New American Poetry," as well as across time, to poets in various lineages of a tradition that extended back from the preceding
generation of modernists to the first bards.

In a 1968 essay, "The Fire," Blaser expounded upon the San Francisco variant of this poetry. "I'm interested in a particular kind of narrative," he says, what Spicer and he had agreed to call the serial poem,
"a narrative which refuses to adopt an imposed story line, and com-
pletes itself only in the sequence of poems, if, in fact, a reader insists
upon a definition of completion which is separate from the activity of
the poems themselves. The poems tend to act as a sequence of energies
which run out when so much of a tale is told." Blaser describes this
"in Ovidean terms, as a *carmen perpetuum*, a continuous song in
which the fragmented subject matter is only apparently discon-
nected." Ovid's words, as Blaser cites them in his own translation, are

> to tell of bodies
> transformed
> into new shapes
> you gods, whose power
> worked all transformations,
> helped the poet's breathing,
> lead my continuous song
> from the beginning to the present world

There's a reason for spelling all this out, about Blaser, Spicer and
others, which has to do with how I see poetry. None of this account
would make much sense unless I believed, as I do, that poetry is a
mode of experience in the world that cannot be subsumed by the other
modes of language, namely, story, discourse, and the mathematical
languages of science. Because, at the beginning of the 21st century,
poetry has been utterly marginalized in the culture in which I live, it
becomes imperative to leave future readers, if there are any, with at
least an echo of an indispensable experience which the present forces
of the world would dispense with and erase. There is nothing outside
of ourselves to require the existence of a mode of experience. That's
especially true under conditions of the decreasing communicability of
that experience, and in a world where the value of such experience has
been debased. So, poetry can be lost, and if not yet lost, is imperilled.

Blaser's *Image-Nations*, which obviously plays on the notion of
"imagination" while demarcating its visual and political elements as
"image-nations," begin with a sense of such peril, when he declares,
"the participation is broken":

that matter of language caught
in the fact   so that we
meet in paradise   in such
times, the I consumes itself

Although subsequent "Image-Nations" will enter more complex
and difficult structures of meaning, the first poems of this continuing
series retain the guise of children's tales, albeit for adults, given the
density of thought, and a narrative that defies prosaic paraphrase.

With *Image-Nations* underway, and *The Moth Poem* completed,
Blaser embarked on a project of translation, the creation of an English-language version of the 19th century mystical poet Gérard de
Nerval's *Les Chimères*. At the centre of this poem, whose eponymous
metaphor of apparitional appearances Blaser would have a natural
affinity for, is a several part poem called "Christ Among the Olives."
The premise of the poem — both Nerval's and Blaser's version of it —
is rooted in the debased spiritual condition of the times.

In Nerval's poem, Christ speaks in a spiritually dead world "whose
shadow is the emptiness." It is Christ himself who is bereft: "seeking
the eye of God / I saw only a socket, / huge, black and bottomless,"
inhabited by night. In a world where "no one heard the grief of the
sacrifice," Christ calls upon Judas, the "only one / awake in
Jerusalem." As in Blaser's later *Last Supper*, the betrayal of Christ is
found in the indifference of those who claim to be faithful rather than
in Judas's "crime . . . in friendship." Blaser's subsequent fierce opposition to "Christianism" is not an argument about metaphysical reality, but an accusation that Christ's "religion of love" has been
misfigured into an absolutism of hatred.

Nerval's *Chimères* ends in a "Golden Poem" recalling the ancient
maxim that "everything is alive."

take the ghost stirring
in an animal   each
flower, a piece of light
scattering love's mystery
asleep in metal   alive
the coherence takes power
over you

Blaser sought an assurance for his version of this strange, unsettling
poem of Nerval's. When I suggested that I bring Spicer to the house to
hear it, even though the two of them were in the midst of some personal quarrel and not officially speaking to each other at the time,
Blaser readily agreed. That day, when I joined Spicer in Aquatic Park

where he frequently spent his afternoons, sitting on sheets of newspaper spread on the damp grass, listening to the baseball game on a transistor radio, drinking beer, and gazing out in the direction of a long pier beyond which was San Francisco Bay, I told him that Blaser had written a new poem and would like him to come up to the house and listen to it. Again, there wasn't a moment's hesitation. Spicer and I boarded the Polk Street bus and made our way up to the apartment on Russian Hill where Blaser and I lived.

It was the year before Spicer's death and he already complained of patches of "fading." When he arrived at the apartment, he asked to take a nap, sleeping for a half-hour on a day-bed in an alcove of books, while our white cat, Tim, snoozed alongside him. When he awoke, he came into the kitchen. Blaser provided drinks, and then read his Nerval poem. Spicer sat silently, occasionally vigorously nodding at some particular line. When the reading ended, there was a moment of silence, and Spicer slowly said, "Wonder-full" — pun intended — then added, "I wish I had written that."

There was an unhappy epilogue to *Les Chimeres*. Once it was published, as a chapbook, Robert Duncan took offence, complaining that the poem wasn't really a "translation." Duncan soon produced his own translation of Nerval, a stilted, wooden transliteration, along with a brief but flamboyant essay attacking Blaser's *Chimeres*. Since Blaser's persona incorporated the notion of the poet as a wounded figure, Duncan's attack naturally caused him untold, unnecessary grief. Duncan's foray in the end came to little — that is, it had no effect on the reading of Blaser's work — so it has to be seen as merely a malevolent aspect of Duncan's otherwise larger personality, a spewing of resentment over the fraying friendship of the former triumvirate of young poets — himself, Spicer and Blaser.

Duncan was at least presciently aware of all this. A couple of years earlier, at the height of his quarrel with Spicer (and Spicer could be as cruel as Duncan), not only were he and Spicer not speaking to each other but Spicer had taken to referring to Duncan in the past tense as if he were a dead poet. Duncan made an unexpected trip across town to North Beach to show Spicer a series of versions or transformations of sonnets by Dante that he'd just written. The third of the series, addressed to Blaser, began:

Robin, it would be a great thing if you, me, and Jack Spicer
Were taken up in a sorcery . . .

Duncan proposed that their "mortal heads" might come under a spell in which they would have no memory of themselves "but the poets we were." In remembering how things had been between old friends, he recalled their poems in which lusts and loves had been entangled, and invoked the figure of Amor, so that "we might have ever at our call / Those youths we have celebrated to play Eros / And erased to lament in the passing of things." Duncan yearned for a moment in the future when each of the three of them "might be glad / To be so far abroad from what he was."

That night, Spicer took me outside Gino's bar and extracted the pages of Duncan's poems, now somewhat crumpled, from his back pocket and handed them to me so that I could read those lines by the light of the neon sign outside the bar on Green Street. Almost predictably, Spicer's approval only incensed Duncan. "I knew he was going to like those poems!" Duncan later complained, still irked by Spicer's rejection of other parts of his work. It was too late to rescue the friendship, but not too late for one last poem to celebrate its memory.

For Blaser, too, there was ultimately "no memory of ourselves but the poets we were." Nothing was forgotten, of course, not the slightest slight, but that wasn't the point. In Blaser's elegy for Duncan — a quarter-century later — written in 1988, just after the latter's death, what comes to mind is the origin of friendship in the poetry:

> the first of your poems
> I read: *Among my friends love is a great sorrow* (brought to me
> in typescript by Jack, 1946, that we three should meet) — no
>   voice
> like it   turns, turns   in the body of thought   *Among*
> *my friends love is a wage . . .*

In the biographies of the poets, most of which are, to my mind, written "upside-down," the point is not that the "life" explains the poems but, rather, that the poems transcend the gossip. The gossip is fun, sure, but if that was all there was, the whole thing would be without purpose. As it is, we already have enough of a problem with life's purposelessness to want to not increase the incoherence delineated by modernity. Above the "oppositions," and much worse, the pettinesses of the merely personal, the gifts of friendship also incur obligations, debts. A decade or so after Spicer's death in 1965, Blaser edited *The Collected Books of Jack Spicer*, to which he appended his own extraordinary account of their relationship in poetics, an essay called "The Practice of Outside." And in mourning Duncan's death, he says:

> *There is no exstacy of Beauty in which I will not remember Man's*
>   *misery,*
> compounded by what we have done   sighted in ruins, neither old

nor discontinuous
>(I smile   it is the thought of you   a happiness
that could not be without your having been
>>there
quarrelling)

In those senses I would say, that with respect to his friends, Blaser
paid the debts of friendship in full, honouring their memories, their
continuing presences/absences. The philosopher Jacques Derrida
makes a similar point in *The Work of Mourning*, a collection of his
elegies for departed friends. He says that the "law of friendship is that
one of you will die, one of you will go before the other." In any
intense friendship we are aware of the inevitable absence of one of the
friends or the other, and thus mourning begins before death. It is an
idea I've "translated" into lines as:

so the sorrow is shared
In the reader's grief
the work of mourning keeps
the dead who never die
alive within ourselves   the world
the poem   at a loss for words

III

I have the idea of the figure of a First Reader, the person to whom the
poem is initially given to confirm that it is a poem, who reads it
before it is read by "the readers of the poem." I've had the fortune to
be a first reader, on occasion, for several writers, including Blaser,
Spicer, George Stanley, Brian Fawcett, and others. At the end of the
1960s, when Blaser and I went our separate domestic ways — but not
really separate, since our lives remained intertwined — I ceased to be
his first reader and joined the ranks of the readers of his poems.

The attention of the readers of the poem, one of intermittencies and
intensities, is different from that of a first reader or the author as
reader of him- or herself. The reader dips into the pages of a large
book, the eye from time to time caught by some particular poem or a
run of them. Now, the reader is lost and found, lost in the poem, and
then found in the room where one is reading, about to prepare a meal
or run an errand, and the book is placed on the pile of other books, or
put on a shelf.

The book in question is Robin Blaser's *The Holy Forest* (1993), a collected poems, from the serial *Cups* to recent works, which the poet and novelist Michael Ondaatje and I edited for its publisher, Coach House Press. I'll return to some of the contents of the book, but first there are subsidiary aspects of Blaser's career that ought to be mentioned briefly in a reading of his poetry.

By the time of the publication of *The Holy Forest*, the Denver-born, Idaho-raised poet had lived and worked in his adopted country, Canada, for more than a quarter-century and, like millions of other immigrants who make up a large proportion of that nation's inhabitants, had long since become a legal citizen of the "True North." Blaser's connections to the country and his community ran deeper than that. As a professor at Simon Fraser University for two decades, he'd been legendary as a scholar and teacher, and for his guidance of a generation of younger scholars and writers who had been his graduate students. As a scholar and editor, he'd been responsible for editions of selected poems of the Canadian modernist Louis Dudek and Blaser's younger Canadian contemporary, George Bowering, as well as producing the requisite array of prefaces, introductions, and volumes of conference papers. There was even a celebration and festschrift held in Vancouver in 1995, organized by friends, colleagues and students, to mark Blaser's 70th birthday.

As a figure of great poetic and intellectual power, over the years of his teaching career Blaser was a kind of magnet who drew, like metal filings, an unusual range of devotions and oppositions. I'll skip most of that — and the gossip and psychological motivations attached to each possible anecdote — as being of little moment, or at least not to my purposes. More important, as many people (including me) are willing to testify, Blaser as teacher and mentor changed or enlarged lives for the better.

If I had to sum up in a phrase what Blaser gave me, I would say, echoing his vocabulary, it is the appreciation of the marvels or "astonishments" of the world — both wonderful and horrific — in ways I never would have imagined on my own. This is a process of enlargement that probably began with the first Mother Goose rhyme I heard or read ("Hickory dickery dock / The mouse ran up the clock"), but the encounter with Blaser's vision was especially transformative. At the intellectual center of his world-view is the injunction "to keep duty and love alive," as he puts it in a poem about one of the grandmothers who raised him. Amid the decay (and defecation) of the world, from which Blaser doesn't at all avert his gaze, he also has an eye that picks out the wonders that gleam in the muck — an appreciation for places, lives, texts, human beauties, objects (among them, moonstones found between the railroad ties when he was a child in Idaho).

It is such appreciation that he transmits to others — poets, lovers, readers, a generation of students — a sense of how to live more fully in one's time. There were poems, readings, formal talks and, as much as anything, excited conversation. The particular character of Blaser's conversation — I often go down the lane to his house for morning coffee — is that it's carefree with respect to temporality, topic and taboo. The conversation has gone on so long that we can shift subjects instantaneously: he and I call up some minuscule incident of shared memory from decades ago and then, without any overt signal, shift to a bit of the day's news that has come in over the radio that murmurs in his kitchen. Ditto for sacred/profane: from "shining masters" to "dirty talk" about the figures in the "comical physical union / our arms like briars / wrapped around." Equally, there is no discrimination culturally between the seemingly most esoteric work of high art and lines from a pop song on the charts ("Let's face it, baby / We're just animal / So let's do it like they do it / on the Discovery Channel," sing the Bloodhound Gang). Nothing has *a priori* intrinsic worth or lack of value. The appreciations open a world whose definition is open-ended. Because of Blaser, I understand it differently, I am different from what I might have been.

No doubt my account or portrait of Blaser makes him out to be more saintly, or at least priestly, than he in fact is. Still, there is something priest-like in his devotions, as well as in his bearing, and his sense of responsibility for that role when he says in *The Moth Poem*, "You, priest, must know why you strike," in an era "when all the world is loved by the / daimon of mediocrity."

But Blaser's biographers need not fear a shortage of suitable material: the poet has drunk the equivalent of an ocean-liner full of martinis (I've made and poured a few of them), he's wept over lost loves not worth weeping over, his passions have escalated into raving and ranting, his quarrels have been as petty as the next person's, he's indulged in countless extravagances, and in the self-portrait of his own poems he's recurrently aware of "tearing, teasing in that silly personality," of "this overweening pride in the peacock flesh," of looking for

> some cinch, some way to live
> entangled and closed in heat
> you were even to yourself
> an ancient face   preening
> before mirrors of comfort

For all that, Blaser has also lived for more than a quarter-century, and counting, with his friend David Farwell, a social worker and therapist who works at St. Paul's Hospital in Vancouver. While to some, Blaser's a creature from outer space, or as he puts it, "the best thing ever said about me / critically was 'alien exotica'," others of us find him more comprehensible. But, as I say, biography is not my business here. Nor is hagiography.

In one of the "Image-Nations" from the late 1960s, which appear among the "books" and serials of *The Holy Forest*, Blaser begins,

> as the image wears away
> there is a wind in the heart
>
> the translated men
> disappear into what they have
> translated
>
> rocking the heart   a childish man
> entangles   an absence   a still-life
> at the edge of his body
> erasing the body   of those opposites
> who are companions
> and also horizons in one another's
> eyes   at the ends of the world
>
> the words do not end   but come back
> from the adventure . . .

The structures (or he might say, the metric) of Blaser's poems become more dense, more complex, but the "adventure" of language and the companions who are "horizons in one another's / eyes" remain. Despite whatever "longing / for completion" there might be,

> the task of a man   and his words
> is at the edge
>   where we are
> translated   restless   men
> the quarrel over the immortal language,
> one may believe in a god-language
> behind us,   but god moves to the end
> of our sentences
>   where words   foment
> a largeness
>   of visible
> and invisible worlds . . .

Certainly, that seems a clear enough credo for a life's work. Among the poets of his generation, the quality and range of Blaser's intellect is notable, and he, along with George Stanley, is probably the best-read, philosophically, of the group of poets with whom he's associated. For those familiar with the thought of the 20th and now the 21st century, Blaser's poetry engages philosophically mainly with a contemporary Continental array of thinkers — Deleuze, Derrida, Serres, de Certeau, Agamben, Nancy, Arendt and others — many of whom are present or at the margins, by way of "borrowings" and citations, in Blaser's poems. I don't think any apology is necessary for the genuine difficulty of thought involved. If life were simple, we would have remained snakes. But as it is, we are not merely reptilian, but slightly more evolved intelligences capable of contact with "shining masters."

    when I tell you what they
    look like   some of it is
    nearly false   their blue hair

    but they are not ourselves   they
    are equivalents   of action   they
    compose forms,   which we hear

    sound within a context
    as if that action we are
    images of   used us
    the body becomes an instrument

    sometimes the harp pierces the body
    and a man only hangs on the strings

The thinking here is paratactic — that is, in Charles Olson's phrase, one perception leads immediately to another — and the meaning unfolds hermeneutically. The shining masters "are not ourselves," rather they are "equivalents" of "action." The concept of action is the philosophically charged term in this conceptualization of how the process of poetic thought works. The action of the shining masters "compose forms, which we hear." We, too, are images of an action, and it's as if the action "used us," used our bodies as instruments to hear the "*sound within a context*." This is one of the more articulated reformulations of what Blaser began with in *Cups*, "The poem / by dictation."

As other images in the same series of poems make obvious, this work is in part a response to the Vietnam War of the 1960s and

1970s. The reason Blaser is so concerned to get clear on the "meta-physics," as I'm calling it, is because "public life has fallen asleep," and the danger of ignorance in the face of the meaning of the war is that we will engage in the *"reduction of horror to sentiment"*. Although Blaser's approach to politics is variously direct and indirect, his poetry is perhaps surprisingly political or, more important, almost always politically intelligent.

In "Even On Sunday," a poem written for the Gay Games held in Vancouver in 1990, Blaser says, "I don't know anything about God but what the human record tells / me — in whatever languages I can muster —" and then moves directly to an attack on the homosexual-hating religious fundamentalists of the day and "that blasphemy which defines god's / nature by our own hatred and prayers for vengeance and dominance — / that *he* (lower case and questionable pronoun) would destroy by a / hideous disease one lover of another or by war, a nation for what / uprightness and economic hide-and-seek — and *he* . . . / is on the side of the always-ignorance of politics / in which we trust." "Blasphemies all, against multiplicity / which is all anyone knows about god," Blaser declares.

In the long "Image-Nation ('oh, pshaw,'" — the phrase is an exple-tive of his great-grandmother Ina — a poem about the sources of one's vocabulary, Blaser returns to the first landscapes found in *Cups*, the sagebrush and aspen valleys in the rural Idaho of his childhood in the 1930s. The dominant figures of the poem are a set of grandpar-ents, great-grandparents and a grandaunt, but especially grand-mother Sophia Nichols, known as Dot for short because she worked as a telegrapher for the railways. The family lived in a series of whistlestops — Orchard, Idaho, even a place named Blaser, Idaho — dwelling in a yellow Union Pacific railcar parked by the tracks, which follow the course of the Portneuf River. In a series of childhood episodes and engagements, the poet he will be takes form:

once the rains were so heavy the water rose up the opposite embank-ment, nearly reaching the railbed, and stayed for days — 'a sea,' Sophia Nichols said, never having seen one, and it was wide and stretched along the tracks as far as I could see — we needed supplies from the commissary across there — Carnation condensed milk, I remember — and we plotted a way to cross that sea — the tin tub and a shingle, just the right size boat and paddle for me, we thought — round and round it went, being round, and drifted from shore meandering — she tossed me a broom, which luckily floated near enough to reach it — 'see if you can touch bottom,' she said — I could — 'so push,' she said — and I made it there circuitously, pulled my tub up on the beach, got the supplies, and returned — 'circuitously Odyssean,' she said, having spent hours those rainy days telling me stories of Odysseus, which were, she said, homeward journeys of the soul . . .

In an earlier poem, Blaser cites his friend, the poet Charles Olson telling him, "I'd trust you / anywhere with image, but / you've got no syntax." This remark is recorded in a book of Blaser's called, appropriately, *Syntax*. Now, in a prose-poem syntax of his own contrivance in "('Oh, pshaw,' ", Blaser makes his Odyssean way homeward to the yellow railcar source of his poetry. In the poem, the images and figures emerge that will be permanent guides in his work:

> the rocking chair from their lost house in Salt Lake City, often talked about, had a painted leather back — the wandering Jew or nomad — whose marvellous, piercing eye followed everyone up and down the boxcar parlour — into corners, even under the library table, also from the lost house — *eros* of wandering — *eros* of being sought in every nook and cranny — that, so far as I'm concerned is where vocabulary begins — fierce eyed — dot – dash – space — and syntax is later and difficult

In the next poem of the Image-Nation series, "(Exody," a poem about Hieronymous Bosch's 16th century painting, "The Garden of Earthly Delight," amid the painter's phantasmagoric rendering of a "bird-headed moth . . . a spotted, kerchiefed cat . . . arrows, flowers, sticks, bird beaks stuck up asses . . . a broken egg shell with a tavern in it" and all the rest, the emblematic Wandering Jew reappears:

> they threw the old rocking chair from the lost house out — but they cut the leather backrest out — with the portrait of the wandering Jew or nomad on it —whose eyes follow me or 'you' — into corners — to the end of the boxcar parlour — even into the brilliance of reading under the library table — and sent it to me

So, at the end of this exegesis, we have Blaser's "exody," his neologism suggesting not the exit of exodus, but an entrance into, or embarkation upon the voyage.

In spring of 2000, the wandering Blaser appeared in Berlin, where the libretto of *The Last Supper* he'd written for composer Harrison Birtwistle's opera received its premiere at the Staatsoperhaus, the 17th century theatre located on the Unter den Linden, east Berlin's grand, stately boulevard. Along with other friends of his, I attended opening night in the old opera house and was present when the silver-haired, tuxedo-garbed poet, just before his 75th birthday, stood on the stage after the performance to receive the audience's applause and to take his bow.

Afterwards, a group of us, including Blaser, wandered next door to the cobbled Bebelplatz, a square named for the founder of German social democracy. In 1933, this was the site of the Nazi book burning. Now, there's an installation there by the sculptor Mischa Ullman. It consists of an unobtrusive marker, noting the historical event that occurred there — accompanied by the poet Heinrich Heine's prophetic remark that people who begin by burning books will end by burning people — and a rectangle of glass.

When you edge up to the glass window set into the rough surface of the square, and look down, you see it is the transparent ceiling of a white, lighted underground room. The room is empty except for, on all four walls, sets of floor-to-ceiling bookshelves, also empty. At night, in the otherwise darkened square, the underground empty library room emits a shaft of light up into the night air, through which, that evening, a thin drizzle was falling. Blaser, as always when in the presence of the "marvellous," as he calls it, was transfixed — curious, moved, joyous, his face reflecting the illumination of the underground library. For a moment, as I stood on the other side of the glass and its shaft of brightness, I glimpsed, as I often have, the figure of Robin Blaser through the shifting light.

Bones

Although his name was Dave Robinson, he was known to everyone in the gay bars of Vancouver in the mid-1980s simply as Bones. He was a slightly misshapen man of spectral thinness and with a barely visible hunchback. He was an old carny — a guy who'd worked in the hustling, nomadic world of fairground carnivals as a youth — and his grating, nasal voice still carried the echo of the pitchman's promise of impossible goods and pleasures, bearded ladies, magic elixirs, two-headed calves.

Bones was rather despised in the bars, bearing the reputation of a con-artist, thief, betrayer, drug-user and drug-pusher. He made his precarious living by a little drug dealing, the sale of various sorts of usually slightly damaged goods, and some amateur pimping. Nonetheless, we struck up an acquaintance and, at times when he was down on his luck, I bought him a drink. I immediately recognized Bones as a go-between, a debased version of the Hermes figure who leads you between the worlds of the living and dead, or at least from place to place.

One night, Bones took me up to a tower apartment in Vancouver's West End, where he was living during a prosperous moment, to introduce me to two young men who he was letting stay there. I was expected to be interested in the younger of the two, but as soon as I saw the other boy, who I'll call Patrick, about 19, with straw-coloured longish blond hair and who was sprawled on a sofa strumming a guitar, I immediately intuited that I was meeting someone who would be in my life for a considerable time. And, as the story prescribes, one thing led to another — adventures, *amor*, scenes, etc., the details of which deserve reticence. More than 20 years later, Pat stays in touch — now married, a father, driving heavy equipment on a pipeline project — phoning from some town in the middle of nowhere in Alberta on a holiday morning, to reassure both of us that we're still friends. He's one of the two or three people I know with whom I can share a memory of Bones, who brought us together.

Although most of the people Bones led me to didn't turn out to be long-term friends like Pat, there were other surprises, ones that even Bones hadn't anticipated. He introduced me to Sean, as I'll call him, a guy in his twenties I'd seen around the bars. Sean was sexually attractive and I liked going with him for that reason, but what was magical about him had to do with something else altogether. Sean was one of those rare people — I've met only three or four of them in a lifetime — who could tell stories about his life with a level of detail that was utterly satisfying. In the middle of a story about how his older brother had first seduced him, I could interrupt and ask, What was the colour of the walls?, or, What was the traffic like outside?, and he would immediately reply, "Yellow," or tell you about an 18-wheel rig idling outside the bedroom window, without wondering for a second why you needed to know. That is, he had the story so completely in mind that every aspect was accessible.

This is an important point, and I don't want to skip over it too casually. Think of the people in your life who told you stories. I grew up in a family in which my father and his brothers and sisters were all pretty good storytellers. Of the great storytellers I've known who come immediately to mind are a shipyard worker I met in Gdansk, Poland, in 1981, who had participated in the famous Solidarity strike, and the Argentine novelist Tomás Eloy Martínez, whom I had asked to tell me about his fellow writer, Manuel Puig, and who not only told me in precise detail about Puig but about the sexual practices of Argentine automobile garage workers, the sort of men Puig sought out. And there is Sean.

I regarded Sean as a gift from Hermes, through his agent, Bones. When I reported to Bones my enthusiasm, he had no idea of the real reason for my delight, but simply regarded it as a future selling point, and whenever he introduced me to someone afterwards, he always assured me, "This guy is as good as Sean." The go-between, however, is not required to fully understand where he has taken you. But with Sean, I wasn't quick enough. At the moment it dawned on me that I had met a real storyteller and decided that I ought to record his tales, Sean disappeared to Calgary on a fool's errand involving girlfriends, drugs, and rock'n'roll. Years later, I ran into him on the streets but, sadly, dope had replaced the muse, and it wasn't possible to continue our conversations. I suppose the moral of the story is, Sure, beware of Greek gods bearing dangerous gifts, but when the Hermes Agency sends you a messenger who can tell you about the world within the world, pay attention.

Through it all, Bones had the soul of a shady salesman. Whether he was peddling drugs, sex, or household goods, there was always a selling point to be made in every offer, and you were always just another rube to be conned a little. His routine must have been persuasive, since I never resented it, even when I knew I was merely being sold on something. Ambiguous intentions apart, his virtue was that of all salesmen: he presented you with a bit of the world in a more promising light than it otherwise would have had. But of course the shadier side was always close to the surface. I remember one time Bones showing me a tweed jacket he was just about to sell to somebody in the bar for $50, and pointing out to me a little burn hole made by a cigarette, just to show me his ability to put one over on his mark. "He'll never notice," Bones cackled with malevolent glee.

Inevitably, one night in the bar — the Dufferin — somebody came up to me and asked, "Have you heard about Bones?" The last times I'd seen him, he'd been even more cadaver-like than usual, and death was visible in his face. Now, he was dead. "What happened?" I asked, and the man reporting the news of the dead said they'd found him in his rooms, sitting in his easy chair before the television, a burned-out cigarette butt between his nicotine-strained fingers, his face in the frozen rictus of a half-grin at some minor deception on the screen that had amused him. "Just like that," the guy said. No doubt, when Bones met Charon, the boatman who takes you across the River Styx to the underworld, and it was time to pay the boatman's fee (2 *obols*, I seem to recall), Bones had patted his empty pockets, and said something like, "How about 1 *obol* and a half?"

Books

Fortress: At whatever writing desk I sit — in Vancouver, Berlin, a hotel room in Siem Reap, Cambodia — I stack up my books, however few or many, in piles, rather than as they're laid out horizontally on bookshelves. Then I see that what I'm making is a child's fortress, or fortified foxhole, like those we dug in the empty lot full of milkweeds behind the apartment building where I lived in Chicago in the 1940s, now reproduced in stacks of books on my desk.

Paradise Library: On my desk in Vancouver, the coffee mug I use during my morning reading was a gift from the Vancouver Public Library (where I had given a talk in one of its lecture series). The mug is white, marked with the logo of the library, and bears the inscription, "I have always imagined that Paradise will be a kind of library," a now famous utterance of the blind Argentine writer and librarian, Jorge Luis Borges (1899-1986).

The line comes from Borges's *"Poema de los Doñes"* ("Poem of the Gifts"), a poem about Borges becoming the head of the National Library of Argentina. "No one should read self-pity or reproach / into this statement of the majesty / of God, who with such splendid irony / granted me books and blindness at one touch," begins one translation. Later in the poem, Borges writes, "Slowly in the darkness, the hollow penumbra, / I explore with a hesitant cane / I, who always imagined Paradise / will be a kind of library." In a 1977 lecture, "Blindness," given in Buenos Aires, Borges says, "In my life, I have received many unmerited honours, but there is one that has made me happier than all the others: the directorship of the National Library ... I received the nomination at the end of 1955. I was in charge, I was told, of a million books. Later I found out it was nine hundred thousand — a number that's more than enough ... Little by little I came to realize the strange irony of events. I had always imagined Paradise as a kind of library. Others think of a garden or a palace. There I was, the center, in a way, of nine hundred thousand books in various languages, but I found I could barely make out the title pages and the spines. I wrote the 'Poem of the Gifts' ... Those two gifts contradicted each other: the countless books and the night, the inability to read them." Paradise as a kind of library or, conversely, how often I've experienced a library as a kind of Paradise.

The Forest: I briefly worked in the University of British Columbia library, shelving books, an employee of the wonderful chief librarian, Basil Stuart-Stubbs. As I made my way through its low-ceilinged, narrow-aisled, sub-basements with my book cart, deep in "the stacks," as they're called, the shelves seemed to me more and more like an oak forest. The stacks stretched out infinitely, the unknown number of sub-basements went deeper and deeper into the earth.

The library becomes all the libraries I have known, from the first one at Sumner Elementary School in Chicago, presided over by Mrs. Spiegal, who had only four fingers on one of her hands, and in which I first encountered the mystery of the Dewey Decimal Classification System (ten categories in which all the books were organized) to Borges's notion of "The Total Library" and the "Library of Babel," fabulist versions of the possibility of a collection of all possible books.

My favourite library building is architect Moshe Safdie's Vancouver Library, with its brown sandstone-like curving walls that make the building resemble a styrofoam version of Rome's Colosseum. Though criticized by architectural critics (for being postmodernist kitsch, I suppose), as soon as I saw it, I knew it was perfect. "It's a fantasia," I thought, "which is exactly what a library is." Institutional libraries, home libraries, and sometimes the temporary library carried around town in a cloth bookbag: a single book, a streetmap of the city, a pocket dictionary.

The Devaluation of Books: One thing I didn't imagine when I was younger was that one day books (and authors) would be devalued, would mean less, would no longer be seen as containing the secrets of the world. Mundane proof of this thesis: there is no object that can be left on the seat of a parked automobile today that you can be more certain will not be stolen than a book.

Reading: My teacher Joseph Tussman's aphorism: "All reading is mind-reading."

Landmark Books: Like the "pantheon" of authors I feel closest to, I maintain, as does each reader, a list of "landmark" books, books that were decisive moments at some point in my life. My father, for example, had introduced me to the writings of Jack London, giving me *Call of the Wild, White Fang,* and *The Sea Wolf* to read. One day, when I was about 12, he said to me, "I've been saving this for you," and handed me London's *The Iron Heel,* a science-fiction political novel in which a socialist revolution is fought in the streets of Chicago, the very streets in which I played.

Other landmark books in my necessarily idiosyncratic list: Balzac's *Pere Goriot*, where the young de Rastignac stands above Paris, its twinkling lights spread below him, and hurls a metaphoric gauntlet at society. Jack Kerouac's *On The Road*, which, on re-reading, proves that landmark books may only be landmarks for the moment in which they're read. George Orwell's *Homage to Catalonia*, introduction to politics; Jean Genet's *Our Lady of the Flowers*, introduction to homosexuality; Proust's *Within a Budding Grove* (whose real title I think of as the opening words of the original French title, *À l'Ombre* ... *In the Shadow...*). Books I've already mentioned here: *Roland Barthes* by Roland Barthes; John Berger's *Photocopies*; *The Symposium* by Plato. Christa Wolf's *Accident*; Marguerite Duras's *The Lover*; Tadeusz Konwicki's *A Minor Apocalypse*; Fernando Pessoa's *Book of Disquiet*; Richard Rorty's *Contingency, Irony, and Solidarity*; Theodor Adorno's *Minima Moralia*, and with it all other "fragments from a ruined" civilization.

Imaginary Books: ever since I began writing, I've always had in my mind a shifting pile of to-be-written "imaginary books," as I call them. Among them: *Cities of Desire*, an erotic auto-geography of the cities where I've been in love; *Reading the Twentieth Century*, a multi-volume, genre-crossing assessment of the writing of the last century; *At the Poets' Table: A White Rabbit Memoir* of the San Francisco poetry scene of the 1960s; *What Does Some of it Mean?*, a philosophy book — a modest version of Thomas Nagel's grander *What Does It All Mean?*; *Democracy and the Body Politic*, a re-write of philosopher Joseph Tussman's *Obligation and the Body Politic* and his *Government and the Mind*. There are others, all of it an imaginary self-produced future library in my head.

The Book: Mallarmé, Borges, Jack Spicer have all imagined The Book. But the greatest imagining of all is Bruno Schulz, the Jewish-Polish author of *Cinnamon Shops* (1934; in English, *The Street of Crocodiles*) and *Sanitorium Under the Sign of the Hourglass* (1937), who wrote in a 1936 letter, "The books we read in childhood don't exist anymore; they sailed off with the wind, leaving bare skeletons behind. Whoever still has in him the memory and marrow of childhood should rewrite these books as he experienced them." But on my shelves in Vancouver, I still have my first books: *Animal Friends* and *Mother Goose's Nursery Rhymes*. On the end pages, my first writing, an exercise in penmanship: unevenly drawn lines on which I practice writing the letters of my name.

In his story, "The Book," Schulz recalls the volume whose magic pages, when rubbed, produce fragments of kaleidoscopic colour. Schulz writes,

Sometimes my father would wander off and leave me alone with The Book; the wind would rustle through its pages and the pictures would rise. And as the windswept pages were turned, merging the colors and shapes, a shiver ran through the columns of text, freeing from among the letters flocks of swallows and larks. Page after page floated in the air and gently saturated the landscape with brightness. At other times, The Book lay still and the wind opened it softly like a huge cabbage rose; the petals, one by one, eyelid under eyelid, all blind, velvety, and dreamy, slowly disclosed a blue pupil, a colored peacock's heart, or a chattering nest of hummingbirds.

Years later, when the young man asks his father what happened to The Book, he is told that it is "a myth in which we believe when we are young, but which we cease to take seriously as we get older." Yet, the young man searches ceaselessly for the lost Book. When he finds some tattered pages that he believes were part of The Book, he discovers that the text has been destroyed, and only old advertisements remain. Yet even the tawdry remnants rise "over the sphere of daily affairs into the region of pure poetry." No image ever appears twice; the writing "unfolds while being read, its boundaries open to all currents and fluctuations." This book, the young man is quite sure, is "the Authentic," to which all books aspire. "They live only a borrowed life, which at the moment of inspiration returns to its ancient source."

George Bowering

Of George Bowering's many books, the one I'm especially attracted to is his picaresque "postmodern" novel about the European discovery of Vancouver, *Burning Water* (1980). In part, that's because its vision of Burrard Inlet in the 1790s is strikingly similar to, but far more imaginative and playful than my own recurrent fantasy about the city of Vancouver before it became a city. At the corner of First and Larch, looking north down the slope (my house is just a half-block below), there's a panoramic view of the inlet basin, along with the 400-hectare dark green patch of the trees of Stanley Park jutting into the water at the end of the downtown peninsula, and across the inlet the ridges and houses of the North Shore (blinking windows caught by the sun in West Vancouver), and behind them, the Coast Mountains. Beyond the mountains, more mountains, further and further north. In my vision of it, modern Vancouver disappears and is replaced by the earlier forested slopes; maybe a native longhouse down on Kitsilano beach.

Bowering's *Burning Water* begins, as it should, on the pristine wooded slopes of Burrard Inlet, where two native men are talking about "whatever it was, the vision, [that] came out of the far fog and sailed right into the sunny weather of the inlet" on a mid-June day in 1792. It is appropriate that the story begins from the perspective of the indigenous inhabitants who watched Captain George Vancouver's tiny ships sail into the inlet. It's here, at the outset, that Bowering makes his first move. Bowering's natives are not Hollywood Indians talking Hollywood Indian talk ("Many moons have I travelled, o Great Spirit ..."). Instead, they're postmodernist 18th century *philosophe* natives, or at least one of them is as he makes the distinction between fact and fancy. "Okay, what do you see?" asks the older, smarter and thoroughly ironic native. "I see two immense and frighteningly beautiful birds upon the water," burbles the younger man, who is naïve, romantic, and filled with horseshit ideas about becoming "a full man of the tribe." In addition to his romanticism, the younger brave is not very good at catching fish, which is the crucial fact in the life of the tribe.

"These young ones could be pretty tiresome," comments the narra-

tor through the mind of the older native. "Full man of the tribe. Talk
talk talk. The second Indian looked over at his companion, who was
now leaning back on a bare patch of striped granite, idly picking at
his navel. And now he is seeing visions."

The young one is impressed by the fact that the vision has been
revealed to him. "Then you do think there is something to facts?"
asks the older native. "Of course," replies the other, "But facts can
only lead us to visions. Some of us, at least, were born to see visions."
"That is perhaps why you have so much difficulty getting a fish to
leave the sea and come home with you," says the second Indian
wryly, adding, "He is a fact whether he is hidden under the surface, or
changing colours on the rocks. To make this fact your fact, you need
skill and a well-made hook." The young one is not only tiresome, but
also obstinate. "But a vision is not a fish, my old ironic friend," says
the youth. Sighs the older native, "I was perhaps making that very
point in its opposite order."

The point is, we don't know what the aboriginals said to each other
when Vancouver's ships appeared in Burrard Inlet, and we need a
storyteller to imagine some sophisticated banter. "You see those
visions of yours?" asks the older man. "Yes, I do see them, and so do
you, so that takes care of your precious facts, too," sneers the younger
one. "'Not quite.' Now he was going to get the brash little squirrel.
Little prick. 'Those are boats,'" says the older native. The younger
one laughs. "Two large dugouts from another people, as I said," the
more experienced man reiterates. "Oh sure, dugouts with wings,"
continues the sneer. "Those wings are made of thick cloth. They catch
the wind as we are supposed to catch fish in our nets, and travel far
out to sea." The younger one complains that the other is only trying
to discredit him. "No, I am discrediting only your fancy. Your fancy
would have the fish leap from the water into your carrying bag. But
the imagination, now that is another matter. Your imagination tells
you where to drop your hooks." Later, the older man adds, "The
vision is made of wood. Hard, smooth, shiny, painted wood."

At the end of the chapter, since this is a postmodernist novel (i.e.,
one that reveals its making alongside its telling), Bowering introduces
us to the author, who is staying in Trieste, Italy, a town where the
writer James Joyce once lived. "In Trieste, it was raining most of the
time, and he would bump other umbrellas with his own on his way
down to the piazza, where he would look out at the fog that had
drifted in across the northern end of the Adriatic. It was his idea,
crazed in all likelihood, that if he was going to write a book about
that other coast as it was two hundred years ago, he would be advised
to move away in space too." The "he" in that passage is Bowering
himself, and the book he's thinking about is the one we're reading.

The Bowering who's a third-person character in Bowering's novel about George Vancouver — a lonely writer in the dismal drizzle of a far-away city — is, in some ways, more present to me than the Bowering I've known in a casual friendship over some 35 years. The Bowering I know is tall, has a mustache, and a craggy face. He's, to my mind, quite shy — what hells reside behind the shyness, I don't know. The shyness accounts, I think, for his manner, which often features the telling of an intentional bad joke (thus making it ironic in its badness), followed by a donkey-bray hee-haw laugh. He has a sort of Donald Duck brightness and tilt. His friends roll their eyes, and say, "Oh, George," forgiving their gawky pal's foibles. But behind the cracker-barrel façade, I remember that a long time ago, at a time in Canada when it was fashionable among writers to display an anti-American literary nationalism, Bowering had the courage not to go along with it. Instead, he insisted that the "New American Poetry" (of Charles Olson, Jack Spicer, Robert Creeley and others) was preferable to a lot of academic Canadian verse, no matter how loyal that verse was. That is, poetry didn't have nationality, it only had reality, or it didn't.

Once Bowering has established the terms of *Burning Water*, the rest is a wonderfully-drawn knockabout account of the 35-year-old Vancouver, who had sailed with the late Captain James Cook; Archibald Menzies, the Scottish ship's botanist who is Vancouver's *bête noire*; and the secret hero of the novel, Vancouver's older Peruvian-born Spanish counterpart, Juan Bodega y Quadra. Behind the historical reconstruction, the postmodern issue of writing nags, or hums. In the historical reconstruction, Bowering makes his characters "real" people rather than realistic figures, and he reminds us that Vancouver's ship, HMS *Discovery*, is ninety-nine feet and a few inches long, the length of two lifeboats on a modern-day B.C. ferry heading to Nanaimo on Vancouver Island. On a 99-foot boat, carrying a complement of 101 officers and men, you can see how the captain might get annoyed at his Scotch botanist. "The little fucker has the deck cluttered up with his stuff, and he is taking over more and more space every day . . . there were the plants, bushes and trees and weeds from New Holland, New Zealand, the Sandwiches, the Societies, and now the North Coast. I cannot set anchor but the little porridge-eater is off in one my boats, having commandeered two of my men, to dig up another obnoxious weed . . . The vessel is ninety-nine feet long, and he hopes to cover all of it, I'm certain."

Meanwhile, the author of *Burning Water* thinks "about the good old days, when the realist novelist just had to describe the setting and introduce into it the main characters. He could have told you a hundred things he had seen in Trieste. For instance, the guy with no legs in the rain on the Corso Italia, with his leather peaked hat, and the dainty man in the hound's tooth suit who crossed the street just before he came to him, pretending that was his car over there, or he had been mistaken in thinking so." Against the mundane moments of Trieste, Bowering spices up the historical tale by imagining a love affair between the elegant Quadra and the practical Vancouver. Like the philosophical conversations of the natives ashore, the erotic invention is a bit of tender slapstick. The narrative plays with the fuzzy border between myth and history, just as the appearance of Vancouver's ships ply the boundaries between fog and clear air.

But Bowering, who later wrote histories of British Columbia and Canada, informal but accurate, is clear enough about the political history of Vancouver's mission: 1) to chart the northwest coast, which he did more accurately than any sailor before him (filling in the gaps left by Cook's earlier mappings); 2) to prove once and for all that the fabled Northwest Passage across North America didn't exist, which it didn't; 3) and to settle the disputed claims to the coast between Britain and Spain, which had established a fort at Nootka on what came to be called Vancouver Island, but which Vancouver named Quadra and Vancouver Island, as a token of his friendship with the Spanish commander. Behind the geopolitics is mercantile capitalism: the political end of Vancouver's mission is designed to set the stage for the dominance of the British fur trade in Canada. Menzies and his botanical expedition is an Enlightenment add-on, and, indeed, it is true that Menzies and Vancouver bitterly quarreled, just as it's the case that Vancouver and Quadra became friends. Bowering sends up both the friendship and the quarrel in good-humoured fashion. The "real" Vancouver died a few years later in England, at age 40, while writing up his *Voyage of Discovery*.

When I stand bemused on the corner of First and Larch, as I have countless times, my imaginings are focused through *Burning Water*, thanks to Bowering. His range is, expectedly, far broader than the single snapshot I've chosen to consider. In "Musing on Some Poets," (1997), he says, "I have no remaining skill for form, / just feel words jostle each other in doorways on the way out . . .," as he sits among friends, who silently agree:

— those poets gave us a way to waste our lives
saying useless things, smiling indulgently at each other's personal
    diaspora,
carrying mismatched goodies on the way to the grave,
trip, fall into hole, write on dirt walls
a first and last sonnet,
solving all, coming to rest, combing hair, adjusting socks,

kissing no one but the image of Jesus, disbursing mind as if it
   were mercury,
listening for the voices to arrive with the worms.

That, too, is what I see, looking from First Avenue toward the
"burning water" of Burrard Inlet.

Richard Brautigan

On the cover of Richard Brautigan's *Trout Fishing in America* there's a photo of Brautigan and a woman friend in Washington Square in San Francisco, posed before a statue of Benjamin Franklin. The photo shows the tall Brautigan, in his early thirties, standing in front of the statue, floppy blond mustache turned down at the corners giving him the appearance of a man trying to look serious for a photograph. He is wearing an open navy peajacket, drawn apart by his hands behind his back, a tan, narrow-brimmed cowboy hat over his straggly blond hair, a buttoned vest, a geegaw necklace worn outside his paisley shirt, and rumpled blue jeans.

In the first chapter of *Trout Fishing*, called "The Cover for *Trout Fishing in America*," Brautigan describes his idea for the cover of his book, "a photograph taken late in the afternoon, a photograph of the Benjamin Franklin statue in San Francisco's Washington Square," in short, a photograph pretty much like the one on the cover of his book, minus Brautigan and his woman friend in their mid-1960s hippie outfits, which make them look, oddly enough, like American Western frontier people that you see in 19th century photographs.

San Francisco's Washington Square is just a couple blocks down from the writers' bars — Gino's, Katy's, one or two others — where we hung out in the early 1960s.

That's where I met Brautigan, although I don't remember him as a regular in the bars. Perhaps he just went occasionally to visit Jack Spicer, who presided at the "poets' table." I got my initial sense of what went on in Brautigan's mind when I read a poem of his that Spicer published in his magazine *J*. The poem was called "The Pumpkin Tide": "I saw thousands of pumpkins last night / come floating in on the tide, / bumping up against the rocks and / rolling up on the beaches; / it must be Halloween in the sea." Not much of a poem, but I liked the image of the orange pumpkins glimmering at night, bumping against the rocks and each other in the waves, brought in by the tide toward the shores of, perhaps, Aquatic Park, where Spicer and the rest of us often spent our afternoons, or maybe further up the coast, at Stinson Beach or Bolinas. I also liked the idea that the sea celebrated Halloween.

Brautigan was a gangly, soft-spoken man and had already acquired a slight stoop. I saw him as a Don Quixote figure who lived by an obscure chivalric code, a notion I got upon witnessing a curious incident one evening. Brautigan was standing outside of Katy's bar getting his boots shined by a black boy (itself an unusual occurrence, since I can't recall any other time when I saw a shoeshine boy in North Beach). The sight of the boy at the lanky Brautigan's feet caused an acquaintance of Richard's, who was going into the bar, to make an obscene remark in passing, suggesting some sexual activity between Brautigan and the boy.

Richard made no reply, but when the shoe shine was completed and paid for, Brautigan went into the bar (I accompanied him), and in a very deliberate manner offered and bought the man a drink. He then demanded that the man apologise for besmirching, not Brautigan's, but the boy's honour. It had been a stupid, vulgar remark, and the guy, of course, should simply have said he was sorry for the thoughtless insult, and that would have been that, but it was one of those emotionally jammed situations. When the man refused, Brautigan, with some formality, invited the guy to go into the nearby alley and settle the matter by means of fisticuffs.

It wasn't until they left the bar that I was struck by the oddness of the incident and the curious complexity of Brautigan's challenge on a point of honour — including the purchase of a drink for the person you're seeking satisfaction from — which Richard had delivered in such a mild-mannered way as to be seemingly without personal hostility. A few minutes later they returned to the bar, only slightly worse for wear, the matter apparently settled to Brautigan's satisfaction. Brautigan, of course, had been in the right, but it was the sort of thing that might as easily have been concluded by Brautigan just calling the guy an asshole. I suppose it is only retrospectively that I see the rigidity of Brautigan's chivalry as a dangerous trait, something that could possibly get you killed, but at the moment I was merely taken by his unusual stance, by his character.

The statue of Benjamin Franklin which, as Brautigan notes in "The Cover for *Trout Fishing in America*," stands in front of three poplar trees, is there because, well, it's there — in Washington Square, a place where Brautigan liked to hang out, as did various local winos — and because Franklin and the statue of him is a notion of America, its industrious, inventive, commercial nature. *Trout Fishing in America* is an elegy for America, for "a pastoral ideal," as one critic put it, "being lost to commercialism, environmental degradation and social decay." That loss is on Brautigan's mind from the beginning.

Across the street from Washington Square is the massive Saints Peter and Paul's Church where, as Brautigan writes, there's "a vast door that looks like a huge mousehole, perhaps from a Tom and Jerry cartoon, and written above the door is 'Per L'Universo,'" a phrase from a line in Dante's *Paradiso*. "Around five o'clock in the afternoon of my cover for *Trout Fishing in America*, people gather in the park across the street from the church and they are hungry. It's sandwich time for the poor." But the poor aren't allowed to cross the street until the signal is given, then "they all run across the street to the church and get their sandwiches [which] are wrapped in newspaper. They go back to the park and unwrap the newspaper and see what their sandwiches are all about. A friend of mine unwrapped his sandwich one afternoon and looked inside to find just a leaf of spinach. That was all." At the end of this bare anecdote, Brautigan drolly remarks, "Was it Kafka who learned about America by reading the autobiography of Benjamin Franklin ... Kafka who said, 'I like the Americans because they are healthy and optimistic.'"

A lot of the stories in *Trout Fishing* are like the one in "The Cover for *Trout Fishing in America*," off-centre in a revealing way. Mostly, the stories, as might be expected (although almost no one mentions this), are fishing yarns. Brautigan knew a considerable amount about trout fishing, and did a good deal of it. In fact, he started writing *Trout Fishing*, his first prose book, in the summer of 1961, during a camping trip with his wife Ginny and their baby daughter, Ianthe, in the wild outback of Idaho. He fished for trout and he wrote on a portable typewriter alongside the trout stream.

What's unexpected about the book, which is often mistakenly billed as a novel, is that its "chapters" are held together, or operate on, poetic principles, and I think it can best be described as a "serial prose poem," no different in spirit from Jack Spicer's *After Lorca* and other serial poems of the time. Not coincidentally, Spicer is one of the book's dedicatees, and apparently edited the manuscript once Brautigan came back to San Francisco from his fishing trip and finished the book.

You can see Brautigan's characteristic poetic move in "The Cover for *Trout Fishing in America*" chapter. At first, the cover is presented as simply a photograph of the Benjamin Franklin statue in Washington Park, a version of which actually ends up being the cover for the book. But in the middle of the story, Brautigan writes, "Around five o'clock in the afternoon of my cover for *Trout Fishing in America*, people gather in the park across the street from the church and they are hungry." That is, the photograph metamorphoses into a living scene, a clip from the life of Washington Square.

Just about any chapter displays Brautigan at work, transforming similes and metaphors into surreal, offbeat realities. Take "Knock on Wood," where Brautigan tells about his first attempt, as a child in

Portland, to go trout fishing in America. In a strange part of town, where "a row of old houses huddled together like seals on a rock," he spots a long, grassy, bush-covered field sloping off a hill, and at a distance he sees "a waterfall come pouring down off the hill. It was long and white and I could almost feel its cold spray. There must be a creek there, I thought, and it probably has trout in it. Trout. At last an opportunity to go trout fishing," something he'd heard about from an alcoholic stepfather when he was seven or eight. "The old drunk told me about trout fishing. When he could talk, he had a way of describing trout as if they were a precious and intelligent metal. Silver is not a good adjective to describe what I felt when he told me about trout fishing. I'd like to get it right. Maybe trout steel. Steel made from trout. The clear snow-filled river acting as foundry and heat."

Early the next morning, the boy goes out with his fishing tackle, which consists of a bent pin tied onto a piece of white string, and a slice of white bread, from which doughballs can be made to be used as bait. "How beautiful the field looked and the creek that came pouring down in a waterfall off the hill." But then, "as I got closer to the creek I could see that something was wrong. The creek did not act right . . . Finally I got close enough to see what the trouble was. The waterfall was just a flight of white wooden stairs leading up to a house in the trees. I stood there for a long time, looking up and looking down . . . Then I knocked on my creek and heard the sound of wood. I ended up by being my own trout and eating the slice of bread myself."

There's an addendum to the chapter, headed "The Reply of *Trout Fishing in America*": "There was nothing I could do. I couldn't change a flight of stairs into a creek. The boy walked back to where he came from. The same thing once happened to me. I remember mistaking an old woman for a trout stream in Vermont, and I had to beg her pardon. 'Excuse me,' I said, 'I thought you were a trout stream.' 'I'm not,' she said." Gradually, we see that a trout stream can be, or can be mistaken for, just about anything. Sometimes, as in "The Hump Back Trout," it can be a string of several thousand telephone booths with their doors off and their backs punched out, and fishing it can be like working as a telephone repair man. In "The Cleveland Wrecking Yard," you can, in a distant corner of the yard, find used trout streams for sale by the foot — birds, bushes, and insects sold separately.

Even more important, the idea of trout fishing in America morphs into various figures and ideas. Trout fishing in America is, first of all, an activity, an almost innocent activity that is America itself. And *Trout Fishing in America* is a book, a serial prose poem, with a cover, but it is also a character named Trout Fishing in America who replies to events in the book, or a legless, ranting wino named Trout Fishing in America Shorty, who Brautigan imagines crating and shipping to the Chicago writer Nelson Algren, and it can even be the gold nib of a pen named Trout Fishing in America Nib, with which to write the book. Often enough, it's just a good fishing yarn in which trout are caught and eaten, but equally, in the tradition of yarn as tall tale, it can be a story about a trout who dies drinking port wine. The wooden streams, telephone booth streams and streams for-sale-by-the-foot, as well as dozens of actual, rushing ribbons of water resonate against each other in the geography of America, just as the winos in Washington Square (and a boy Brautigan knew as a kid who was a Kool Aid wino) correspond to the trout who dies drinking port wine.

If the tall tale and the pastoral are among America's fundamental literary forms, it's easy to see *Trout Fishing*'s lineage going back to Henry David Thoreau and Mark Twain. It was Thoreau who wrote, "Time is but the stream I go a-fishing in. I drink at it; but while I drink I see the sandy bottom and detect how shallow it is. Its thin current slides away, but eternity remains." Among humorous writers of his own time, Brautigan's "trout stream of consciousness," as someone once called it, connects to a range of kindred spirits from Kurt Vonnegut to William Saroyan.

In 1962, Brautigan gave a reading of *Trout Fishing in America* over two nights at a former church located at the intersection of Market, 16th, and Noe streets in San Francisco. I was there, along with most of the other writers I knew, but the only one I remember, apart from Brautigan himself, was Jack Spicer, the brooding angel presiding over Brautigan's book, who sat there enthusiastically nodding his head over some accurate, unexpected metaphor, or laughing uproariously at something funny. The reading in the church was like a combination of Black Mass and a constitutional convention ratifying *Trout Fishing in America* as a work of art.

Trout Fishing had a complicated publishing history. It was only published in a commercial form in the later 1960s, about a half dozen years after it had been written. It arrived in the midst of the hippie and anti-Vietnam War movements, and struck some kind of chord, with its oddball humour that appealed to people smoking marijuana, and its lament for lost American innocence. It sold two million copies and Brautigan became a cult, a legend, and a book-producing industry. He was rumoured to be living on a ranch in Montana, where a group of other American novelists lived on similar ranches; he was said to be spending time in Japan; he had a house in Bolinas; the books continued to appear and different women friends appeared on the covers alongside Brautigan. But at a certain point, Brautigan ceased to be fashionable (the literary critics had never been interested in him), the books stopped selling, and the publishers no longer wanted them, or perhaps Brautigan was having trouble writing them.

I hadn't seen Brautigan for many years. Jack Spicer had died, the poets I'd known had moved out of San Francisco to nearby towns like Bolinas or distant New York, and I had become a college teacher in northwestern British Columbia. In spring of 1977, I traveled with a group of political activists from B.C. on a three week tour of China. On the way to Shanghai, there was a stopover in Tokyo, and for some reason, we were billeted for the night in an expensive hotel tower, the New Otani. The next morning, I went up to the restaurant on the hotel's 31st floor where the breakfast buffet was served. Standing in the entrance to the restaurant, I became aware, through their alcoholic smell, of two men standing next to me. One of them was wearing a sort of cowboy hat and had a floppy blond mustache. "Richard?" I hesitantly asked. It was Brautigan. He and the other man, a British engineer he'd met in the course of the evening's wanderings, had been up all night drinking, and had now landed at the New Otani for breakfast. I joined them at a table after we'd filled up our plates from the line of silver serving trenchers loaded with scrambled eggs, baked beans, potatoes, bacon, and the rest. I only recall one fragment of the conversation, as we sat at the table, looking out the wraparound windows at Tokyo thirty stories below. I wanly asked, "How's the fishing?" Brautigan blearily gazed at me, and said, "I can hear your mind going. Tick-tock, tick-tock."

That was the last time I saw him. Of course, he couldn't hear my mind, but perhaps he heard something going tick-tock. I soon left to catch the flight to Shanghai.

Some fifteen or so years after Brautigan's death in 1984, I read an essay by a San Francisco poet, August Kleinzahler. The occasion was the posthumous publication of Brautigan's last manuscript, and a memoir by Brautigan's daughter, Ianthe, who I'd known when she was a baby. Kleinzahler (I've met him once) begins, "Bolinas is a sleepy little seaside community about an hour's drive north of San Francisco, at the end of a long, windy road over the hills," which is how I remember it, just beyond the long beaches and town of Stinson Beach, and not far from an egret sanctuary that I used to visit. He notes that the turn-off isn't easy to find, and has been further obscured by residents who have camouflaged the road signs to discourage tourists. For many years, Kleinzahler says, a fair number of artists and writers have made Bolinas their home, and Brautigan was one of them. Kleinzahler recalls that when he gave a reading at the Bolinas library many years ago, a couple of Brautigan's friends from his San Francisco North Beach days in the 1960s mentioned that Brautigan had recently turned up in town.

"I remember hoping that he might come to the reading if he had nothing better to do," Kleinzahler writes. "But there was little chance of that. Brautigan was lying dead in his Bolinas house, having taken a .44 calibre handgun and shot himself in the head. His body lay there for weeks until finally discovered by friends."

That stark memory serves as an introduction to the essay, which is one of those periodic literary soundings about a half-forgotten writer. "Time has not been kind to the writings of Richard Brautigan," Kleinzahler reports, recalling that the critics were already having a go at his inflated reputation by the early 1970s. The critics were, he agrees, "on the whole, quite right: he really wasn't very good after all. The work is not without charm or felicities of style, but it is pretty thin stuff: precious self-indulgent fluff." I didn't pay much attention to Brautigan's later books, but I'm prepared to take the critics' and Kleinzahler's word for it. However, that judgment fails to take account of *Trout Fishing*. Later, Kleinzahler remarks that "the poetry is just flat awful, no two ways about it, and now embarrassing to read, not least, I suppose, because I was so infatuated with it thirty years ago." As for the posthumously published manuscript, a collection of diary entries from 1982 that revolve around the death of a woman friend, Kleinzahler says, "It was unkind of the publishers to release the book. Brautigan is now exhausted and in despair. Two years later, he will be found dead . . . Only some of the tired old mannerisms identify the author, but these, too, have grown faint."

Like others, Kleinzahler wonders what happened. Clearly, the huge success of *Trout Fishing* took its toll on Brautigan. "For someone as gentle, bewildered, alcoholic and vulnerable as him, it must have been powerfully upsetting to be taken up so fast, then dropped so hard," Kleinzahler remarks. That's one of the reasons that Brautigan makes me think of William Saroyan, another California writer, from the generation before Brautigan, the 1930s and 1940s, who employed a somewhat similar faux-naïve manner, and rocketed to celebrity with a book called *The Daring Young Man on the Flying Trapeze*, a title borrowed from a hit song of the period.

What I'm thinking about is not so much the inevitable fading popularity but the danger in a certain kind of voice. Unlike Brautigan's violent end, Saroyan went on churning stuff out in his distinctive style, for an increasingly indifferent readership. But there's something about an overly recognizable voice that invites parody, and worse, as the writer loses energy and something to say, a self-parody within which the writer is finally trapped. It was one of Jack Spicer's more intransigent lessons to us younger writers: Don't repeat yourself, don't write the poems you already can write. Finding oneself cornered in such a situation, mixed with a quixotic ethical code, and a lot of alcohol, might produce a fatally combustible outcome. In any case, Kleinzahler's account of Brautigan's troubled life and end comes out sounding a bit like one of those tearjerker country and western songs that ends with an empty bottle and a bullet.

I thought that Kleinzahler, who I tend to think of as a bit of a Grumpy Gus, might have been a bit more, what?, forgiving, or generous, but on re-reading him, I notice that he does allow that *Trout Fishing in America* "is arguably Brautigan's best book, and although largely rough going forty years later, the writing remains highly original and inventive." Mainly, he remembers the effect of *Trout Fishing* at the time: "There was in the writing something that felt new and fresh . . . Brautigan had a lightness of touch, gorgeous timing and a delicious off-handedness that always managed to hit all the right notes, in just the right sequence . . . Breathtaking stuff." Well, that's fair enough. But, still, it's not enough. Maybe the only difference is that I think that *Trout Fishing* is still pretty breathtaking stuff, a moment of American vision that sees right to the bottom of time's stream, where the current slides away, but eternity remains. Brautigan may have had only one great book, but as those of us who drink at the trough fed by the muses say, One great book is better than no great books. At the end of his essay, Kleinzahler cites William Carlos Williams's remark that "The pure products of America go crazy," then adds, "Sometimes they are simply overwhelmed."

In San Francisco's Washington Square, it's probably around five o'clock in the afternoon again, and the people are no doubt restlessly milling in the park on the cover of *Trout Fishing in America*, across the street from the church where they give out the sandwiches wrapped in newspaper. I hope the sandwiches have more in them than just a leaf of spinach.

Buchenwald

When I walked through the black wrought-iron gate, I expected to see the famous and bitterly ironic slogan of the Nazi concentration camp at Auschwitz, *Arbeit Macht Frei* ("Work makes [one] free"). But at Buchenwald the entrance gate bears the puzzling inscription, *Jedem das Seine*, "To Each His Own," which could also be translated, "To each, what he deserves." Inside the enclosure, the sites of the once-crowded prisoners' barracks are marked by rectangular beds of black stones, amid paths laid with white and grey pebbles, the whole giving the effect (to postmodern eyes) of a large minimalist earthworks sculpture.

From the slope of the camp, beyond a small wood, you look down into a farming valley with a patchwork of neat green and yellow fields. That afternoon, the sun momentarily broke free of the cloudy sky, illuminating the velveteen fields beyond. My first thought was incongruous: "How beautiful it is here!" It's a view shared by writers going all the way back to Goethe, who often strolled on this patch of ground. Later, wandering between the beds of black stones where the barracks had been located — along with other visitors, pilgrims, and groups of adolescent German schoolkids — I felt the urge to tell myself, "This is where it happened," as if I had to insistently remind myself of a fact that's impossible to grasp.

When I travel in Europe and occasionally seek out the sites of my tribal ancestors, I usually visit the old Jewish quarters of cities — Krakow, Vilnius, Budapest — rather than the concentration camps; I prefer the remnants of places where Jews lived and flourished rather than those where they were slaughtered. But some five or six kilometres outside of Weimar, the small German city in Thuringia where Goethe lived, and the place whose name was given to the Weimar Republic of the 1920s, the most notorious concentration camp in Germany is located on a slope of Ettersberg Hill.

Now, more than a half-century after the execution of over 50,000 prisoners there, what remains are the entrance gate buildings, surmounted by a squat clocktower, some concrete posts on which was strung the barbed wire around the 200-hectare enclosure, as well as a few preserved and restored sample barracks, the crematorium and a memorial at the site where the ashes of the incinerated dead were dumped into an accumulating mass grave.

The singularity of the Holocaust in the 20th century, in which six million Jews were murdered by the Nazis, is pinpointed by cultural critic George Steiner. The *Shoah* (as the Holocaust is known in Hebrew) was driven, says Steiner, by the unique principle that "a category of persons, down to infancy, was proclaimed *guilty of being.* Their crime was existence, the mere claim to life."

Not only Jews perished at Buchenwald — also gypsies, prisoners of war, homosexuals, and political prisoners. The best account of what happened there —as much a masterpiece as Primo Levi's *Survival in Auschwitz* — is former political inmate Jorge Semprun's *Life or Literature.* There, Semprun sees himself not so much as a "survivor" but — in contradistinction to Wittgenstein's claim that "death is not an event in our life" — as someone who "crossed through death, which had been an experience of my life."

No one of Jewish descent growing up in America in the 1940s and 1950s could be entirely unaffected by the Holocaust. Indeed, in the necessary Jewish insistence on remembering it, there could even be a kind of mis-use of memory, a nagging for attention. I like the brutal Jewish quip criticising the excesses of exploitation of Holocaust memories, cited by Jacobo Timerman in his book *The Longest War,* "There's no business like *Shoah*-business." After all, 20th century politics produced sufficient millions of other deaths, driven by various comparably evil principles, that the Holocaust claim of uniqueness need not be an appropriation of exclusivity with regard to suffering.

In my family, Uncle Walter and Aunt Holla were presented to us (I'm tempted to say, exhibited to us) as our survivor relatives. They had managed "to make it out just in time," I was repeatedly told, in what became a recitation of a family legend, whose moral concerned the dangers of procrastination and the vagaries of luck. Yes, Uncle Walter and Aunt Holla, now placidly seated on a sofa across someone's large living room (that of my mother's brother, Irving, perhaps), had sailed on "the last boat out of Europe." As a ten-year-old, I somewhat confusedly tried to imagine a Europe out of which no more boats sailed.

In the late afternoon, under a lowering sky over Buchenwald, I rode the bus back to Weimar, and quickly returned to its tourist-crowded quaint streets and town squares bordered with outdoor cafés. I lingered in the sunshine (it had reappeared), sipping cappuccino, far from history's darkest shadows.

Budapest/Bucharest

Dream city, nightmare city:
The first time I went to Budapest, in 1990, shortly after the end of communism, I stayed in an apartment just below one of the squares near the Danube River, the great river that runs through the city and is spanned by a series of bridges. From the beginning, I saw Budapest as the kind of city you find in dreams. Because you had to walk up a little hill to get to the square by the river, I always had the sense that the city was somehow under water.

Recurrently, little incidents occurred that were like scenes from sleep. One night, with my travelling companion, Tom Sandborn, I walked out into the narrow street outside our apartment building, looking for a place to have a drink. Although we had walked up and down that street several times without ever finding a bar or café, suddenly there appeared, just across the street, a shoebox-sized bar which we hadn't previously noticed. Above the door, there was a hand-daubed circular sign with the words "Orpheus Drink-Bar" on it, as if it had been hastily painted and hung minutes before our arrival, a dream sign for aspiring poets. Inside, they served a liquor called Unicom, a Hungarian specialty.

Again and again, I found myself walking over the hump of one of the bridges over the Danube, as you do in dreams, crossing from the Pest side to the Buda side, or vice-versa, the water far below. The city is aqueous, punctuated by temple-like buildings housing thermal baths, ranging from elegant spas like the one at the Hotel Gellert to ordinary, everyday establishments, like the Rudas, where Tom and I went one afternoon. The vast central pool is located under a cathedral dome, with bits of translucent coloured glass in the ceiling. Through the fog rising from the heated water, you catch glimpses of middle-aged men in loincloths, reading newspapers while half-submerged in the pool, or younger male couples, perched on the bath's edge, like water nymphs.

The people we talked to were also like figures that your unconscious mind presents while you're sleeping, but they were magical and reassuring rather than the frightening demons produced in nightmares. The first person I met, on the night of the first free Hungarian elections since the political collapse of communism, at the headquarters of the youth party, was a beautiful boy, about 19, who became my guide to the city for the rest of the time I was there. He was as striking as an Hermes statue, with black, curly hair, but when he turned his full face to you, there was one brown eye, and the other was completely occluded, like a milky moonstone.

When I returned to Budapest a few years later, it was as dreamy as before, even as Hungarians were waking from the fantasy of freedom into the realities of international capitalism. The one-eyed boy had become a computer technician at an advertising agency. I was staying in an old Jewish quarter, on the hilly, Buda side of the river. My host, a man named Christoph, who lived in a garret above the apartment I'd been given (he came downstairs from time to time at night, to use the kitchen), was a composer of a visionary kind of music he called "Refulgence." He played it for me on the baby grand piano that had been winched into his tiny studio.

There were long, engrossing conversations with intellectuals whose books and articles I had admired — Miklos Haraszti and Gaspar Tamas, among them — but to find them, I had to wander at night through narrow, dark, Kafkaesque streets just off the Danube. Then there was an unexpected jump-cut transition, as in a dream, and I emerged into a lighted, book-stuffed study, lined with shelves from floor to ceiling. In addition, piles of books and journals occupied every available surface, spilling onto chairs, tables and a small day bed against the wall. "Here, let me," said my host, Gaspar, hauling away a tottering heap of volumes to make a space for me to sit down, again as in a dream. Or, another time, I stepped into a sun-drenched square high above the Danube, on my way to a lecture at the newly established Budapest Collegium, and at the same moment, entering the square from the other side was the lecturer, the American philosopher Richard Rorty, in a light-coloured suit, floating like a person met in dreams. I went up and introduced myself, as I have in other dreams to statesmen, writers, movie stars.

On my last night in Budapest, I went to dinner at a neighbourhood restaurant with my composer acquaintance Christoph. On the way home, walking through the dark streets, he stopped to show me something I would have otherwise missed. It was a five-storey apartment building, set back from a tram stop in a little square. An ornate metal grille gate opened into the courtyard, around which rose several floors of apartments. There were lights here and there, laundry hanging to dry, bits of sound from television sets, the normal life of a block of flats at night. But in the centre of the courtyard, instead of a tree or patch of cement, there was a dimly visible, squat, round building. What is it? I wondered. As I drew closer, I saw that its window frames of crumbling cement held a Star of David motif, as did its locked entrance. It is a synagogue, Christoph informed me, and in the darkness I had the sense of encountering a temple underwater, as if from a Jewish Atlantis.

In Bucharest, Romania in spring 1990, no one I met was really certain about what had happened, whether it had been a popular revolution or an internal Communist Party coup or some other sort of plot-like conspiracy that had violently overthrown the previous government only three months ago. On our first afternoon, Sandborn and I, having barely settled into a 19th century inn Tom had discovered in a guidebook, took a neighbourhood walk through the narrow, twisting streets. We came out of the labyrinth into a boulevard where a memorial had been established at the edges of a traffic round. There were candles in glass holders, vases with flowers, and at one place a thick line of red paint had been brushed across the road. The nearby sooty buildings were scarred with bullet marks. But when we talked to some people holding a vigil there, we were unable to determine exactly what was being memorialized or why. We met a man and his wife in their thirties and struck up a conversation. He was a lecturer in a technical faculty at one of the universities. They invited us to visit them at their apartment. But the explanations we were seeking remained elusive.

Is that where we first saw the legless beggar, hauling himself up the cobbled street on a kind of leather apron, using wooden clogs that he clashed down to propel himself forward? Or was it later?

The only thing that was clear was that the former communist dictator, Nicolae Ceausescu, and his wife had been executed by firing squad in an underground room. We had seen that on television, back home, around Christmas time, a repeated clip of the dictator and his wife toppling over and crumpling to the floor. But now that we were here, the rest of the story was murky.

In the centre of Bucharest, we found the architectural remnants of Ceausescu's megalomaniacal intentions. A whole neighbourhood, filled with old houses and a 19th century tangle of narrow streets and lanes, had apparently been leveled, and cleared away. In its place, a monstrous square was laid out, filled with huge mosaic-decorated reflecting pools and dozens of fountains, adorned with sculptures of gargoyles, mermaids and dolphins from which water was supposed to spout. At one side of the square, ranks of six-storey apartment buildings for the Communist Party's officials, not yet finished, had been constructed in white marble, their facades designed in undulating waves. Across the square, on a slight rise, was an even larger structure, also incomplete, Ceausescu's palace, in the same white marble and unique architectural undulations. The whole thing was grotesque, but had a sort of chilling grandeur, like the models for the city of Germania, Hitler's notion for the Nazi transformation of Berlin. Here, it wasn't just an architectural model, but an actual construction site. Everything was unfinished, abandoned; there was no water, the reflecting pools were empty, baking in the sun, the spouts on the sculptures of the gargoyles and mermaids were not yet connected to water pipes, the fountains were dry. The skeletons of buildings remained in their incomplete state. For a moment, seeing the site was like peering into the mind of the madman who had envisaged it.

We retreated to the inn. It was a three-storey enclosed wooden structure, like something left over from the Ottoman Empire. Once inside its gates, there was a large circular courtyard in the centre where a bustle of activity unfolded through the day — the delivery of goods, cackling chickens scampering under the feet of a tethered donkey and wagon, carpet-beating, dogs barking at imaginary caravans, women carrying baskets of laundry. Around and above the courtyard were the facilities of the inn, corridors with rooms to let containing sleeping divans, and a restaurant whose tables spilled out onto a terrace from which to view the scene below. The stairways to the terrace were made of weathered, rotted wood. Several of the steps had been punched through, threatening to plunge you into the melee below. It was timeless, indifferent to empires, communism, or whatever rule was now taking its place. The communists had given way to a mafia whose local representative, as far as we could tell, included the captain of the waiters in the inn's restaurant.

He was an ominous figure, his obsequious service masking his powers. I observed him one evening serving a table of drunken English louts, who were shouting for this and that, making vulgar joking remarks about sex and the defeated Russians, bellowing, "Russkie, Russkie!" at him. But the head waiter was also the source of various goods — items not listed on the menu, bottles of expensive whiskey, drugs, sex. He was equally imperturbable whether dealing with visiting yobs or local oily businessmen, but he seemed to me like a man into whose debt I wouldn't want to put myself. The inn was an enclosed world, far from whatever else was going on in Bucharest, yet reproducing the city's mentality.

It was a city caught in a swirl of rumours, rife with superstition, paranoia, conspiracy theories. We visited a government ministry and talked with a man who dealt with ethnic minorities. We entered a large room with a conference table, and the government official introduced us to a visitor with whom he was finishing some business, an elderly heavy-set man in an old-fashioned suit and wearing a bowler hat, apparently an important gypsy chief. When the chief left, we interviewed the ethnic minorities official, who told us he was part-gypsy himself. He was a sophisticated, witty man, who readily confirmed, with a certain amusement, the great confusion about who was in control of the government. At one moment in the transition, he told us, he had been held at gunpoint, suspected, because of his swarthy appearance, of being a Libyan agent. In the end though, he didn't say who he represented. He said, "A Romanian is a man who, just before he leaves his house, looks in the mirror, and winks. And sometimes the reflection in the mirror winks at him."

Before we left Bucharest, we visited the couple from the technical university who we'd met the first day at the memorial. They received us at their apartment, and gave us coffee and little cakes. At first, the conversation proceeded normally as we talked about Romanian politics. But then they began to talk about shadowy figures who were behind recent events. Gradually it came out that the ones pulling the strings were Jews, connected to an international ring of fellow Jewish bankers and dealers. The man said something to his wife, and she went out of the sitting room for a moment, and then returned with a book. "It's all in here," he said, as she nodded in agreement. The book was a volume of the 500-year-old prophecies of Nostradamus, some of whose lines he read to us and then interpreted in terms of Romanian politics. Afterwards, outside their building, Tom and I exchanged a glance, gritting our teeth, raising our eyebrows, and almost simultaneously shuddering.

Finally, one night towards the end of our stay, we were coming back to the inn after a long, hot day of travelling through the city and interviewing people with whom we had appointments. We were physically weary and thirsty, exhausted in the particular way that is produced by working through a baffle of half-comprehended languages and explanations. It was dark and we entered a narrow lane that was just a street or two away from the inn. We turned a corner, then another, and then we were unsure of where we were. Even Tom, who has a sure sense of direction that allows him to plunge into a strange city for a morning's jog, certain of finding his way back, was momentarily baffled. The streetlamps were dim or out, the winding streets were empty of people, there was only the occasional skinny dog, skulking along the base of a building. Tom asked for my cigarette lighter to hold up to a street sign, but the flame flickered, sputtered. Is that when we heard the wooden clogs crashing on the cobblestones? Did we glimpse the legless beggar disappearing around a corner? And for a moment, only a moment, we were lost in the maze, tantalizingly close to our destination but infinitely far from it, trapped in the nightmare of Bucharest.

C

Café Bonaparte

The Café Bonaparte in Paris, where a good part of my sexual education was initiated in 1960, is located on the Rue Bonaparte at the edge of Place St.-Germain-des-Prés. The square features the oldest medieval church in Paris. The café is still there today. I recently found a contemporary photo of the five-storey building at 42 Rue Bonaparte in which it is housed on the main floor. There's a new garish awning in the blue, red and white French national colours, but the tables and chairs on the tiny terrace appear to be little changed, and as fully occupied as they were in 1960.

Cafés and bars are among the social institutions by which I make sense of the world, and have been since I was in my teens. They have multiple functions, beginning with the simple sociability of being a place where you can meet friends and acquaintances. They also offer both public solitude in which you can read, write, and meditate, and a shifting scene of unexpected encounters. In each of the cities where I've lived or visited, I've found suitable cafés in which to hang out. I began in San Francisco's North Beach in 1958 at the Co-Existence Bagel Shop, where I talked to a black painter called Mad Alex, and played chess with a Persian chess master. Almost a half-century later in Berlin, I go to Kastanie (the Chestnut), Zwiebelfisch (the Onionfish), and Pinocchio, a café-bar named for the Italian children's tale. Even in Vancouver, which I don't think of as a café city, I prefer to meet people at coffee shops in either the Kitsilano neighbourhood where I live or on Commercial Drive. When I visit Brian Fawcett in Toronto, we go to his regular neighbourhood hangout, or "office" as he sometimes calls it, Dooney's Café on Bloor St., a café we have extended into a website magazine of that name.

The Café Bonaparte in Paris opened a previously mysterious and scary aspect of reality to me. I was 19 and visited Paris on several month-long furloughs from the naval air base outside of Naples, Italy, where I was stationed for two years. At first, I went to Paris alone, later I brought navy mates from the base, Larry Ray and David Martin. In Paris, I lived in the Beat Hotel at 9 Rue Git-le-Coeur, a little street in the student and artist quarter behind the Place Saint Michel, from which one could see the Seine River at the end of the block. My room was next door to that of the poets Allen Ginsberg and Peter Orlovsky, who were friends from San Francisco. Gregory Corso, William Burroughs and Brion Gysin also had rooms in the hotel, which was presided over by the grey-haired Madame Rachou, who provided café-au-lait and croissants in the breakfast room café below.

I found the Bonaparte more or less by accident. On the main boulevard of the St.-Germain were the famous cafés, the Deux Magots and the Café Flore, where Jean-Paul Sartre and Simone de Beauvoir spent much of their time when they were in Paris, and where Roland Barthes could also be found. It was at the Deux Magots that Ginsberg one day introduced me to the elderly Dada poet Tristan Tzara.

The Café Bonaparte was on the corner of a narrow street at the bottom of the square. The Bonaparte was a hybrid café-bar, and attracted a mixed crowd of local artists and intellectuals, some foreign visitors, and a gang of French boys and girls my age who occupied some tables near the pinball machines, which they played. The first people I met in the Bonaparte one afternoon were an English couple living in Paris, two men in their late thirties (I thought of them as middle-aged), who were in the art business. The Bonaparte had sets of glass doors that extended around the café and could be opened, giving the place an open-air quality. Soon I joined the two men, who I'll call Lindsay and Clive, since I can't remember their names, at their regular table, facing the street. The striking and at the time exotic aspect of the two men was that they were homosexual queens, a breed of man I didn't know much about, but that fascinated me.

Lindsay and Clive took me in hand, taught me to drink Pernod, helped me with my French (which quickly became passable, at least for street use), but more important, through their conversation they began to educate me about how things worked. One of the ways things worked at the Bonaparte, I learned, was that it was possible to go with the boys there. Some were students, others were what we would now call Parisian street kids, who hung out at the Bonaparte with their girlfriends and sometimes went to bed with the customers at the bar when they needed a place to stay, or pocket money. Lindsay and Clive gradually explained all this to me, and satisfied themselves that my pronounciation of the sentence *"Voulez-vous coucher avec moi?"* (a version of which later became the title of a pop song) was acceptable, as I became friends with a guy my age named Luc. Finally, one day, I took a little walk around the square with Luc and I tried out my magic sentence, which seemed to me like a daring thing to say to another person. *"À condition,"* Luc amiably replied, which mainly had to do with whether I had a place we could go. I did — the Beat Hotel — but I also absorbed the larger point that all of life is presented to us "on condition."

The next afternoon I reported my adventure to Lindsay and Clive, who approved of my choice. Soon, I was part of the gang of Luc's friends, and could sit at the tables near the pinball machines as well as with my English acquaintances. My friends Harold and Dora Dull were also in Paris at the time and I took them to the Bonaparte one crowded evening — we were all at the bar drinking Pernod — and I pointed out Luc. They too approved of, and were amused by my new-found affection. Dora put her imprimatur on this new part of my life with an encouraging "Ooh la la." I think Ginsberg was also at the Bonaparte one evening, perhaps after some art event in the neighbourhood, since he didn't go to bars much.

All of this approval from people older than me, whether six or seven years in the case of Harold and Dora, or 15 or so years in the case of Allen and the English queens — approval from elder siblings, mentors, substitute parents — was enormously important. Going to bed with people of the same sex was at that time an officially forbidden and socially disapproved activity, about as disapproved a sexual activity as could be imagined. I had had sex before, but always under terrifying conditions. The difference here was that it was guilt-free, shame-free, playful. It didn't matter whether or not anyone else knew, and those that did regarded it completely without censure. Most important, Luc treated it as natural; he had a quality of sexual calmness just like the characters in Jean Genet's *Our Lady of the Flowers*, which Ginsberg had instructed me to read. All this resounding approval gave me courage to explore my desires, to follow my nose, and other appendages.

Nowadays, the young sailor I was then seems like another person, with his tremulous desires and naïve intelligence. It would be handy, if like Christopher Isherwood at the beginning of *Goodbye to Berlin*, I could say, "I am a camera with its shutter open, quite passive, recording, not thinking ... Some day, all this will have to be developed, carefully printed, fixed." Isherwood is the literary spirit hovering over this particular set of memories. But there was no camera, and my mind doesn't work like one. The circumstances are closer to what Isherwood says about his younger self in *Down There On a Visit*, a novel written at the very time I was going to the Bonaparte: "For, of course, he is almost a stranger to me. I have revised his opinions, changed his accent and his mannerisms, unlearned or exaggerated his prejudices and his habits. We still share the same skeleton, but its outer covering has altered so much that I doubt if he would recognize me on the street."

My younger self had a sturdy body, on the edge of husky (a word used in those days for young men who were likely to run to fat later on), and I can see, from photographs, that he had a kind of beauty, somewhat in the style of the then-popular singer, Elvis Presley. But he was no doubt preoccupied with his imperfections, adolescent pimples or something like that, and thus had no idea that others might see him as attractive. I don't know what these experiences were for Luc. We went together many times, but his image has merged with those of other boys I met at the Bonaparte, so that when I look into the recesses of memory, there is an image, not merely an idea of him, but a felt presence, a tangible body across whose bare chest, barely rising and subsiding in sleep, my arm is draped, yet the image is generic rather than specific.

What is specific are the interior architectures of the Bonaparte and the room in the Beat Hotel. In the room, there are sheets of newspaper spread on the windowsill above the bed where the two of them are sleeping late, and on the paper the socks and underpants they washed in the room's little sink the night before are drying in the morning breeze. The door opens a crack and Madame Rachou's head appears, checking to see if the room is free so she can make the bed. The boy I barely recognize half-wakens for an instant, while the other boy, the French one, continues to sleep, and Madame Rachou discreetly and quietly shuts the door. Later, in the afternoon, or evening, having gone their separate ways during the day, the two young men will see each other again, through the thicket of customers, across the tables and pinball machines of the Café Bonaparte, and greet each other by formally shaking hands and exchanging the frank but private looks of those who know each other.

Italo Calvino

I

Often, when I find myself contemplating a scene, whether of people at a dinner table, or an advertisement I'm watching on television, or some ducks in the lake I'm looking at from a park bench in the Tiergarten in Berlin, I begin constructing a logic for the occasion. I make observations, and ask questions: Why does the gray duck have dark green iridescent dorsal feathers? I attempt generalizations: Whether you account for them as caused by a god (dubious) or generated by evolution (likely), those iridescent green feathers remain mysterious. Why green? Why iridescent? Why there? I lament my failings. I should have taken the nature course at school. Eventually, and inevitably, I reach a tangle of hopeless absurdity and give up. I allow the world to reappear in its ordinariness, with the ducks bobbing around and hunting for food. At that moment, I realize I have been looking at the world through the eyes of Mr. Palomar, the eponymous character of Italo Calvino's novel, *Mr. Palomar* (1983).

Mr. Palomar is Calvino himself, as the American novelist and essayist Gore Vidal mentions in his essay, "Calvino's Death" (1985), and Calvino's short book, the last one he completed, consists of a number of meditations on different subjects. A photograph of Calvino shows a man in his fifties, with a high forehead, black hair plastered back on either side of his head, heavily-lidded eyes, a wide mouth, lips narrowly pursed shut, a slight chin and cheeks going jowly — the total effect bears a slight resemblance to a contemplative iguana.

The settings of Mr. Palomar's meditations, according to Vidal, are the familiar landscapes of Calvino's life. Although born in Cuba — his father was an agronomist working on the island at the time, 1923 — Calvino's home was the town of San Remo, on the Italian Riviera, in the province of Liguria, adjacent to France's Côte d'Azur. The scenes in Mr. Palomar take place on the beach at Castiglion della Pescaia, in Calvino's nearby house in the woods at Roccamare, at his flat in Rome (where Vidal also had an apartment), and in such other places as a food specialty shop in Paris, a city where Calvino spent much of his time, or a zoo in Barcelona, or amid the Tula ruins in Mexico.

Mr. Palomar begins his adventures on the beach where he is looking at a wave. "It is not 'the waves' that he means to look at," Calvino notes, "but just one individual wave." Naturally, that leads to trouble, because "it is very difficult to isolate one wave, separating it from the wave immediately following it, which seems to push it and at times overtakes it and sweeps it away; just as it is difficult to separate that one wave from the wave that precedes it and seems to drag it towards the shore, unless it turns against its follower as if to arrest it." Nor is that the extent of the difficulties in looking at a wave for this "nervous man who lives in a frenzied and congested world." There are countless considerations to take into account.

At one point, while concentrating his attention on the backward thrusting of waves, "it seems that the true movement is the one that begins from the shore and goes out to sea." Calvino asks, "Is this perhaps the real result that Mr. Palomar is about to achieve? To make the waves run in the opposite direction, to overturn time, to perceive the true substance of the world beyond sensory and mental habits?" If so, Mr. Palomar has no more success than anyone else who attempts to command the waves of the sea. Instead, our wave-watcher, just like us, most likely, loses patience and gives up. "Mr. Palomar goes off along the beach, tense and nervous as when he came, and even more unsure about everything."

There are further adventures on the beach, but the one I like best, because it encapsulates almost everything Calvino is trying to do in his book, is called "The Naked Bosom." Mr. Palomar is walking along a lonely beach where there are few bathers. However, "one young woman is lying on the sand, taking the sun, her bosom bared. Palomar, discreet by nature, looks away at the horizon of the sea." As a proto-feminist, Mr. Palomar is sensitive to the situation in which a strange man approaches and the bare-bosomed woman feels obliged to hastily cover herself. "This does not seem right to him: because it is a nuisance for the woman peacefully sun-bathing," and so he turns his gaze on the outline of a bronze-pink cloud in the distance (which happens to also have the shape of a naked female torso); at least he has shown his "civil respect for the invisible frontier that surrounds people."

But having passed the young woman and resumed his stroll, it occurs to him that in acting as he has, "I display a refusal to see; or, in other words, I am finally reinforcing the convention that declares illicit any sight of the breast ... My not looking presupposes that I am thinking of that nakedness, worrying about it; and this is basically an indiscreet and reactionary attitude."

So, returning from his walk and again passing the bather, "this time he keeps his eyes fixed straight ahead, so that his gaze touches with impartial uniformity the foam of the retreating waves, the boats pulled up on the shore, the great bath towel spread out on the sand, the swelling moon of lighter skin with the dark halo of the nipple, the outline of the coast in the haze, gray against the sky." Mr. Palomar is satisfied with himself. He has succeeded "in having the bosom completely absorbed by the landscape." But wait a minute, he further reflects. "Does it not mean flattening the human person to the level of things, considering it as an object, and, worse still, considering as object that which in the person is the specific attribute of the female sex?" Isn't he simply perpetuating the old habit of male superiority?

He is compelled to turn and retrace his steps. This time, while gazing at the beach with neutral objectivity, "he arranges it so that, once the woman's bosom enters his field of vision, a break is noticeable, a shift, almost a darting glance." Now, he's made his position quite clear, with no possible misunderstandings. But hold on. "Couldn't this grazing of his eyes be finally taken for . . . an underestimation of what a breast is and means, a somehow putting it aside, on the margin . . . relegating the breast again to that semi-darkness where centuries of sexomaniac puritanism and desire considered as sin . . ." No, it won't do. He does an about-face. "With firm steps he walks again towards the woman lying in the sun." This time, giving the landscape a fickle glance, his gaze "will linger on the breast with special consideration, but will quickly include it in an impulse of good-will and gratitude for the whole, for the sun and the sky, for the bent pines . . . ," etc.

Well, that's it for the bather. The moment he approaches, she springs up, covers herself, and goes off in a huff, knowing she's been ogled by a dirty old man, with "the tiresome insistence of a satyr." As for Palomar, he bitterly concludes that "the dead weight of an intolerant tradition prevents anyone's understanding . . . the most enlightened intentions." He, too, shuffles off, along the beach. And we, the readers, smile or chuckle, understanding that we've been presented, in a sophisticated comic mode, with a survey of one of the great issues of the era, the critical evaluation of the asymmetric equalities of women and men.

What gradually becomes clear, through the story about the bosom, and succeeding ones about copulating turtles, looking at the moon in the afternoon, listening to whistling blackbirds in the garden where Palomar sits and his wife weeds, going to the zoo to see the giraffes and the iguanas, and all the rest, is that Calvino is providing an almost complete, albeit hilarious, course in philosophy. You could teach Mr. Palomar in an introductory course on reality and knowledge, raising all the basic questions about perception and illusion, time and space, understanding and mortality, with Calvino's slapstick thrown in for free. One semester I did just that, and it was just as successful (or unsuccessful) as when I teach Thomas Nagel's *What Does It All Mean?*, or some other standard textbook.

The stories in Mr. Palomar are organized, as Calvino explains in an "Index" note, in an ingenious, tripartite schema. There are three sets of nine stories each, and each of the parts, "Palomar's Vacation," "Palomar in the City," and "The Silences of Palomar," correspond to the three thematic areas of the book, each of the sets numbered 1, 2, 3. For instance, "those marked 1 generally correspond to a visual experience, whose object is almost always some natural form; the text tends to belong to a descriptive category." Stories marked 2 have cultural or anthropological elements and take the form of a story. Those designated with a 3 involve more speculative experience, and are inclined to be meditative. What's more, each of the parts is subdivided into three parts, also numbered, and each of the subdivisions contains three stories, further numbered.

It sounds a bit complicated, but it's quite simple. The first story, about looking at a wave, is in the first part, which emphasizes visual descriptive experience, and it's also in the first subdivision, and it's the first piece in that subdivision, so it's numbered "1.1.1." Whereas, the second story about the naked bosom is mainly visual and descriptive, but contains an element of the anthropological and cultural, so it's marked "1.1.2." In the second part, which emphasizes the cultural, all the stories begin with the number 2, and a story about Mr. Palomar being in a specialty cheese shop in Paris, which is the second story in the second subdivision of part 2, is designated "2.2.2," and of course there are other stories that have markings like "2.1.3" or "2.3.1," etc., until we get to the last story, "Learning to be dead," a meditative work through-and-through, marked "3.3.3." Thus, there are "three kinds of experience and enquiry that, in varying proportions, are present in every part of the book." Of course, Calvino's "Index," though accurate, is also part of the fun, though neither Calvino nor Mr. Palomar are in the least fooling around.

Throughout, there are sharp-eyed observations and illuminating aperçus. In the story about the mating tortoises ("1.2.1"), amid the clacking turtle shells, Mr. Palomar asks, "What does eros become if there are plates of bone or horny scales in the place of skin?" Considering blackbirds ("1.2.2"), Palomar notices that the blackbird's whistle "is identical with a human whistle, the effort of someone not terribly skilled at whistling," and he begins to imagine that if humans "were to invest in whistling" everything normally entrusted to words, "and if the blackbird were to modulate into his whistling all the unspoken truth of his natural condition, then the first step would be taken towards bridging the gap between . . . between what and what?

Nature and culture? Silence and speech?" In the end, they simply "go on whistling, questioning in their puzzlement, he and the blackbirds."

Visiting the Vincennes zoo (a story called "The Giraffe Race," number "2.3.1"), Mr. Palomar observes that "every now and then the adult giraffes start running, followed by the baby giraffes; they charge almost to the fence, wheel around, repeat the dash two or three times, then stop. Mr. Palomar never tires of watching the giraffes race, fascinated by their unharmonious movements." And while Mr. Palomar is pondering the "complicated harmony that commands that unharmonious trampling," I, as the reader, who am also especially fond of those long-necked, ungainly creatures, start thinking about giraffes too. I see the running giraffes as letters of the alphabet, specifically as *h*-shaped animals, and more specifically as lower-case *h*'s in italics (to account for the shorter back legs), and all the italic *h*'s are moving backwards across the page, from right to left. Then I catch myself, whoops, realizing I'm turning into Mr. Palomar once again.

At the Ryoanji Zen Buddhist garden in Kyoto, Japan, which consists of raked white sand and groups of positioned rocks, Mr. Palomar tries to get into the meditative spirit of the place and "allow the indefinable harmony that links the elements" of the garden to gradually pervade him. "Or rather, he tries to imagine all these things as they would be felt by someone who could concentrate at looking at the Zen garden in solitude and silence. Because — we had forgotten to say — Mr. Palomar is crammed on the [viewing] platform in the midst of hundreds of visitors, who jostle him on every side; camera-lenses and movie-cameras force their way past the elbows, knees, ears of the crowd, to frame the rocks and the sand from every angle ... Swarms of feet in wool socks step over him ... numerous offspring are thrust to the front row by pedagogical parents ..." Just try to meditate.

Finally — and I say finally because any proper consideration of *Mr. Palomar* would, in a Borgesian manner, simply present the entirety of the text — there is one story in the book which cannot be passed up. Every reader of *Mr. Palomar* will have his or her favourite piece, the one that somehow sums up everything. (A friend of mine, for example, who is particularly partial to birds, and who lives in an apartment with an observation terrace, just like Mr. Palomar's terrace in Rome, would no doubt choose a bird story, since *Mr. Palomar* is filled with thousands of birds, and since she too is always noting the doings of birds.) Mine is "Serpents and skulls" ("3.1.2").

Mr. Palomar is visiting the ruins of Tula in Mexico, the ancient capital of the Toltecs, in the company of a friend who is an impassioned and eloquent expert on pre-Columbian civilization, and can tell Palomar everything about what it all means. This is quite handy, since "in Mexican archeology every statue, every object, every detail of a bas-relief stands for something that stands for something else that stands, in turn, for yet another something. An animal stands for a god who stands for a star that stands for an element or a human quality and so on." Fortunately, Mr. Palomar's friend is there to explain what each thing stands for and what it means.

While wandering through Tula, Mr. Palomar and his friend cross paths from time to time with another party of sightseers. "A group of schoolchildren moves among the ruins: stocky boys with the features of the Indios, descendents perhaps of the builders of these temples." They're in school uniforms, and resemble Boy Scouts. "The boys are led by a teacher not much taller than they are and only a little more adult, with the same round, dark, impassive face. They climb the top steps of the pyramind, stop beneath the columns, the teacher tells what civilization they belong to, what century, what stone they are carved from, then concludes, 'We don't know what they mean,' and the group follow him down the steps." At each stop, the teacher supplies some facts, and then invariably adds, "We don't know what it means."

Though Mr. Palomar continues to follow the wonderful and rich explanations of his expert friend, filled with a wealth of mythological references, allegorical readings, and the play of interpretation, he always ends up crossing the path of the schoolboys and overhearing the teacher's words. At last they're at the Wall of the Serpents. It is perhaps the most beautiful piece in Tula: a relief-frieze consisting of a sequence of serpents, each holding a human skull in its open jaws.

At that moment, "The boys go by. The teacher says, 'This is the wall of the serpents. Each serpent has a skull in its mouth. We don't know what they mean.'" This time, Palomar's friend can no longer contain himself. "Yes, we do!" he bursts out. "It's the continuity of life and death; the serpents are life, the skulls are death. Life is life because it bears death with it, and death is death because there is no life without death . . ."

The boys listen, "mouths agape, black eyes dazed." Palomar reflects that maybe the "refusal to comprehend more than what the stones show us is perhaps the only way to evince respect for their secret; trying to guess is a presumption, a betrayal of that true, lost meaning." Once the school group has disappeared around the corner, leaving the Wall of Serpents to Palomer and his guide, Palomar hears "the stubborn voice of the little teacher resume: 'No es verdad, it is not true, what that señor said. We don't know what they mean.'" That's the story's last word.

II

When Italo Calvino suddenly and unexpectedly died of a cerebral hemorrhage in September 1985, just three weeks short of his 62nd birthday, his friend Gore Vidal hadn't yet read *Mr. Palomar*. On the morning of the funeral, to be held in the beach town of Castiglion della Pescaia, "the first equinoctial storm of the year broke over the city of Rome," and Vidal woke to thunder and lightning, "and thought I was, yet again, in the Second World War." Shortly before noon, a car and driver arrived to take Vidal up the Mediterranean coast to the burial.

Vidal remembered their last meeting earlier that spring, when Calvino was working on lectures he planned to give at Harvard University in the winter, a series titled *Six Memos for the Next Millennium*, of which only five were completed. Vidal commended Calvino on his bravery, for he intended to lecture in English, a language he spoke hesitantly, compared to his fluency in French and Spanish. "Italo smiled," Vidal recalled, "and when he smiled, suddenly, the face would become like that of an enormously bright child who had just worked out the unified field theory." "At Harvard, I shall stammer," Calvino said, "but then I stammer in every language."

But now Calvino was dead. His dying and death were treated in the Italian media as a national calamity for Italian culture. For, "unlike the United States," remarks Vidal acidly, "Italy has both an education system (good or bad is immaterial) and a common culture, both good and bad." When Calvino died, Vidal notes, "Italy went into mourning, as if a beloved prince had died. For an American, the contrast between them and us is striking. When an American writer dies, there will be, if he's a celebrity (fame is no longer possible for any of us), a picture below the fold on the front page; later, a short appreciation on the newspaper's book page (if there is one), usually the work of a journalist or other near-writer who has not actually read any of the dead author's work but is at home with the arcana of gossip . . . and that would be that." Whereas, when Calvino died, the European press regarded his passing as an event that required daily reports from the hospital, the hauling out of actual literary critics, as opposed to journalists or theorists, to assess the author's work over a half dozen pages of the paper, extensive coverage of the funeral. Well, *vive la différence* of Old Europe.

In the car taking him north through the rain, Vidal took up the last novel, *Mr. Palomar*. Calvino had inscribed a copy to Vidal almost two years earlier, and now, with some guilt, he read for the first time the inscription, "For Gore, these last meditations about Nature, Italo."

"Last" is a word artists should not easily use, Vidal reflected. What did this "last" mean?, he wondered. Latest? "Or did he know, somehow, that he was in the process of 'Learning to be dead,' the title of the book's last chapter?" On the way to the cemetary at Castiglion della Pescaia, Vidal read and reflected on his friend's short final novel.

Suddenly, up ahead, on a hill overlooking the sea, there was the town. "To my left is the beach where Palomar saw but sees no longer . . . The sea has turned an odd disagreeable purple color." The cemetery is on another hill in back of the town. "We park next to a piece of medieval wall and a broken tower. I walk up to the cemetery which is surrounded by a high cement wall [and] am reminded of Calvino's deep dislike of cement," which he saw as the emblem of an economic boom burying the Italian Riviera where he had grown up. "To the right of the cemetery entrance a large section of wall has been papered over with the same small funeral notice, repeated several hundred times. The name 'Italo Calvino,' the name of Castiglion della Pescaia, 'the town of Palomar,' the sign says proudly."

Inside, there are a row of vast floral wreaths, "suitable for an American or Neapolitan gangster," Vidal remarks, and a new grave, "the size of a bathtub in a moderately luxurious hotel." The TV camera and photographers are there. Vidal is interviewed by a young journalist. At the foot of the cemetery hill, a van filled with police arrives, for crowds are anticipated. Eventually several hundred friends of Calvino, writers, editors, publishers, press, local dignitaries, fill up the cemetery. The ceremony unfolds.

Calvino is known for the oddly realistic surreality of his most famous books: *Mr. Palomar*; *Invisible Cities*; and above all, *If On a winter's night a traveller*. The latter book begins with a self-reflexive flourish: "You're getting ready to read the new novel by Italo Calvino, *If on a winter's night a traveller*. Relax. Collect yourself. Put all other thoughts aside. Let your surroundings fade." In this paean to the art of reading, which underscores the entire book, Calvino discusses the business of buying and reading books, from adventures in the bookstore, where you're assaulted by bestsellers, and books-you've-meant-to-read, and books-you-should-read, and all the rest, to the dangers at home. You especially have to watch out for the television. "Tell the others, 'No I don't want to watch television!' Raise your voice, or else they won't hear you. 'I'm reading! I don't want to be disturbed!' Maybe they haven't heard you with all the noise, so say it louder, shout, 'I'm just beginning to read the new novel by Italo Calvino!' Or say nothing, if you don't want to; hopefully, they'll leave you in peace."

Like a great shaggy-dog story comic, Calvino can run his routine through all the aspects of the activity of reading, from finding a com-

fortable position to getting the right light. And when we get to the
first chapter of the novel proper, which opens, "The novel begins in a
railway station ...", with locomotive smoke enveloping "part of the
first sentences," even as we make our way into the station café, we
know we're in for something other than a conventional tale. That's
enough to get one started, I can skip the full-blown précis.

What is less known about Calvino's writing, at least outside of his
native land, is how precisely, without surreality or slapstick, he writes
about political issues and his literary apprenticeship in the 1940s and
'50s. *Hermit in Paris*, a posthumous gathering of scattered autobiographical pieces, provides a nice sense of how Calvino got to *Mr.
Palomar*. Several of the essays recount the experience of a provincial
boy in obscure San Remo who, toward the end of World War II, is
drawn into the nearby hills, fighting as an anti-fascist partisan for
some 20 months. He becomes a youthful, non-ideological member of
the Communist Party, and moves to the great city of Turin. There, he
acquires a mentor, the Italian novelist Cesare Pavese, writes cultural
journalism for *L'Unita*, the Communist newspaper, and gets a job in
publishing.

It's interesting, especially now, some fifteen years or so after communism, when we can be ideologically more neutral, to recognize
how for post-war European intellectuals, not only in Italy, but elsewhere (in France, say, for Sartre and Camus), that the central question that everyone had to respond to was what was one's relationship
to communism, the one plausible alternative to both the recently-
defeated fascist totalitarianism and to looming international capitalism. Calvino remained in the Communist Party until 1957, leaving it
in the wake of the Soviet invasion of Hungary in 1956, and the failure
to reform communism after the death of Joseph Stalin. Still, as late as
1980, he asks in the title of one essay, "Was I a Stalinist, Too?", and,
as might be expected, the answers are subtle. Other essays are simply
enjoyable for their mastery: the title piece, "Hermit in Paris," that
deals with his long residency in that city, or "The Duce's Portraits,"
an account of the iconography of Mussolini that pervaded his youth.

In his later interviews, the self-mocking mode is tempered by
melancholic irony. For somebody's idiotic project called *Behind the
Success*, a collection in which "some of the most important people of
our time" reveal "the secrets of their success," Calvino says, "I would
very much like to be one of those writers who have something really
clear in their head to say and throughout their life they promote this
idea in their works. I would like to be like that, but I am not ... I
always think of the pros and cons in everything and each time I have
to construct a very complex picture. This is the reason why I can even
go many years without publishing anything, working on projects

which constantly end up in crisis. So you see that coming to interview me on the subject of success is really barking up the wrong tree." He concludes, "Perhaps the time has come for me to accept myself as I am, and write just as it comes, for the remainder of the life that is left to me, or even to give up there and then if I saw that I had nothing more to say."

Meanwhile, at the funeral in Castiglion, where Calvino has nothing more to say, but Vidal does, "with a crash, the pallbearers drop the box into the shallow bathtub. Palomar's nose is now about four inches beneath the earth he used to examine so minutely. Then tiles are casually arranged over the coffin; and the box is seen no more . . . We look at one another as though we are at a party that has refused to take off." Vidal gazes around at well-known writers; he recognizes Natalia Ginzburg, and sees "someone who looks as if he ought to be Umberto Eco, and is." Calvino's daughter "and buckets of cement arrive simultaneously. One of the masons pours cement over the tiles; expertly, he smooths the viscous surface with a trowel. Horrible cement." The cement Calvino hated.

Then there's a final Calvinoesque moment. Vidal looks up "from the gray oblong of fresh cement and there, staring straight at me, is Calvino. He looks anguished, odd, not quite right. But it is unmistakably Mr. Palomar, witnessing his own funeral. For one brief mad moment we stare at each other; then he looks down at the coffin that contains not himself but Italo." The man is Calvino's younger brother.

I look at the photo of Calvino again, the one that makes me think of a contemplative iguana. But then I think, Do photos really tell us anything about what someone thinks, or what he is like? Isn't too much made of interpretive descriptions of photographed faces?

Just then my eyes happen to light on a nearby photo of the writer Primo Levi, Calvino's compatriot, on the cover of a book of Levi's to which Calvino has contributed an afterword. There is Levi, survivor of Auschwitz, who died two years after Calvino, in 1987, in a fall believed to have been suicide. He sits at a desk with his hands resting passively on its surface; he's wearing a short-sleeved shirt and a sleeveless sweater over it, and you notice his somewhat hairy forearms. Is there a faint tattoo on one of them, from Auschwitz? His face is a burnished tan, his grey hair is in a brush cut, he has a mustache and a trimmed white beard. Behind his glasses, his eyes are intense and possibly anguished; altogether, he has a spidery quality . . . Then, just as I'm about to arrive at an enthusiastic generalization, I once more catch myself: Aha, I'm looking at the world through the eyes of Mr. Palomar.

Canada

I often find myself thinking about Canada around Thanksgiving time because it is one of those count-your-blessings holidays. The Thanksgiving holiday tends to inspire national musings, especially if you're a Canadian who immigrated from the United States. One of the first things you notice is that while Canada and the U.S. both celebrate Thanksgiving and gobble up turkeys, they do so on different days, more than a month apart. At first, if you're an American immigrant to Canada, you think of the second weekend in October as "Canadian Thanksgiving," in contrast to "Thanksgiving," i.e., the "real" (American) Thanksgiving. After a few decades of dwelling north of the U.S. border, you eventually get the idea that Thanksgiving occurs somewhere around Columbus Day in October and that there's also something you now think of as "American Thanksgiving," which consists mainly of American football games on television. So, I've been reflecting on the True North, Strong and etc. Here's what I've been thinking.

I

John Ralston Saul's book about Canada at the end of the 20th century, *Reflections of a Siamese Twin*, begins with a consideration of national myths and their relation to the reality of the country they concern. Though I normally tend to think of mythology in a literal sense as the stories and figures of pre- and quasi-history — Hermes, Orpheus, Odysseus, etc. — Ralston Saul uses the term to refer to distorted ideological images of Canada. To that sort of "mythology," he sensibly counterposes a re-reading and remembering of the actual past. I should note, by way of a declaration of interests, that I'm a friend of Saul and an acquaintance of his wife, Adrienne Clarkson, who was named Governor-General of Canada in the late 1990s (with Saul thereby becoming His Excellency, the Governor-General's consort). The two of them seem to me the most intelligent and intellectually elegant people to occupy high office in the country since Prime Minister Pierre Elliot Trudeau in the 1970s.

Saul's *Reflections* enumerate and challenge a number of national myths, starting with the notion that Canada was founded on the basis of a conquest by the British of the French. Other "myths" include the claim that Canada is a land of two (or more) solitudes and pervasive isolation; that Western Canadian and other regional alienation is a simple fact rather than an ideological position; that the country's allegedly natural north to south ties are distorted by the imposition of its east to west boundaries; that Canada is constructed on a classic European nation-state model; and finally, that Canada finds its sole *raison d'être* in being not-American. Saul argues that all of those ideas are distortions of reality. Interestingly, another recent book that challenges ideas about Canadian-American similarities, Michael Adams's *Fire and Ice*, which I've discussed elsewhere (see "Dave Barrett"), uses the term "myth" in its subtitle. Adams's book counters "the myth of converging values" between the two countries, and demonstrates a growing divergence of attitudes and values between Americans and Canadians in recent years.

Saul launches his argument for the unusual character of the country by noting that "Canada, like other nation-states, suffers from a contradiction between its public mythologies and its reality." He recognizes that mythology can have its good and bad days, as can various nationalisms. It can help "citizens to summon up enough energy to consider the public good," but it can also encourage a denial of reality, in whose atmosphere "a rising undercurrent of fear creates the self-demeaning need for certitude. Absolute answers and ideologies prosper" in the place of healthy doubt. Flag-waving and chest-thumping also flourish. "In this way mythology becomes not so much false as mystification."

Mythologies gone wrong, Saul argues, tend to turn on heroics and victimization. "The very act of brandishing slogans and flags, when done in the name of heroics or victimization," he says, "necessitates the identification of villains." Even though the need for villains is often denied, there's usually a "code" by which "to identify the enemy, unnameable because they are a race or a language group or believers in another religion."

In Saul's view, the fundamental complexities that characterize Canada are a) its crosscutting founding linguistic groups, including its aboriginal inhabitants; b) its geographic northernness and particular accomodation to place and circumstance; and c) its social democratic ameliorative character. Such complexity can be lost in "the dangerous false clarity of mythological truth." Of course, "we need a reasonable level of identity, nationalism, self-respect, pride and, for that matter, fantasy"; but, taken beyond the reasonable, we're in trouble, and the country is then dominated by "the provincial, colonial mind at its most insecure." Distorted mythologies subsume reality. "How is this done? Practical memory is eliminated. The modern tools of communication become the tools of propaganda. And fear of the consequences of non-conformity is propagated."

Deformed mythology inspires a sense of victimization (each group sees itself as a victim of something or someone else), and a pervasive sense of victimization produces unrealistic, usually simplistic, imaginary options. Trivial contemporary examples of "imaginary options" range from the cries of victims of alienation who call for an independent "Cascadia" (or western Canada) to the straining of various Canadian cities to be "world-class," a sort of wannabe mythology that bears little relation to reality. Saul historically locates much of this problem in the dominance and negative nationalism of two racist, anti-democratic 19th century movements, the Ultramontanes in Lower Canada, or Quebec, which resisted modernization and fought for Catholic Church control of education and politics, and the Orange Order in Upper Canada, or Ontario, which provoked the persecution of the Métis people, attacked francophone rights, and brought the Protestant prejudices and divisions of Ireland to Canada, *circa* 1830. Their legacy is no longer dominant, although it remains alive in contemporary Canada in the form of a neoconservative political party and the most negative elements of Quebec separatism.

Saul opposes both the mythologies of a founding conquest and a contemporary need to be not-American. By the latter, he means, Canadians *are* not-American, but their differences from Americans are not driven by a neurotic need to be not-American. As a by-the-way — and I'll just cite this as a single example of method rather than reprise the entire text — Saul notices that the alleged founding British and French were not really all that British or French, but were actually "Scots and Irish, Bretons and Normans. In other words, on both sides the origins were largely northern (Viking) and Celtic. And on both sides these Celts were the descendents of the losers in the wars waged by London and Paris for central control and the elimination of both regional cultures and languages inside Britain and France. There could be no more eloquent illustration of the colonial mind-set than a bunch of Celts and Vikings in a distant northern territory insulting each other as *les anglais* and *the French*, as if they were the descendents of the people who had subjected and ruined them. But then racial interpretations always end up as farce or black comedy."

Against the colonial mind-set, Saul counterposes the reformers who sought some form of independent, reconciliatory, "responsible" government, government that was inclusive not only of francophones and anglophones, but the aboriginal inhabitants. He identifies the figures of the 1837 Rebellion, the Confederation of the mid-1860s, and their successors over the next century and a half, as those with an authentic vision of the country. He particularly focuses on the formal agreement in 1842 (for the unification of Upper and Lower Canada) and the "binding handshake" of Louis-Hippolyte LaFontaine and Robert Baldwin, the country's original "Siamese twins."

The title metaphor of Saul's book is inspired by Jacques Godbout's novel *Les Têtes à Papineau*, an allegorical tale about Siamese twins with two heads, one body, and two separate but interrelated personalities, whom most everyone wants separated, or "normalized . . . banalized," as Saul remarks. I'm not especially taken with this metaphor, considering the real-life difficulties of conjoined twins. Still, I'm persuaded by Saul's argument about the character of Canada, which differentiates it from both the United States and Europe, excepting some of the Scandinavian countries. The latter share with Canada its northernness and its social democratic political solutions, but not its multi-ethnic, multicultural population. Overall, Saul consistently argues for Canada's uniqueness as a national formation.

I particularly like Saul's theoretical framework. His tropes of mythology, victimization, false options and the rest seem to me effective and accurate. This is not academic theory in the sense produced by departments of professional historians (though Saul has a history PhD), but popular and conversational thinking. Saul is a quirky thinker, which is to say imaginative, but the point is that he actually thinks about Canada, rather than accepting the shibboleths that have been concocted for it, which is a rarer virtue, in or out of the academies, than one might expect. He makes me think afresh about the history of what seems like, at first glance, a minor national backwater whose past is a dull replication of other colonial traditions. Under his convincing definitions, Canada turns out to be one of the most interesting, complex, and so far successful experiments in nation-building available. Since Saul's reading is not a neutral interpretation, but a polemic or normative presentation, naturally his opponents are driven crazy by his contrarian claims.

What's more, Saul brings to his *Reflections* some of the major themes of his earlier 1995 Massey Lectures, published as *The Unconscious Civilization*, and applies them directly to the Canadian context. One of Saul's big ideas in his previous work is that modern democracies are increasingly subject to "corporatism." He defines "corporatism" not just as business corporations, but as any body (trade unions, occupational organizations, religious entities, advertising agencies, and a host of sectoral elites) whose attention is directed to self- and other partial, private interests rather than concern for a public, common good. Although "there is nothing wrong with business," Saul points out that business is not in the business of democracy. "[Business] has nothing to do with defining the public good in a democracy, let alone defining a democratic nation-state." The same applies to other forms of corporatism.

As against corporatism, Saul poses the figure of the individual citizen and the possibilities of his or her government. One of Saul's unusual insights about individualism is that it is more effectively and properly expressed through citizenship than as a consumer of goods and entertainments. Thus, for Saul, the issue of public citizenly education, education for something more than vocation, is at the heart of the development of democracies. In *Reflections*, Saul notes that "everywhere the [pupils-per-]class numbers are creeping up, everywhere the amount spent per capita on students is declining and governments everywhere are attempting to replace teaching with technology." For all that, Canada persists as a vibrantly unfinished, complex, non-conforming political and geographical entity. That likely accounts for the unexpected enthusiasm many of us have for it these days.

II

Just prior to my arrival in Vancouver in 1966 — an event that, like a lot of the major occurrences in my life, was more accident than intention (I really am one of those people who backs into life-situations) — I embarked upon an autodidactic course of reading about the physically vast, sparsely-populated nation-state to the north of the United States. When I signed up to become a student at the University of British Columbia that first rainy autumn, the reading continued. My becoming a student, by the way, was also partially accidental — I was required by Canadian Immigration to have some justification for my presence in the country, and it so happened that since I was a U.S. military veteran, a portion of my university tuition fees would be paid for by the GI Bill. In reading about the place I was coming to, it was as if I intuited that I might be staying longer than I had at first planned.

I began by reading the journals of early European explorers and visitors to what would become British North America. The first book I found was a recently published volume of the journals of Alexander Mackenzie, *First Man West*, edited and introduced by a historian named Walter Sheppe. MacKenzie reached the Pacific overland better than a decade before the Lewis and Clark expedition in the U.S.

Sheppe's introduction to and annotation of Mackenzie's journal of his voyage to the Pacific coast of Canada in 1793 was so compellingly intelligent that my imagination was instantly engaged, and I followed this explorer/businessman along his circuitous route to the coast, all the way to the moment where he wrote, "I now mixed up some vermilion with melted grease, and inscribed in large characters, on the South East face of the rock on which we slept last night, this brief memorial — 'Alexander Mackenzie, from Canada, by land, the twenty-second of July, one thousand seven hundred and ninety-three.'"

Then I read the journals of George Vancouver, Simon Fraser, David Thompson, and some others — the raw materials that contemporary Canadian writers like George Bowering in *Burning Water*, and Brian Fawcett in *The Secret Journal of Alexander Mackenzie* and *Virtual Clearcut*, would turn into literature.

Having acquired an initial sense of the lay of the land from primary sources, I turned, for a broader view of the country, to the works of contemporary historians and thinkers, such as Donald Creighton, Harold Innis, Stanley Ryerson, George Grant, Farley Mowat, Pierre Berton, and C.B. Macpherson, whose views covered a spectrum from conservatism to Canadian Marxist historiography. This unwitting apprenticeship in becoming a Canadian took a further turn when I went to UBC and, again luckily, studied with Michael Kew, an anthropologist who knew a great deal about the aboriginal peoples of British Columbia, and geographer Richard Copley, who had an acute perspective on the local landscape. His geography class field trip into the Fraser Valley, east of Vancouver, showed us the Sumas moraine, the leavings of the last ice age from 15,000 years ago, a literal lay of the land. In more mundane fashion, there were the 8:30 morning classes in the rain-sodden, small wooden amphitheatre of UBC's geography building, amid the smell of damp cordoruy and wool clothes being dried by the body heat of the students. As Copley and Kew lectured, I took notes on where I was.

About five or six years later, I walked into one of those institutional buildings with pea-green walls and grey cubicle dividers which housed the local Canadian Immigration bureaucracy, and I applied to become a Canadian citizen. In the interim I'd become, among other things, a fairly notorious student and civic radical whose pontifica-tions had been regularly reproduced in print and on the air. I handed my application to a man whose desk nameplate said Mr. Eliot, and who was as unprepossessing as his name and surroundings suggested.

He had a question for me. His hand rested on a file that contained a thick pile of clippings that had been gathered for him by one of the nation's branches of the constabulary. "Are you a homosexual?" Mr. Eliot asked. At the time, the early 1970s, homosexuality in Canada had been recently legalized when the prime minister, Pierre Trudeau, declared that "the state has no business in the bedrooms of the nation." His omnibus bill, striking down proscriptions against homo-sexuality, was passed by parliament with less fuss than might have been anticipated. However, the immigration laws still contained an anachronistic prohibition against immigrants who were homosexuals. I told Mr. Eliot that, given the implications, I'd better consult a lawyer and come back later to answer his question. That was fine by him.

I was just buying a little time in order to figure out what he was actually asking me. I figured out that he certainly wasn't asking me, "Are you a homosexual?" Mr. Eliot and Canada couldn't care less about that. Instead, he was asking, "Are you planning to make a fuss about the homosexual clause in Canada's immigration laws?" I wasn't, at least not at that moment. No political martyrdom, thank you. At an even deeper level, the answer was, It's none of your business. A few days later I was back in Mr. Eliot's cubicle. He looked as though he hadn't left his desk in the intervening days. "I'm ready to answer your question," I said. "Mm-hmm," he said, politely not repeating the offending question. "No," I said. That was evidently good enough for him. He seemed rather relieved (Canadian culture tends to eschew unpleasant confrontation). In due course, I was sworn in.

Most Canadians weren't particularly interested in my sexual orientation, but were more curious about whether I was a draft-dodger, on the run from the American war in Vietnam. Nope, military veteran, I reported. Of course, every time I opened my distinctive yap, Canadians did say, Oh, you're American, eh? No, I'm Canadian, I said, but that's not what they meant. They meant that I had an audible American accent, despite my efforts to pronounce "about" and "been" in a Canadian accent. Perhaps they also meant, Once an American, always an American. In reality, I'm probably not a citizen of anywhere, but instead a "rootless cosmopolitan," a Wandering Jew. Still, some Canadians have noticed, in the intervening three decades, that rootless cosmopolitans and Wandering Jews tend to be better Canadians than most.

The striking thing I've noticed about Canada is, as Saul points out, its fundamentally social democratic character. That is, most of the country's political parties, and the majority of its polled population, accept capitalism, however grudgingly, but favour some regulation of the marketplace. The country also thinks some goods ought to be in the public domain, including a segment of the media. And it believes there ought to be a collectivization of some of the risks of living, in the form of public health care, welfare, and education. Unlike European social democratic nations, its population is not ethnically homogenous and yet, as a multicultural assemblage it has managed to avoid ethnic riots and large-scale slaughter. Yes, plenty of injustice — against aboriginal peoples, ethnic groups (Japanese-Canadians were interned in camps during World War II), religious minorities, women, the poor, etc. — but no mass violence, at least not so far. And there is a tangible will to keep it that way.

Since the completion of Canada's more than century-old constitutional process in 1982, another legacy of Trudeau, to be a Canadian means to speak one of the two national languages, and to formally adhere to the Canadian Constitution and its values. But there is no official Canadian national identity, unless one takes seriously the beer-guzzling, toque-wearing "hoser" comedians on TV who do sketches about typical Canadian louts. National identity in Canada is consciously weak, especially compared to countries like the U.S., Germany and France where there is a strong sense of being French, German, and American, even if more in myth these days than in reality.

Once, I was on a literary panel that was prattling on about "the writer and the state in Canada." An elderly woman in the audience couldn't stand it any longer, and got to her feet to ask, while literally pointing a finger at us, "What makes you proudest of being a Canadian?" My fellow panelist, Brian Fawcett, a Prince George, B.C.-born, dyed-in-the-wool, authentic Canadian (if there is such a thing), didn't pause as long as the blink of an eye to reply, "What makes me proudest about being a Canadian is that I don't have to be proud of being a Canadian." The audience, which burst into the laughter of self-recognition, thought that was a good thing, too.

III

Being an immigrant to Canada and a Canadian who lives outside of the country a good part of the time has concentrated my attention on Canada, perhaps more so than for those who take it for granted. It accounts for my periodic but steady bits of writing about it for some three decades. I noticed that phenomenon again, in Berlin in spring 2003, during a "Kanada Week" cultural offensive put on in the German capital, which included a conference on German and Canadian relations with the U.S., lectures on "Citizenship and Multiculturalism in Canada" at Humboldt University, a retrospective of a Canadian filmmaker at the local art film house, as well as a lecture-reading tour by Ralston Saul. At the foreign relations conference, an old friend of mine, Phil Resnick, a UBC political science professor, turned up to give a paper delineating some of the differences between Canada and the U.S.

Resnick was giving his talk just a month after the U.S. invasion of Iraq, an imperial excursion which the Canadian government, like those of much of "Old Europe," had declined to join. On my way to Resnick's talk, I'd been held up a few minutes because the police had blocked off the streets so that the black limo cavalcade of the visiting U.S. Secretary of State could zoom through Berlin's thoroughfares unimpeded.

"Canadians, in general," Resnick observed, "have been worried by the tendency of the Bush administration to act as sheriff of a new world order" in the period since the terrorist attack on the U.S. in 2001. "Instinctively, Canadian public opinion, despite strident support . . . for the American position" by the some of the media and the business sector, "has been closer to European public opinion," he added.

Three striking and deep distinctions between Canada and the U.S. are observable, Resnick argued: first, the Canadian constitutional emphasis on "peace, order, and good government" contrasted with the "life, liberty and pursuit of happiness" phraseology of the American founding documents. The difference shows up in everything from "the wild west" of American legend compared to the more sedate taming of the Canadian prairies, to contemporary differences in attitudes toward capital punishment, guns, and the culture of violence. Second, "there has historically been a different balance between state and market in Canada and the U.S." Like Saul, Resnick cited Harold Innis's half-century-old argument that conditions in Canada necessitate a more significant role for the state than in the U.S. Canada, by circumstance rather than "political virtue, genetic predisposition, or chemicals in our drinking water," is a social democratic country. This feature of the society shows up in Canada's early adoption of welfare state policies, from health care to public broadcasting.

Finally, while "the appeal to patriotism in American politics is omnipresent, even embarrassing," by contrast, "the Canadian temperament is less given to patriotic excess." Even recognizing that Canada, as a minor power, is less tempted by such patriotism (and its corruptions), the deeper fact is that "Canada, in practice, is a multinational state with fault-lines of language running down the middle. This leads to the elevation of compromise into a high political art domestically," Resnick said, echoing Saul's refrain of reform and reconciliation as the historic authentic themes of the country.

About a thousand conceptual kilometres from the gathering of political scientists, but only a short physical distance away, the basement art-movie theatre in Potsdamer Platz was showing the films of Toronto director Bruce LaBruce. Resnick had pointed out that in Canada culture was a crucial and necessarily state-supported sector that preserved useful differences, and it was the case that the cultural attaché of the Canadian Embassy was footing the bill for the after-show drinks, but still it was odd to imagine Canadian government backing for LaBruce's films.

If Canada is typically all about moderation, reticence and compromise, LaBruce's movies are typically about excess. They intentionally verge on gay porn, deal with homosexual fascism, and graphically portray full-frontal sadomasochistic sex, right-wing homosexual skinheads, and various other obsessions. They also happen to be fairly funny. Oddly enough, LaBruce's sexually extreme movies are not atypical of Canadian cinema, which is what gets my attention. LaBruce's preoccupations aren't all that different from other Canadian fare, such as Atom Egoyan's *Exotica*, Denys Arcand's *Love and Human Remains*, Robert Lepage's *The Confessional*, John Grayson's *Lilies*, or a Lynne Stopkewich film, *Kissed*, based on a Barbara Gowdy story that's about necrophilia (it's strange, but strangely, not implausible). Naturally, that's not the only thematic of Canadian film, but the field is small and independent enough that it is noticeable. Although Canadian literature is competent and interesting enough, I'm especially taken with the aspects of Canadian feeling that emerge from the country's comedians and its filmmakers. Under all that "whoops, sorry" Canadian reticence, there's a lot of curious passion.

Finally, that week, I tagged around with Ralston Saul for a couple of days as he gave talks and readings at a number of venues. What he had to say, expectedly, were mainly turns on his argument in *Reflections*. In discussing the tripartite aboriginal, Anglo, and French-speaking founding peoples, he even included a footnote of approval for historical inter-ethnic "sleeping together," which received an appreciative chuckle at an early morning seminar at Berlin's Free University.

Saul also shrewdly observed that the successful "psychological trick" of Canada is "to immediately treat immigrants as citizens." Altogether, this fortnight of Canadian rah-rah seemed to me persuasive that there is something profoundly interesting about Canada as a political entity. Although one wag has remarked that Canadians are a people who, without a trace of irony, love to yell about how modest they are, nonetheless, it's the case that the prizewinning entry in a recent radio contest to define Canadian identity in a single, short sentence, was, "As Canadian as possible under the circumstances." Again, that line produced a national chuckle of self-recognition.

A long time ago, during a protracted Canadian debate about the adoption of a national anthem, a mischievous friend of mine proposed a tuneless refrain that went: "Canada, it's the same country / all over the world," a sentiment that nicely captured Canadian self-mockery of national blandness. In the tuneless official song we ended up with, "Oh, Canada," it warbles of "true patriot love," but the reality is closer to affectionate fondness. We prefer, apparently, to reserve "love," patriot or otherwise, for other venues.

Capilano College

Coming from a classroom on the south, or lower side of the Capilano College campus, where I've just taught an 8:30 morning class, I'm heading up the hill towards the northside Fir Building. I have a cubbyhole office there on the fourth floor. On my way, I pass the music rooms at the base of the building. Pouring out of the practice cubicles, whose windows are partially open on this Indian summer September morning, is an astonishing cacophany of sound — rippling piano scales, horn blurts, the tooting of woodwinds, and human voices running through arpeggios. I'm half-distractedly thinking about whatever happened in the classroom a few minutes ago, when I'm suddenly startled by the overlapping melodies wafting out of the bunker-like building, as if I'd never heard them before. Transfixed for an instant by the pleasure of hearing the wave of sounds, it's as if I am listening to a local version of the music of the spheres.

My relation to Capilano College, over the more than twenty years that I've taught there — first politics, then philosophy — has a lot of the quality I experience when hearing that music. I find the sounds and the musicians reassuring: as they earnestly toot and ripple and warble, I feel reasonably certain that they're not planning to punch anyone in the nose — which is my line-drawn-in-the-pine-needles definition of civility. The music students wander around campus, moving up and down the alpine hill like humpbacked pack animals, with guitar bags and tuba cases slung on their backs, along with the other rucksack-carrying students, giving the whole place a bucolic air. (Sudden memory of singing "The Happy Wanderer" hiking song, as a child in elementary school music class: "I love to go a-wandering / Along the mountain track / And as I go, I love to sing / My knapsack on my back / Val-deri, val-dera . . .")

The geography of the college also contributes to that pacific sense. Capilano is located on the first ridge of hills on the north shore of Burrard Inlet across from the city of Vancouver, just beyond North Vancouver's industrial foreshore, where piles of sulphur are heaped on the docks. The college, which you arrive at by a canyon road that runs up to the top of a hill, is set within a stand of mostly evergreen forest. Beyond the college are more ridges and canyons, and further to the north, range after range of mountains. A hundred and fifty kilometres north of Capilano, once you're past the mill-town at Squamish and the ski-resort at Whistler, it's pretty much pure wilderness.

Apart from my somewhat sentimental idea of the charm of the place — which, admittedly, is just plain gloomy during the rainy season, when the whole institution huddles miserably under a steady, chill drizzle for weeks on end — what I'm interested in is the main activity of the college, namely, teaching. From most of the public and media discussion of education, you'd never imagine that teaching is what Capilano and similar schools are all about, or that the teaching is aimed at developing the sort of person who can assume a place as a citizen in a democracy. Even we teachers occasionally forget that. Instead, there's an enormous preoccupation with whether students are being properly trained for various jobs, and such other diversions as whether or not the college is suitably online. The latter refers to a concern about the use of technology in teaching, a subject I crankily regard as a euphemism for replacing teaching. But as one of my favourite newspaper columnists (John Doyle, the TV writer for the Toronto *Globe and Mail*) says when he recognizes he's just about to launch a rant, Don't get me started.

My friend Ryan Knighton and I once collaborated on a mock-book called *Teaching Is Easy*. Ryan is a colleague at Capilano College, a writer who teaches in the English department. He's 30-something, one of the new generation of instructors, with a shaved head, a gym-fit body, and a white cane to get around because he's blind. We drive to work together in the mornings, since we both teach morning classes. My one-liner is, We're a carpool, but I don't let him drive very much. We're both pretty good at irony, the alternative to which, I point out, is suicide. I also have a one-liner about teaching, which I contributed to our mock-book: Teaching is easy because anything you say in class these days is news to the students. We both agree that the hardest part of teaching is leaving the coffee kiosk on the way to a rainy morning class because you need three hands to carry the book bag, the cup of coffee, and the umbrella. Four hands, if you're also tapping around with a white cane, Ryan adds. After that, as we say, it's all downhill.

Jokes aside, the first issue is the conditions of teaching. Again, this is seldom publicly discussed, but there's a major difference between teaching in a university and teaching in a college, the two parts of the Canadian post-secondary education system. Typically, in North American universities these days, introductory classes (in biology, psychology, physics and other disciplines) are conducted in amphitheatres that can hold up to 800 students. From some vantage points, the professor in the pit doing the lecturing appears to be about the size of an insect, so a large screen behind him is often provided on which a magnified TV image is projected. A good deal of the lecture occurs in half-darkness because the professor is using an overhead projector to provide notes on the screen for the students to copy down. The professor will have teaching assistants to deal with the students. The teaching assistants are senior graduate students and they mark the student papers and exams, and, at what are considered good schools, they may conduct seminars with smaller groups of students. The professors have little contact with the introductory students beyond answering a handful of questions at the lectures.

The students in these huge introductory classes are fiscal cannon-fodder to pay for the university's often excellent graduate schools. At best, then, you get great lecturing. And while great lecturing is nothing to sniff at, it's also a very small part of teaching. At worst (and worst may be the norm), what you get is the equivalent of those country schools in benighted countries where students spend the day performing en masse rote recitations of religious texts. I regard most of what goes on in undergraduate education of this sort as a scandal, something just short of criminal activity, but the habit is so entrenched, it's seldom even remarked upon. Inevitably, sooner or later, some educational mad scientist appears on stage and proposes that there's no need for the mass lectures, that the whole performance can be digitally repackaged, and the students can stay at home and watch it on their TVs or computers (this would also save institutional janitorial costs). Worse, such dotty proposals become rational in the light of actual teaching conditions. Most of the current talk about the use of computers in teaching (or replacing teaching) is an outgrowth of this situation.

At Capilano College, I teach classes with about 35 students. The numbers creep up a little when there's a budget squeeze on and the administration pleads with us to take in two or three extra students per course. Unlike the hermetic amphitheatres of the university, I teach in rooms, not necessarily great rooms for teaching, but often good enough that they have windows, and I can point outside to our little glade of woods and intone sentences like, "So, we all agree that the trees out there are real, right?" (It's a sentence that occurs in introductory metaphysics courses more often than one might expect.) In short, I'm able to engage in something that resembles conversations with the students. I know their names, I read their work, I mark their papers, I talk to them in my office or on the phone or by e-mail. After a few weeks, I know them well enough that I'm able to shape the lessons towards who they are and what they can understand, rather than what, as a professor, I understand. By the end of the term, I have a pretty good idea of the minds, personalities, and stories of the people I teach. I don't want to make any exaggerated claims about results, but I think these conditions of teaching produce slightly better "outcomes," as they say in the education business, than the alternatives.

Compared to the universities, the colleges, according to the unspoken wisdom that governs the matter, are second-rate schools for second-rate students who can't get into university or who can't afford to pay the more expensive tuition fees of the university. In reality, the colleges are about the only place in undergraduate education where teaching is still permitted. But I gloomily view the colleges, as I do spotted owls, as an endangered species.

I'm a pluralist on the question of how to teach. I take the position that there are lots of good ways to teach well. For example, John Dixon and I teach in what's known as the "Socratic style." Dixon is my best and oldest friend at Cap College, a colleague of mine in the philosophy department. He's a tall, white-haired, bearded, outdoorsy type. In former years, when we were both more mobile, we were a familiar sight on campus, walking around together like classic peripatetic philosophers, the statuesque Dixon and his pudgy bald companion, a real Mutt and Jeff team. The only thing missing was the togas.

Dixon and I were both students in Bob Rowan's political philosophy classes at the University of British Columbia in the 1960s, and we both learned to teach from Rowan in the Socratic manner (although the term perhaps flatters us). I was notorious for having burst into Rowan's class one day when we were reading Plato's *Republic* and announcing, "Plato is wrong, Thrasymachus was right!", praising the world's first renowned pragmatist, who had argued that might is right, there are no eternal verities, against Socrates's wily defense of the moral life. Well, that was then. The Socratic method was reinforced for Dixon and me when we both studied briefly with the magisterial Joseph Tussman at the University of California in Berkeley. Tussman was Rowan's teacher, and Tussman's teacher was a philosopher named Alexander Meiklejohn, so there's a continuous line of transmission of both mode and thought (though, again, this probably flatters the feeble heirs).

What the Socratic manner amounts to is that the fulcrum of the class rests not on the lecture but on the conversation in which we engage the students. Sometimes I "lecture" for a while, if I have something particular I want to say, although the lecturing has more the character of performing an improvised operatic aria than the Powerpoint presentation taught in business schools. There are also texts that provide the foundation for the conversation, and the texts matter.

But in our reading of the books, I'm not trying to "get through" the text with a view to having "covered the material" in preparation for the final exam. The texts are usually not "textbooks," but real books by real writers, and I use them as entrances into the world and into the minds of their authors.

One of the features of Socratic-style teaching is that you don't know in advance precisely what's going to happen in the classroom or where the conversation is going to go. That doesn't mean it's loosey-goosey, adlibbing, stand-up philosophy, but it does require a certain degree of "adamant confidence," as Dixon calls it, that you can provide a measure of disciplined guidance to the conversational journey. (Our detractors occasionally describe our confidence as "arrogance.") Once we're all settled into the room and the students are nibbling on their morning muffins, I may kick it off by saying, "On the way into school this morning, I was thinking about something we said last time about whether it's possible to really be a solipsist about reality. Now, my idea is . . ." And after I've rattled on for a bit, somebody in class asks a question, makes an observation, is provoked to challenge something outrageous I've said, and we're off. Sometimes, I'll say, "Well, you've read chapter two of Nagel's *What Does It All Mean?*, right? What is it about?" At other times, I'll just ask, "Where did we leave off last time?", and then, liked stoned people trying to remember what they were talking about five minutes previously, we'll fumble around a bit until we find the thread back into the labyrinth. Sometimes, when the class has coalesced into a group (about a third of the way into the semester), and things are going really well, I walk into the room and only have to say, "Well . . .?", and we're on the way.

It is not the only way to teach, as I've said, and it's more exhausting or nerve-wracking than coming in with a well-planned, neatly packaged talk, complete with overhead transparencies on which the main points of the lecture can be projected onto the screen. To make matters a bit more challenging, at the start of each teaching season, I try to forget everything I think about teaching, and start all over again. I tend to think of my method as "non-algorithmic" teaching. That is, it's designed to be difficult for a computer to simulate (since I'm paranoid about teaching machines replacing teachers). Gradually, over the years, I've abandoned most of the technology used in teaching. I don't show movies or television documentaries, though the room is equipped with an overhead TV. I don't give final exams (the students write essays), and therefore I don't need to provide transparencies for overhead projection and note-taking. Lately, I've stopped writing in chalk on the blackboard, except once or twice a year (at the beginning to write my name, and in the middle to draw a Venn diagram, if

I'm talking about logic). Chalk, I've decided, is the final barrier between us and the abyss; I prefer the abyss. I don't even wander around the room. Instead, I just sit there, at a table, and we talk.

Jean Clifford, a colleague in the English department, teaches in a style she describes as rather different from how I teach (but she enthusiastically approves of my successes in engaging students, as do I of hers). Despite our differences, one thing we agree on is how to deal with students who miss classes and then turn up later to ask what happened. On her door, she's taped up a poem by Tom Wayman (from his book, *Selected Poems 1973-1993*) to which she refers students who have just asked,

Did I Miss Anything?

Question frequently asked by
students after missing class

Nothing. When we realized you weren't here
we sat with our hands folded on our desks
in silence, for the full two hours

    Everything. I gave an exam worth
    40 per cent of the grade for this term
    and assigned some reading due today
    on which I'm about to hand out a quiz
    worth 50 per cent

Nothing. None of the content of this course
has value or meaning
take as many days off as you like:
any activities we undertake as a class
I assure you will not matter either to you or me
and are without purpose

    Everything. A few minutes after we began last time
    a shaft of light suddenly descended and an angel
    or other heavenly being appeared
    and revealed to us what each woman or man must do
    to attain divine wisdom in this life and
    the hereafter
    This is the last time the class will meet
    before we disperse to bring the good news to all people on
      earth

Nothing. When you are not present
how could something significant occur?

    Everything. Contained in this classroom
    is a microcosm of human experience
    assembled for you to query and examine and ponder
    This is not the only place such an opportunity
        has been gathered

but it was one place

And you weren't here

The one thing today's students are pretty good at has to do with
psychological astuteness, which probably comes from having
watched lots of psychological talk-show television, like the Oprah
Winfrey program. So, they can tell the difference between friendly
fooling around and faculty hostility. I do a lot of fooling around, and
I wouldn't want it mistaken for hostility. Most of the students are
able to tell that I like them. When I say that teaching is easy because
anything we say is news to the students, I'm simply referring to the
fact that the students are inevitably ignorant (but not stupid). On the
whole, it's not their fault. Most of their education, up to age eighteen,
was conducted in competition with television and video games. TV
and the games won.

But now they're not watching much television anymore. Oh, a few
of them are, and I can refer to their experiences to make a point in
class. The programs change every couple of years. For a while it was
90210, a sex-and-soap opera for post-adolescents, then there was *X-
Files*, a pernicious program encouraging belief in paranormal phenomena and conspiracy plots, then came *Touched by an Angel*, a
soppy religious show that arrived at about the same time as a horrible
hit song called, "What If God Was One of Us?" Now there's "reality
TV," a combination of game show and softcore pornography. This is
the junk that shaped their minds. But now that they're in college, TV
viewing time is down; they're too busy with part-time jobs, parents,
interpersonal relations and, if we're lucky, us.

Some teachers don't like the students' ignorance, and resent having
to do "remedial work." I don't. If I mention Samuel Beckett's name (I
may be trying to say something about existential absurdity in the
metaphysics class), and I notice that they don't recognize the reference, I'm perfectly happy to stop and enthusiastically explain who
Samuel Beckett is and why he's so great. I remember we're being paid

lots of money, have great working conditions, good pensions, etc., so why should I resent dispelling ignorance? It's useful work.

The students, for all their ignorance, have passed through lots of filters to get here, and tend to be friendly, well-behaved, and perfectly amenable to teaching. They're the 20 per cent cream of the crop of their age aggregate. I regard them as the right people in the right place at the right time. Admittedly, I'm preternaturally cheerful when I'm at school and with the students. Sometimes, according to my colleagues, spookily cheerful. I'll eventually have to figure out why.

A few years ago, the faculty discovered the problem of "disruptive students," and several meetings and committees were devoted to figuring out what to do about them. I occasionally run into students who are nuts or inexplicably hostile, but I seldom locate any disruptive ones. Sometimes, there are students chattering away in some corner of the class, distracting me from whatever I'm going on about, and I've apparently invented various clever techniques to deal with them. Mostly, the techniques have to do with cajoling them out of their own distractions. If I read someone's moving lips, asking someone else, What time is it?, because they're thinking about their day instead of metaphysics, I'll jump in and announce, "It's nine-thirty, about a half-hour left." Or, if it's more elaborate gossip, I'll ask, "Pardon? Did you want to say something?" I have physically big ears, and am very sensitive to sound, so I tend to hear a lot of the whispers and murmurs, which pop up on my bat-like echolocation radar system, thus making intervention fairly easy and automatic. When they arrive at class with their headphones on, listening to digital music, I always ask them what they're pumping into their heads, because I'm culturally interested.

Sometimes, there's a student who wants to answer every question. I deal with that through my only ground rule about public talking: you have to raise your hand to talk, and I keep a speaker's list in my head, and if I see a hand for the first time that day, even if there are other hands up belonging to people who have already spoken, I move the first-time hand up to the top of the list to maximize the number of students who get to speak. The students seem satisfied with the justice of the procedure. When things are going well, they don't even have to raise their hands, I can read who wants to speak just from their eyes and eyebrows. On the whole, I'm inclined, if anything, to encourage disruption. I worry more about the "glazed donut" problem, students who politely sit there for weeks on end and give no indication of what's happening for them.

For me, the main thing that goes on at school is what happens after we teachers close the door behind us and begin the class. I have, on the whole, shied away from the internal politics of academia, which is often a source of agony that permeates academic life. As a result, I tend to see my colleagues more favourably and charitably than some others do. Though I don't want to administer, or sit on committees, and I find the meetings a chore, I admire those who are good at administration, and I'm happy to raise my hand whenever a vote is taken to support them and give them "release sections" (time off from teaching). I wander along the corridor and stop at faculty offices to chat with colleagues, who come in a diverse assortment of temperaments and states of mind, and end up at my pal Dixon's cubbyhole, where he's usually boiling a kettle of lunchtime water to make a bowl of instant noodle soup. There are about 50 or so teachers about whom I have a fair idea of what's on their minds. When I run through their names in my mind — Reid Gilbert, Yolande Westwell-Roper, Mark Battersby, Wayne Henry, Dan Munteanu, Pierre Coupey, Bob Sherrin, Bill Shermbrucker, Melanie Fahlman-Reid, and others — I have a rich album of images, personalities, and ideas they're interested in. But I'll save the encomiums for the retirement parties. The heart of the school is inside the classroom.

I only lecture twice a year, on the first day, the introduction to the course, and the last day, the Goodbye Class. Since very little has been written about actual classroom teaching (aside from the professional literature on the subject, which tends to be technique- and technology-driven), I'll say a couple of things. I have an unwritten imaginary book about teaching called *The Horses of Instruction* (from William Blake's "The tygers of wrath are wiser than the horses of instruction"), but this is not the place for it.

Inside the room, after I write my name, telephone number, and name and number of the course on the blackboard (which is actually green), and sit down behind my table, I ask, "Is there anybody here who hasn't taken a philosophy course?" I know perfectly well that almost nobody has taken a philosophy course, but when most of their hands shoot up, I affect slight surprise, and say, "Oh?! Well, then I better say a few things about philosophy, and then something about how this course fits into philosophy, and then what this course is specifically about." The theme of my sermon is that philosophy is the most important subject we teach at Cap College. I say, "Well, the first thing to say about philosophy is that it's the most important subject we teach at Cap College." I allow a micro-pause for them to get the joke about my possible self-interest in this assertion, and once I've heard the chuckle, I add, "I actually mean it." Then I quickly amend that, pointing out that there are a lot of other great things taught at school, and give some examples, but nonetheless insist that philosophy seems to me the most important subject. I have two arguments for that.

The first is that philosophy is the only subject taught at school which is primarily devoted to discussing the questions that human beings have historically come to regard as the deepest, most central, and important: questions about how to live our lives, what the universe is all about, gods, selves, and all the rest. There's an internal debate in philosophy about whether these questions are intrinsic, eternal, or natural to our condition as human beings, or whether they're an historic artifact. I tend to think the latter, but for my purposes here an agnostic view is sufficient. It doesn't matter whether the questions really exist independently of us or whether we make them up. They're the questions that people have come to care about and philosophy is the only place in school completely devoted to them.

My second argument is that philosophy is very old, and I tell them all about my teacher, Socrates, although I quickly concede that arguments from authority and age are not as strong as arguments from good reasons. Even though I supply some dates and contrast Socrates to Jesus — pointing out in passing that it's easier to understand Socrates than Jesus, i.e., he sounds more like us, and that we have better historical evidence for Socrates's existence than Jesus's — some of them are probably left with the impression that I know Socrates personally and talk to him pretty regularly on a cellphone. All of this occasions some self-told jokes about my advanced age.

The point is simply to establish the tone and the pace of the class, to indicate that we're not merely pushing Sisyphus's stone up the hill, that we're looking for a state of mind in which it's possible to think. The semi-serious point about Socratic longevity is that most of the other disciplines taught at Cap College and elsewhere are in some way spin-offs from philosophy, and fairly recent spin-offs at that (I note that "recent" in philosophy is a word that can mean "within the last four or five hundred years"). My closer to this pitch for the importance of philosophy is that despite philosophy's importance, it doesn't provide "right answers," and therefore, the students are not required to agree with anything I say or that other students say and, conversely, I'm not required to agree with what they say. However, I urge, we should treat our disagreements with a modicum of civility because we're all decent people. And that's about it.

The rest of the talk is practical stuff. I use the practical stuff (answers to questions like, "How long should the essays be?", "How many references do you want, and in what style?", etc.) to do a lot of "positioning," as I call it. Positioning has to do with how you want the students to think about the material, the teacher, the whole project. Most of it is jokey. I'm letting them know that I'm really available to be "the teacher," if that's what they're looking for. So, I repeat my phone number several times, as if they should memorize it in case of emergencies, assure them they can phone at any time, nothing is too trivial or too large, and provide examples. The examples range from, "You want to know whether to write on one side or both sides of the paper?", and then I recite the phone number, to "You're driving along the Upper Narrows Highway at 3 a.m. in your Porsche, and the nice policeman stops you, tells you to open the trunk of the vehicle, and discovers the funny white powder. You don't want to discuss this with the folks just yet." Chuckles. Then I recite the phone number, as the punchline. Laughter. "I'm very good at giving advice about your legal rights, available attorneys, and bail procedures." Point taken.

If there's time the first day, I may "do" some philosophy, as Dixon and I have learned to call it, as a sample of what's going to go on for the rest of the semester. It can be as straightforward as asking, "What do we mean when we say that these chairs and tables, or those trees outside the window there, exist?" (That's when the classroom window comes in handy.) "What makes us so sure?" Or it can be that I'll point to some guy who was listening to (fill in the current fashionable blank, some rap or hiphop group) when he came into the room, and ask him, "What is it that leads to your listening to X rather than Mahler's 'Fourth Symphony'?", which then leads to, "What do you mean by 'I like it'?", which then leads to a discussion of the differences between "art" and "entertainment," which then leads to, How do we become the persons who have acquired the tastes we have?, etc. In short, let the conversations begin.

Most of the rest of the days are devoted to doing philosophy. I spend a considerable amount of class time in metaphysics debunking unlikely beliefs — everything from astrology to Zoroastrianism — and presenting arguments for what constitute good reasons for believing in something. When students start talking about weird kinds of "energy" that they believe in, I get Mike Freeman or Stan Greenspoon from the physics department to come in for expert advice, even though the idea of reality in physics these days is stranger than any cultish beliefs in aliens, astral travel, or near- and after-death experiences. If the students are balky about fossils, radio-carbon dating, and our relationship to other hominids, a teacher in the biology department, Paul McDonald, is usually kind enough to come in and explain the fine points of evolution.

I'm a moderate on epistemology. I certainly don't think we absolutely know what the world is like from a god's eye view, independent of our consciousness and use of language, and I equally don't think that whatever you believe is "what's real for you," or that all beliefs are equally well-held. I'm what might be called a "local realist": within the realm of tables, chairs, trees outside the window, and other local phenomena, what we know is good enough, and it doesn't matter whether it is absolute or ultimately relative. The knowledge of science may not be absolute either, but it's helpful, and I've no big objection to privileging it insofar as it "works." Knowledge about politics, ethics, and human relationships is shaky, and it's only possible to have better or worse arguments rather than knowledge. Claims to paranormal knowledge — from god(s) to God — ought to be resisted, unless the person making the claim can provide a good reason to believe. Various knowledges and various false beliefs make a practical difference to how we live our lives. People who think God wants them to blow up buildings, other people, and themselves ought to be discouraged. Insofar as there is a politics of metaphysics, mine is fairly middle-of-the-road. The direction we're moving in is: if it's possibly the case that there are no gods to provide purposes for our lives, and if the accounts of evolution and physics are reasonably true, and if there's no good reason to believe in an afterlife, then what are the possible meanings (and selves) that we can construct for ourselves, both individually and as a society, to make our lives worthwhile?

In recent years, I notice, I've been making use of local geographic metaphors. I find myself arguing that, "up here, on the hill" — since the college is on a hill — life is different from and, I imply, better than "down there, at the bottom of the hill." Down at the bottom of the hill is a big parking lot attached to something called The Real Canadian Superstore, and I portray the parking lot as a kind of hellish purgatory, where people aimlessly push their basket-carts, or read no more than the statistics in the sports pages of the tabloids, or eat burgers in their overly large vehicles, and various other awful things happen. Whereas, up here, we read terrific books, talk about important stuff, meet interesting people, get ready for great jobs, and what's more, the murder rate is lower up here on the hill than down in the lot at the bottom of the hill. A lot of other arguments flow from that, about language, the making of the self, and society, but I needn't rehearse them here. If someone notices that I'm being "elitist," I permit myself a rare political remark. I concede that the students are indeed an elite, representing only about 20 per cent of their age aggregate, and that being a democrat myself, I wish it were otherwise, but it isn't, not yet. I also note that their being an elite who will get better jobs, exercise more power, and have more leisure time than the people at the bottom of the hill, is probably not a matter of intelligence, but does imply responsibility. (I then have a riff on the difference between ignorance and stupidity, but we can skip that.) I conclude, a little sadly, Well, if there is going to be an elite, I'd prefer that it be an informed rather than an ignorant elite.

There's another point to my "life up on the hill" metaphor that I usually don't talk about, but I notice it. It's that I really do believe all the stuff I say about life on the hill. Both the activity and the manner of interaction on the hill seem a model of human civilization. As Dr. Pangloss keeps insisting to Candide in Voltaire's *Candide*, life up on the hill is the best of all possible worlds . . . at least of the worlds that are possible right now. Then it occurs to me, as I wander around Cap College, listening to the music of the spheres, teaching, drinking my coffee and holding my umbrella and bookbag — and this, I realize, is what accounts for my preternatural cheerfulness when I'm at school — I've come to regard life here (and at similar institutions, not all of them schools) as utopia, as the actual nearest approximation to utopia we'll experience in our lives.

I also give a talk at the Goodbye Class, in which I try to figure out what's happened in the course of the semester just concluding. It's not a very strenuous pitch, though sometimes I get worked up. Mainly, though, I'm just underscoring that goodbyes matter and that parting really is a sweet sorrow. By then, if things have gone well, the class has become a group, and the barbarians who arrived at the gates at the beginning of the semester have now become civilized. If things have gone really well, the shaft of light in Tom Wayman's poem doesn't "suddenly descend" from the heavens, but arises from the room and reveals, not a divinity, but what each man or woman among us must do.

That only happens when things are going really, really well.

Notes on Capitalism/Communism

Capitalism, the philosophy of our time: At the college where I work, I've occasionally taught the political philosophy course. Like most political philosophy profs, I've used the standard textbooks: Plato's *Republic*, Hobbes's *Leviathan*, Rousseau's *The Social Contract*, Marx and Engels's *The Communist Manifesto*, and sometimes a contemporary work like Joseph Tussman's *Obligation and the Body Politic*.

But I think that if I were teaching political philosophy today, I would focus on books propounding the tenets of capitalism, which is the philosophy of our time. Instead of concentrating on traditional topics in political philosophy such as the state, authority, obligation or even democracy, I would examine the picture of the world as seen by proponents of capitalism. Although such texts, whether classics like Adam Smith's *The Wealth of Nations* or contemporary works like economist Milton Friedman's *Free to Choose* and *Capitalism and Freedom*, are more polemical tracts than works of philosophy, they're probably more relevant than standard political philosophy for what students need to know in order to understand the world.

I'd also include books challenging capitalism, such as Benjamin Barber's *Jihad vs. McWorld*. My strategy would be to criticise the ideas of capitalism sufficiently that I would eventually be able to re-introduce the political ideas of social democracy, in which the capitalist market at least comes under public regulation. Admittedly, this is a weak strategy, but I think it's the most realistic one we've got if we're to have a hope of recovering a public world.

The astonishing intellectual development of the last quarter of the 20th century, as far as political philosophy is concerned, is that capitalist thought has replaced or subsumed democratic politics. Although capitalist polemics may pay lip service to democracy, issues like legitimate authority have been displaced by the tenets of capitalism, in which authority is founded in ownership of property in some form. Capitalist thinking provides a more or less complete philosophy about human nature, individual freedom, rights (mainly of property), as well as a theory of collective, social life. Global capitalism has simply underscored and extended capitalism's ideosyncratic view of the world.

I'm in the ranks of those opposed to capitalism, but it seems to me necessary not only to provide a critique of the philosophy of our time, but also to recognize the power of capitalist thinking and doing. What most of my fellow capitalist opponents are loath to do is to appreciate the accomplishment of an economic system that has changed human relationships. These notes aren't intended to be a treatise, so I'll confine myself to one example.

ATMs: Of all the features of current capitalist societies, the one that leaves me most in awe is the ATM. An "ATM" is the acronym for "automated teller machine" or "asynchronous transfer mode." This device, as my dictionary has it, is "an unattended electronic machine in a public place, connected to a data system and related equipment and activated by a bank customer to obtain cash withdrawals and other banking services." It is also called a cash machine, money machine, and bank machine.

There are several other similarly astonishing technologies available in contemporary society, like computers (and the associated software, Internet, email, etc.), cellphones, and the ubiquitous private transportation vehicles, but it is the ATM that impresses me as the characteristic technological instrument of capitalism. You can have the computers and cellphones and cars in non-capitalist societies. But money is the commodity emblematic of capitalism, and the ATM is its individualized instrument of dispersal.

There are several remarkable things about ATMs, and they are both social and technological. It is my emotional response of stunned awe that I want to underscore, as I stand in the neighbourhood temple before one of these electronic altars. The ATM branch is like an unattended church where worshippers enter, kneel, pray and light a candle before their favourite saint. A similar awe to the one that compels religious submission hovers around the bank machines, even for critics of capitalism.

In the years before ATMs, I went to my credit union on 4th Avenue in Vancouver or the one on Bismarckstrasse in Berlin (because I bank at credit unions), lined up before a row of wickets attended by human tellers, stood in line for a couple of minutes, and then spoke to a teller to withdraw money or do whatever other fiscal transaction was on my agenda. It wasn't a major human interaction, but it was the case that some of the tellers and I came to recognize each other, and there were often greetings and bits of gossip exchanged, just as there are at the local supermarket with the cashiers in the checkout line. The

ATM eliminated those social exchanges and literally privatized "private enterprise." In the most advanced bank branches, there are no people present at all except the customers. The workers and their managers have been eliminated at the fully automated branches.

This unattended character is also psychologically significant. The fantasy is that large stacks of the most important commodity in the culture have been left lying around and you can go in and take however much you desire. It's the old communist slogan brought to life: "From each according to his ability, to each according to his need." Except, of course, the machines aren't unattended. They're protected by electronic gates that require the customer to enter a correct code to get access to the money, by a surveillance camera system connected to human-staffed security agencies, and the ATMs are physically designed to withstand middle-of-the-night bankrobbers taking a sledgehammer to them. At some eureka moment in the evolution of the machine, the bankers sitting around the table were able to triumphantly declare, Shazam! We can leave them unattended.

It is also awesome how well they work. I'm not thinking so much here about the data system as about the physical delivery of the money. I worked as a printer for a while, and one of the problems of operating a printing machine is paper delivery. The paper feeder operated on a suction system, and the little suction cups lifted up a single sheet of paper and fed it into the press. No matter how good the machines were, the paper delivery system inevitably made mistakes. It missed a sheet, or it grabbed a heap of sheets and fed them into the press, jamming the machine, etc. What compels my professional awe about the ATMs is that the engineers have produced a paper delivery system that almost never makes mistakes. You never hear, except in urban legends, of the machine sucking up and delivering a big wad of bills in error. Again, at a certain point in the development of the machine, the bankers were able to say, We can leave this machine unattended as it spews out the money, secure in the knowledge that we won't lose a penny.

When I embark on my recurrent fantasy of the overthrow of capitalism, I remember the ATMs — fortresses of capital.

Capitalist desire: I'm puzzled, both emotionally and intellectually, by the motives that drive capitalism. I don't understand why someone wants to maximize profits to an infinite degree, why they want to control the market to the point of absolute monopoly, or what they want to do with the power they can wield as "masters of the universe." I just don't get it; my bafflement is a blindspot in my understanding of how things work. I understand spiritual desire. If someone tells me they want to go to some remote place to listen to obscure lectures about the meaning of the idea of "emptiness" in 6th century BCE Buddhist texts, and then visit nearby ancient caves to see the drawings made by neolithic hunter-artists, that makes sense to me. (My friend Thomas did exactly that in the Dordogne region of France, where some Tibetan Buddhists have a community, and sent me a postcard from a prehistoric cave that he visited that had a 15,000-year-old drawing of a rhinocerous on a cave wall. Curiosity, in other words, is perfectly understandable to me.) I also get the point of sexual desire. Ditto for artistic desire. I understand scientists, and most other kinds of knowledge-seekers. I understand the desire to do good. But capitalist desire remains mysterious.

As I say, I appreciate the capitalist ability to efficiently produce a cornucopia of goods and services, something that other modern economic systems have signally and dismally failed to do. But at the same time, I see that the capitalists exercise more or less complete control of where, how, and under what conditions the goods and services are produced. They show only minimal concern for the lives of the workers who carry out the capitalists' projects. So how can this economic mode possibly foster, say, democratic societies, or literate cultures? Matters are made worse when the preoccupations of capitalist economics absolutely subsume the affairs of people living together, a.k.a. politics. Finally, when the capitalists are allowed freedom to locate cheaper labour markets (I think that's what meant by the euphemism "globalization"), although theoretically in the long term it might conceivably lift or equalize global standards of living, in the short term, life is further destabilized for workers in existing capitalist societies.

Speaking of long and short terms, capitalism also poses a problem about time and time-frames. Since the managers of the corporations are primarily concerned with short-term profit maximization, they tend to be indifferent to long-term planning. Even in sectors such as forestry, where the long-term renewability of the resource requires steady care for sustainability, in practice, the focus is largely on current market prices, the present "annual allowable cut," and a steady increase in productivity through the elimination of the labour force in favour of technological improvements. I don't think the managers of capitalism have any particular interest in seeing beyond their own careers, a time-frame of about twenty-five years, unlike, say, a prime minister proposing a charter of rights and freedoms for a national constitution, or parents raising a child.

Finally, there's a contradiction between capitalist desire and consumer need. Friends of mine who describe themselves as "anarcho-capitalist libertarians" and argue for absolutely unrestricted free markets claim that individual consumers freely buy the goods and services they want (within the constraints of their purchasing power), but I find that hard to believe. It seems obvious that a large part of the consumption process consists of the manufacture of needs in consumers, and that the desires are created with indifference to the harm they cause to individuals or the society. A vast mechanism of capitalist advertising and publicity is solely devoted to pumping up the volume of desire, without qualms about psychological distortions and manipulations. I realize that there are more sophisticated arguments justifying capitalism against the objections I've raised. There are claims that capitalism is ultimately aimed at human good within the limitations of "human nature." The more elaborate, seemingly deeper arguments suffer from the same defects as the simpler, shallower ones. All of the above seems fairly obvious, yet it is almost never discussed on the evening news.

Communism, Version 1.0: I'm the sort of person that Karl Marx, the first great theoretician of communism, scornfully dismissed as a "Utopian communist." That is, although I'm a mild-mannered social democrat in practice, I continue to dream of a world in which all resources, commodities, and planning for the production of goods (including the determination of needs) is primarily a matter of public and collective ownership and decision-making rather than a process carried out under laws of private ownership. Marx was the 19th century thinker who most successfully recognized capitalism as a system, and who proposed a political program to replace it with a form of socialism. Since he viewed social and economic development in evolutionary, Darwinian terms, his expectation was that socialism would develop in the most advanced capitalist countries, such as England. In political history, among the most suggestive of developments occurred in Germany toward the end of the 19th century, which saw what appeared to be the inexorable electoral growth of social democratic political parties, and whose representative thinker was Eduard Bernstein, the author of *Evolutionary Socialism.*

As it happened (and "happened" is the right word to indicate its accidental, historical character), actual socialism first politically triumphed, as we know, in "backward" Russia (soon to become the Soviet Union) in 1918 in a revolution led by V.I. Lenin, leader of the brutal Bolshevik wing of the nascent Communist Party. Most of the remainder of 20th century politics was given over to the struggle between the Soviet Union and its satellite countries and parties, and the developing empire of the United States. Under the rubric of the Cold War, the struggle between Soviet-style communism and American capitalism reached levels of near-insanity as the contending powers threatened "mutually assured destruction" (MAD).

The conditions for the development of socialism in the Soviet Union, as historians have emphasized, were not propitious. A war-ravaged, barely capitalist, non-democratic political entity attempted, in the wake of World War I, to create socialism *ab ovo*. Not only did the attempt ultimately and miserably fail, but it quickly turned monstrous. Within a decade of its founding, the Soviet leader Joseph Stalin had brutally eliminated his most plausible rivals, Leon Trotsky, and his followers, as well as suppressing the most fundamental democratic freedoms. The ideas of Marx and others were transformed into religious texts and the character of the movement became that of a totalitarian religion. By the late 1930s, there were show trials of imaginary enemies of the state, as portrayed in Arthur Koestler's novel, *Darkness at Noon*, as well as the mass imprisonment and murder of suspected opponents in a system of camps documented by Alexander Solzhenitsyn in *The Gulag Archipelago*. Stalin could and did make an alliance with Hitler and Nazism because communism and fascism were ultimately two sides of an ideological coin.

Even after Stalin's death in 1953, attempts at reform of the Soviet system in Poland, Hungary, and Czechoslovakia were crushed by military force in the 1950s and 60s. Communist Parties in capitalist countries nonetheless remained abjectly subservient to the central control of the Soviet Union, even after the revelations about the gulags.

The dream turned into a nightmare. Even those who weren't supporters of Soviet-style socialism — from wacky left-wing political splinter groups to social democrats who subscribed to the dream of public ownership — suffered the effects of the disastrous Soviet course. Weighed down by its own productive and intellectual failures, communism sank into a period of stagnancy until, in the late 1980s, it finally collapsed, and the Berlin Wall, its most repressive emblem, was taken down. This is the briefest, but hopefully not inaccurate, capsule history possible, and no account of the 20th century, however idiosyncratic, can be imagined that doesn't contemplate it.

Since 1989, the imperial power of the United States has grown, religious fundamentalisms have revived (both in the Islamic and American realms), and various vain announcements of the "end of history" have been made, both in economic and cultural terms. While I continue to argue for social democracy in the present world, I retain the intuition (not a religious notion of inevitability, certainly) that something like Communism, Version 2.0 will be invented by future human beings. In dreams begin responsibilities, one poet (Delmore Schwartz) reminded us: perhaps the next dreamers will remember that one of the responsibilities is not to realize the dream as a nightmare.

Constantine Cavafy

The poet Constantine Cavafy (1863-1933), one of the writers to whose work I feel close, lived most of his life in the Greek-speaking diaspora in Alexandria, Egypt. He was born and died there, oddly enough, on the same day, April 29, 70 years apart. His apartment was located in the Rue Lepsius, situated between the red-light Attarin district, with its taverns and bordellos (one of which was housed on the main floor of his apartment building), the Greek Orthodox church, and the Greek hospital, which he characterised, respectively, as "the Temple of the Flesh," "the Temple of the Soul," and "the Temple of the Body." Or, as Cavafy put it another way, looking out from his balcony above Lepsius St., "Where could I live better? Below, the brothel caters for the flesh. And there is the church which forgives sin. And there is the hospital where we die."

Sexually attracted to young men, Cavafy wrote frankly about what he called "deviate, sensuous delight" (what we might call today "queer, sensuous delight"), long before almost anyone in the 20th century. He described this desire in himself as "An erotic bent of his / one sternly forbidden and most scorned / (but innate nevertheless)". Those of us who have lived similar erotic lives, though under different and more favourable historical circumstances, and have written about our experiences, are naturally drawn to Cavafy's poems, few of which were published during his lifetime.

Cavafy was the ninth son of a prosperous Alexandrian merchant family, but his father died young, leaving his wife and children in difficult financial circumstances. From ages nine to 14, Constantine lived in England where there were family connections. Later, he spent three years in Constantinople (now Istanbul), the home of his grandparents. But from age 22 on, except for a couple of literary visits to Athens around age 40 and other brief travels in Europe, Cavafy seldom left Alexandria, where he worked as a provisional clerk for 30 years in the Ministry of Irrigation, translating documents and handling correspondence.

A contemporary visitor to Alexandria, Duncan Sprott, reports that although the city has changed in the 70 years since Cavafy's death, there still remain parts of it that "feel like his city. The cafés where he watched the world go by are still in business. The street markets and flaking 19th century apartment blocks have not been swept away. Deep underground lies the buried city of the Macedonian Greeks and, somewhere, the lost tomb of Alexander the Great. Being here is like walking about inside Cavafy's poems."

As narrowly circumscribed, orderly, and quiet as his life appeared to be, Cavafy's world was a great deal wider and more turbulent, both geographically and temporally. In his own life, it is triangulated, in terms of family and literary connections, by three cities: Alexandria, Istanbul and Athens. In his imagination, it spread more broadly than that, extending throughout the Hellenistic realm, "trawling the history of the Hellenic world for subject matter—Athens, Rome, Antioch, Rhodes, Beirut, Byzantium," Duncan Sprott observes, "but always returning to write of the glorious Greco-Roman past of Alexandria."

Its time frame moves episodically, but seamlessly, from Alexander the Great in roughly 330 BCE through the succeeding Ptolemaic Egyptian and Seleucid near-East dynasties. It takes in the Roman Empire and its outposts, especially in the time of its decline; the rise of Christianity and medieval Byzantium; and it goes right up to contemporary Alexandria, that "capital of memories," where Cavafy recorded the presence of one or another "flawlessly beautiful" boy encountered in a bar, a shop or on the street in the Quartier Attarine. "Often he recycled his experiences," says Sprott, an historical novelist who has also written about the city named for Alexander, "turning his beautiful boys, his furtive embraces, into poetry: always he kept up this parallel outpouring of subtly erotic poems about the Alexandria of his own time."

Cavafy's single most famous poem, "Waiting for the Barbarians," written fairly early in his career, permanently defined for us an image that haunted the 20th century. "What are we waiting for, assembled in the public square?" the poem asks. "The barbarians are to arrive today," it replies. The anticipation of the crisis affects everything in the city. The senators pass no laws, because "when the barbarians come they will make the laws." The emperor sits on his throne at the principal gate of the city because he waits to receive the barbarian chief — "Indeed he has prepared to give him a scroll." The consuls and praetors have bedecked themselves in jewels "because the barbarians are to arrive today, and such things dazzle the barbarians." But the streets and squares clear out by the end of the day, the people return to their homes, deep in thought, "because night is here but the barbarians have not come." At the end, the poem asks, "And now what shall become of us without any barbarians?" It ruefully replies, "Those people were a kind of solution."

In the contemporary "war on terrorism" of the 21st century, we, too, continue to wait for the barbarians; daily, the officials of the "Homeland Security" office raise or lower the colour-coded threat alerts of the barbarians' anticipated appearance. What kind of a solution are they for us?

Cavafy is one of those poets for whom all of historical time is omnipresent, a claim verified by fellow poets who heard his conversation on Lepsius St. and in the bars. In the poem "Philhellene," written in the persona of a minor puppet monarch of the Seleucid kingdom (*circa* 250 BCE), the status-anxious satrap instructs the minter of his coinage, "See that the engraving is artistic / The expression serious and stately . . . / The inscription, as usual in Greek; / not exaggerated, not pompous — / lest the proconsul who is always poking about / and reporting to Rome misconstrue it . . . /

> Above all I charge you to see to it
> (Sithaspes, in God's name, let this not be forgotten)
> that after the words King and Savior,
> there be engraved in elegant letters, Philhellene.
> Now don't try your clever sallies on me,
> your "Where are the Greeks?" and "Where is anything Greek
> behind Zagros here, beyond Phraata?"
> Since so many others more barbarous than we
> write it, we too shall write it.
> And finally do not forget that at times
> sophists from Syria visit us,
> and versifiers, and other comedians.
> So we are not un-Greek, I reckon.

Cavafy reaches into the past with the same magic that the mythological Greeks in Jean Cocteau's *Orpheus* films enter the mirrors through which they pass to the underworld, their hands plunging into the liquefying glass. How intimately Cavafy hears those voices, confidently providing a parenthetical aside — "(Sithaspes, in God's name, let this not be forgotten)" — and recording precisely Sithaspes's scornful ripostes, his sneering "Where are the Greeks?" in a debased age when the glory of Greece is past. But since the others proclaim their love of the Greeks, so too will we. After all, are we any less Greek than the other imposters who stamp "Philhellene" on their coinage? Cavafy returns from the mirror with a slice of the past, as easily as someone at the end of dinner casually cutting a sliver from a round of cheese to go with a Mediterranean wine.

Cavafy makes his method explicit in "Caesarion," when he says, "Partly to verify an epoch, / partly also to pass the time / last night I picked up a collection / of Ptolemaic inscriptions to read." Their "plentiful phrases and flatteries" are familiar. But as he's about to put the book aside, a passing mention of an obscure king, Caesarion, attracts his attention. "In history only a few / lines are found about you, / and so I molded you more freely in my mind,"

And so fully did I envision you,
that late last night as my lamp
was going out — I deliberately let it go out —
I thought I saw you enter my room,
you seemed to stand before me as you must have been
in vanquished Alexandria . . .

There is a complicated internal history to Cavafy's poems and nighttime forays whose facts I don't command, but which would be interesting to learn. (Robert Liddell's *Cavafy* is the extant, somewhat tendentious, biography.) There are poetic and life crises, quarrels over readings of history, the elegant mixture of colloquial or demotic language with literary Greek, periodizations to discern. The year 1911, at age 48, is some sort of dividing line between earlier poems and the ones he henceforth logs annually. And within a given year, there are other years recalled; in 1927, "Days of 1896"; in 1917, "Days of 1903," and so on. He lived with his mother, waiting until she had gone to bed before going out to cruise the taverns in the Attarine district; then, after her death, with one or another of his unmarried brothers; eventually, alone, on Lepsius St.

The "parallel outpouring of subtly erotic poems about the Alexandria of his own time" begins in evanescent memory, already "Far Off," as the title of these lines from 1914 has it (the ellipses are Cavafy's):

I should like to relate this memory . . .
but it is so faded now . . . scarcely anything is left —
because it lies far off, in the years of my early manhood.
A skin as if made of jasmine . . .
that night in August — was it August? — that night . . .
I can just barely remember the eyes; they were, I think, blue . . .
Ah yes, blue; a sapphire blue.

The ellipses are the key to reproducing the process by which the faintest of memories gradually yields "a skin," a possible time of year, barely remembered eyes that were, "Ah yes, blue," and then suddenly, precisely: "A sapphire blue." And that's it.

After that, the recollections and presences become more frequent. In "At the Café Entrance" (1915), "Something they said beside me directed / my attention towards the café entrance. / And I saw the beautiful body that looked / as if Eros had made it from his consummate experience ..." Or "On the Street" (1916), "he is twenty-five years old, but looks more like twenty; / with something artistic in his dress / — a touch of color in his tie, a bit of shape to his collar — / he walks aimlessly on the street, / as if hypnotized still by the deviate sensual delight, / by the so deviate sensual delight he has enjoyed." And "They stood among many others / near a lighted tobacco-shop window. / Their glances chanced to meet, / and they timidly, haltingly expressed / the deviate desire of their flesh. / Then a few steps uneasily taken on the sidewalk — / until they smiled, and gently nodded" ("The Tobacco-Shop Window," 1917). Or at "The Next Table" (1918), "Ah see, now that he is sitting down at the next table / I know every movement he makes — and beneath his clothes, / once more I see the adored bare limbs."

Again and again, the poems have their origins in "the fulfillment of their deviate, sensual delight," and though the two lovers rise from the mattress, dress hurriedly, and "leave the house separately, furtively," it is the poet who returns to the scene of their pleasures, and registers "how the life of the artist has gained. / Tomorrow, the next day, years later, the vigorous verses / will be composed that had their beginning here" ("Their Beginning," 1921). Repeatedly, Cavafy affirms that "The joy and essence of my life is the memory of the hours / when I found and sustained sensual delight as I desired it" ("Sensual Delight," 1917).

It was around that time, toward the end of World War I that, through a mutual friend, Cavafy was introduced to the English novelist E.M. Forster, who had volunteered for the Red Cross and was stationed in Alexandria. They immediately hit it off, the author of those poems about "deviate, sensuous delight" and the author of *Maurice* (1913), the forbidden homosexual novel Forster kept in a drawer, leaving it to Christopher Isherwood, who saw to its posthumous publication at the beginning of the 1970s. Did Forster — I seem to remember this from one of the biographies — have a little affair with an Alexandrian streetcar conductor, someone he met in the taverns Cavafy frequented? Later, it was Forster who, after the war, brought Cavafy's poems to Eliot and D.H. Lawrence, Forster who, in *Pharos and Pharillon* in 1923 (later he wrote *Alexandria: A History and a Guide*) left us this indelible portrait:

> ... a Greek gentleman, in a straw hat, standing absolutely motionless at a slight angle to the universe. His arms are extended, possibly. 'Oh, Cavafy ...!' Yes, it is Mr. Cavafy, and he is going either from his flat to the office, or from his office to the flat. If the former, he vanishes

when seen, with a slight gesture of despair. If the latter, he may be pre-
vailed upon to begin a sentence — an immense, complicated, yet
shapely sentence, full of parentheses that never get mixed and of
reservations that really do reserve; a sentence that moves with logic to
its foreseen end, yet to an end that is always more vivid and thrilling
than one foresaw. Sometimes the sentence is finished in the street,
sometimes the traffic murders it, sometimes it lasts into the flat. It
deals with the tricky behaviour of the Emperor Alexius Comnenus in
1096, or with olives, their possibilities and price, or with . . . It is
delivered with equal ease in Greek, English, or French. And despite
the matured charity of its judgments, one feels that it too stands at a
slight angle to the universe: it is the sentence of a poet.

As the contemporary visitor to Alexandria, Duncan Sprott,
observes, "Here in Egypt, Cavafy seems very like the last contributor
to the Greek Anthology, reinventing for modern times the exquisite
ancient Greek erotic poem . . . He is the heir and true successor to the
great ancient Alexandrian poets Callimachus and Theocritus." In an
early poem about the art of poetry, when a young poet who has only
accomplished one idyll complains to Theocritus that he stands on
"the first step . . . I shall never ascend," Cavafy has Theocritus reply,
"If you are on the first step, / you ought to be proud and pleased. /
Coming as far as this is not little; / what you have achieved is great
glory / . . . even this first step." Cavafy's poems, Sprott notes, "are
delicate, usually short — like snapshots, like broken fragments, like
sparkling bits of mosaic."

In a 1961 introduction to Cavafy's poems, W.H. Auden admits that
"I can think of poems which, if Cavafy were unknown to me, I
should have written quite differently or perhaps not written at all."
Pondering the untranslatable character of poetry, Auden nonetheless
finds that "there must be some elements in poetry which are separable from their original verbal expression and some which are inseparable." Obviously, we lose the associations created by homophones
in the original language; much of the metric is uncapturable; and the
mixture, both in Cavafy's vocabulary and syntax, "of demotic and
purist Greek is untranslatable." What, then, Auden asks, "is it in
Cavafy's poems that survives translation and excites? Something I
can only call, most inadequately, a tone of voice, a personal speech,"
what we today call a "sensibility."

Something else, too. Sprott, visiting Cavafy's apartment (now a
museum), sees "the death mask, his brass bed, desks, books, and family photographs." Actually, although some books and photos were
saved, the furniture was sold off, and today they have been replaced
with reproductions, reconstructed from the photographs. Looking

out from Cavafy's balcony, Sprott remembers a remark of Cavafy's about his neighbours in the brothel below: "They receive some disgusting people, some monsters, but they receive some angels . . . some angels." Sprott adds, "Cavafy's angels are still everywhere in Alexandria." Elsewhere, too, I think.

The translatable sensibility and the recurrent presence of human beauty is what makes possible a writing *after Cavafy* (in the sense that Jack Spicer called his book *After Lorca*). Reading "Days of 1903," "1904," we imagine "Days of 2004," "2005," recording equally handsome youths, the "faded cinnamon-colored suit" of "Days of 1908" replaced by some artless garb of today. Both then and now, the beauty of the figure of desire requires little attention to fashion. The differences, if any, are mostly technological: today the young are ubiquitously armed with cellphones; a digital miniature music-player hangs on a cloth necklace, a black wire caresses a collarbone, silver earphones pour the melodies of the day into their heads. But then and now, "your image watched over him / when he took off . . . / the worthless clothes . . . / And he remained entirely naked; flawlessly beautiful, a marvel / His hair uncombed, standing up a little . . ." About an adolescent youth, just 17, and the older man to whom he has given himself, Cavafy (and I), then and now, can declare:

> Philostratus says the gods see
> future events, people only what is happening
> now, but older men see approaching things.
> He is 17 and will disappear
> into manhood. This, the older man
> sees. Will he remember himself at 17,
> when he is 24,
> when he is 40?

The injunction remains: "Try to guard them, poet, / however few there are that can be kept. / The visions of your loving. / Set them, half hidden, in your phrases. / Try to sustain them, poet, / when they are roused in your brain / at night, or in the glare of noon." ("When they are roused," 1916.)

Toward the end of his life, Cavafy was horrified by the decay of the flesh. "The ageing of my body and my beauty," one of his personae lamented, "is like a blow from a frightful knife." He abandons the dyed hair of middle age, the requests to have the wrinkles left out of his portraits. The memoirs of a young contemporary, preserving the cruelties of our fate, claims that Cavafy's "whole soul concentrated in his glance and the touch of his hand, ready to hazard in my direction a movement as of a carnivorous plant."

Later, throat cancer left him with only a whisper. After a tracheotomy he was silenced and communicated by means of pencilled notes. On Cavafy's 70th birthday in 1933 — perhaps the story is apocryphal — he wrote a period, a full stop on a sheet of paper, and drew a circle around it, Sprott reports, then adds, "That afternoon he was buried." But as Cavafy says in "The Tomb of Iases," one of many poems speaking from the grave: "Traveler, / if you are an Alexandrian, you will not condemn. You know / the rushing torrent of our life, what ardor it has; what supreme / pleasure."

Cecilienhof

The mythological figures to whom I'm most drawn are not the great gods (though, if I were to believe in any divinities, it would be the Greek ones), but the spirits, demi-gods, rare mortals and beasts who move between them and us — Eros, Orpheus, Pegasus, the Furies, Hermes, Narcissus.

Each year, when I'm in Berlin, I make at least one visit to Cecilienhof, a Tudoresque manor on the edge of Potsdam, just beyond the Berlin city limits, to pay homage to one of those mythic forms. Cecilienhof was built during World War I by Kaiser Wilhelm II for his son, Crown Prince Wilhelm, recently married to Duchess Cecilie von Mecklenberg-Schwerin, and is known as the last castle of the Prussian kings, because the calamitous war ended monarchy in Germany and drove its inhabitants into exile. Even more historically notable, Cecilienhof was the site of the Potsdam Conference (July 17–August 2, 1945), in which Stalin, U.S. President Harry Truman, and Clement Atlee, representing Britain after Winston Churchill had been defeated in the 1945 election, formally ended World War II and drew up the boundaries of their new world order.

But none of that is why I go to Cecilienhof. Rather, I make my pilgrimage in order to see the 19th century bronze statue of Narcissus, draped over the rim of a sculpted well or raised pool in which he can gaze upon the reflection of his face in the water. Although as a work of art, this Narcissus, situated in a small garden at the back of the manor, is neither great nor famous, it exerts an enduring fascination upon me. So much so that I pestered a kindly art librarian at the city library in east Berlin to provide me with whatever scraps of information about it might be available. They were few.

The obscure sculptor is Hubert Netzer, who specialized in the subgenre of the art known as fountain-sculpture, an apparently lucrative trade during the late 19th and early 20th centuries, when burgeoning, unified Germany could afford such artifacts to decorate its urban squares. There's a date — 1897 — but it's uncertain, and a place, Munich. The sculptor studied there with the now equally obscure Adolf von Hildebrand. Netzer was still alive in the 1920s, teaching at Düsseldorf, where his one dubious claim to fame is that one of his students was the Nazi sculptor Arno Breker. Beyond these bits, the sculptor of this Narcissus, like so many other forgotten makers of public works, is almost anonymous. The summer tourists who visit the statue do not stay as long as I, they go on to look at the rooms of the Potsdam Conference, or to have an ice cream in the courtyard café.

I remain there to think about the mystery of Narcissus. It is a strange story, told by Ovid in his *Metamorphoses*, of a beautiful child fathered by a river god and born to a water nymph, or naïad. When he is 16 years old and "might seem both boy and youth," many of his age-mates, both boys and girls, desire him. However, Ovid tells us, "there was such intense pride in that delicate form that none of the youths or young girls affected him." The one most smitten is the nymph Echo, who one day sees Narcissus hunting deer with his nets.

Here, Ovid pauses for a digression to tell us about the girl "of the echoing voice, who cannot be silent when others have spoken, nor learn how to speak first herself." Echo still had a body then and was not just a voice. It was Juno, or Saturnia, queen of the gods, who curtailed her speech, because when Juno might have caught the nymphs "lying beneath her husband Jupiter on mountain slopes," Echo held her in long conversations while the nymphs fled. When Juno realized this, she condemned Echo to have "less power over that tongue by which I have been deluded, and the briefest ability to speak," reduced, as we know, to only being able to repeat the last of what is spoken.

When Echo sees Narcissus wandering through the fields, she is inflamed, follows him secretly, and yearns to get close to him with seductive words. But her tongue-tied condition prevents it and will not let her begin. However, when the boy is separated from his mates and calls out, "Is anyone here?", Echo replies, "Here." "Let us meet together," he calls. "Together," she replies, and comes out of the woods to put her arms around his neck. But upon seeing her, he flees, and says, "May I die before what's mine is yours." She answers only, "What's mine is yours." Scorned, Echo wanders in the woods, her unrequited love and sleepless thoughts waste her form, until only her voice is left.

Meanwhile, Narcissus continues to reject those who desire him. One of those mocked lovers cries to the gods, "Then, let him love himself, and fail to command what he loves," and is heard by the goddess Nemesis, who thus curses Narcissus. Then Ovid takes up the part of the tale that those of us who read the old stories know best.

One day, Narcissus, tired by the heat and his enthusiasm for the chase, comes upon an unclouded fountain and desires to quench his thirst. Instead, Ovid says, a different thirst is created. As he drinks, "he beholds himself / reflected in the mirrored pool — and loves; /

loves an imagined body which contains / no substance, for he deems
the mirrored shade / a thing of life to love . . .”

All that is lovely in himself he loves,
And unknowingly, he desires himself . . .
He seeks, is sought, he burns and is burnt.

Narcissus gives his lips in vain to the deceptive pool, he tries to
embrace the neck he sees, and plunges his arms into the water, but
cannot catch himself within them. “What you search for is nowhere:
turning away, what you love is lost,” declares the poet. Ovid suggests
that Narcissus at some point knows, “I am he. I sense it and I am not
deceived by my own image.” Yet he can’t leave the image, and like
Echo, wastes away. When he cries out, “Alas!”, she repeats with her
echoing voice, “Alas!” In the end, “death closes those eyes that had
marvelled at their bearer’s beauty.” Even when Narcissus is received
into the underworld, the house of shadows, he continues to gaze into
the Stygian waters; the water nymphs cry out in sorrow, and Echo
returns their laments. Eventually, the body of Narcissus is transformed into the small, white flower that is named for him.

There, in a back garden at Cecilienhof, is Netzer’s Narcissus,
sprawled on the rim of a raised pool, a statue gazing into real water at
its reflection, as we contemplate the bronze image of him. The fascination is in the complex play between reality and imagination; artifact and actual youth; self and other; between the phantasm of love
and the experience of eros. We want to know if love is real or not. Or,
perhaps love is real, but the image we seek is a phantasm. Worse,
what if what we think is love is merely self-absorption, even an
inability to see the other person?

As with all powerful stories, there are recurrent versions of the Narcissus myth. He is a figure among the ancients; he reappears in late
medieval love poetry, as philosopher Giorgio Agamben tells us in
Stanzas: Word and Phantasm in Western Culture; and the story is
made especially problematic in the 20th century by Sigmund Freud’s
essay, “On Narcissism” (1914). There, Freud suggests that a primary
narcissism — a self-absorption that substitutes for the love of the
mother — is natural, and is normally transcended by self-recognition
or what the later psychoanalyst Jacques Lacan called “the mirror
stage,” a recognition of self in a world of others. But, Freud continues,
there is a troubling secondary narcissism, an “arrested development”
or personality disorder, in which the narcissist, in devoting his energies to maintaining an idealized self-image, proves incapable of genuine love for other people. Worse, Freud associates this narcissism
with homosexuality. By the late 20th century, the notion of narcissism

as a pattern of traits and behaviours which involve infatuation and obsession with one's self to the exclusion of others is popularised, dumbed-down, and inscribed in the psychoanalytic diagnostic manuals as a mental disorder. Finally, it is socialized, in Christopher Lasch's *The Culture of Narcissism*, to describe a self-absorbed, greedy, and frivolous society, dependent on consumerism.

There are puzzles in each of the versions. Why, in Ovid's telling, is there such "intense pride in that delicate form" that Narcissus is unaffected by his desiring age-mates? Is it pride, or is Narcissus merely innocent of desire? Why the violent rejection of Echo? Can we read it as simply fear in the presence of awakening desire, hers and his, that he doesn't understand? Why, once he knows that "I am he," is he unable to break away from the reflected, watery image of himself?

And isn't Freud's reading of narcissism as arrested homosexual desire a fundamental confusion of the alleged desire for the self with the homosexual desire for the same gender (not the same person)? In reply to Freud's suggestion that homosexuality is caused by some inner psychic disturbance, a poet friend of mine naughtily quips, "Homosexuality is caused by pretty boys," i.e., it is their beauty, not our psyches, that inspires desire. But naughtiness aside, homosexual desires, despite personal ads that claim "WM, 35, enjoys candlelight dinners, movies, walks in the park, seeks same," are desires for others, just as much as heterosexual desires.

The solutions to the mystery of Narcissus are, like the questions, legion. Oscar Wilde, as usual too clever by half, even considers the problem from the perspective of the reflecting pool or mirror. With characteristic irony, he proposes (in a brief prose poem, "The Disciple") that the beauty is not Narcissus's image in me/the pool, but my beauty reflected in Narcissus's eyes. But Wilde can be excused, having had his fair share of torment in loving the eternally narcissistic boy named Bosie.

Giorgio Agamben is the most careful reader of the story, tracing the psychology and physiology of the late medieval troubador love poets back to Plato. In Plato's *Philebus*, Socrates observes that "memory unites with the senses, and the passions connected with these write words in our souls, so to speak." What's more, the artist of the soul "draws in the mind the images" of things said and seen. He "sees within himself in some way the images of these objects." These pictures, Agamben reports, are thereafter defined as "phantasms." The central theme of the dialogue, Agamben reminds us, "is not knowledge, but pleasure, and, if Plato evokes the problem of memory and phantasm, it is because he is anxious to show that desire and pleasure are impossible without this 'painting in the soul,' and that a purely corporeal pleasure does not exist" without images. Both our own incessant fantasies and the ubiquitous availability of explicit erotic images in our era display the self-evident connection of Plato's argument to contemporary experience.

In the medieval reception of Plato, Agamben argues, "the whole cognitive process is conceived as speculation in the strict sense, a reflection of phantasms from mirror to mirror." Eyes and senses are both mirror and water that reflect the form of the object. So is fantasy, "which 'imagines' the phantasms in the absence of the object." Finally, eros is necessarily a matter of literal speculation, and its site is the fountain or mirror. "Medieval psychology," Agamben concludes, "conceived of love as an essentially phantasmic process involving both imagination and memory in an assiduous circling around an image painted or reflected in the self." So, despite the interpretations of modern psychology, Agamben urges us to remember that "Narcissus was, after all, not directly in love with himself, but with his own image reflected in the water, which he mistook for a real creature"; that is, he was in love with what he thought was someone else, since he had never seen himself before.

As I see them, the young are, by nature, self-distracted. Their pronouncements of boredom or interest in the world are made from the location of self, rather than from the perspective of being in the world. They are both self-conscious and unself-conscious, if we recognize the contrasting senses of that term. Mortified by self-consciousness, they return to the mirror, combing their hair, checking their complexions, matching their clothes to fashion, and are trapped in themselves. But in the other sense of becoming conscious of self-in-the-world, they wait to be led out of themselves.

In the garden of Narcissus at Cecilienhof, I identify with Echo, since who or what is a writer but Echo herself? Echo, in my version of the story, doesn't waste away, but persists, reminds, re-iterates, and ultimately, with luck (Fortuna), rouses Narcissus from self-distraction and brings him into the world. In the triangulations of Eros, Narcissus is roused/aroused, and often embraces Echo, at least for a while. That is why, I assume, Agamben cites Dante's *Purgatorio*, as do the proponents of a "dictated" poetry:

I am one who, when
Amor inspires me, takes note, and in the mode
that he dictates within me, I go signifying.

In Dante's Italian: "*Vo significando.*"

Chicago

One Saturday afternoon in Chicago in 1948, when I was seven years old, my mother Ida took me downtown to the Loop. It's known as the Loop because of the elevated urban railway. The tracks of the "El," as it's called, are raised on black metal pylons and form a loop around part of downtown Chicago. We went to the big Marshall Field and Carson's department stores and, after shopping, to the movie theatres on State Street. I recently found a night-time photo of that street while I was thinking about this incident — it's on the cover of Alan Ehrenhalt's *The Lost City*, a book about Chicago in the 1950s. The lighted marquees of the Chicago and State-Lake theatres face each other across the traffic-crowded thoroughfare.

My mother took me to the Chicago Theatre for the matinee. In those days they still had live stage shows before the movie was shown. That afternoon the star act was Carmen Miranda, the Portuguese-born, Brazilian samba singer who wore elaborate, glamorous costumes, and was famous for headdresses on which a pile of fruit was arranged atop her thick red hair. She performed a couple of numbers and entertained the crowd with some between-songs patter, which included an invitation for children in the audience to come up on stage. The ploy was Miranda's refutation of the claim that she was wearing a wig, that her lush, red hair wasn't her own.

The theatre's ushers quickly herded a half-dozen of the children in the audience up on stage. I was one of them. We ordinary, real kids suddenly crossed the boundary of footlights into the magic world of the stage and its larger-than-life figures. There I was, tugging on a proferred lock of Carmen Miranda's red hair, and offering mutely nodded testimony in reply to her question, "Ees it real?"

I can't remember if I was frightened by the amusement of the audience of mostly women shoppers or if I was thrilled to touch Carmen Miranda's hair. Nor can I remember my mother's reaction after I came down from the stage and was back in my seat next to her. The distant memory isn't enlivened by a feeling, but is more like a fact I might read in a book. Of course, I didn't know that Miranda was "a Brazilian samba singer" or anything else. I probably thought of her as a fairy-tale princess come to life. I'm more interested in what my mother felt than my own response. That's the emotional hole in the memory. As for myself, what's interesting to me now is seeing that this incident has a meaning, has something to do with who I am and how I see Chicago.

Carmen Miranda was my first encounter between the magical and the mundane. But it was at another stage venue, when I was 14 or so, that I glimpsed the idea of the city as a theatre of history. What I saw was a production of Tennessee Williams's play *El Camino Réal* (The Royal Road), in which characters both real and fictional, from all periods of history, appeared on Williams's road of life: Don Quixote, Casanova, Lord Byron, Marguerite Gautier from Alexandre Dumas *fils's Camille*, and even a post-World War II GI that Williams called Kilroy, named for an ubiquitous chalked graffito of the era that declared "Kilroy was here."

An older, "artistic," second cousin of mine, Anne Thompson, gave me the ticket to the theatre because she saw in me a potential literary sensibility. The play was considered to be a failure (too sprawling, too "ambitious"), and Williams was critized for his pessimism in the mid-1950s era of President Dwight Eisenhower's America. But I was completely entranced by the possibility that time and person were far more fluid than the linear version of our experience. This time I knew I was understanding something beyond the dramatic scenes on stage. I transformed the idea of time-shifting history on a theatre-stage into the city itself as a theatre in which, as Czeslaw Milosz puts it, "Daily occurrences lean every day into history."

I

Time turns hometowns into memory palaces and ghost cities. I was born and raised in Chicago, and left it in summer 1958 when I headed out into the world at age 17. It now appears to me retrospectively in two ways. First, I see that theatre of history populated by all the figures who were present but unknown to me during my years there. Second, in a more literal sense, the city returns in the details of the narrow, but specific geographic zones of childhood and adolescence.

So, for instance, in the romantic sense of Chicago I've invented for myself, I'm a six-year-old in spring 1947 on my way to Mrs. Valentine's first-grade class at Sumner Elementary School on the West Side, confident reader of the *Dick and Jane* first-grade textbook ("See Dick run. Run, Dick, run. See Spot run. Run, Spot, run. See Jane . . ."). I was a confident reader because my father had already taught me to read, so I was spared puzzling over the inanities of Dick and Jane, but I was puzzled by why we had to read about them.

Meanwhile, partway across town, around the intersection of Milwaukee and Division streets, the Polish section of the city (where my Uncle Gob has his drygoods store), the novelist Nelson Algren, soon to be the author of the 1950 National Book Critics' award-winning *Man With the Golden Arm*, a novel about the hell of heroin in Chicago's back streets, is in the midst of a passionate transatlantic affair with the French existentialist writer Simone de Beauvoir. She's about to write the *The Second Sex*, the founding document of modern feminism. He's showing her around the grubby taverns, backroom gambling dens, and B-girl hotels that are his bailiwick, and the elegant, brainy Parisian is swept off her feet by the rough-edged authenticity of her Chicago boyfriend. Chicago as a city of literature and romance.

Or, I'm 14 years old, in fall 1955, in love for the first time with a schoolmate, and we're erotically horsing around in the boy's gymnasium locker room at Marshall High School, with barely a language in which to recognize our incipient desire. And somewhere out there in a swanky Chicago-area mansion ("swanky" is a word from that era), there's the sophisticated Hugh Hefner, puffing a pipe, garbed in a brocade bathrobe, the recent founder of *Playboy* magazine, a glossy, cleverly respectable, and very profitable packaging of soft-core porn with fashionable fiction and interviews. He's lounging at his heated swimming pool, surrounded by a "bevy" of "Playboy bunnies."

That night, in my bedroom, I've unfolded the picture of the nubile *Playboy* centrefold-of-the-month, and as if I were doing an experiment in chemistry class, I'm checking my reactions to make sure I'm "normal." The experiment is technically a gooey success, but with the cool objectivity of a budding scientist, I recognize that I prefer the locker room to the Playboy mansion, and I say to myself, foreseeing future social difficulties, "Uh-oh, this is going to be a problem." Chicago as a city of desire.

Or, I'm within a year of graduation from Austin High School, the 1957-58 school year, and I'm deciding whether to "Join the Navy and See the World" (as the recruiting poster has it) or to make use of an invitation from the University of Chicago to drop out of high school and join the university's innovative "accelerated program" as an undergraduate. Meanwhile, on the far South Side of Chicago, even further south than the black ghetto where my father's grocery and meat market is located at 45th and Prairie Avenue, there are a host of people in the classrooms of the University of Chicago whom I'll eventually come to know through their books.

Although I'd never been to the University of Chicago campus, during those years I was growing up, the future philosophers and social critics Richard Rorty and Allen Bloom, then grad students, are listening to the lectures of Leo Strauss. Is aspiring novelist Philip Roth there, too? What about Saul Bellow? Bellow will become a friend of Bloom, and decades later write a very good, late novel about him, *Ravelstein*. In my reconstructed mirror of the past, he has already published the prize-winning *Adventures of Augie March*, whose opening lines declare, "I am an American, Chicago born — Chicago, that sombre city — and go at things as I have taught myself, free-style, and will make the record in my own way . . ." Chicago as a city of the mind.

Even an odd television incident fits into this picture of imagining a larger Chicago than the one I knew. On the city's new educational channel one evening in 1957, the city's great architect Frank Lloyd Wright, and its most famous poet, Carl Sandburg ("Chicago, city of big shoulders . . ."), now respectively 88 and 79 years old, are chatting amiably and blandly about the prospects for the city. After the moderator signs off, and the old guys think they are off-air, Wright turns to Sandburg and says, "We'd better get out of here, Carl, before somebody starts telling the truth." The point is that there wasn't a lot of public truth-telling in the Chicago of that era. And elsewhere on that soon-to-be-pervasive TV, far from the truth, lurks the jowly bulk of recently elected Chicago Mayor Richard J. Daley.

II

The literal city begins for me in an empty lot behind the three-storey apartment building and its navy-grey wooden back porches at 1110 South Keeler Avenue on Chicago's West Side where I lived with my parents. In the post-war summer of 1946, the lot is filled with tall milkweeds, there's a raggedy path diagonally bisecting it, and we dig foxholes from which to replay imaginary scenes of the just-concluded World War II. Kitty-corner across Fillmore Street is the sandlot baseball field belonging to the adjacent red-brick Calumet Baking Powder factory. The cans of baking powder are dark red and have a drawing of the head of a Calumet Indian on them.

The outfield boundary is a cement railroad viaduct, and when one of the local heroes, a 16- or 17-year-old kid named Archie, with muscular biceps and wearing a white T-shirt, hits the ball onto the tracks, it's a home run, and one of us younger kids has to go around behind the viaduct, climb the grassy slope, retrieve the ball from the tracks, and toss it back onto the field. The viaduct runs through the neighbourhood, and where Keeler Avenue crosses under it there's a dip in the asphalt so trucks can get through without their roofs scraping the viaduct overhead. During the summer rains the dip gets flooded and cars are shipwrecked.

From our empty-lot foxholes amid the milkweeds, armed with wooden toy rifles, we can see the railroad viaduct, and occasionally, running on the tracks, long dun-coloured passenger trains. In their windows, we can see the uniformed soldiers coming home from World War II, like my older cousin Herb Kane. The boy in the foxhole with me is six-year-old Johnny Tallone, who lives with his parents in a semi-basement flat in our apartment building. Johnny's father, Frank, works in a metal fabricating factory, and from the lead scrap, he makes toy soldiers for us. I have a Lionel electric toy train, and Johnny and I stuff the lead soldiers into the windows of the passenger cars, so that the train looks like the ones we see on the railroad viaduct.

This is my world, the tiny patch of less than a square block, my Chicago, whose gradual expansion I can trace year by year, as I venture out from the empty lot. In one direction, north, I walk under the viaduct along Keeler toward Sumner Elementary School located on the diagonal-running Fifth Avenue. In the other direction, south, I head toward the main neighbourhood intersection of Roosevelt and Pulaski Roads. It is a world of origins: first friends, first learnings, first city (even though Chicago was known in America as the "Second City," second to New York). The details of it, which flood in at the instant of recall, explain almost everything about the shaping of self: sex, adventure, relationships, intellect. The images are like a Tinkertoy set from which I can put together my childhood past. Tinkertoys were a package of wooden spokes and wheels out of which one could construct buildings, trains, Ferris wheels, and imaginary animals. In the contemporary world, they've been replaced by video games in which kids practice killing other people.

I have a tricycle, Johnny Tallone has a red wagon. The older boys in the neighbourhood, like teenage slugger Archie and his pal, Jackie, conduct races by pushing me on my tricycle and Johnny on his wagon as fast as they can along the sidewalk on Fillmore Street. The speed is incredible, the ride precarious, the tricycle tipping onto one wheel as we make a perilous corner. Then comes the crash, we've hit the stanchion of a metal fence enclosing a patch of grass. There's blood everywhere. Mine. A gash just below the knee. I still have the faint scar, the first scar.

I'm of two minds about the specificity of those images that spill out of the cornucopia of the past. There's Callico, my first stuffed toy animal with its multi-coloured, slightly greasy oilcloth covering. I see the dented two-cup tin coffee pot with a crystal glass knob that violently jiggles when my father's coffee brews. Then, the second-hand Tom Mix and Red Ryder and Little Beaver comic books being resold for a nickel from the top of an orange crate by one of the Murphy kids down the block and which I urgently need to buy. I'm looking at the framed photo of me at age 4 in a sailor suit, the picture sitting on a spinet piano, my cheeks and eyes colour-tinted by my cousin Bob's mother, Marge, at the photo shop that she and her husband, my father's brother Lew, run at the intersection of Van Buren and Canal Streets downtown near the Passport and Immigration office. Finally, in this strange sequential rush of objects, there are the John R. Tunis sports novels with shortstops named Bucky and outfielders called Jeff and Chad that I devoured as an adolescent reader, and which I've only seen referred to once in my entire subsequent reading career, in Philip Roth's novel *American Pastoral*. On the one hand, these things, and dozens of others, are irreplaceable, are what the real is made of. On the other hand, they're just lost, obsolete, meaningless (or only idio-syncratically meaningful) artifacts, the stuff of elderly nostalgia.

The first enlargement of my backyard world is a few paces south along Keeler. There's another empty lot, grassless, which backs onto the three-storey windowless rear brick wall of our building. You can throw a rubber ball high up against it, without any fear of breaking a window, since there aren't any. I play games of solitary imaginary baseball, or if there's a playmate to act as a combination infielder-outfielder, then, as the batter-first baseman, I also have to be the radio announcer broadcasting the game as we play it — my first idea of narration.

Behind the batter's box of this imaginary field are the wooden back porches, painted with the same Navy-surplus grey paint as the ones on our building, of another three-storey apartment building that fronts on the next street, Grenshaw. The paint blisters in the summer heat and one of our games is to break the bubbles of paint. I only know the back of the building. That's where the Murphys live — three brothers, Steve, Johnny, and Tommy, a sister, the parents — all crammed into a small basement flat that I see as being so poor that I think it has a hard-packed dirt floor, rather than the linoleum kitchen floors in our building (the actual floor must have been cement). Through the open door, I spy Johnny Murphy, the brother closest in age to me, walking around in the gloom of their cave-like dwelling, wearing white underpants. He's exotic, and because he's tough, also a little scary. Once, referring to some adventurous feat he was prepar-ing to attempt, jumping off a high diving board I think it was, he said to me, "If I can't do it, I'll kiss your ass." In the erotic confusion of age 10 or 11, I didn't realize he meant the phrase figuratively rather than literally, and I was uncertain if he was threatening that I would have to kiss his ass if he succeeded.

On the corner of Keeler and Grenshaw, on the main floor of the building where the Murphys live, is the grocery store where I take my pennies to buy gummy candies, licorice strips, Popsicles in summer — two columns of flavoured, sugary water frozen on two pine wood sticks. Discarded Popsicle sticks are everywhere and easy to collect. When you have 20 or so, the flexible pine wood can be plaited (my first craft) into a toy raft that floats in rain puddles — not much different in principle from plaiting these bits of childhood into a life-raft floating on a sea of time.

Chicago now includes friends, a gang of neighbourhood kids, but it also embodies a first sociological recognition. It's a neighbourhood more or less evenly divided between Jews and Irish. When we choose baseball teams to play on the sandlot — late into long summer evenings until the ball at last becomes invisible in the darkness — a meritocracy of hitting and fielding skill reigns, indifferent to ethnicity. Everybody wants Eddie Lacy on their team. But there's also an underlying rivalry of religion and class, and the occasional scrap between leaders of the hostile ethnicities. Bobby Greenspan, Jewish, who lives next door to me, and Steve Murphy, Irish, are rolling around in the dirt of the lot between our buildings, one of them with a bloodied nose that stains the other's dirt-smeared, white T-shirt.

What strikes me now is how little I knew of the city's geography. The literal city returns to me in the form of non-contiguous island neighbourhoods. There's a horizon: to the northwest on summer evenings, a glow of fire from the steel mills in nearby Cicero (or is it more distant Gary, Indiana?), and from the south, on those same hot summer nights, an olfactory horizon as the smell of the Chicago stockyards wafts across the city, comes in the open kitchen window.

I have almost no sense of direction in the city — even now, to read the past, I need a streetmap of Chicago at my side. My fuzzy sense of geography and direction, even in places I supposedly know, is one of the motifs of my life. I never know where I am and I'm always afraid of being abandoned in the middle of nowhere. Yet, I plunge deeper and deeper into far-flung urban jungles in a nutty effort to be somewhere. I think that explains some of my persistent fascination with cities, and why portraits of cities are so often part of everything I write.

Though I'm fuzzy on geography, I know some of the transportation corridors that connect one relevant island-neighbourhood to another. For instance, I know how to get from my house to my father's economically precarious corner store on the South Side, where I help out after school and on weekends. Looking at another photograph in Ehrenhalt's *Lost City*, this one of the intersection of 43rd and Prairie, just two blocks from my father's store — a photo taken in 1954 when I was 13 — I strain to identify the corner restaurant/drug store where I went up to the counter and ordered lunch (macaroni and ground beef in tomato sauce), almost unaware of being the only white person in a sea of black people. I can see the black woman in her starched uniform putting the plate on the counter before me and saying, "Here you go, sugar."

But all I see in this photo are the sun-bleached sidewalks, the wide traffic-free street, with its brick paving and embedded streetcar rails, on what could be a spring Sunday morning. The few people out walking are so distant that I can't identify them by skin colour. I've already spoken of my sense of black people (see "Of African Descent"), but the point to reiterate is that my experience is phenomenological rather than political. My nascent politics, shaped by my father's sense of respect for people and by what I've seen on television, are liberal, supportive of the civil rights movement on the march in a distant, feudal, anachronistic American South. But my sense of that, while I'm delivering a bag of groceries up a rickety flight of back porch wooden steps to a black middle-aged couple and am rewarded with a shiny 25 cent tip, is simply that these are people. So are the black young men in the neighbourhood who work in the store, and teach me to shoot a basketball in the alley. The baskets aren't nets, but peach baskets with their bottoms punched out, nailed up to telephone poles.

The other distant neighbourhoods simply float like islands, sudden landfalls that we unexpectedly arrive at in my father's car. Uncle Gob — he's another of my father's siblings, three brothers and four sisters — has his drygoods store in the Polish neighbourhood on Division Street. That's where I learn to say, "How are you?" in Polish and where they call me "Staš" or "Stashu." Cousin Marge, the "highstrung" daughter of my mother's Aunt Dora and Uncle Docky, and her husband Harry Fertig, a soft-spoken insurance salesmen at Prudential Life who always asks me how I'm doing in school, live in a high-rise apartment on Lake Shore Drive along Lake Michigan, a status-conscious address that Marge has anxiously insisted on acquiring. Her anxiety will eventually turn into "mental illness." I remember the distinctive, individual sounds of their laughter better than I do the geography. Downtown is the Hamilton Hotel, site of the monthly Cousins' Club meetings that brings together my mother's extended family. Eventually, I learn how to get downtown by myself, to go to Kroch and Brentano's bookstore.

III

There's also a real, larger, historical city that I was only dimly aware of during my years there. It's run by two great entities, The Machine and The Mob. The Machine is the Democratic Party of Chicago and Cook County, and its Boss, as of 1955, and for the next 20 years (until he died in office), is Richard J. Daley. One middle-of-the-road account of Daley's long tenure that I've been reading just to fill in the facts I didn't know as a kid is Adam Cohen and Elizabeth Taylor's *American Pharoah*. A more pungent, harder hitting biography is Chicago journalist Mike Royko's *Boss*.

Daley rose to a position of almost absolute power from the humble Irish-Catholic, bungalow neighbourhood of Bridgeport, north of the stockyards. The machine he came to control, abetted by church and business elites, consisted of his lieutenants, city aldermen and county commissioners, thousands of "precinct captains" responsible for getting out the vote at election time, and an even vaster population of people holding patronage jobs — city clerks, garbagemen, building inspectors, judges — doled out by the machine. The corruption was deep and the pay-offs huge. Though Daley's minions regularly got scooped up in periodic waves of moral fervor and even went to jail, Daley himself was untouchable. That's because the secret of his politics was not stealing money, but exercising power — and Daley's power was almost as absolute as that of any feudal ruler who ever lived. His lieutenant in the Jewish ward where I lived was Alderman Jake Arvey, whose name was uttered in tones of reverence. If the local precinct captain couldn't get your parking ticket fixed, your alley paved, your kid into summer camp, he would utter the magic formula, "I'll talk to Jake Arvey, don't worry."

I knew even less about The Mob. An Italian kid at school might boast of some cousin or uncle with mob connections, but it was an invisible power, like the grace offered by the Catholic Church. The Chicago Mafia's dramatic glory days of the 1920s and Al Capone had been succeeded by a quieter, more businesslike generation, headed by Tony Accardo and the younger Sam Giancana. Accardo, like Daley, lived a long life and died peacefully, still in office. Between The Machine and The Mob was the institution that served both masters, the doubly corrupt Chicago Police Department. It was, by all accounts, perpetually on the take, racist, and vicious. A decade after I left Chicago, it would be found guilty of a "police riot" against protestors at the 1968 Democratic National Convention held in Chicago.

The Lost City by Alan Ehrenhalt is a book about the allegedly "forgotten virtues of community in America." The reason I'm reading it is because I'm trying to figure out how to understand the past, including my own past. When people talk about their childhoods, they invariably get onto the subject of whether there was something wonderful about their childhood neighbourhoods and times that have now been irretrievably lost. When I listened to such talk as a kid, I rather typically regarded the adults' memories as mere nostalgia. Ehrenhalt's book is set in various neighbourhoods in Chicago in

1957, the year I was preparing to head out into the world, and Ehrenhalt offers a political defense of what he believes are lost virtues. The lost virtues he laments are authority, religious belief, loyalty, obedience and the value of community.

Ehrenhalt is no dummy. He's an intelligent conservative. His lament has some appeal, and isn't mere nostalgia. Rather, it is the political proposal to somehow restore those lost virtues, which is what makes him dangerous in my eyes. Ehrenhalt is what's known as a "communitarian" thinker, part of a school of contemporary political philosophy that had some prominence in the closing years of the 20th century. I'm reading him as a negative example of how to see mid-20th century American life. I think that what he has in mind leads to a political dead end, one that is still popular in contemporary American urban life.

Ehrenhalt remembers that the Chicago Cubs' black shortstop of the late 1950s, Ernie Banks, loyally stuck with the team, despite being drastically underpaid during a decade or more of annual Most Valuable Player-level performances. Ehrenhalt also remembers Chicago alderman and congressional representative, John Fary, a tavern owner by trade, whose claim to fame was his humble boast that he had faithfully supported Mayor Daley for over 20 years and "the mayor was always right." As Ehrenhalt more broadly puts it, "People just stayed married in the 1950s, to their spouses, to their political machines, to their baseball teams," and he suggests that that was basically a good thing.

"If it is true to say of 1950s America that it was a world of limited choices," he says, "it is also fair to call it a world of lasting relationships." What grieves Ehrenhalt is a contemporary world of bewildering, unlimited, individual choice and the concomitant loss of authority, faith, and community that it entails. He blames this loss on the coming of age of the self-indulgent Baby Boom Generation of the 1960s.

Ehrenhalt's paean to lost values and virtues is clever. Not only is he aware of the danger of mere nostalgia, he also knows that a great deal of the loss he grieves over was primarily caused by the developments of American capitalism during its mid-20th century boom years. Ehrenhalt recognizes that the responsibility for moving factories to regions with cheaper labour costs was purely a capitalist decision, not something decided by communities. The cosy corner stores he lyrically recalls, like my father's, were doomed not by the neighbours, but by the advertising and pricing power of national supermarket chains. But his partial recognition of capitalist power also serves to cover up that power. Instead of saying that neighbourhoods were irrevocably changed for the worse by capitalism, Ehrenhalt blames the abstraction of "choice," which is tied to the willful, rebellious youth of the succeeding decade. It is true that the next generation challenged complacent authority, and that we made stupid mistakes of our own. But the point is that the authority we challenged was unreasonable, and not some beneficent form of order whose passing should be lamented.

Ehrenhalt is also shrewd enough to note that "there are few among us . . . who mourn for the rigidities and constrictions of American life in the 1950s." But there is a mourning, he says, for a sense of community that many remember to have existed in their childhoods and no longer exists now. "Authority," he admits, "is something else again. It evokes no similar feelings of nostalgia." Ehrenhalt's argument is that one can't have the virtues of community, without also endorsing, in some significant measure, the virtues of authority, faith and loyalty.

Yet, when Ehrenhalt looks at "the whole array of social institutions [that] still stood outside the grip of the market and provided ordinary people with a cushion against it," something curious happens. The authority of the day, whether embodied in Mayor Daley, the bishop of the archdiocese, or the cop roughing up a black motorist, is monstrous, undemocratic, and far from reasonable. The faith with which people were imbued, whether embodied in the Catholic catechism or the revivalism of black storefront churches, was bizarre, authoritarian, and if not plain false, a permanent mystification. Finally, his defense of the virtues and pleasures of the oppressed black community is risible at best, and never comes close to recognizing that virulent racism in Chicago was part of the nation's national disgrace. Ehrenhalt's political project is to restore authority, but the actual authority he examines as a historian is hideous.

Ehrenhalt tends to gloss all the imperfections over, but he concedes that "there is no point in pretending that the 1950s were a happy time for everyone . . . For many, the price of the limited life was impossibly high. To have been an independent-minded alderman in the Daley machine, a professional baseball player treated unfairly by his team, a suburban housewife who yearned for a professional career, a black high school student dreaming of possibilities that were closed to him, a gay man or woman forced to conduct a charade in public — to have been any of these things in the 1950s was to live a life that was difficult at best, and tragic at worst." He, nonetheless, continues to mourn. I don't think we should mourn this particular past. Chicago, though it wasn't all that different from other big American cities in the peaceful, prosperous era of President Dwight Eisenhower, was an authoritarian, racist, corrupt model of life. For us kids, it was just life, filled with the little, specific objects and relationships that make up childhood. That's not a cause for mourning, either. We ought to save our mourning for things that matter to us — for the dead, for faded beauty, for *temps perdu*.

IV

What interests me is not elegy but what I think of as "windows" into a world that I might enter. I found those windows more in painted images, books, and conversation that I did on television, in the movies, or from the radio, although I duly absorbed the stories they told. At around age six, I was stirred by a reproduction of John Everett Millais's *The Youth of Raleigh* — the first painting I ever "saw" — that hung in the waiting room of my Uncle Docky's medical office. Two boys sit in the sand, along the seashore, at the feet of a veteran sailor, who sits on a log and points out to sea as he recounts an old salt's tale, inciting them (and me) to adventure.

The emotional charge I get from painting is explicitly connected to the initiatory childhood experience of being taken to see the sumptuous collection of the Art Institute of Chicago – the Impressionists, Picasso, Georges Suerat's pointillist *La Grande Jatte*. The idea I crudely developed had to do with the way art reflects the world to create another heretofore non-existent world. What begins as a mirror or representation of the world becomes an independent landscape, one whose figures and objects we can enter in imagination so that we, too, are doubled, multiplied, as either personae or as an additional figure in the new landscape. At the same time, the painting and our psychological relationship to it are simply part of the world, but our conception of reality has become more complicated. That idea was barely articulated at, say, age 12, but I was intuitively certain that I was seeing something from "out there."

Even more fundamental to my developing sense of a geographic outside and a temporality behind and/or under us, were the books my father gave me to read and those I found on my own in the public library. The library was the one "social institution outside the grip of the market," as Ehrenhalt puts it, that was of use to me. My sense of Chicago expanded beyond its present-day streets to Frank Norris's *The Pit*, about the Chicago wheat pool traders; Upton Sinclair's *The Jungle*, about the Chicago stockyards; and Jack London's *The Iron Heel*, with its imagination of socialist revolution in Chicago. Soon I found the books of Bellow and Nelson Algren, set in present-day Chicago.

Equally important as the books about Chicago were the sea stories my father started me reading to give me an idea of the wider world:

London's *The Sea Wolf*, Jules Verne's *Twenty Thousand Leagues Under the Sea*, Richard Henry Dana's *Two Years Before the Mast*, and Melville's *Typee*, and then *Moby Dick*. My father's personal repertoire of stories about running away from home and riding box-cars across America in the 1920s also had their effect. When I eventually announced that I wanted to go to sea, he wasn't surprised, or displeased. What's more, I could count on my father's authority — the sole authority I trusted to be reasonable — to fend off dissenting relatives who knew that aspiring children went to college, not to sea. "It's what he wants to do," my father declared, settling the familial matter, as he had earlier settled the matter of my not wanting a bar mitzvah.

My literary interests were crosscut by the lure of the media. I didn't understand the difference between real writing and slick journalism until much later, when I actually worked as a journalist. Both serious books and sensational tabloids seemed like equally glamourous instances of being in print. So, for example, my first book review (I think it was in 5th grade, age 11), based on a patchy reading of *Moby Dick*, was titled, "Bloated Whale Beached." I got the idea for the snappy title from the headlines of the tabloids. The teacher was impressed, I believe, by this hatchet job, at least in light of my youth, but I now cringe at what I see as a tendency towards glibness. It only meant I would have to read *Moby Dick* again, later, and this time pay attention.

I was also a reader of the *Chicago Tribune*, and its tabloid sibling, the *Chicago Sun-Times*, which I was soon inspired to emulate. I became the publisher, editor, writer, and sole reader of the *Oswego Times*, named for the obscure town of Oswego, New York, which I had goofily selected at random from the Rand-McNally Atlas of the United States. Since I was simultaneously reading John R. Tunis sports novels and running an imaginary baseball league, the *Times*, under my editorship, mostly reported sports scores.

The imaginary baseball league was based on a board game called "All-Star Baseball." The game consisted of circular cards of famous ballplayers, which were divided up into a map of their actual records. If they hit lots of home runs, or struck out a lot, the respective spaces for home runs and strike outs on the card reflected that. The cards were placed on a cardboard mount to which was attached a metal spinner. You flicked the spinner with your fingernail — it hurt a little — and wherever the spinner stopped on the card determined whether it was a hit or an out or a walk. I dutifully kept the stats on the teams I made up, and faithfully reported the results of the games the teams played in the *Times*. The interesting feature of the game, and the point of this memory, is that it included players from all historical eras. So it was possible for Babe Ruth, Honus Wagner, or Rogers Hornsby, all historical figures, to play in the same imaginary games as such contemporary players as Johnny Mize, Ted Williams, or Ernie Banks of our own Chicago Cubs. The sole reader of the *Times*, namely, me, was immersed in this time-shifting theatre of baseball history.

Finally, I put imaginary print behind me for real print. My first publication was a letter to the editor of the *Chicago Sun-Times*, *circa* 1952-53, in which I urged readers to take a balanced view of the congressional hearings pitting anti-Communist Senator Joseph McCarthy against Joseph Welsh, counsel for the U.S. Army, an institution that the senator alleged harboured thousands of Communist agents. I had even too-cleverly figured out that appending the words "8th grade" to my signature would significantly improve my chances of appearing in print.

My first reader was an older, Jewish highschool kid in the neighbourhood, Ben Rubin, who coolly asked me, "Did you write that letter?" "Yes," I proudly replied. He didn't say anything more, he just went on his way. I was never able to determine whether he was simply verifying my authorship, or displaying a young radical's contempt for liberal wishy-washiness. But his tone made me suspect that appearing in print wasn't so great if what you wrote was stupid. I suppose, in my defence, it could be said that at least all these activities kept me out of trouble, and spared my parents the fashionable worry of the day, namely, "juvenile delinquency."

Fortunately, beyond my flair for the merely facile, I had some idea of wanting to be a writer. In the last years of high school, ages 16 and 17, having settled in at school with the bohemian crowd who hung out in drama class — I appeared as a prosecutor in Ayn Rand's play, *The Night of January 16th* and as a sheriff in William Saroyan's *Hello, Out There* — I began writing a series of prose poems, sketches, vignettes, and verse. After I had written a sufficient amount, 25 pages or so, I stapled it all together under the title, *How the Night Comes to Me*. My first book.

My cousin Anne Thompson, the one who gave me the ticket to Tennessee Williams's *El Camino Réal*, also gave me a subscription to a magazine, the *Saturday Review of Literature*. One day in 1957, I read a review in that magazine of Jack Kerouac's novel, *On the Road*. The reviewer hated it, describing Kerouac's stories of his and his friends' madcap adventures across America as tiresome, amateurish and jejeune. I had to look up "jejeune" in the dictionary, but it got my attention. The reviewer also made the mistake of quoting sizeable chunks of Kerouac's breathless prose to make his critical point.

Those quotes were enough. I had now read books by most of the major contemporary American writers and I had never seen any prose like the quoted paragraphs of Jack Kerouac. I didn't hesitate. I put down the magazine, left my room, and got on the Washington Boulevard bus (we were now living in a neighbourhood slightly west of our original apartment) and went straight downtown to Kroch and Brentano's bookstore. I was as excited as I was the time I rushed down with a nickel in my hand to buy a used copy of the Red Ryder and Little Beaver comic book the Murphys were selling. By the time I was back on the Washington Boulevard bus, reading the first pages about Sal Paradise and Dean Moriarity, the book's main characters, I was in Jack Kerouac's America.

Soon after reading *On the Road*, I also found the *Evergreen Review* at Kroch's, a magazine that published Kerouac and a group of his friends — Allen Ginsberg, William Burroughs, Gregory Corso, and others. A widely scattered community of the very people I might be looking for existed. Like someone on a desert island putting a message in a bottle, I put my own pamphlet of writing, *How the Night Comes to Me*, in an envelope, along with a note explaining that I was a 16-year-old in Chicago who had read *On the Road* and wanted to be a writer, and I sent it to Kerouac at his publisher's address in New York.

A week or so later, I came home from school, opened the family mailbox to which I had a key, and inside I found a postcard filled with typed writing from top to bottom, and along the sides. "Dear Stan," it opened, "You neednt ever worry about not only your reputation as a poet but about my great wild admiration of your poetry and I think the same will be said by Ginsberg, Corso et all, when they see your stuff." It was from Jack Kerouac. The "outside" had sent a message in a bottle to my desert island in "Chicago, that somber city." The rest of the message contained similar enthusiasms, practical advice, Ginsberg's address, and noted that my "great name" had a ring similar to that of "Johnny Pesky," third baseman of the Boston Red Sox, 1942-1954.

I was soon on the road myself. My first stop: Great Lakes Naval Training Center, which put me on a bus and shipped me to the U.S. Navy boot camp in San Diego, California. The rest is, well, a history that I've documented elsewhere.

V

My cousin Bob Perrey is the family chronicler, archivist, and ringmaster of our particular familial circus. I'll skip the story of how he got to be a Perrey instead of a Persky, except to note that the name change was predicated on a grain of half-truth connected to his parents' exaggerated fears about how anti-Semitism might affect their offspring's career. Bob is a year or so older than me, and the person in the family closest to me in terms of irony, wariness and intellectual interests. There are others in our clan who have the same kind of minds Bob and I do, particularly the daughter of Aunt Emma, our younger cousin Karen Loeb, also a writer and teacher, and Joe Persky, who teaches economics at the University of Illinois in Chicago. Joe is the son of my father's youngest brother, Harold, a biochemist who was the first person in the family to go to university and become a professor. But Bob is the one I hear from most often.

Bob stayed in Chicago twenty years longer than I did, leaving only in mid-life, in the late 1970s, for California, where he and his wife Heidi raised a sizeable brood of children. He has a sharper sense of Chicago than I do because he lived there and was politically active during the 1960s and '70s. He is one of those talented people who has been a jack of many trades, from college professor to theatrical producer to technical manual writer to proprietor of a tobacco shop. More to the point here, he's also an enviably competent composer-musician and at one stage in his career he portrayed Chicago as a theatre of history in a cabaret-style political satire. Produced soon after the 1968 riots in Chicago, his theatre piece, *City in a Swamp*, took a dig at the civic motto, "City in a Garden," and played on the aboriginal word, Chicago, which meant something like "stinking swamp." The show was also a local hit, sometimes even outdrawing the road company production of the Broadway musical of the moment, *Hair*.

So, Bob does other things besides remembering family lore and keeping the rest of us up to date on whereabouts, marriages, births, and deaths. But it was in his role as family ringmaster that he gradually cajoled us all to Chicago for a couple of days at the end of summer 1999. I was in Berlin that summer, and would return there a few days later. But for a little while, for the first time in decades, there we all were in my cousin Joe's living room in a Chicago neighbourhood on the North Side, close to Lake Michigan. There were now only cousins, spouses and their children, who were also cousins. All of our parents were dead. They were the ghosts in the circus tent.

We hadn't all been together for at least 30 years, yet everyone was instantly recognizable and we were, in the family tradition, as garrulous as I remember our parents being when they were all gathered at my Aunt Emma's house telling tales, arguing about who was born when, and who lived where, and where the stars were to be seen on a summer night.

By mid-life, most people have acquired a veritable sea chest — just like the locker at the foot of my bunk in the Navy barracks — full of yarns, our own and those we've acquired from other people, and we continue to add to them into old age. We tell those stories again and again, more than twice-told tales, recycling them for new acquaintances. But the art of that storytelling is in the interpretation of their point, the discovery of a detail that changes the story's meaning. It's not a matter of "stop me if you've heard this one before," but of what we see in them at any given moment. So, for example, I've often told the story of how I decided not to have a religious confirmation (see "Bar Mitzvah"), but it wasn't until this telling that I suddenly remembered what I'd forgotten up til now, that I still retained the words of the Hebrew prayer, "*Baruch ata Adonai . . .*" And now, the point of the story wasn't only my refusal to be bar mitvah'd, but also the way memory keeps, not the faith, but the melody of those exotic words.

It was at these various houses, Emma's, or my uncle Gob's, where all of the Persky siblings were gathered (minus Aunt Jane, who was crazy and institutionalized, and Aunt Babe, who had moved to California), along with their husbands and wives and us children, that I first heard the uproar and cacophany of this great repertoire of stories rolled out, interrupted with gales of laughter, urgent interventions, disputed meanings. I was my father's son, and the great family divide for me was between my mother's family, who were mostly shopkeepers I wasn't interested in (with the exception of Uncle Docky and Aunt Dora), and my father's family, who were all fabulists. From the beginning, I recognized that I belonged to my father's tribe. Now, here we were, their descendents, as loud, raucous, and laughter-filled as they had once been.

As well, there was Chicago, a big, prosperous American city. I was unaware of its politics, except to note that the mayor was now Richard Daley, son of the former Mayor Daley, and perhaps that was all one needed to know. Bob, Heidi, and their kids went with me on an architectural boat ride up the Chicago River (I'd never been on the Chicago River before), and I took a trip out to the University of Chicago for the first time, and was eventually the only white person on the bus as it moved south through battered black neighbourhoods. On the last day, the whole family reunion boarded a chartered bus and drove through the old districts, none of which I recognized.

The area where I grew up, on Keeler, had been levelled during the city riots in the wake of Martin Luther King's assassination in 1968, and anyway, the ghosts I wanted to see, principally my father, were only available in the photos Karen Loeb had collected for us. It was probably exactly like all family reunions, except that it was *us*, and it was perhaps slightly more jovial than the average such gathering. In each person, I could see both the trace of the child I had known, and the parent from whom he or she had come. So, Bill looked like Bill, the present-day successful commodities trader and parent, and also like the chipmunk-cheeked kid I remembered, and in him I could also hear an echo of the laughter of his father Gob, standing in his double-store on Division Street in 1952 and calling to me, "Hey, Stashu, come over here for a minute."

Sometimes the cities we describe are the fabled, distant metropolises that the 13th century Venetian traveler Marco Polo spoke of, and that Italo Calvino reconstructs in *Invisible Cities*. Sometimes they are just our own little Venice — not the famous canals and the doge's palace, though they are present, too, in the background — but some otherwise forgotten alleyway where we kicked a ball, or a neighbourhood bridge against whose railing we rattled our stick. As Calvino's crafty Marco Polo says to Kublai Khan, intending exactly the opposite meaning of his utterance, "No one, wise Kublai, knows better than you that the city must never be confused with the words that describe it."

Contingency

For about 15 years now, I've been reading and re-reading Richard Rorty's *Contingency, Irony, and Solidarity* (1989) and all of his previous and subsequent writings. I think he's the most interesting philosopher of the last quarter of the 20th century, at least in America, if not further afield. Rorty is the object of controversy and considerable misunderstanding, both within and outside of philosophy, but his ideas are absolutely relevant to our time, so it's worth taking a look at some of them.

In terms of a brief overview of what Rorty believes, he begins by taking the position that there is no common human nature, apart perhaps from a few evolutionary features of human beings, such as a capacity to acquire and use language, making us more complex beings than other animals. Like his existentialist predecessor, Jean-Paul Sartre, Rorty believes that "existence precedes essence" and that we have no shared essence. Instead, "socialization and thus historical circumstance, goes all the way down — there is nothing 'beneath' socialization or prior to history which is definatory of the human." We are contingent, or accidental, beings, the result of a process of evolution that is impersonal and has no particular intentions.

As for the universe we live in, there is no one way that it is that we can know, there are only our successive historical descriptions of it, some more or less useful to our developing purposes. There's no good reason to think that the world is the creation of a divinity, especially not one which has a truth of its own that we merely have to discover in order to get things right once and for all. Not even science provides an objectively true final account, according to Rorty. His broad argument is, "We need to make a distinction between the claim that the world is out there and the claim truth is out there." With respect to the latter, "truth cannot be out there — cannot exist independently of the human mind ... The world is out there, but descriptions of the world are not ... The world does not speak. Only we do." Nor should we make the mistake, he adds, of "divinizing" language to produce truths outside of ourselves.

Like some other contemporary philosophers who emphasize the distinctiveness of human language, Rorty subscribes to Hilary Putnam's dictum that "elements of what we call 'language' or 'mind' penetrate so deeply into what we call 'reality' that the very project of representing ourselves as being 'mappers' of something 'language-independent' is fatally compromised from the start." While sentences in a description or vocabulary can be true or false, there is no total description of reality or a final vocabulary whose truth can be determined, and no way one can step outside the given language or "language-games" (as Wittgenstein called them) in which we participate.

Just to give a homely contemporary example: while it is true or false that Iraq possessed weapons of mass destruction when the United States invaded it in 2003, it is not a determinable objective truth that the U.S. doctrine of "pre-emptive war" is right or wrong, although a majority of us may believe that it was wrong in the given instance.

Since there is no large truth about the meaning of life, Rorty suggests that, just as many of us have given up asking about the nature of God (because there's no good reason to think there is one), we also ought to abandon the notion that the goal of inquiry is the discovery of such a pre-existent truth that will provide meaning to our lives. Instead, we ought to turn our attention to our social hopes and practical projects for realizing them. We ought to focus — "we decent, liberal humanitarian types" — on achieving social solidarity, rather than being obsessed with a fruitless quest to discover the truth about how things are. Finally, since there is no truth about life that others can be made to see as "objectively true," the most we can do is to persuade various groups of people that the descriptions and vocabularies we employ are more interesting and useful than other available accounts. We can offer justifications for our arguments, but no proofs from outside of us are available.

What I've just laid out is the short version of my reading of Rorty. To unpack some of what it might mean, one of the better places to start is an autobiographical essay that Rorty wrote a couple of years after *Contingency*, called "Trotsky and the Wild Orchids" (which can be found in his *Philosophy and Social Hope*). In it, we learn that Rorty was born in 1931, and raised in a small New Jersey town, not far from New York, by parents whose left-wing politics provided a curious ideological childhood for their son. Within the homocidal political split between the Soviet Union's Joseph Stalin and the exiled Leon Trotsky, and its repercussions among obscure American political groupuscules, Rorty's parents were devotees of Trotsky. In the red-diaper politics of his youth, Rorty recalls that "the most salient books on my parents' shelves were two red-bound volumes" that made up the report of American liberal philosopher John Dewey's commission of inquiry into Stalin's Moscow show trials that had condemned Trotsky to exile (and eventual assassination), and millions of others to the firing squad, concentration camps, and psychiatric prisons.

Even though the Dewey commission report was but one more failure among many efforts to resuscitate the reputation of the doomed Trotsky, Rorty regarded those books the way "other children thought of their family's Bible: they were books that radiated redemptive truth and moral splendour." In the 1940s, the Russian Revolution and its betrayal by Stalin were for the adolescent Rorty "what the Incarnation and its betrayal by the Catholics had been to precocious little Lutherans 400 years before." A good part of Rorty's youth, in which he "grew up knowing that all decent people were, if not Trotskyists, at least socialists," was given over to working in this obscure political movement. He devoted a lot of after school time to delivering pamphlets to, among others, the New York office of Norman Thomas, the perennial Socialist Party candidate for president of the United States during that era.

"So, at 12, I knew that the point of being human was to spend one's life fighting for social justice," Rorty says. He then adds, "But I also had private, weird, snobbish, incommunicable interests." One of those interests involved the mountains and woods of northwest New Jersey, near Flatbrookville, where Rorty's parents spent part of their time. The mountains were where one could find orchids. "Some 40 species of wild orchids occur in those mountains, and I eventually found 17 of them. Wild orchids are uncommon, and rather hard to spot." Young Rorty wasn't "quite sure why those orchids were so important, but I was convinced that they were."

At age 15, in 1946, Rorty went off to become one of the precocious students at the University of Chicago, in the accelerated program established by university chancellor Robert Hutchins. "Insofar as I had any project in mind," says Rorty, "it was to reconcile Trotsky and the orchids. I wanted to find some intellectual or aesthetic framework which would let me — in a thrilling phrase which I came across in Yeats — 'hold reality and justice in a single vision.' By reality I meant, more or less, the Wordsworthian moments in which, in the woods around Flatbrookville (and especially in the presence of certain coralroot orchids, and of the smaller yellow lady slipper), I had felt touched by something numinous, something of ineffable importance. By justice I meant what Norman Thomas and Trotsky both stood for, the liberation of the weak from the strong. I wanted a way to be both an intellectual and spiritual snob and a friend of humanity — a nerdy recluse and a fighter for justice. I was very confused, but reasonably sure that at Chicago I would find out how grown-ups managed to work the trick I had in mind."

The rest of Rorty's autobiographical account is the story of how the quest to "hold reality and justice in a single vision" didn't pan out. At Chicago, Rorty studied philosophy, eventually moving on to Yale to acquire a PhD in the subject, but always increasingly disillusioned about "what, if anything, philosophy is good for." For a long time, Rorty found himself stranded between a notion of " 'understanding the world' in a Platonic sense — an understanding from a position outside of time and history," and a position he had picked up from hints in Hegel, in which philosophy is, at best, "its time held in thought." Still, that might be enough, Rorty thought. "For by thus holding one's time, one might do what Marx wanted done — change the world."

It was this hint that led Rorty to diverse other voices, principally the American pragmatism of John Dewey and William James from the early part of the 20th century, and the contemporary Continental philosophers, like Heidegger, Jacques Derrida and Jürgen Habermas. Rorty's ruminations led to his first book, *Philosophy and the Mirror of Nature* (1979), an historicist critique of conventional, or analytic philosophy, as it's known in North America. Though its success gave Rorty some needed self-confidence, it didn't do much for his adolescent ambitions. "I was no closer to the single vision which, 30 years back, I had gone to college to get." By then, Rorty had had a successful career as a philosophy professor at Princeton, and subsequently, as a humanities professor at Virginia, as well as distinction within the professional associations and journals of his discipline.

As Rorty tried to figure out what had gone wrong, he came to what for him was the intellectual breakthrough that reshaped his life as a philosopher. He "gradually decided that the whole idea of holding reality and justice in a single vision had been a mistake — that a pursuit of such a vision had been precisely what led Plato astray." Only something like religion could perform that trick, and Rorty wasn't religious. "So I decided to write a book about what intellectual life might be like if one could manage to give up the Platonic attempt" of a single vision. That book, *Contingency, Irony, and Solidarity*, "argues that there is no need to weave one's personal equivalent of Trotsky and one's personal equivalent of my wild orchids together. Rather, one should abjure the temptation to tie in one's moral responsibilities to other people with one's relation to whatever idiosyncratic things one loves with all one's heart and soul or mind (or, if you like, the things or persons one is obsessed with). The two will, for some people, coincide ... But they need not coincide, and one should not try too hard to make them do so." I should underscore that such a view is not a suggestion either to abjure one's moral responsibilities or one's loves.

I found Rorty's pluralistic way of looking at life exhilerating for a number of reasons. The idea of not holding reality and justice in a single vision, once you get it, seems rather common-sensical, almost banal, but to get to that idea and articulate it, Rorty had to climb over an enormous amount of philosophical wreckage insisting on the opposite. The idea that we have different, sometimes incompatible interests, appealed to me, and seemed practically useful (a way of ceasing to worry about some things not worth worrying about), given my own experiences. The idiosyncratic preferences of my own life for certain books, philosophical views, and people were preferences and passions that were often technically illegal and shameful in the societies in which I had lived, and at times seemed at a considerable distance from my democratic commitment. Even when I could make a connection between my desires and my public commitment by arguing that those desires ought to be included within a democratic society, there was still a distance between the argument, a rather abstract set of reasons, and the actual phenomenological experience of what the poet Cavafy called "deviate sensual delight." In any case, I had some first-hand experience that inclined me to favour Rorty's notion.

At its grandest, the idea of not requiring that reality and justice be held in a single vision seems to make sense in terms of one way of looking at the human condition, namely, that we live together but die on our own, or, to put it another way, we converse with one another, but we dream alone. Rorty also emphasizes that this way of looking at things is a way of accepting your finitude, and that of the world, within time, chance, and history. Not only is there no power outside of ourselves, either spiritual or natural, that determines the meaning of our lives, but there is no one way that the world or reality is. There is only a long, historical, intersubjective negotiation about the way things are and might be. Rorty insists that we pay more attention to the way things might be rather than to worrying about whether we've got reality absolutely right or if we've discovered the truth.

This practical approach to our shared and individual lives, and the rejection of absolute or foundational truths about ourselves is known in philosophy circles as "pragmatism" or "neo-pragmatism." On the personal level, accepting your finitude "means, among other things, accepting that what matters most to you may well be something that may never matter much to most people. Your equivalent of my orchids may always seem merely weird, merely idiosyncratic, to practically everybody else. But that is no reason to be ashamed of, or downgrade, or try to slough off, your Wordsworthian moments, your lover, your family, your pet, your favorite lines of verse or your quaint religious faith. There is nothing sacred about universality which makes the shared automatically better than the unshared. There is no automatic privilege of what you can get everybody to agree to (the universal) over what you cannot (the idiosyncratic)."

Just from the passages of Rorty I've quoted so far, you can get an idea of another of his virtues, one that's relatively rare among philosophers and even poets. Rorty writes in a style that most educated readers can easily understand. What's more, though he writes simply, he's not simplistic. It quickly becomes clear that he has read as much philosophy and literature as any philosopher of his time, and he has the ability to "translate" very dense, technical writing by other writers into satisfyingly plain English. Although it's not all that often admitted in the philosophy business, even philosophers like to understand what the hell is being said as much as non-philosophers do.

Along with his comprehensibility, Rorty is also capable of engaging with his fellow philosophers in the sort of abstruse discussion that marks much of the discipline. For readers interested in the more technical level of argumentation, there's *Rorty and His Critics*, edited by Robert Brandom, in which Rorty is in discussion with some of the leading philosophers of the times, including Jürgen Habermas, Donald Davidson, Daniel Dennett, Hilary Putnam, and others, itself an indicator of the seriousness with which Rorty is taken by major practitioners in the field.

Rorty's views also have implications for how we read other writers, and solves a problem that many readers feel. Rorty says, in *Contingency*, there are two kinds of writers, and he urges that "we not try to choose between them but, rather, give them equal weight and use them for different purposes." For example, authors like Kierkegaard, Nietzsche, Baudelaire, Proust, Heidegger, and Vladimir Nabokov are useful "as illustrations of what private perfection — a self-created, autonomous human life — can be like." Others, like Marx, Mill, Dewey, Habermas, and John Rawls "are fellow citizens rather than exemplars. They are engaged in a shared, social effort — the effort to make our practices and institutions more just and less cruel. We shall only think of these two kinds of writers as opposed if we think that a more comprehensive philosophical outlook would let us hold self-creation and justice, private perfection and human solidarity, in a single vision."

But Rorty doesn't believe that philosophy, or any other theoretical discipline, will ever let us do that. "The closest we will come to joining these two quests is to see the aim of a just and free society as letting its citizens be as privatistic, 'irrationalist,' and aestheticist as they please so long as they do it on their own time — causing no harm to others and using no resources needed by those less advantaged." If we can adopt this viewpoint, we will see that "one sort of writer lets us realize that the social virtues are not the only virtues, that some people have actually succeeded in re-creating themselves ... The other sort reminds us of the failure of our institutions and practices to live up to the convictions to which we are already committed by the public, shared vocabulary we use in daily life."

Apart from observing that Rorty is fond of making lists, it should also be noted that he tends to think of writing as "writing," and doesn't think that the categorization of writing into "genres" is particularly important or useful, a view that accords with my own.

When Rorty turns his attention to the public sphere, readers often begin to get uneasy because what he says is not reassuring or comforting. It's at that point that he tends to be misunderstood. What makes such readers uncomfortable is that Rorty doesn't think that "people like us" — "we decent, liberal humanitarian types" — are absolutely or even fundamentally right.

Rather, "representatives of the moral community to which both my [readers] and I belong, are just luckier, not more insightful, than the bullies with whom we struggle." Rorty is often dismissively read as being a "cultural relativist," someone who believes that all views are equally valid. But he explicitly denies being a relativist of any sort, "if that means saying that every moral view is as good as any other. Our moral view is, I firmly believe, much better than any competing view, even though there are a lot of people whom you will never be able to convert to it. It is one thing to say, falsely, that there is nothing to choose between us and the Nazis. It is another thing to say, correctly, that there is no neutral, common ground to which an experienced Nazi philosopher and I can repair in order to argue out our differences. The Nazi and I will always strike one another as begging all the crucial questions, arguing in circles."

There is, according to Rorty, simply no neutral ground, period. There is no objective truth about moral beliefs "out there," apart from ourselves, to which we can appeal.

If that's true, it raises several questions. The most troubling one, I suppose, is, Does this mean, then, that there's no guarantee that our decent, liberal humanitarian views will prevail? The answer is, Yes, no guarantees. The most we can hope for is that in the course of history we will succeed in persuading more and more people to adopt our views. To dispel the ensuing gloom, it should be noted that Rorty holds the rather chipper view of history that we have been, in recent centuries, doing precisely that. We've been making, in that sense, "moral progress." What's more, he cheerfully believes that we can do without moral certainties, and can successfully proceed on the basis of our social hopes.

At his bluntest, Rorty asserts that "there is no answer to the question, 'Why not be cruel?' — no noncircular theoretical backup for the belief that cruelty is horrible. Nor is there an answer to the question, 'How do you decide when to struggle against injustice and when to devote yourself to private projects of self-creation?' . . . Anybody who thinks that there are well-grounded theoretical answers to this sort of question — algorithms for resolving moral dilemmas of this sort — is still, in his heart, a theologian or a metaphysician. He believes in an order beyond time and chance . . ." Rorty doesn't.

As discomfiting as Rorty can be, he has a good head for practical politics. Writing in the 1990s, at the height of both religious fundamentalism and a form of tribalism rampant in academia and spilling over into society at large, Rorty shrewdly noted in his "Trotsky and the Wild Orchids" essay, "At the moment there are two cultural wars being waged in the United States." The first war, he said, is the important one. It's the one between "decent, humanitarian liberals" and fundamentalists of various stripes. The outcome of that cultural war "will decide whether our country continues along the trajectory" of everything from the Bill of Rights to the New Deal to the civil rights, feminist, and gay movements of our own era. "Continuing along that trajectory would mean that America might continue to set an example of increasing tolerance and increasing equality." Rorty sees the fundamentalists, "the people who think hounding gays out of the military promotes traditional family values, as the same honest, decent, blinkered, disastrous people who voted for Hitler in 1933." Rorty sees the humanitarian liberals "as defining the only America I care about."

The second cultural war, he argues, is being waged primarily in the universities and its attendant intellectual journals. "It is between those who see modern liberal society as fatally flawed (the people handily lumped together as 'postmodernists') and typical left-wing Democrat professors like myself, people who see ours as a society in which technology and democratic institutions can, with luck, collaborate to increase equality and decrease suffering. This war is not very important," Rorty declares. It is, he says, "just a tiny little dispute" within the ranks of "upmarket progressives."

People on the postmodernist side operate from the perspective that the U.S. "is not so much in danger of slipping into fascism as it is a country which has always been quasi-fascist. These people typically think that nothing will change unless we get rid of 'humanism,' 'liberal individualism' and 'technologism.' People like me," Rorty admits, "see nothing wrong with any of these -isms, nor with the political and moral heritage of the Enlightenment." He also admits that most people with his views have given up on socialism. "We are willing to grant that welfare state capitalism is the best we can hope for" at the moment.

Unsurprisingly, given his views, Rorty notes that he is distrusted by the fundamentalist side "in the important war and the 'postmodernist' side in the unimportant one." Although Rorty is often tagged as one of the seminal thinkers of postmodernism and his philosophical views are often close to the postmodernists, he regards most of what got to be called "political correctness" and "identity politics" in the 1990s as "politically silly." Besides quickly picking up on the early-warning signs of academic tribalism, Rorty conversely saw that many of those attacking postmodernism were prone to a sort of "Blimpishness". They tended to ignore the criticisms of injustice that had motivated the postmodernists in the first place. Over all, Rorty demonstrates a level-headedness when it comes to the less important academic disputes. As for the important cultural war with the fundamentalists, he thinks "they are philosophically wrong as well as politically dangerous." Although the high-tide waters of the unimportant cultural war have receded since Rorty made those initial observations, the flood waters of the important cultural war continue to rage.

If our vocabularies, selves and communities are accidental in the sense of being historically conditioned and not grounded in absolute truths, that holds consequences for how we view ourselves and our beliefs. In *Contingency, Irony, and Solidarity*, Rorty sketches a figure whom he calls the "liberal ironist." His definition of "liberal" is borrowed from the political thinker Judith Shklar, who says that liberals are people who think that cruelty to other people is the worst thing we do. As for "ironist," Rorty uses that term "to name the sort of person who faces up to the contingency of his or her most central beliefs and desires — someone sufficiently historicist and nominalist to have abandoned the idea that those central beliefs and desires refer back to something beyond the reach of time and chance."

Our selves, Rorty suggests, do not consist of an essence or a unique "soul," but are simply webs of beliefs and vocabularies that we have idiosyncratically acquired in the course of our lives. "All human beings carry about a set of words which they employ to justify their actions, their beliefs and their lives." Rorty calls that set of words a person's "final vocabulary," and it is final not in the sense that it can't change, but in the sense "that if doubt is cast on the worth of these words, their user has no noncircular argumentative recourse. Those words are as far as he can go with language: beyond them there is only helpless passivity or a resort to force."

An "ironist" in terms of "final vocabularies" is a person who fulfills three conditions. First, he or she "has radical and continuing doubts" about his or her own final vocabulary, because such persons have "been impressed by other vocabularies taken as final by people or books" they have encountered. Second, such people realize that arguments phrased in their present vocabulary "can neither under-write nor dissolve these doubts." Finally, insofar as such people philosophize about their situation, they don't think their vocabulary "is closer to reality than others, that it is in touch with a power not [themselves]." Thus, such people who renounce the "attempt to formulate criteria of choice between final vocabularies" are put in the position that "Sartre called 'meta-stable': never quite able to take themselves seriously because always aware that the terms in which they describe themselves are subject to change, always aware of the contingency and fragility of their final vocabularies and thus of their selves." Ironists recognize the contingency and historicity of language and "our inability to step outside our language in order to compare it with something else."

Irony "results from awareness of the power of redescription." That's a problem because "most people do not want to be redescribed. They want to be taken on their own terms — taken seriously just as they are and just as they talk." Rorty also recognizes that there is something potentially cruel about telling people that their final vocabularies are up for grabs, since one way of humiliating people is "by making the things that seemed most important to them look futile, obsolete and powerless." Rorty has various solutions to this problem — mostly "elitist" ones of reserving irony to private self-creation rather than promoting social solidarity, and confining it to a restricted class of intellectuals. I'll skip the details of those solutions, and merely note that ironic or not, Rorty hopes it is possible for large, general publics to take a view that is contingent and historicist. At bottom, Rorty thinks there is some practical advantage to people taking that view, and a lot of the debate about Rorty's ideas starts at that point.

Finally, there is Rorty's notion of "solidarity," which he urges in preference to ideas about truth or getting reality right. "The traditional philosophical way of spelling out what we mean by 'human solidarity,'" he says, "is to say that there is something within each of us — our essential humanity — which resonates to the presence of this same thing in other human beings." He also concedes that "at times like that of Auschwitz, when history is in upheaval and traditional institutions and patterns of behavior are collapsing, we want something which stands beyond history and institutions." But in his book, Rorty urges "that we try not to want something which stands beyond history and institutions." After all, even without something beyond history, "a belief can still regulate action, can still be thought worth dying for, among people who are quite aware that this belief is caused by nothing deeper than contingent historical circumstance."

What solidarity comes down to is a "process of coming to see other human beings are 'one of us' rather than as 'them'," and that process is mostly a matter of "detailed description of what unfamiliar people are like and a redescription of what we ourselves are like." It is an expansive view of "us" that is to be achieved "not by inquiry but by imagination, the imaginative ability to see strange people as fellow sufferers." Rorty suspects that this expansive view of us is less accomplished by theory than by the narrative arts — reportage, novels, movies, TV and the like.

Finding Rorty to be "the most interesting philosopher in the world today," as the literary critic Harold Bloom once described him, does not entail agreeing with him about everything. I have an odd response to Rorty's ideas: I think most of them are true, but I'm not sure what practical difference it makes to believe such ideas. Since he believes that there aren't such things as grand or large truths, and he also believes that things have to make a practical difference to be useful, my response is truly and literally ironic. It also means I have questions for Rorty.

Many intellectuals think Rorty doesn't believe in any form of truth, and I've read longish articles earnestly arguing that there is a truth to such things as whether or not there were weapons of mass destruction in Iraq in 2003, and that Rorty's denial of truth is wrong, irresponsible and dangerous. I think that's just a misreading of Rorty. He believes in the same "local truths" as most of the rest of us, and he believes sentences in a given vocabulary or language can be contextually true or false; he just doesn't believe there are large or universal truths, whether we're talking about science, morality, politics, or art.

A lot of what I do as a philosophy teacher of undergraduate students is to debunk views they might hold — about everything from astrology and alien abductions to god and goddesses — when they don't have good reasons for thinking such beliefs are true. I think there's a practical advantage to not believing unlikely beliefs. If you don't believe that a god wants you to blow up other people and yourself, and if you don't believe that you'll land in paradise as a result of suicide bombing, then you're less likely to engage in such acts.

Further, I argue that there are pretty good reasons for thinking that a lot of things, like tables and chairs and the trees outside the window, are real enough. The aliens and the gods don't provide much evidence of their existence, but insofar as our senses are reliable, insofar as there is nearly unanimous intersubjective agreement, and insofar as there are no good reasons to think otherwise, the tables, chairs, trees, and other people do provide good evidence that they're real. This way of looking at things — a sort of "local realism," as I think of it — doesn't require a notion of absolute truth or a strong notion of mind-independent reality, but it favours the idea that within our way of using language ("our" here means something like "Western civilization"), some arguments are better than others, even if there isn't a way of absolutely grounding them.

I think that what I want is Rorty-*lite*. While it isn't necessarily an essential or eternal feature of human beings to want to know what is real, nonetheless questions about how the universe does or doesn't hang together have a long, human history, and there's a lot of inter-subjective agreement about the desire to know What It All Means. There may even be an evolutionary feature of humans that inclines us to want to know what's going on beyond our immediate spheres of effect. I think Rorty underestimates the practical usefulness and pleasure people take in pondering the universe, even though it doesn't necessarily increase human solidarity. That underestimation on his part may be a grumpy result of his experience among professional philosophers.

One of Rorty's claims irks a lot of people. It is his claim that science isn't much different from interpersonal relations, morality, politics or art when it comes to "truth." Now, it's true that when I talk to physi-cists at the school where I teach, they don't, these days, make too much of the matter of truth. In a field where they regularly talk about "string theory" and "quantum particles," where time, space, energy and matter are up for grabs, and where much else is uncertain, I appreciate their modesty about how to characterize the grand scheme of things. Still, scientific descriptions of bits of the universe are con-sistently better (even if "better" only means "useful") than other descriptions (descriptions that merely suggest that "god-dunnit"). And since moral and political descriptions of bits of the universe are notoriously not consistently better, then I don't see what the practical advantage is of not allowing science some privilege, at least with respect to the bits it is characteristically interested in describing. In the end, I don't quite understand Rorty's assault on scientific truth and philosophy.

When it comes to morality and politics, I think things are much fuzzier, though I'm not a relativist any more than Rorty is. I think cer-tain ways of behaving and living together are better than others sim-ply because they invoke less violence. But I don't think there is anything close to an absolute grounding for my views. How we come to choose the "values" we adhere to seems a contingent matter, but once we've identified with some values or images of human life, then there are arguments within that system of values that are more coher-ent and better than others, and within that system of values there are also ways of negotiating with people who don't share those values that are less likely to end up with people killing each other. But the "value" doesn't seem to be inscribed in and/or beyond the world.

Take the current popular value of "equality." There is nothing, or very little, about us that presupposes equality — either of opportunity, or equality before the law. In terms of abilities, we are obviously unequal. There is no built-in feature (or nature) of human beings that requires equality. It is strictly historical contingency or "progress" that has gotten us as far as we have with equality — and it didn't have to be that way.

One metaphor that recurrently appears in Rorty's writings, and which I'm taken with, is the notion of beauty versus the sublime. Among metaphysicians, Rorty observes, there's a perennial hankering after the sublime. In contrast, a novelist like Marcel Proust is willing to settle for the merely beautiful. Once Proust "had put the events of his own life in his own order, made a pattern out of all the little things . . . his job was done." Rorty says, "Beauty, depending as it does on giving shape to a multiplicity [of little things], is notoriously transitory . . . Beauty requires a frame, and death will provide that frame." By contrast to the modesty of beauty, "sublimity is neither transitory, relational, reactive nor finite." The theorist, even ironists such as Nietzsche or Heidegger, "is continually tempted to try for sublimity, not just beauty. That is why he is continually tempted . . . to try for one big hidden reality rather than for a pattern among appearances . . . To try for the sublime is to try to make a pattern out of the entire realm of possibility, not just of some little, contingent actualities."

In an essay called "Universality and Truth" (which is in *Rorty and His Critics*), the beauty versus sublimity metaphor comes up in another context. Among some philosophers, Rorty notes, there are what they call "impossible, indefinable, sublime objects of desire . . . In my view, truth is just such an object. It is too sublime, so to speak, to be either recognized or aimed at. Justification is merely beautiful, but it is recognizable . . . Sometimes, with luck, justification is even achieved," even if only temporarily.

I think the preference for beauty over sublimity also provides a clue about what to do with our yearning for transcendence, something beyond time and history. It suggests that if there is something transcendent, and there certainly seem to be things that transcend our mundane experience, then transcendence must be in the world, not beyond it. The candidates for such transcendence, then, must be found in activities like art — music, dance, visual art, writing — and science, or in experiences like finding wild orchids, having sex or climbing mountains.

I've been present on a couple of occasions, in Budapest and Berlin, when Rorty lectured. I was at the Budapest Collegium in 1993 when Rorty gave a talk that eventually became his essay, "Universality and

Truth." He argued before a group of Hungarian intellectuals, who had recently seen the end of communism in their country, that he didn't think that the notion of "truth" was particularly relevant to democratic politics, although of course he thought democratic politics were very relevant. Rorty's manner is a charming, informal American style that adopts the tone of what was once known as "cracker barrel" philosophizing, although in the face of technical questions, he's willing to stiffen a bit and act the role of a more formal academic. In any case, it has a twangy appeal.

At the end of his talk, I had a question. It went roughly like this: if there is no neutral ground from which to argue for kindness over cruelty, and if there is no neutral ground by which to justify one argument over another, and if we can only persuade one audience after another, why should I think that Rorty was more likely to persuade people than, say, Hitler, or Disney productions, or some major Islamic ayatollah, all of whom had far more access to audiences and far more powerful media for delivering their messages? Rorty leaned back. "Gee," he admitted, "that's the 64-dollar question."

What struck me as odd was the monetary amount. *The 64 Dollar Question* was an American radio quiz show back in the 1930s Depression, when 64 dollars was a considerable sum of money. It turned into a catchphrase, meaning any ultimate question. Later, when television and inflation came along in the 1950s and 1960s, the show became *The $64,000 Question*, and since then, contestants have sweated over the answers to trivial questions that yield prizes much larger than $64,000.

While I was pondering Rorty's folksy phrase in a rather nonplussed way, he was patiently waiting for me to provoke him further. The next question could only be a variant on the perennial political favourite, "What is to be done?" But I more or less knew Rorty's answer to that, having read *Contingency*, where he says that we've been sent back to the drawing board, and "we still are there. Nobody has come up with a large framework for relating our large and vague hopes for human equality to the actual distribution of power in the world."

Since the Hungarian intellectuals in the room seemed gloomy enough in the wake of Rorty's pronouncement that they couldn't look to truth to help them shape democracy, I decided not to depress them further by asking a "What should we do?" question, a question that Rorty or any of the rest of us could only answer, "The best we can." Outside the Budapest Collegium, which is located on the heights of the Buda hills, there was a view of the great Danube River below, flowing through the city, at sunset. I was willing to settle for the beautiful rather than pursue the sublime.

Continued

I remember how thrilling it was as a child to come to the conclusion of something I was reading, a story or a book, and discover, at the end, that it wasn't "The End," but that there might be more to come. More Walter Farley *Black Stallion* stories, more *Wizard of Oz* books, more John R. Tunis sports novels or *Amazing Adventures*. Ever since I began to write, I've always wanted to end a book with the magical promissory words:

To be continued ...

Index

Atom Egoyan, 260
Alan Ehrenhalt, 174, 293, 299, 301-304
Albert Einstein, 169
Dwight Eisenhower, 294, 303
Mr. Eliot, 256, 257
T.S. Eliot, 284
Lew Ellingham, 72, 73, 174
Ralph Waldo Emerson, 133
Friedrich Engels, 176, 274
Eros, 288, 292
Clayton Eshleman, 174
Euripides, 74
Jan van Eyck, 11

Melanie Fahlman-Reid, 269
Walter Farley, 174, 325
David Farwell, 202
John Fary, 302
Brian Fawcett, 10, 70, 174, 200, 237, 256, 258
Lawrence Ferlinghetti, 19
Harry Fertig, 181, 300
Marge Fertig, 181, 300
Johann Fichte, 159
Ernst Fischer, 147
David Fisher, 163, 177
Lisa Fittko, 160, 175
Gustave Flaubert, 175
Maurice Flood, 37
Theodor Fontane, 168
E.M. Forster, 122, 175, 284
Michel Foucault, 124, 175
Benjamin Franklin, 220, 221
Ruth Franklin, 175
Simon Fraser, 256
Frederick the Great, 158, 164
Mike Freeman, 271
Sigmund Freud, 12, 168, 175, 290, 291
Milton Friedman, 175, 274
Rose Friedman, 175

Allen Gardner, 61
Beatrice Gardner, 61
Jon Gates, 36
Marguerite Gauthier, 294
Dan Gawthrop, 10, 44, 83, 84, 85, 86, 89, 90, 91, 92, 93, 97, 98
Jean Genet, 175, 213, 239
Sam Giancana, 301
André Gide, 125, 175
Reid Gilbert, 269

Fred Gilbertson, 36
Anton Gill, 156, 175
Allen Ginsberg, 19, 23, 24, 133, 134, 135, 175, 196, 238, 239, 307
Natalia Ginzburg, 250
Jean-Luc Godard, 14
Jacques Godbout, 175, 254
Johann von Goethe, 228
Elliot Goldman, 12
Barry Goldwater, 72
Cy Gonick, 111
Paul Goodman, 138, 177
Barbara Gowdy, 260
George Grant, 256
Günter Grass, 4, 160, 168, 175
John Grayson, 260
Bob Greenspan, 12, 299
Stan Greenspoon, 271
John Grisham, 45
Brion Gysin, 238

Jürgen Habermas, 314, 316
Miklos Haraszti, 231
Mr. Harris, 17
Chuck Harris, 12
Nathaniel Hawthorne, 133
Ralph Hefferline, 138, 177
Hugh Hefner, 295
Georg Hegel, 38, 168, 169, 314
Martin Heidegger, 314, 316, 323
Heinrich Heine, 207
Wayne Henry, 269
Hermes, 251, 288
Jim Herndon, 131, 132, 154, 175
Franz Hessel, 158, 175
Stefan Heym, 160
Charles Higham, 49, 51, 52, 53, 54, 175
Adolf von Hildebrand, 288
Magnus Hirschfeld, 166, 168-169
Adolf Hitler, 170, 233, 279, 318, 324
Thomas Hobbes, 175, 274
E.T.A. Hoffman, 168
Aunt Holla, 229
Homer, 147
Rogers Hornsby, 306
Roger Horwitz, 29, 30, 31, 33
Richard Howard, 122, 173
"Hube the Cube", 19
Robert Hutchins, 313

Indravarman, 52
Harold Innis, 256, 259